Computers:
Concepts and Implications

Computers: Concepts and Implications

Fritz J. Erickson
Millersville University of Pennsylvania

John A. Vonk
University of Northern Colorado

B&E TECH Business and Educational Technologies

B&E TECH Business and Educational Technologies

Vice President and Publisher *Susan A. Simon*
Acquisitions Editor *Paul Ducham*
Managing Developmental Editor *Linda Meehan Avenarius*
Advertising/Marketing Coordinator *Jennifer Wherry*
Product Development Assistant *Sandy Ludovissy*

WCB Wm. C. Brown Communications, Inc.

Chief Executive Officer *G. Franklin Lewis*
Corporate Senior Vice President and Chief Financial Officer *Robert Chesterman*
Corporate Senior Vice President and President of Manufacturing *Roger Meyer*
Executive Vice President/General Manager, Brown & Benchmark Publishers *Tom Doran*
Executive Vice President/General Manager, Wm. C. Brown Publishers *Beverly Kolz*

Copyright ©1994 by Wm. C. Brown Communications, Inc.
All rights reserved

A Times Mirror Company

Library of Congress Catalog Card Number: 93-74091

ISBN 0-697-23945-4

No part of this publication may be reproduced, stored in a retrieval system, or transmitted, in any form or by any means, electronic, mechanical, photocopying, recording, or otherwise without the prior written permission of the publisher.

Printed in the United States of America by Wm. C. Brown Communications, Inc., 2460 Kerper Boulevard, Dubuque, IA 52001

10 9 8 7 6 5 4

To Kelly, Kaela, Sam, and Sasha
For their loyalty, enthusiasm, and devotion

Preface

COMPUTERS AS TOOLS

Not so long ago, the use of a computer to solve a problem was big news. Today, however, computers affect so many aspects of our daily activities, we sometimes hardly notice their benefits. This is not to say that the world of computing is no longer interesting; hardly! The pace of innovation and potential applications make the study of computers more exciting than ever. The goal of this text is to share that excitement with students by showing them the far-reaching effects of computers and technology, and the applications that computers have to their own lives.

THE TOOLS FOR UNDERSTANDING CONCEPTS

Students are motivated by success. By introducing ideas in manageable doses, this text allows students to succeed with each topic, building confidence to move to the next. In addition, we have created the following learning system to help students effectively comprehend computer concepts.

- *Extensive examples.* Throughout every chapter, each example is designed to encourage student interest and motivation and support topics presented in the text. These examples have been chosen for their relevance and interest to freshman or sophomore students.
- *Emphasis on microcomputers.* With more efficient microprocessors available each year, the microcomputer is the dominant tool of the end-user. To reflect this shift away from mainframes, we have focused exclusively on microcomputers (PCs and Macs) and their relevance to the college student and professional.
- *Integrated history.* History adds flavor and personality to most disciplines. Computing is no exception. Unfortunately, few instructors can devote significant class time specifically to the history of computers. That is why we have included a boxed insert on history within each chapter. Students will learn about the evolution of computing and the people behind the changes without searching through an appendix.
- *Easy-to-understand language.* We made a considerable effort to make technical information comprehensible to the student. We made no assumptions about jargon, technical terms, or industry names. As a result, students will be less intimidated and will understand more.

Interesting marginal notes •••

• CHAPTER 2: Microcomputer Hardware •

ROM is used in many specialized computers in which instructions must be stored permanently, such as automobile computers that store instructions that control gasoline and air flow to the engine.

Additional Chips. What chips are there other than RAM, ROM, and CPU? Expansion boards typically contain chips that provide additional storage or memory and control monitors, printers, modems, and facsimile (fax) transmission.

Disk Drives

Typically microcomputer systems use magnetic disk storage; as the technology improves and prices decline, optical storage devices are becoming increasingly popular.

A magnetic disk is a direct-access storage device (DASD) that lets the computer directly locate a record of information. This differs from magnetic tape storage, in which records can be accessed only sequentially—one after the other. Thus, to access the last sequential record, the computer must first read all prior records.

The surface of a magnetic disk is read as concentric circles, called *tracks*, where data is stored as magnetic spots. The same amount of data is stored on each track, whether it is an inner or outer circle.

The disk drive is the device that allows data to be read from or written to a disk (Figure 2-6). It has an access arm equipped with read/write heads that move on the disk. The read/write head either reads (that is, obtains data from the disk and sends it to the CPU) or writes (that is, transfers data from the CPU to the disk). Reading makes a copy without altering the original data. Writing replaces—actually writes over—the original data, like recording a new song over an old one on a tape recorder or cassette player.

The typical microcomputer has one or two floppy disk drives and one hard disk drive.

Multimedia's Pictures Are Worth How Many Words?

Thanks to CD-ROM and interactive video storage disks, huge amounts of information, especially visual information—photos, TV, and film, for instance—can now be stored on personal computers. A computerized book or catalog can now be more realistic, to say nothing of user-friendly. Taking advantage of this technology, Kodak has joined forces with L.L. Bean to scan its catalog onto disks that can be mailed to customers. By typing the words "red" and "dress" a customer can view all the red dresses in the catalogue. Encyclopedias on CD-ROM can include short animation segments to illustrate the functioning of a heart valve or the formulation of cumulus clouds, for instance. History texts can include newsreel footage of historical events, bringing a sense of immediacy to students.

Easy-to-understand language •••••▶

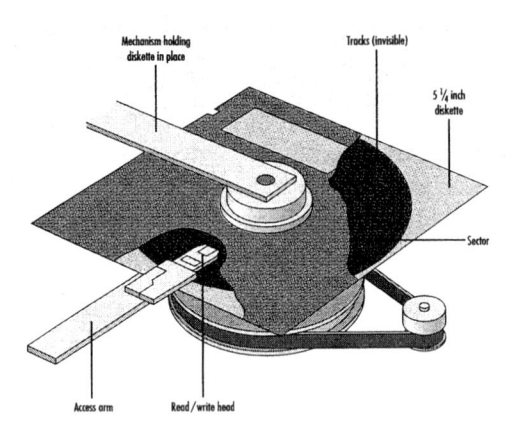

Figure 2-6
The essential parts of a floppy disk drive: a motor to spin the drive, a mechanism to hold the disk in place, and a read/write head to transfer data to and from the disk. Data on the disk is organized into tracks (concentric circles) and sectors (pieces of each circle).

Clear illustrations and descriptions ••••••••••••••••••••••••••••••••••••••

• PREFACE •

> HISTORY

Altair and the Birth of the Microcomputer

Although computers have been around since the 1940s, the first microcomputer—or personal computer—appeared in 1975. In fact, the Altair computer made its debut on the January, 1975 cover of *Popular Electronics* magazine. Like so much else in the early days of the computer industry, its appearance was part luck, part genius, and part necessity.

Altair's "father" was Ed Roberts, a six-foot, four-inch man who weighed close to 300 pounds. A gadget nut, Roberts had an insatiable appetite for information and had joined the Air Force to learn more about electronics. Eventually posted at Kirtland Field, near Albuquerque, New Mexico, he started a company called Model Instrumentation and Telemetry Systems, or MITS, which sold model rocket equipment Roberts made in his garage.

In 1969, Roberts moved MITS (by then "Micro" had replaced "Model" in the company's name) to what had been a restaurant called The Enchanted Sandwich Shop just off Route 66, and sank all his money into making a commercial calculator. MITS was the

> *Its appearance was part luck, part genius, and part necessity. The railroad lost the world's first personal computer.... The Altair had rather limited appeal. There was no software to run on it, and it did not even have a keyboard.*

culator. MITS was the first U.S. company to sell calculator kits, so it was extremely successful at first. Unfortunately, when larger companies such as Texas Instruments entered the market, the ensuing price wars devastated MITS.

Desperate to save his company, Roberts decided to build computer hobby kits in 1974. He browbeat Intel into selling him its 8080 chips in volume for $75 each (rather than the usual $350), so he could market his kits for $375.

Roberts was still building his prototype machine when he was contacted by the technical editor of *Popular Electronics*, Les Solomon, who was looking for a computer to run on the cover of the magazine. Roberts promised that his machine would be ready by the end of 1974, and Solomon decided to feature it on the January 1975 cover.

Solomon's 12-year-old daughter, a "Star Trek" fan, came up with Altair after a star to which the Starship *Enterprise* had been heading. As part of the Altair ad campaign, Roberts himself came up with the term "personal computer."

Roberts shipped Solomon the only Altair in existence so the editor could test it—but it never arrived in New York. The railroad *lost* the world's first personal computer. Readers of *Popular Electronics* didn't know the couple even flew to Albuquerque hoping to get their Altair sooner by appearing in person.

For all its historic importance, the Altair had rather limited appeal. There was no software to run on it, and it did not even have a keyboard. Moreover, it was sold unassembled—to assemble it, you had to be able to solder. And to use it, you had to be able to program it in complex 8080 machine language by flicking a row of switches on its front panel. Blinking red lights were the only display Altair could show. It had only 256 bytes of memory, though there were 18 slots for more memory boards that would increase its capacity to 4,096 bytes.

Among those who saw that January *Popular Electronics* were two Harvard students, Bill Gates and Paul Allen, who decided to provide a programming language that would allow the Altair to actually do the work of a computer. Without an Altair to work on (Roberts had

◀······ Easy-to-find History inserts appear in every chapter

> SECOND OPINION

Multimedia: A Bandwagon or a BMW?

Multimedia presentations! The words conjure the image: smooth, glamorous, and very, very effective. I used to have a coffee mug with the motto, "Nothing is as easy as it looks."

It's not as easy as it looks, and it's not simple in any way, to produce glamorous, smooth presentations, or tell when it's worth it. We in the computer field are all too prone to fall in love with our own technical capabilities, producing solutions in search of a problem. Is multimedia just the next techno-fad, a bandwagon to be abandoned in a couple of years, or something more? And how do we tell?

First, let's look at the downside. There are hard technical problems to be solved in order to put together a multimedia device. The computer has to operate fast enough, it has to have enough storage, it has

Second Opinions provide a balanced perspective ·····▶

> *Is multimedia just the next techno-fad, a bandwagon to be abandoned in a couple of years, or something more? And how do we tell?*

to have the right kind of peripheral devices (like high-quality stereo speakers), and so on. That much good hardware costs more than a bare-bones PC.

Also, producing a good multimedia product is very much like producing a motion picture. It is a specialty in its own right, involving a great deal of knowledge and skill that you simply do not have if you are an accountant, a fashion designer, a programmer, a computer scientist, or even a multimedia systems expert. Making a movie is trivial; making a good movie is very hard; making a good movie that works together with everything else happening on the screen of a multimedia workstation is harder yet. There isn't a program available that can turn an amateur into a professional producer.

A third problem involves a different kind of technical issue. A frequent claim for multimedia is that it allows for highly interactive products. Well, sometimes. Think of it this way: It's easy for us to interact with a computer; it's very hard for the computer to interact with us. It knows only what keys you're hitting, and perhaps the pauses between keys. It's tremendously difficult to interpret such limited data.

Okay, there are obstacles. But aren't there benefits too? Absolutely! If you're trying to decide on a multimedia project or system, you have to balance the costs against the benefits. The catch is this: to estimate the benefits, you have to use some imagination, some skill, and some old-fashioned intuition. You have to have a vision of how things would be improved for you and your audience by developing a multimedia product. Maybe in spite of all those difficulties mentioned earlier your multimedia product can do a much better job that really needs doing.

In determining the merit of multimedia, concreteness and technical details are marvelous things, but not if you leave out the vision. ■

H. Joel Jefferey, Ph.D.,
Northern Illinois University

- *Guest essays.* Three guest essays provide a broadened range of information and perspective. In the chapter on selecting hardware and software, Joey George of Florida State University explains the impact of software/hardware upgrades on the end-user. In the graphics chapter, Joel Jeffrey of Northern Illinois University discusses the criteria for evaluating the merits of multimedia. And in the communications chapter, Janet Whitaker of Mesa Community College tells how colleges in Arizona are using their network to enhance learning.
- *Pedagogy.* Each chapter contains an Introduction, Vignettes, Learning Objectives/Outlines, Chapter Summaries, List of Key Terms, Discussion Questions, Self-Quiz, and Study/Review Questions.
- *Marginal notes.* Throughout the text, interesting marginal notes include tips on avoiding microcompter problems, stories about historical figures in computing, and real-life applications of the chapter subject.

ANCILLARY MATERIALS

Knowing that *Computers: Concepts, Implications, and Applications* is just one component of the course, we have developed several instructional tools with utility and value in mind.

- *Instructor's resource disk.* Available to instructors only, this IBM disk contains lecture outlines, solutions to end-of-chapter questions and exercises, teaching tips, and additional test questions. The disk is in ASCII format, so it's easy to modify, add additional material, or print sections as needed.
- *Transparencies.* A set of full-color acetates, one for every line drawing, has been provided to facilitate lectures.
- *TestPak.* This computerized classroom management system includes a database of questions, reproducible student self-quizzes, and a grade-recording program. No programming experience is necessary.
- *Custom test/quiz service.* Instructors can choose questions from the printed Test Item File and phone or FAX in their request for a printed exam. The exam will be sent within 48 hours.

CUSTOMIZE YOUR TEXT

If you find that none of the titles in the Erickson/Vonk series meets the needs of your course exactly, Business & Educational Technologies will create a book especially for you. Simply call your B&E Tech sales representative at (800) 258-2371, choose the exact content necessary for your course, and we'll do the rest. Your students will receive a text custom-fitted to your course needs. You can even include your own materials.

Acknowledgments

One of the joys of working on this book was having the very capable assistance of reviewers, editors, students, and colleagues. Although they are too numerous to mention by name, we are grateful for their help and guidance throughout the development of this project; their unselfish contributions made this book possible. Our special gratitude goes to the efforts of Susan Simon, Paul Ducham, Linda Meehan Avenarius, Jennifer Wherry, Sandy Ludovissy, Julie Fleege, and all of our new friends at Business & Educational Technologies. We are also indebted to Karen Hawk for her friendly voice and dedication to keeping this project on track and on time. Most of all we would like to thank our families. No author could develop a project of this nature without the loving tolerance of family members. Thanks, Jan, Jenna, John, Arlo, Petie, Jennifer, Julie, Jacqui, Joey, Clancy, Torrie, and Riley.

Photo Credits

Chapter 1 Opener Sean Arbabi/Tony Stone Images
Figure 1-1 Photo courtesy of Motorola
Figure 1-2 Poulides/Thatcher/Tony Stone Images
Figure 1-3a Photo courtesy of Unisys Corporation
Figure 1-3b & c Courtesy of International Business Machines Corporation
Figure 1-3d Photo courtesy of Cray Research, Inc.
Figure 1-4 Photo provided by The Computer Museum, Boston
Figure 1-5 Courtesy of International Business Machines Corporation
Figure 1-7 David Joel/Tony Stone Images
Figure 1-11 Screen shot reprinted with permission from Microsoft Corporation
Figure 1-13 Courtesy of International Business Machines Corporation
Figure 1-14 Courtesy of International Business Machines Corporation
Figure 1-15 Courtesy of International Business Machines Corporation
Chapter 2 Opener Reg Watson/Tony Stone Images
Figure 2-3a, b, & c Courtesy of Intel Corporation
Figure 2-4 Courtesy of International Business Machines Corporation
Figure 2-7 Photo by Pat Martin
Figure 2-8 Photo courtesy of Seagate Technology, Inc.
Figure 2-9a & b Photo by Pat Martin
Figure 2-10 Photo courtesy of Radius, Inc.
Figure 2-11 Photo by Pat Martin
Figure 2-12 Photo courtesy of Logitech, Inc.
Figure 2-13 Photo courtesy of Logitech, Inc.
Figure 2-14 Photo courtesy of Intermec Corporation
Figure 2-15a Photo courtesy of Hewlett-Packard Company
Figure 2-15b Photo courtesy of Logitech, Inc.
Figure 2-16a Photo courtesy of Radius, Inc.
Figure 2-16b & c Courtesy of International Business Machines Corporation
Figure 2-18a & c Photo courtesy of Epson America, Inc.
Figure 2-18b Photo courtesy of Xerox Corporation
Figure 2-21 Photo courtesy of Scitex
Figure 2-22 Photo courtesy of General Motors
Chapter 3 Opener Courtesy of International Business Machines Corporation
Figure 3-4 ©American Mega Trends, Inc.
Figure 3-11 Courtesy of Sun Microsystems
Figure 3-12 Courtesy of International Business Machines Corporation
Chapter 4 Opener David Joel/Tony Stone Images
Figure 4-1 Courtesy of International Business Machines Corporation
Figure 4-2 Courtesy of Lotus Development Corporation
Figure 4-3 Photo courtesy of Adobe Systems Incorporated
Figure 4-4 Photo courtesy of Aldus
Figure 4-5 Courtesy of Lotus Development Corporation
Figure 4-6 Courtesy of Borland International

• PHOTO CREDITS •

Figure 4-7	Courtesy of Lotus Development Corporation
Figure 4-8	Courtesy of Apple Computer, Inc.
Chapter 5 Opener	Tim Brown/Tony Stone Images
Figure 5-1	Courtesy of International Business Machines Corporation
Figure 5-2	Photo Courtesy of Smith-Corona
Chapter 6 Opener	Lonny Kalfus/Tony Stone Images
Figure 6-1	Photo courtesy of Adobe Systems Incorporated
Figure 6-2	Photo courtesy of Adobe Systems Incorporated
Figure 6-9	Photo courtesy of Nikon Inc.
Figure 6-10	Courtesy of Wacom Technology
Figure 6-11	Courtesy of Lotus Development Corporation
Figure 6-13	Photo courtesy of National Center for Supercomputing Applications/University of Illinois
Figure 6-14	Photo courtesy of Microtek
Figure 6-15	Photo courtesy of Adobe Systems Incorporated
Figure 6-16	Fractal Design Corporation—Fractal Design Painter® 2.0
Figure 6-18	William S. Helsel/Tony Stone Images
Figure 6-19	Tim Brown/Tony Stone Images
Figure 6-20	Used with permission of Macromedia
Chapter 7 Opener	Jim Cambon/Tony Stone Images
Figure 7-1	Jon Riley/Tony Stone Images
Figure 7-2	Photo by Pat Martin
Figure 7-3	Photo courtesy of Quark
Figure 7-16	Jon Riley/Tony Stone Images
Chapter 8 Opener	Courtesy of International Business Machines Corporation
Figure 8-1	Courtesy of Lotus Development Corporation
Figure 8-2	Courtesy of Lotus Development Corporation
Figure 8-11	Don Smetzer/Tony Stone Images
Chapter 9 Opener	Courtesy of International Business Machines Corporation
Figure 9-1	Stan Fellerman/Tony Stone Images
Figure 9-2	Photo courtesy of Claris Corporation
Figure 9-3	Jim Pickerell/Tony Stone Images
Chapter 10 Opener	Roger Tully/Tony Stone Images
Figure 10-1	Courtesy of Lotus Development Corporation
Figure 10-2	Photo by Pat Martin
Figure 10-3	Courtesy of Prodigy
Figure 10-4	©Copyright 800-Software, 1993. 800-888-4880.
Figure 10-5	Courtesy of Compuserve
Figure 10-6	Courtesy of Prodigy
Figure 10-7	Courtesy of Hayes Microcomputer Products, Inc.
Chapter 11 Opener	Chip Henderson/Tony Stone Images
Figure 11-1a	Jon Riley/Tony Stone Images
Figure 11-1b, c, & d	Courtesy of International Business Machines Corporation
Chapter 12 Opener	Terry Vine/Tony Stone Images
Figure 12-1	© 1983 United Artists and SLM Entertainment, Ltd. All rights reserved.
Figure 12-3	Photo courtesy of Central Point Software, Inc.
Figure 12-5	Courtesy of International Business Machines Corporation
Figure 12-6	Courtesy of International Business Machines Corporation
Figure 12-7	Photo supplied by MicroComputer Accessories, Inc., a Rubbermaid Office Products Company

Table of Contents

1 Introduction to Microcomputers	**1**
What Is a Microcomputer?	3
Why Focus on Microcomputers?	5
Hardware and the Computing Process	6
Software	7
How Application Software Was Used to Make this Book	8
Many Users, Many Uses	13
2 Microcomputer Hardware	**19**
Hardware Devices	23
Peripheral Devices	32
3 Microcomputer Operating Systems	**41**
Common Operating Systems	43
Utility Programs	52
4 Selecting Software and Hardware	**57**
Evaluating Your Needs	59
Selecting a Family	59
Choosing the Software First	59
Selecting Hardware	67
Where to Buy Your Computer	72
5 Working with Word Processing	**77**
Types of Word Processors	79
Choosing a Word Processor: Uses and Users	80
Using a Word Processor	81
6 Working with Graphics	**97**
What Are Graphics?	99
Data-Generated Graphics	106
Device-Generated Graphics	109
User-Generated Graphics	111
7 Working with Desktop Publishing	**117**
What Is Desktop Publishing Software?	119
Page Layout	121

Typographical Controls	125
Graphics Controls	128
Desktop Publishing Output	131
A Tool of Expression	132
Designing with Desktop Publishing Software	133

8 Working with Spreadsheets — 139

Spreadsheet Functions	141
Setting Up the Worksheet	145
Entering Data	146
Ranges in Formulas and Functions	148
Manipulating Data	148
Special Functions	151
Save, Save, Save	154
Printing the Worksheet	154

9 Working with Databases — 157

Electronic Databases	159
Database Design	160
Data Entry	164
Sorting and Indexing	164
Data Queries	167
Generating Reports	169
Database Organization	170

10 Working with Communications — 177

Telecommunications	179
Telecommunications Hardware and Software	184
Networking	190

11 Programming — 197

Programs and Programming	199
The Programming Process	199
Types of Programming Languages	204

12 Microcomputers and Social Issues — 217

Computer Crime and Security	219
Personal Information: Storage, Use, and Abuse	225
Guarding Our Privacy	227
People and Computers	229

Index — 233

1

Introduction to Microcomputers

OBJECTIVES

After completing this chapter, you will be able to
- Name the four types of general-purpose computers.
- Name two types of software and the four stages of computing.
- Describe at least six types of application software and how each is used.
- Explain the importance of learning about microcomputers.

FOCUS

The introduction of the microcomputer in 1975 revolutionized the world of computers and in the process has brought about vast changes in the way people live and work, as microcomputers have developed from toys for hobbyists to powerful and versatile tools used in thousands of different ways (Figure 1-1).

In this book, you will look at the fundamental nature of microcomputers: the hardware devices that make up the physical machine; the operating systems and the six major types of application software that make microcomputers the profoundly useful tools they have become; and some of the issues surrounding microcomputer use today. Along the way we will explore innovative ways of using the microcomputer, understand some of the most important events in the development of microcomputers, and hear the viewpoints of industry experts on microcomputing.

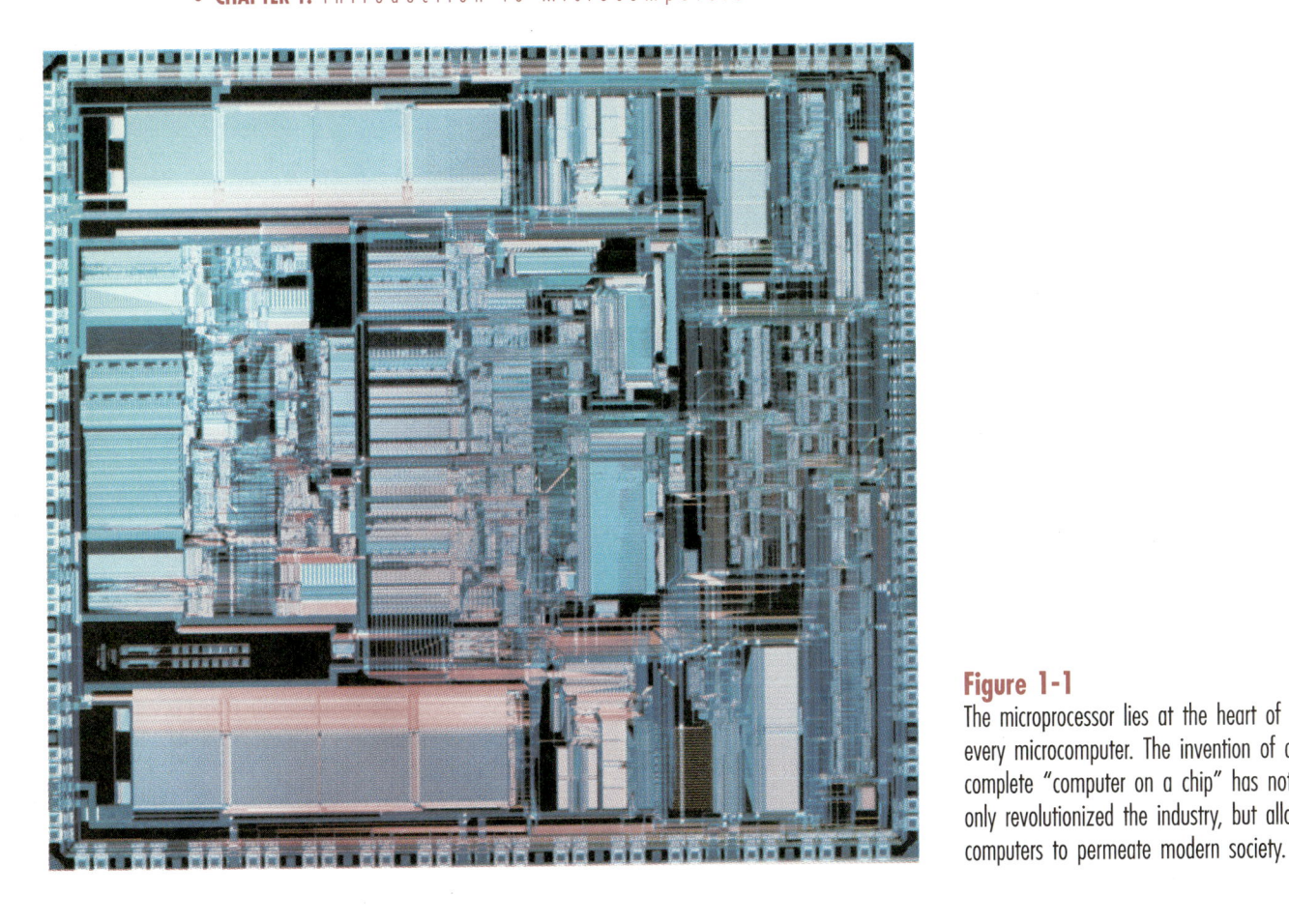

Figure 1-1
The microprocessor lies at the heart of every microcomputer. The invention of a complete "computer on a chip" has not only revolutionized the industry, but allowed computers to permeate modern society.

WHAT IS A MICROCOMPUTER?

There are many different kinds of computers in the world today. Computers are operating at the bank (Figure 1-2), in your car, and at the grocery store. Many of these computers are **special-purpose computers;** that is, they serve specific functions. There are also **general-purpose computers** in the office, at home, and at school, versatile enough to handle all kinds of tasks. The existence of all these different types of computers raises an important question: What *is* a computer? Simply put, a **computer** is a device that processes raw data into useful information. But from that perspective, a typewriter, a calculator, or even an abacus could be called a computer. What distinguishes a computer from other information-processing devices are three basic characteristics:

- A computer is completely electronic. That is, all its functions are carried out with electrical signals.
- A computer can remember information and hold it for future use. Computers do this on a temporary basis with memory circuits and permanently with storage devices such as magnetic disk and tape.
- A computer is programmable. Unlike other devices built to perform a single function or limited range of functions, a computer can be instructed to do whatever task we tell it to do. This opens up a vast realm of possibilities for computers to solve problems for us in everyday life: at home, in school, or at work.

Figure 1-2
An automatic teller machine is an example of a special-purpose computer; it is controlled by computer circuitry that communicates with the bank's account database, giving you access to cash and banking services.

• **CHAPTER 1:** Introduction to Microcomputers •

a

b

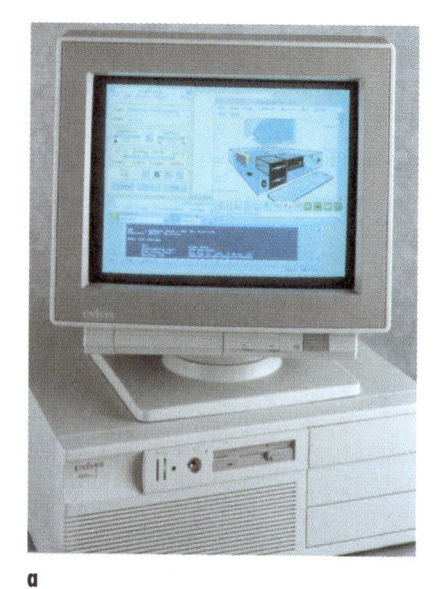

c

d

Figure 1-3
The four types of computers find use in different working environments. (a) Microcomputers are most often found at home, school, or on the desk at the office. (b) Mainframes are typically used in large business, academic, or scientific settings with huge amounts of data where many users need access to the computer. (c) Minicomputers are often used as multiuser computers in business and academic environments. (d) Supercomputers, designed for maximum computing capability, are most often used for research and simulations such as weather prediction, wind-tunnel simulation, and weapons systems simulation.

The most common kind of general-purpose computer in use today is the personal computer or microcomputer (Figure 1-3a). It gets the name **microcomputer** from the tiny electronic device, called the *microprocessor*, that does the actual processing. The use of personal computers has grown greatly during the last ten years. Only a few million personal computers were in use in 1980, so they were a relative novelty. Now there are almost a hundred million in this country alone.

Microcomputers form the most common of the four classes of general-purpose computers; the other three classes are minicomputers, mainframe computers, and supercomputers. Microcomputers, besides relying on a microprocessor, are the smallest and are generally designed for a single user. Minicomputers, mainframes, and supercomputers all use processors built from a large number of components. **Minicomputers,** larger than microcomputers (up to the size of a refrigerator) are generally intended for small- to medium-

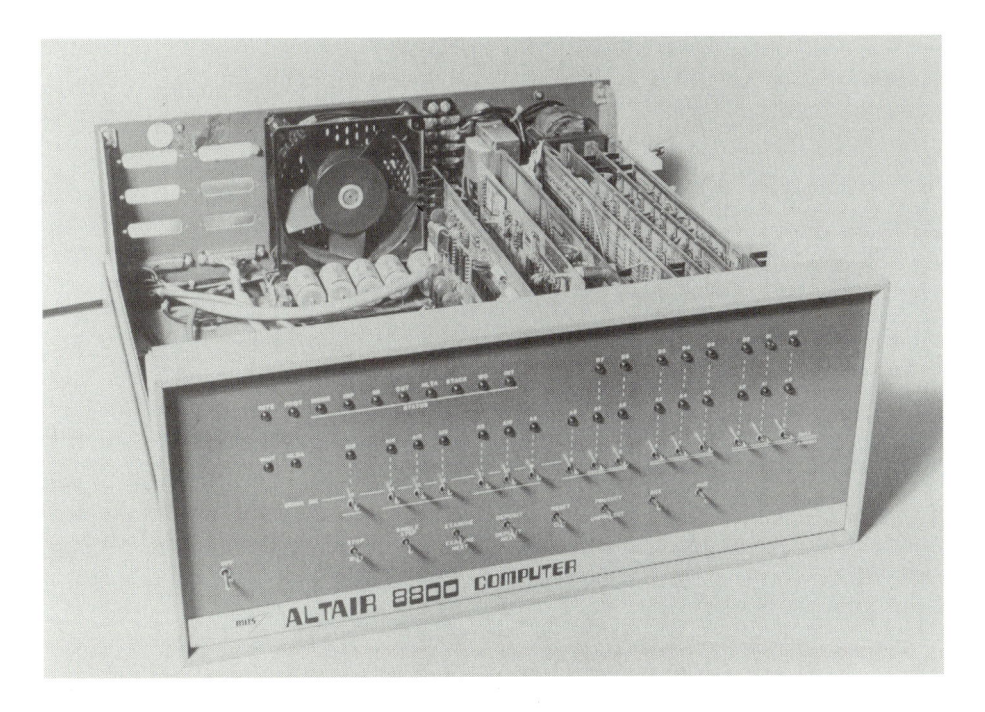

Figure 1-4
The MITS Altair 8800 was the first microcomputer, announced on the cover of the January 1975 *Popular Electronics*. It was based on the Intel 8080 microprocessor and was sold as a kit.

sized groups of users in businesses and other organizations (Figure 1-3b); their processing abilities are more robust than those of microcomputers. **Mainframe** computers (Figure 1-3c) can take up a whole room and can handle the needs of many simultaneous users while processing large volumes of data; they are most often used in large organizations and institutions. **Supercomputers**, the most sophisticated computers (Figure 1-3d), are designed for extremely high-speed processing of huge amounts of data, often using multiple processors working together. They are most often used for performing complex computations by the government, research organizations, and large industrial groups.

WHY FOCUS ON MICROCOMPUTERS?

Fifteen or twenty years ago, most books on computers described mainframes, because mainframes were the most common. Today, though, you are more likely to use a microcomputer. The first micros were sold to computer hobbyists in 1975 (Figure 1-4). In 1977, Apple entered the market with the Apple II, and in 1981 IBM joined the race. Apple released the Macintosh, the cornerstone of its current computer line, in 1984. During the 1980s, literally hundreds of manufacturers began making microcomputers. The competition kept prices down, and millions of people and businesses bought micros.

As the microcomputer industry grew, computer makers constantly tried to lure new customers with more powerful machines. The typical microcomputer sold today can work with more than 200 times as much data as the first IBM PC, and it can work with that data at least 200 times as fast. In fact, many of today's laptop (Figure 1-5) and desktop microcomputers are more powerful than the minis and mainframes that dominated the market only fifteen or twenty years ago.

The power of the modern microcomputer enables it to be used for all kinds of tasks. For a couple of thousand dollars, you can buy a computer and use it to write papers, perform mathematical computations and analyses, and conduct research. At home, you can use the same computer to communicate with

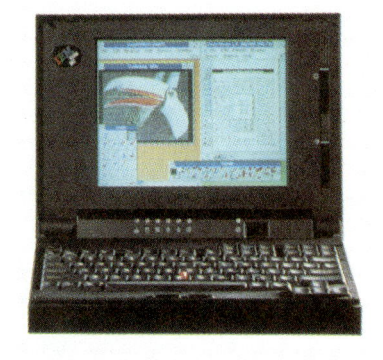

Figure 1-5
It's a long way from the Altair to modern laptop computers based on the latest microprocessors: these have more processing power than many mainframes of 15 or 20 years ago.

Computers and Natural Disasters

Scientists at Livermore Labs in California used computerized wind and weather data to guide Air Force pilots through volcanic ash clouds as they evacuated people from the vicinity of erupting Mount Pinatubo in the Philippines. Over 20,000 people were evacuated. Every 12 hours scientists sent their predictions—which later were confirmed by satellite photos—to Air Force pilots. Earlier, the scientists had computed the path of clouds of radiation released by the explosion of the Soviet nuclear reactor at Chernobyl, which sent plumes of radiation up to 50,000 feet into the atmosphere. More recently, the same team of scientists provided forecasts of the dense clouds made by oil wells set on fire by the Iraqi army as it began fleeing Kuwait during the Gulf War.

friends, play games, buy airline tickets, and keep track of finances. The same computer can be used again at work for correspondence, financial analysis, compiling and analyzing data, communicating with clients, and a thousand other tasks.

HARDWARE AND THE COMPUTING PROCESS

All computers consist of **hardware.** This includes the computer itself and all other related physical devices. The other pieces of the computer system include software, the instructions that tell the computer what tasks to perform; data, the information the computer works on; and you, the user, who ultimately tell the computer what to do, and for whom the computer does all its work.

All computers use the same basic techniques for carrying out the tasks we give them. The computer takes in data through input devices, it manipulates the data according to its instructions, it outputs the results of its processing, and it stores data for later use. These four processes together are known as the **computing cycle** (Figure 1-6).

Input is the process of entering data into the computer. The most common device used for input on microcomputers is the keyboard. Computer keyboards include many special command and function keys to perform specialized input tasks as well as the usual typewriter layout. Other input devices include a mouse, which manipulates a pointer on the computer screen for giving commands and entering data; a scanner, which reads graphic images and pages of text and sends them to the computer; a modem, which receives data over phone lines; and several other devices.

Once data is in a microcomputer, it is **processed** by the microprocessor and its associated integrated circuit chips. Microprocessors perform all calculations and manipulations necessary to transform data into meaningful infor-

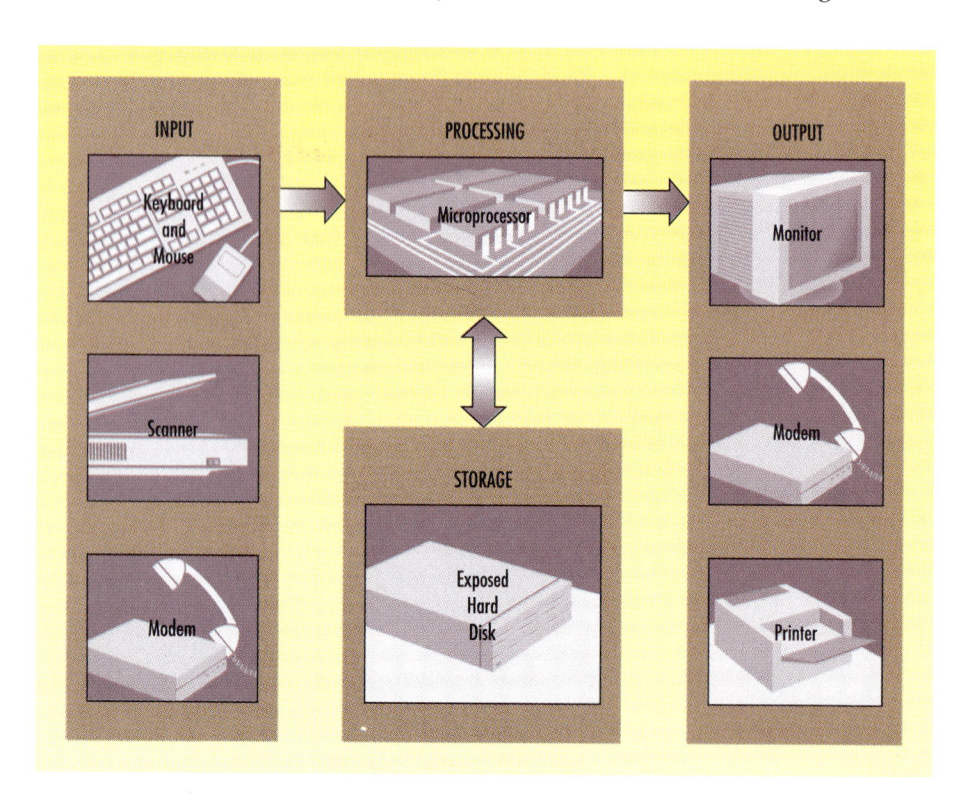

Figure 1-6
The computing cycle. The microprocessor (CPU) receives data from input devices, processes it, and sends the data to output devices for display, printing, or communication. Along the way, the CPU stores data temporarily in memory or permanently on a storage medium such as magnetic disk, tape, or optical disk.

mation. Associated with the processor is the computer's memory, which is used for storing data and programs while they're being used by the processor.

Getting processed data out of the computer is the job of **output** devices. The computer can display the data on a monitor screen, of which there are several types: color or monochrome, flat-panel or picture tube, desktop or portable. You can also send data to a printer or plotter to make a paper copy, use the modem to send the data over a phone line to another computer, or use any number of specialized output devices.

What do you do if you want to keep the data in a permanent form? That's what **storage** devices are for. Storage devices hold data permanently, so you can save it and retrieve it later. All microcomputers use disks to store data magnetically. Each type of disk is used by its corresponding disk drive to read and write information. Floppy disks are used for easy, portable storage, and built-in hard disks are used for more permanent storage of larger amounts of data and programs for fast access. Other common storage devices include optical discs (such as CD-ROM) and magnetic tape.

SOFTWARE

A **program** is a group of instructions that tells the processing devices what to do. **Software** can be a single program or a set of programs that work together. Because their meanings are very similar, the terms *software* (or *a piece of software*) and *program* are often used interchangeably.

Two types of software are necessary to make the computer capable of performing useful work. They are the operating system and application software. The **operating system** contains basic instructions that tell the CPU how to use other hardware devices, where to find programs, and how to load and keep track of programs in memory. Because it includes basic instructions that are vital to the internal functioning of the computer, the operating system is the first program to be processed after the computer is turned on, and it remains in memory until the computer is turned off.

For the computer to perform useful tasks, it needs application software (Figure 1-7) in addition to the operating system. An **application** is a job that

The Language Barrier

One of the most difficult hurdles facing multinational companies is the language barrier. But software companies face an extremely unusual challenge with the Japanese language because of its complex alphabet. English uses only 26 letters. The Japanese written language uses over 6000 separate symbols. Also, it takes twice as much memory and storage space to hold each Japanese character as it does to hold each English character.

The difficulties of translating such a complex language into computerese have been both a help and a hindrance to the Japanese computer market. Their software market has developed slowly because the first computers used English ASCII code. But the Japanese have been way ahead in graphics displays, largely because of the problems associated with displaying complex characters clearly.

Figure 1-7
The microcomputer's versatility has enabled it to replace many traditional tools.

Talking Books

Thanks to the rapidly increasing storage capacity of hard disks, as well as the expanded capabilities of CD-ROM, more and more reference books are being issued in electronic format, such as Grolier's Encyclopedia, which has over 33,000 articles and 10 million words. Many of the electronic reference books are more than just books to be read on screen instead of on paper. They utilize computer technology to enhance their effectiveness: *Webster's Ninth New Collegiate Dictionary* talks and can pronounce 160,000 root words. A complete edition of Shakespeare's works is available with texts in both Elizabethan English and modern English versions. Numerous style guides and collections of quotations, literature, and philosophy, as well as databases of historical events, can be accessed in a variety of ways. That's the good news. The bad news is that you still have to write your own term papers.

---

a computer can perform, such as creating text documents, manipulating sets of numbers, creating graphic images, and communicating with other computers. **Application software** is the term used to describe programs that tell the computer how to perform such jobs. The six most common types of application software are

- Word processing software
- Graphics software
- Desktop publishing software
- Spreadsheet software
- Database management software
- Communications software

Application software is what makes a computer a tool for performing the tasks we most often need to complete at school, at home, or at the office.

HOW APPLICATION SOFTWARE WAS USED TO MAKE THIS BOOK

Because of the variety of application software available, the microcomputer is much more than just a flexible tool. In many cases it can be integrated into every aspect of a complex endeavor. Take the making of this book, for example. Virtually every step of the way, we used microcomputers. To give you a better sense of how a complex process can be accomplished using microcomputers, we'll describe the four stages of making a textbook: planning, research, development, and production.

Planning

Like any other business, making books requires financial planning. Before officially launching the project, the publisher of this book had to project revenue and costs from the proposed book in a budget. Twenty years ago, budgets were created entirely by hand—an unpleasant task considering how many individual expenses had to be figured in. Even worse than creating the budget by hand was revising the budget. Usually, a budget has to be manipulated and fiddled with for quite a long time before the numbers are acceptable. And each time the numbers are changed, all the totals need to be recalculated. Doing budgets by hand was like getting an arithmetic assignment that took a week to finish.

When our publisher calculated the budget for this book, a spreadsheet program helped a lot. The publisher still had to estimate each cost, enter it into the budget, and then plug in the formulas that were needed. But the computer, with instructions from the application software, did all the math (Figure 1-8). If the totals weren't acceptable, the publisher decided where costs could be cut and then changed the numbers, and the totals were calculated again automatically. A recalculation that would have taken a person with a calculator an hour to figure out probably took the computer less than a second.

Once the budget was done, it was time for the publisher to draw up contracts for the authors. Here again, the publisher had application software to make the job easier: in this case, a piece of word processing software called Microsoft Word. The publisher didn't even have to do much typing, because most author contracts are similar. All the publisher had to do was edit a generic contract by filling in the names, some figures, and the dates.

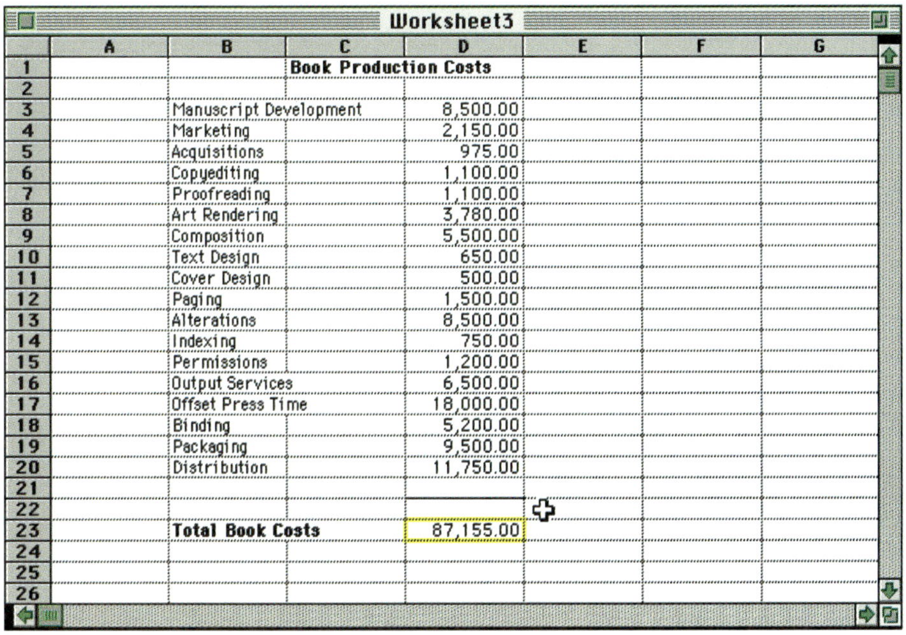

Worksheet3

	A	B	C	D	E	F	G
1			Book Production Costs				
2							
3		Manuscript Development		8,500.00			
4		Marketing		2,150.00			
5		Acquisitions		975.00			
6		Copyediting		1,100.00			
7		Proofreading		1,100.00			
8		Art Rendering		3,780.00			
9		Composition		5,500.00			
10		Text Design		650.00			
11		Cover Design		500.00			
12		Paging		1,500.00			
13		Alterations		8,500.00			
14		Indexing		750.00			
15		Permissions		1,200.00			
16		Output Services		6,500.00			
17		Offset Press Time		18,000.00			
18		Binding		5,200.00			
19		Packaging		9,500.00			
20		Distribution		11,750.00			
21							
22							
23		Total Book Costs		87,155.00			
24							
25							
26							

Figure 1-8
Creating a budget for this book was as simple as entering the numbers in a budget template and having the budget automatically calculated by the spreadsheet software.

Research

With contracts in our hands, we were ready to get to work. Time was of the essence, and we had a schedule to keep. But you can't just sit down and write a textbook off the top of your head. You need to do some research. Fortunately, you can do a lot of research in your home or office with a microcomputer, a modem, and a piece of communications software. A **modem** is a hardware device that lets your computer communicate with another computer over the phone lines. The communications program is the application software you use to control your modem.

We used Crosstalk for Windows to control our modems. With these tools we accessed information services and bulletin boards (Figure 1-9, p. 10), where we could ask questions of other microcomputer users and gain valuable information. If we found information that might be useful to a third party, we used the modem of the holder of the information to send directly to the third party's computer. Not only did we save a lot of time this way, but we also saved a good deal in mailing costs.

The piece of database software called Paradox also saved us time in our research. The only way to keep up with the ever-changing computer industry is to read a lot of newspapers and magazines. Every time we found an interesting or useful article, we entered data about the article in a database. When it came time to write about, say, graphics software, we were able to search our database for all the articles on the subject.

Development

With enough research amassed, it was time to start writing the manuscript. This is where we really put our word processing software to work. We outlined, wrote, revised, wrote some more, outlined again, and revised again. Whenever one of us finished a chapter, he used the modem to send the chapter to the other to check and revise the work. With the help of the word processing program, WordPerfect, we streamlined much of the writing process. For example, we checked our spelling electronically, thus avoiding the embarrassment of

Pedal While You Write

Steve Roberts decided to create a life out of his three passions: travel, technology, and bicycling. The result is the world's smartest bike, the 350-pound Behemoth (big, electronic, human-energized machine, only too heavy), which comes complete with stereo, refrigerator, solar power, and a word processor. The keyboard is built into the handlebars of the bicycle and doubles as a musical instrument. Actually, there are about a half-dozen computers on board, one of which allows Roberts to hook into the Navstar satellite system and pinpoint his location to within 50 feet. There is also a top-notch security system. If the bike is stolen, it can alert the police, and if anything is not functioning properly, it can alert Roberts. What else could a self-confessed "yuppie hobo" want?

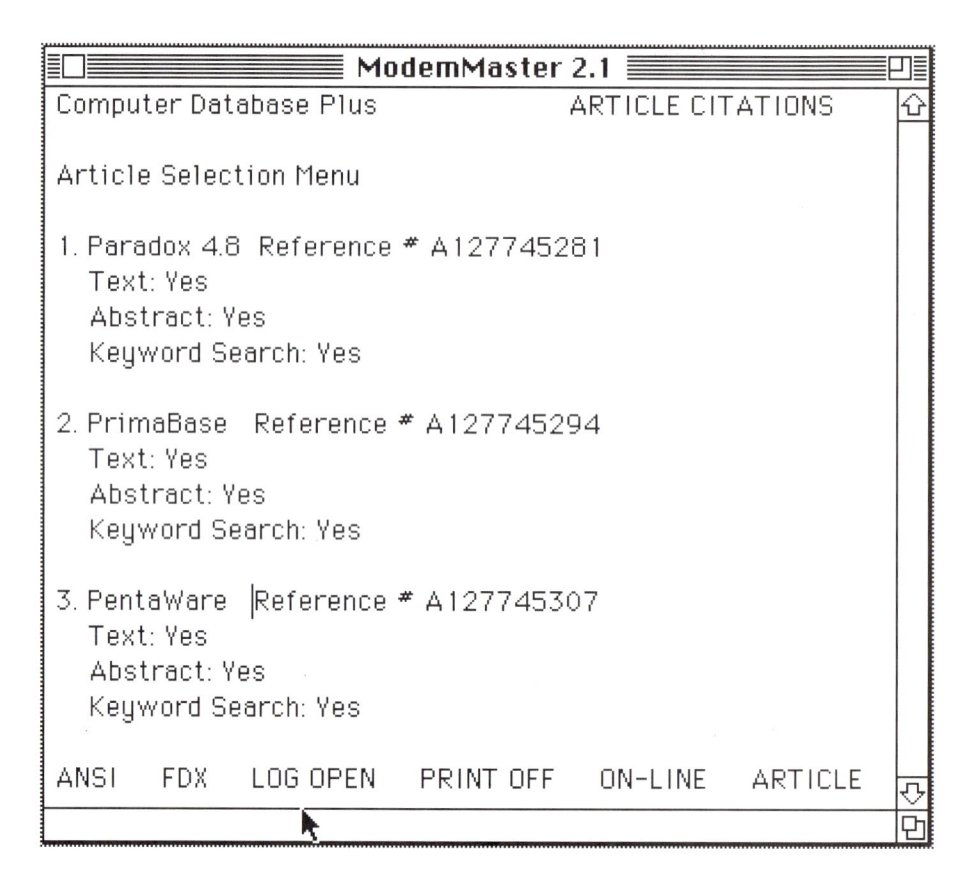

Figure 1-9
Using a modem and communications software to call online services, such as Compuserve, gave us instant access to large volumes of information for research.

sending the publisher a manuscript full of typos and misspelled words (Figure 1-10).

Each time we finished a chapter, we used another piece of application software called Rightwriter, which is a grammar checker. It searched our prose for nonstandard usage, bad sentences, and all kinds of other problems.

After completing about half the manuscript, we printed it out and sent it to a group of reviewers that teach classes like the one you are in now. While the reviewers critiqued our work, we plunged ahead with the rest of the manuscript. When the reviews came back, we went back to the same word processing files to revise our work again. We went through the same process a second time, with the second half of the manuscript.

Production

As soon as we were done writing the manuscript, production began and a lot more people—and computers—got involved. This book was produced using

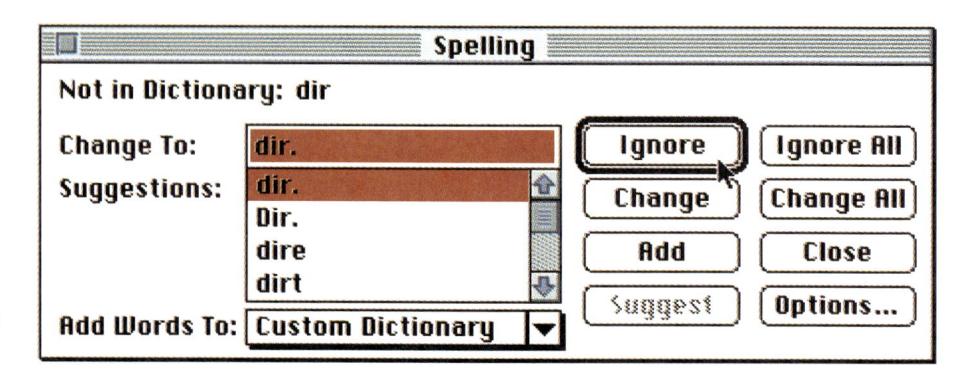

Figure 1-10
Microsoft Word's spell checker was invaluable in preparing the manuscript.

• CHAPTER 1: Introduction to Microcomputers •   11

the techniques of **desktop publishing**, or **DTP**. Desktop publishing is a process in which microcomputers, high-quality printers, and advanced text and graphics software are used to produce complex professional documents, such as books, advertisements, pamphlets, and magazines. The techniques of DTP have literally revolutionized the book-publishing industry. Books such as this one can now be produced in far less time and for less money than is required by traditional book-making practices.

As production began on this book, a production manager took over the job of coordinating everyone's efforts and keeping everyone on schedule. To help her in her work, she used a piece of project management software called Microsoft Project (Figure 1-11). Project management software keeps track of schedules, budgets, and vendors. Not only does it help the manager, but it also helps the vendors get paid on time.

The first group of people to be hired by the production manager were the copy editor, the input editor, and the proofreader. The copy editor wrote corrections on the manuscript to make it logical, consistent, and grammatically accurate. The input editor entered the changes into the word processing files, and the proofreader checked the input editor's work.

While the copy editor, input editor, and proofreader were working on the text, an illustrator and a photo researcher were making or finding all the illustrations you see in this book. The illustrator worked with a graphics program called Adobe Illustrator to create the line drawings and another program called Hijaak to create the screen captures. The photo researcher used a database of photos, listed by subject matter, that she created with a program called FoxPro.

When the proofreader, the illustrator, and the photo researcher were done, the manuscript went into page makeup. In this stage, the word processor files and the electronic illustrations were imported into another type of application program, known as desktop publishing software. DTP software is a powerful tool for formatting pages that will be used in books, pamphlets, ads—anything that needs to look professional (Figure 1-12, p. 13). Word processing software contains some of the same features as DTP software, but the latter

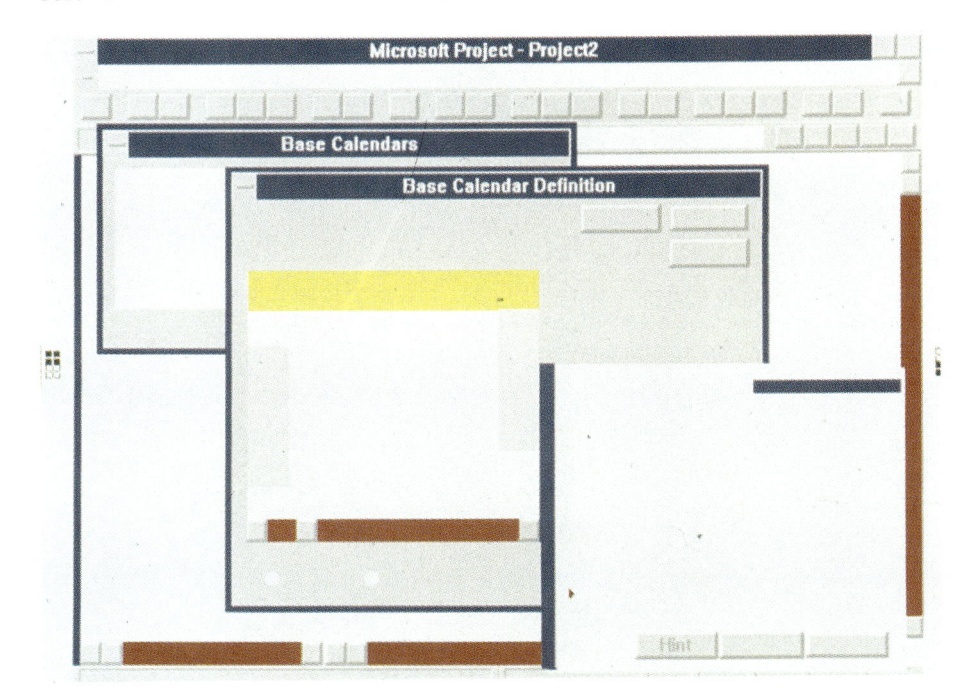

A Street Map for the Whole Country

Not all databases are filled with information about companies, business transactions, or scientific research. Some are filled with graphic images, and one new application for such graphic databases involves maps. Street Atlas USA from Delorme Mapping Company comes on a single CD-ROM and has street maps for the entire country—over one million maps in all. The maps include the address ranges along each street, ZIP codes, and area codes, as well as names of mountains, rivers, lakes, and other geographical features, all in full color. Users can search all this data for specific geographical names or street addresses, use a zoom feature to display various levels of detail, and even copy sections of maps onto other documents—all for only $99.

Figure 1-11
Keeping track of all the little tasks related to producing the book was made a lot easier with project management software; we used Microsoft Project.

HISTORY

Intel and the Birth of the Microprocessor

In 1969 a Japanese firm called Busicom was working on a new low-cost, desktop printing calculator. Looking for a custom chip manufacturer, Busicom approached one-year-old Intel, a company that had spun off from Fairchild Semiconductor. It was only one of the new companies that had sprung up dedicated to the idea that the future lay in semiconductors, not in the magnetic core memories then in use.

At the time, Intel had no in-house expertise in random-logic design and was in no position to bid on the project, which would involve approximately 10 custom circuits. However, Ted Hoff, then manager of Intel's Application Research Department, thought the Busicom project was an opportunity to define a small set of standard components designed around the possibility of a central processing unit (CPU) on a chip.

Late that year Hoff and an application engineer named Stan Mazor defined an architecture consisting of a 4-bit CPU, a RAM to store data, a ROM to store program instructions, and several I/O parts to interface with such external devices as a keyboard, printers, and switches. Working with Busicom engineers, the two men also defined and verified the CPU instruction set.

By the following spring, Federico Faggin had joined Intel and begun designing a calculator chip set. While at Fairchild, Faggin had developed a new process, called *silicon-gate technology* for fabricating high-density, high-performance metal-oxide semiconductor integrated circuits. He set to work using this technology on the Busicom project.

With his silicon-gate technology Faggin had to develop a new methodology for random-logic design—something that had never been done before. Since the circuits had to be small, it was necessary to use bootstrap loads, which no one at Intel thought could be done with silicon-gate technology. Once Faggin demonstrated it would work, bootstrap loads were incorporated into the memory designs as well.

The chip set, which Faggin called the 4000 family—consisted of four 16-pin devices. The 4001 was the first chip designed and laid out. It consisted of a 2K ROM with a 4-bit mask-programmable I/O port, and when it came out in October 1970 it worked perfectly. But not until the end of February 1971 did the developers get all of the other chips working as well. In mid-March 1971 Busicom received the full kits of components and verified that the calculators now worked perfectly. The first microprocessor was a reality.

The designers were full of plans for the chip set, but Intel's management decided that the 4000 family was only good for calculators. Management also pointed out that the product had been designed under exclusive contract to Busicom—it could not be sold, or even announced, to anyone else.

A little later, when the need for a production tester arose, Faggin decided to demonstrate that the 4000 family could, indeed, be used for noncalculator uses. He successfully used the 4004 as the tester's main controller. Intel negotiated with Busicom a lower price for the chip set in exchange for the right to market the 4004 for noncalculator uses. In November 1971, the 4000 family, known as the MCS-4 (for microcomputer system 4-bit) was officially introduced.

Meanwhile, Computer Terminal Corporation (now Datapoint) had asked Intel to integrate the CPU of the company's new intelligent terminal into a few chips and to reduce the cost and size of its electronics. Intel's Hoff came up with a more complex version of the 4004, an 8-bit device Intel called the 1201, later renamed the 8008. Although other companies, such as Texas Instruments, advertised that they had a central processing unit on a chip, none were ever marketed.

Intel introduced the 8008 in April 1972, and two years later the 8080—a vastly improved chip that allowed several applications not possible before—was brought out. With the 8080, the microprocessor had come of age. ∎

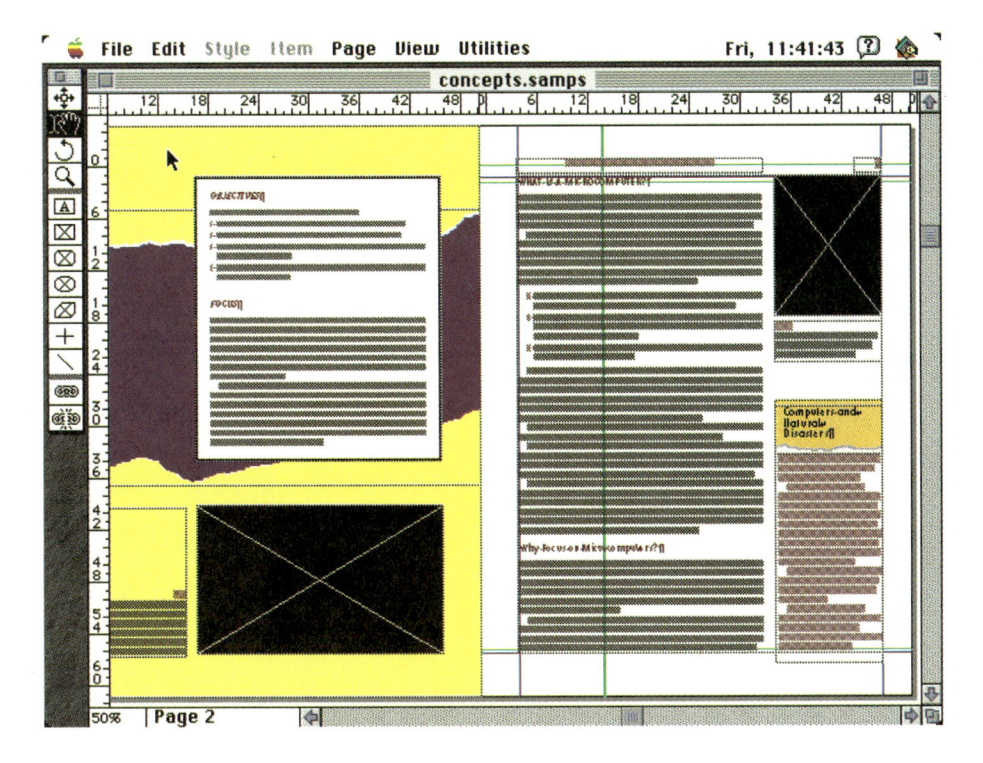

Figure 1-12
QuarkXPress is a powerful DTP program that integrates text and art electronically and prints the pages directly to film.

specializes in text formatting and the ability to combine text and graphics on the same page.

Page makeup was the last major phase of production before printing, although the phase includes several cycles before it is completed. Each cycle is called a *pass*. After the production team members finished each pass, they printed out copies of the book's pages on a laser printer. Different types of quality checks were performed each time a new pass was printed.

Finally, after the last quality check, the book was printed. Even this step involved computers. The laser printer that printed the different passes produced a print of quality high enough to check for errors, but not high enough to print books from. Book printing required projecting the electronic page makeup files onto photographic film. The film was then passed through an offset printer, the printed pages were cut, and the book was bound. Voilà! You see the result before you.

MANY USERS, MANY USES

Publishing, of course, isn't the only business that uses microcomputers extensively. If you look closely, you will find that almost every business has been, at the very least, affected by their use. Equally important are the effects the microcomputer has had on homes and schools. Let's take a look at some of the varied applications that computers have in these three areas.

In the Schools

You have undoubtedly seen a few of the ways in which computers are used on campus (Figure 1-13). For writing papers, typewriters are becoming a thing of the past. Most students find that using a word processor is much faster and far more convenient, especially when it comes to editing and revising. But besides the ubiquitous word processing program, what other types of application software do students use in their studies?

Figure 1-13
Students have found microcomputers to be very useful in nearly all academic disciplines.

Where in the World Is—Who?

Carmen Sandiego, that's who, a now-legendary crook who does things like attempting to steal the Taj Mahal or the original copy of the Magna Carta. She's glamorous, hip, and, thanks to the fact that children interact with her on their computer in a series of bestselling games (sales of over 1 million), she can travel anywhere in the world and visit any time. Oh, and yes, along the way children learn a lot about geography, history, and a variety of other subjects. And that's the real purpose of the games from Broderbund Software. Each player is a detective from Acme Detective Agency and must capture all of Carmen's gang to win. Each game comes with a reference book, appropriate to the storyline, which provides clues. Kids love the games, and parents love the fact that their children are learning—schools have even had Carmen Sandiego Day, complete with an actress dressed as the crook arriving by helicopter. No one is saying where the next Carmen Sandiego game will be set, but there are a lot of people who can hardly wait to find out.

Figure 1-14
Microcomputers in the home provide both practical applications and entertainment value.

In writing papers, another useful tool is hypermedia software, such as HyperCard for the Macintosh. Hypermedia programs are similar to database programs but less rigidly structured. HyperCard, for instance, allows writers to create a set of electronic note cards and then create links between them. Using such a tool, a writer can work out the structure of an argument or presentation before writing it.

The most widely used application after the word processor is the electronic spreadsheet. In addition to helping students keep track of finances, spreadsheets are invaluable as research tools. This is especially true in the sciences, where empirical evidence is often numeric. For example, if you are conducting a psychological study, the quality of your research depends largely on the number of people in your study. But as your sample size grows, the amount of math involved in analyzing your study grows too. Spreadsheet software is designed to make this kind of work easier. Most programs, in fact, have statistical functions built in. And not only does the software speed the numeric calculations, but with a few commands you can also generate graphs and charts that summarize your data or your analyses.

Another common application used in research is the database. In much the same way that we collected data about articles we read during the research phase of this book, students use databases to organize their own research. Whereas the spreadsheet is good for organizing numeric data, database software is excellent for collecting many kinds of data, including numbers, text, graphic images, and even sound. Once you have collected a large body of data, you can use the software to search through it, organize it, and pick out specific subsets of related data.

Computer graphics software is even used in the arts at school. Fine arts majors can create startling images using computers. They can even combine more traditional formats with electronically generated material.

At Home

The first place that microcomputers appeared was in the home. Today, applications geared for the home market are more diverse than ever (Figure 1-14). One popular type is software that helps you figure your taxes. For people who own a home, or work at home, or have outside investments, these programs can help identify items on which taxes must be paid and where deductions can be listed. These programs can save you incredible amounts of both time and money.

Games are also popular on home computers. Some of the best-selling types are adventure games, flight simulators, and sports games such as golf and football.

Databases have proven to be invaluable in the home. People find it very convenient to organize data about their books, their recipes, or their collections (such as stamps). Insurance companies encourage their customers to keep a careful inventory of their valuables in case of fire or theft, and database software is an excellent way to do it.

In addition, people at home use all the same types of software as they do at school or at the office. They use word processors to write letters, spreadsheets to keep track of finances, and communications software to access information services.

Figure 1-15
The office environment has been revolutionized by the pervasive use of microcomputers for all aspects of business, increasing productivity and communication.

At the Office

The biggest market for application software is the office, and the uses for microcomputers are as varied as the businesses that use them (Figure 1-15). As in schools, the most widely used applications are word processors and spreadsheets. Creating documents (correspondence, reports, and so on) and managing finances are the two most commonly pursued tasks in an office.

Another application that has steadily grown with microcomputer use is electronic mail, or E-mail. E-mail lets one computer user send a message to another user on the other side of the building—or the other side of the planet. As long as both users have access to a common computer network, they can communicate. Using E-mail is a lot like using a modem, except that the two users don't have to be using their computers at the same time. With E-mail, a businessperson just types a message to a client or associate and sends it. When the recipient next accesses the E-mail application, the message will be there waiting. Businesses have found that this type of communication can save large amounts of time and money.

Another application for which businesses have found great use is presentation graphics. Whether you are selling an idea or product to your boss or to a potential customer, presentation graphics software can help get your point across. These programs give you a great deal of power to create and format charts, graphs, and accompanying text.

SUMMARY

A wide variety of computers are used today, but they can be broadly classified as special-purpose and general-purpose computers. Special-purpose computers, such as the bank's ATM, accept only certain types of input and present a narrow range of outputs. In this book, we will be focusing on a type of general-purpose computer, the microcomputer. Microcomputers are the logical choice of

Grandmaster Computer

The age-old question, "Which is smarter, man or machine?" has just been answered, at least when the application involves a chess game. The computer can now beat the grandmaster. Since computers are faster at calculating, they can test every possible move and every possible outcome for any given position of pieces on the board. Although a grandmaster has more familiarity with what may work and what may not, a human cannot exhaust every possibility each time it is his turn. But does the computer enjoy the game?

Computerized Travel Guides

Let's say you are visiting New York City for the first time and would like to visit a Thai restaurant that offers dancing and nearby parking, is close to your hotel, and allows two people to enjoy an evening for under $50. Thanks to a computerized version of the famous Zagat travel guides, you can punch in your requirements, and if such an establishment exists, the computer lets you know. And if you need directions from your location to the restaurant, a little red Porsche zooms around the screen to show you the way. CityGuide (as the computer guide is known) currently offers help for three cities—New York, Los Angeles, and Chicago. Guides to 27 other U.S. cities should be available soon, with Europe and Japan following—as will CD-ROM versions of the information. Random House is converting its famous Fodor's travel books onto software that can be used with handheld computers. The Official Airlines Guides, published monthly, is now available on diskettes and CD-ROM. Some software suppliers are even looking ahead to a guide with an electronic voice for car computers so that the driver doesn't have to look at the map.

computer studies today because they are capable of performing so many tasks that are relevant to modern workplaces, schools, and homes.

The computing cycle includes four kinds of hardware device: there must be input, processing, output, and storage devices. To be capable of performing useful work, a computer also needs two kinds of software. The operating system includes basic instructions that are vital to the internal functioning of the computer. Application software tells the computer how to perform a certain type of job. The six most common types of application software are word processing, graphics, desktop publishing, spreadsheet, database, and communications software.

Microcomputers were used throughout the making of this book. The publisher used spreadsheet software to generate the budget and word processing software to draw up contracts. The authors used communications software to communicate with each other and access information services and bulletin boards. They also used database software to keep track of articles. Finally, they used word processing software to write the manuscript. The book was produced using the techniques of desktop publishing, the cornerstone of which is DTP software, used for page makeup. The production process also required project management software, graphics software, and database software.

Microcomputers are used in thousands of ways at schools, in homes, and in offices. At school, students use them to write papers and conduct research. At home, they are used to figure taxes, play games, keep inventories, write letters, and keep track of finances. Businesses use microcomputers in countless ways. The two most common applications are word processing and spreadsheets. E-mail is also a growing application. Presentation graphics are used to convey ideas. In all these ways and more, microcomputers are becoming a permanent part of our world.

KEY TERMS

application	hardware	output
application software	input	processing
computer	mainframe	program
computing cycle	microcomputer	software
desktop publishing (DTP)	minicomputer	special-purpose computer
E-mail	modem	storage
general-purpose computer	operating system	supercomputer

REVIEW QUESTIONS

1. Is a calculator a general-purpose or special-purpose computer? Why? Explain your reasoning.
2. How might you use a word processor, spreadsheet program, and database program in the classes you are currently taking at school?
3. Even if minis and mainframes were inexpensive, why is it unlikely that you would buy one for your home?
4. What is a scanner? A mouse? A modem? What functions does each serve?

5. If you wanted to create a professional-looking brochure to advertise your carpentry business, what kind of application software would you use?
6. How could you use database software to help you write a term paper?
7. Describe the individual processes of the computing cycle.
8. What are the major types of application software?

Microcomputer Hardware

2

OBJECTIVES

After completing this chapter, you will be able to

- Define the term *hardware*.
- Identify the parts of the computing process.
- Identify the basic components that make up a microcomputer system.
- Distinguish between random access and read-only memory.
- Discuss the different types of disk drives.
- Explain the uses of the various kinds of peripheral devices.

FOCUS

Computer hardware is usually considered to be the physical devices—those that we can see and touch—of a computer system. Hardware for a typical microcomputer includes the microprocessor itself, its associated processing and memory circuits in the system unit, storage devices such as hard and floppy disk drives, and peripheral devices for input and output, such as keyboards, monitors, and printers.

Despite the many sophisticated tasks they are capable of performing, all computers operate using a simple set of electrical signals; all the computer has to know is whether a given circuit is on or off. Using these two choices to represent data in binary format, the computer can manipulate information nearly any way we ask it to in order to solve a problem or perform a task.

Microcomputers today can use many specialized hardware devices for performing the tasks of the computing cycle: input, processing, storage, and output. We will look at a number of these devices to understand what they do and how they work together.

Input

Human data is a series of complex thoughts and ideas, but computer data is nothing more than a series of electrical signals. To convert human data into a form the computer can understand, each number, letter, or any other input is converted into a specific combination of electrical signals in binary format.

A signal in binary format is either on or off, connected or not connected, open or closed. The **binary system**, which uses only 0 and 1 to represent all numbers, is perfect for computers, which can understand only two states. The number 0 represents an off signal and the number 1 represents an on signal. The number 3 in the binary system is 11; that is, a series of two on electrical signals. Similarly, one on and one off electrical signal converts to the binary number 10, equal to the number 2 in the base 10 system.

What about all the letters, punctuation marks, keystrokes, and so on? Computer code simply combines each of these into a unique combination of 0s and 1s.

Each 0 or 1, the smallest piece of data used by the computer, is known as a **bit**—short for *binary digit*. Data from an input device enters the computer in groups of 8 bits, called a **byte**. For this reason, computer code generally assigns each letter, number, and symbol a unique combination of eight 0s and 1s.

For example, the word HELLO, typed on the keyboard, enters the computer as five separate bytes—one for each letter:

Byte	Character
01001000	H
01000101	E
01001100	L
01001100	L
01001111	O

Several binary codes exist; however, the most common code, which all popular U.S. microcomputers can use, is the **American Standard Code for Information Interchange (ASCII)**. Table 2-1 shows the ASCII code, which includes letters, punctuation marks, other keystrokes, and control codes.

Processing

Once it has been converted to binary form, data is available for processing. The **CPU (central processing unit)** performs this function in conjunction with memory and storage (Figure 2-1, p. 23). The CPU, the "brains" of the computer system, consists of a **control unit** and an **arithmetic/logic unit** (**ALU**).

- The control unit controls the computer system, acting like a traffic cop directing the flow of data throughout the system.
- The ALU performs all mathematical and logical functions.

Memory is the area of the computer that stores data. **Random access memory** (**RAM**, discussed later in more detail) temporarily stores data needed for the current processing task. When the computer's power is turned off, the data vanishes. **Storage**, by contrast, is the area where data permanently resides, whether the computer's power is on or off.

Table 2-1
ASCII Codes

Decimal	Character	Decimal	Character	Decimal	Character	Decimal	Character
0	NUL	32	(SP)	64	@	96	`
1	SOU	33	!	65	A	97	a
2	STX	34	"	66	B	98	b
3	ETX	35	#	67	C	99	c
4	EST	36	$	68	D	100	d
5	ENQ	37	%	69	E	101	e
6	ACK	38	&	70	F	102	f
7	(BEL)	39	'	71	G	103	g
8	(BS)	40	(	72	H	104	h
9	(HT)	41	)	73	I	105	i
10	(LF)	42	*	74	J	106	j
11	VT	43	+	75	K	107	k
12	(FF)	44	,	76	L	108	l
13	(CR)	45	-	77	M	109	m
14	SO	46	.	78	N	110	n
15	SI	47	/	79	O	111	o
16	DLE	48	0	80	P	112	p
17	DC1	49	1	81	Q	113	q
18	DC2	50	2	82	R	114	r
19	DC3	51	3	83	S	115	s
20	DC4	52	4	84	T	116	t
21	NAK	53	5	85	U	117	u
22	SYN	54	6	86	V	118	v
23	ETB	55	7	87	W	119	w
24	CAN	56	8	88	X	120	x
25	EM	57	9	89	Y	121	y
26	SUB	58	:	90	Z	122	z
27	(ESC)	59	;	91	[	123	{
28	FS	60	<	92	\	124		
29	GS	61	=	93	]	125	}
30	RS	62	>	94	^	126	~
31	US	63	?	95	_	127	

Column 1: Control characters.

Ones in parens are most commonly used on micros.
BEL = BELL   FF = FORM FEED
BS = BACKSPACE   CR = CARRIAGE RETURN
HT = TAB   ESC = ESCAPE
LF = LIVE FEED   SP = SPACE

Changing Keys

When the typewriter was first invented in 1867, the letters on the keyboard were arranged to slow down the typist. Why? If typists went too quickly, the keys would jam, so letters that were usually next to each other in a word were placed far apart on the keyboard. However, when the electronic typewriter was introduced this was no longer a problem, so a new keyboard, called the Dvorak keyboard, was introduced. It had the letters that normally followed each other next to one another. But the Dvorak keyboard did not catch on for the simple reason that generations of typists were used to their QWERTY system (named for the first six letters on the typewriter keyboard). Now a new keyboard has been developed to help users avoid carpal tunnel syndrome. A common, debilitating malady for many people who use a keyboard over an extended period of time, carpal tunnel syndrome is caused by the continuous flexing of the wrist. To avoid this, the new keyboard splits the traditional keyboard into two sections, one for each hand. It also has an extended lip for the wrist to rest on. Will it replace the entrenched QWERTY keyboard? That depends on the users.

Data typically flows throughout the system in the following way:

1. The control unit directs the transfer of data from an input device to either memory or storage. For example, the text that appears on the screen as you type is placed in random access memory.

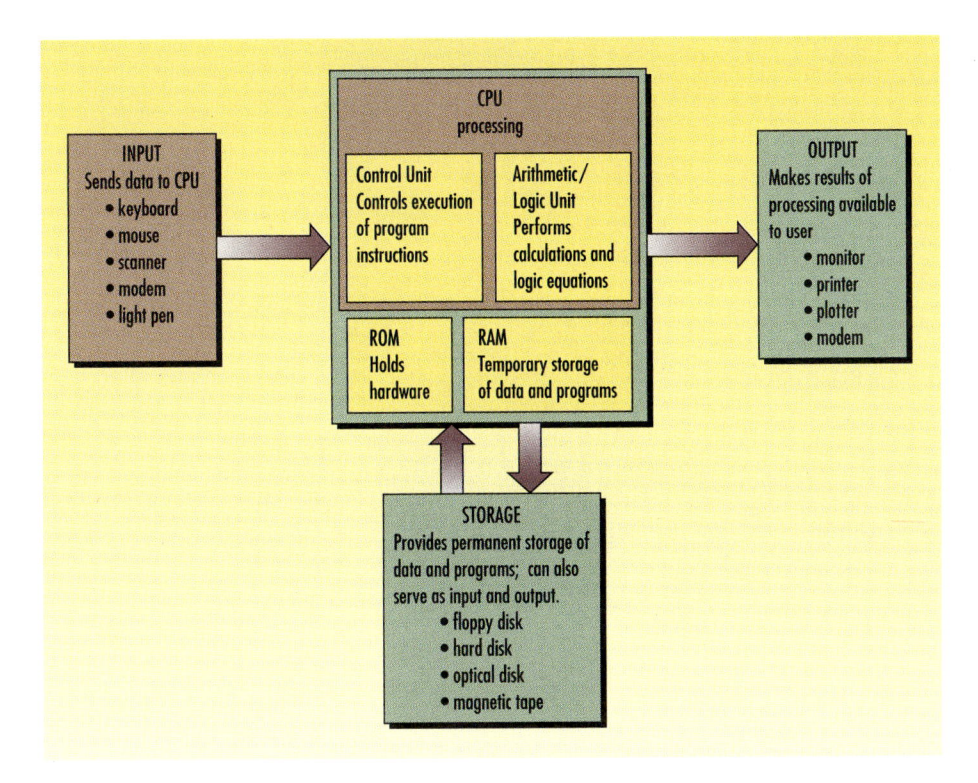

Figure 2-1

Interactions among computer hardware: the CPU's control unit orchestrates the computing process, accepting data from input devices, giving instructions to the arithmetic-logic unit, storing data temporarily in memory and permanently on storage devices, and sending data to output devices.

2. Data in storage remains there until it is needed for the current processing task. Then the control unit transfers the data from storage to memory. When you select a spreadsheet program and budget report, for example, they are loaded from storage to memory.

3. The control unit sends the required data from memory to the arithmetic/logic unit. For example, the formula and data you need to calculate the return on investment are placed in the ALU.

4. The ALU makes the necessary mathematical and logical computations as you enter data and formulas.

5. The control unit sends the results to memory. It can also send them to storage or to a printer. It erases the data from memory when instructed to do so or when the computer's power is turned off.

Output

The result of processing is called **output**. The output of the processing just described is a new budget report that can be saved magnetically in storage and printed on a printer.

HARDWARE DEVICES

Using this basic understanding of input, processing, and output, we can now look at a microcomputer's specific hardware devices.

System Unit

The system unit, sometimes called the "box" or the processing unit, houses processing devices, various electronic circuits, and other components (Figure 2-2, p. 25).

HISTORY

Altair and the Birth of the Microcomputer

Although computers have been around since the 1940s, the first microcomputer—or personal computer—appeared in 1975. In fact, the Altair computer made its debut on the January, 1975 cover of *Popular Electronics* magazine. Like so much else in the early days of the computer industry, its appearance was part luck, part genius, and part necessity.

Altair's "father" was Ed Roberts, a six-foot, four-inch man who weighed close to 300 pounds. A gadget nut, Roberts had an insatiable appetite for information and had joined the Air Force to learn more about electronics. Eventually posted at Kirtland Field, near Albuquerque, New Mexico, he started a company called Model Instrumentation and Telemetry Systems, or MITS, which sold model rocket equipment Roberts made in his garage.

In 1969, Roberts moved MITS (by then "Micro" had replaced "Model" in the company's name) to what had been a restaurant called The Enchanted Sandwich Shop just off Route 66, and sank all his money into making a commercial calculator. MITS was the first U.S. company to sell calculator kits, so it was extremely successful at first. Unfortunately, when larger companies such as Texas Instruments entered the market, the ensuing price wars devastated MITS.

> Its appearance was part luck, part genius, and part necessity. The railroad *lost* the world's first personal computer.... The Altair had rather limited appeal. There was no software to run on it, and it did not even have a keyboard.

Desperate to save his company, Roberts decided to build computer hobby kits in 1974. He browbeat Intel into selling him its 8080 chips in volume for $75 each (rather than the usual $350), so he could market his kits for $375.

Roberts was still building his prototype machine when he was contacted by the technical editor of *Popular Electronics*, Les Solomon, who was looking for a computer to run on the cover of the magazine. Roberts promised that his machine would be ready by the end of 1974, and Solomon decided to feature it on the January 1975 cover.

Solomon's 12-year-old daughter, a "Star Trek" fan, came up with Altair after a star to which the Starship *Enterprise* had been heading. As part of the Altair ad campaign, Roberts himself came up with the term "personal computer."

Roberts shipped Solomon the only Altair in existence so the editor could test it—but it never arrived in New York. The railroad *lost* the world's first personal computer. Readers of *Popular Electronics* didn't know the computer on the cover was actually a metal shell hastily put together by MITS engineers.

Within weeks, more than 4,000 orders for the Altair had been placed with MITS. A few people even flew to Albuquerque hoping to get their Altair sooner by appearing in person.

For all its historic importance, the Altair had rather limited appeal. There was no software to run on it, and it did not even have a keyboard. Moreover, it was sold unassembled—to assemble it, you had to be able to solder. And to use it, you had to be able to program it in complex 8080 machine language by flicking a row of switches on its front panel. Blinking red lights were the only display Altair could show. It had only 256 bytes of memory, though there were 18 slots for more memory boards that would increase its capacity to 4,096 bytes.

Among those who saw that January *Popular Electronics* were two Harvard students, Bill Gates and Paul Allen, who decided to provide a programming language that would allow the Altair to actually do the work of a computer. Without an Altair to work on (Roberts had the only working model in existence), they invented what became MITS BASIC—and in the process laid the foundation for Microsoft Corporation. ∎

• CHAPTER 2: Microcomputer Hardware •

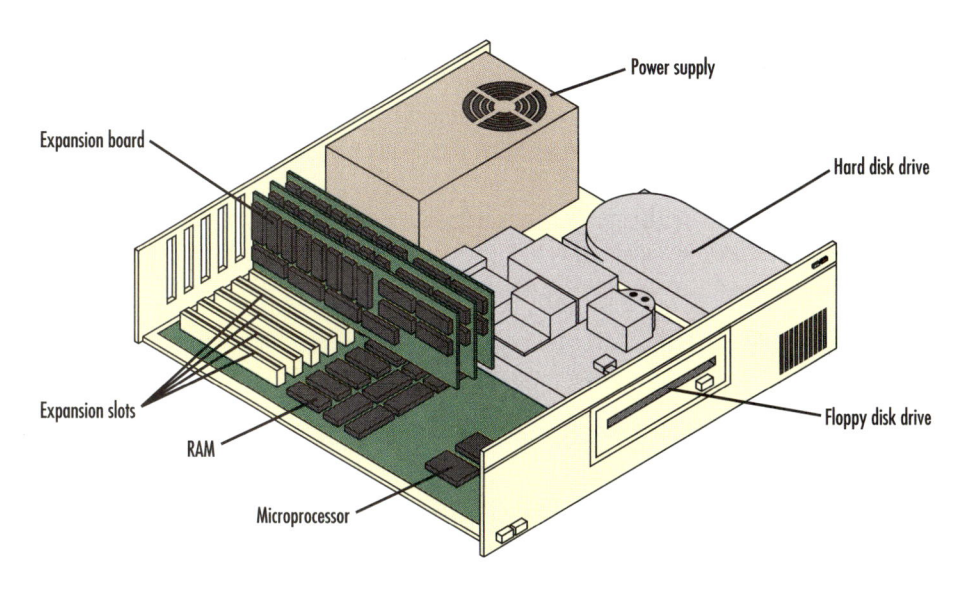

Figure 2-2
This view of the inside of a typical microcomputer shows the major parts of the computer system.

Chips, Printed Circuit Boards, and Slots. Many of the computer's operating parts, such as the CPU and memory, consist of tiny silicon **chips**, also called **semiconductors** or **integrated circuits** (ICs). Chips are enclosed by a carrier package called a **DIP (dual-inline package)**. Users commonly do not distinguish between DIPs and chips; generally the entire enclosed package is referred to as a chip.

Each enclosed chip plugs into a socket on a **printed circuit** board (PC board, also called a **card**). Printed on each board is a series of metallic lines that act like embedded wires; these provide the hard-wired (directly connected) interconnections between different circuit elements (Figure 2-3).

Figure 2-3
(a) An integrated circuit chip; the tiny circuits are photographically etched into the silicon. (b) The chip is encased in a plastic cover called a dual-inline package (DIP), which provides electrical connections for the chip. (c) Circuit boards, such as this one here, provide places to insert the DIPs and circuit paths connecting them.

Responding to the Master's Voice

Computer technology has often improved the quality of life for those who are disabled, but simply using the computer can sometimes be a problem. The introduction of the graphical user interface put blind people at a distinct disadvantage; how to operate a computer that graphically displayed options? One solution is to use a voice synthesizer to describe icons. And rather than a mouse, keyboard commands can direct the computer.

However, this approach will not work for everybody. Consider Dennis Muchen, a counselor who is blind, wheelchair-bound, and missing some fingers. He first used a computer with a speech output that read back his work to him, but the state of his hands made this work slow and difficult. He now uses a desktop microphone to verbally command his computer to dictate letters and reports. The computer reads them back so he can verbally edit and format them.

The printed circuit board containing the CPU is the **system board** or **motherboard**. A microcomputer's motherboard can have a number of additional slots, called *expansion slots*. Each expansion slot can accept a separate printed circuit board. The additional printed circuit boards are called *expansion boards*, *plug-in boards*, or *cards*, and each can hold various combinations of chips. Computers with an **open architecture** allow users to add expansion boards themselves, providing the flexibility of adding new chips with different functions.

Microprocessor Chips. The fundamental difference between a microcomputer and a mainframe computer is that a microcomputer's CPU is contained on one chip. This chip is called a **microprocessor**. Various manufacturers produce a number of microprocessors with differing capabilities and capacities. A microprocessor's capacity is based on the number of bits it can process in one computing cycle and the speed with which it performs a computing cycle. Microprocessors originally processed 4 bits in one processing cycle. Today, chips are available that process 8, 16, 32, or 64 bits. In short, advances in microprocessor chip technology results in more data per cycle at higher speeds.

Types of Microprocessors

16-bit	Intel 8086, 8088, 80286
32-bit	Intel 80386, 80486
	Motorola 68000, 68010, 68020, 680030, 680040
64-bit	Intel Pentium
	Motorola Power PC

As data moves through the computer system, it travels along paths on the PC boards in a prescribed format. The electrical pathway for transporting data from one location to another is called a **bus** (also called a *system bus* or *bus line*). The bus consists of a set of parallel wires on the motherboard that connects the CPU with memory, other control chips, and expansion boards. The first 8-bit microprocessors used a bus with 8 wires (an 8-bit bus). Most of today's 16-bit microprocessors use 16-bit buses; most 32-bit microprocessors use 32-bit buses and so on.

Each microcomputer has a system clock. The system clock sends a continuous rhythmic series of electrical pulses, much like a metronome, which the other circuits use to stay in synchronization with each other. The speed of

Figure 2-4
The 80486, or just 486, microprocessor is a popular microprocessor for the IBM-compatible family of microcomputers. The actual circuitry is on a silicon chip less than 1/2" square; the package is about 2" square to provide room for all the electrical connections that are needed.

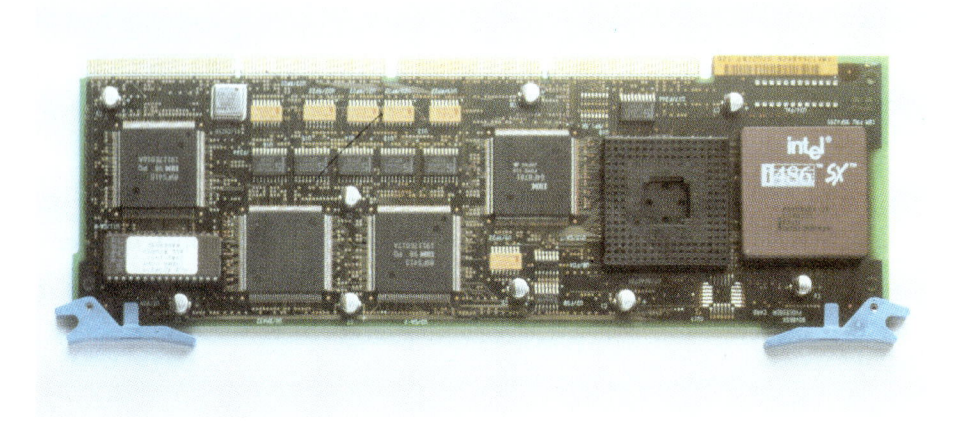

the clock's pulses sets the operating speed of the computer: the faster the clock pulses, the faster the computer can process data. Clock speed is measured in megahertz (MHz; 1 MHz equals 1 million cycles per second). Early microcomputers, such as the Apple and Apple II, used a clock that ran at 1 MHz. Today's microcomputers operate at speeds up to 66 MHz.

These two factors, the width of the bus and the speed of the clock, together determine to a large extent the computer's power. Think of the bus as a highway. The number of bits it can carry at one time is the number of highway lanes, and clock speed is the speed limit. With a higher speed limit, the cars travel faster; with more lanes, more cars can travel simultaneously. A computer's processing power is largely the product of clock speed and the number of bits processed simultaneously; however, the question "How fast is the computer?" is still difficult to answer. Speed is a somewhat elusive term when you are dealing with computers. It is influenced by the microprocessor, the clock speed, the bus, the amount of time needed for information to flow from a disk drive into RAM, the amount of time it takes to move data from RAM through the CPU, and even the amount of time required to display information on a monitor. Leading industry periodicals often provide comparison tests of computer speed for different brands of microcomputers, using as criteria the computer's speed in processing text and numeric data, manipulating databases, displaying graphics, and transmitting data to and from peripheral devices. These tests give the consumer important performance information for making a buying decision.

RAM Chips. RAM (random access memory) is the temporary memory where the computer holds data for the current processing task. The computer can read data from and write data to—that is, change—RAM. When the computer's power is turned off, all data in RAM is erased. For example, when you type a term paper, the words on the screen reside in RAM. If you turn off the computer without saving the data in permanent storage, the term paper is lost.

RAM, also known as *memory*, *main memory*, *primary memory*, or *internal memory*, is measured in kilobytes (K), megabytes (Mb), and gigabytes (Gb):

$$1 \text{ kilobyte (K)} = 2^{10} \text{ bytes (approximately 1,000 [actually 1,024] bytes)}$$
$$1 \text{ megabyte (Mb)} = 2^{20} \text{ bytes (approximately 1 million bytes)}$$
$$1 \text{ gigabyte (Gb)} = 2^{30} \text{ bytes (approximately 1 billion bytes)}$$

Asking how much memory is enough is like asking how much money is enough. The larger the memory, the greater the computer's ability to perform complex tasks. For example, the desktop publishing program Ventura Publisher uses about 584K of memory. If it is used on a computer having 640K of memory, only 56K will be left for text and graphics. Yet a single figure can use far more memory than this; a full-color photograph can use several megabytes. Thus the greater the memory, the more efficiently Ventura can handle large documents.

The various computer systems use memory differently. For example, an Apple Macintosh uses memory as a continuous set. That is, although there are upper limits on the total amount of RAM possible in Macintosh computers (it differs from model to model), there is no differentiation between the types of RAM. This is not the case with IBM-family computers.

What Price Memory?

As sophisticated new software is developed for the computer, users with older PCs are sometimes discovering they do not have enough memory to run the programs they most need. Graphic-intensive programs are real memory hogs, so software for desktop publishing programs, computer-aided design programs, scientific modeling, and even complex business analysis often requires users to add memory to their machines. Fortunately, the cost for adding memory has steadily declined. In 1988, 1 megabit of memory cost $42. By 1994 it was less than $3.75. It is relatively easy to add memory because the trend is to open architecture in PCs, and memory comes in modules that snap into a computer's motherboard. But what to do when you need more memory on your laptop or palmtop computer? An IC DRAM (integrated circuit dynamic random access memory) card can help you. About the size of a thick credit card, it is inserted into your laptop like a floppy disk and can boost memory 1 to 8 megabytes.

It Looks Kinda Familiar...

Imagine the Mona Lisa, the da Vinci painting with the tantalizing smile, with someone else's face. Imagine the image suddenly deconstructing electronically. By using an electronic scanner, artists can now incorporate images created by the great masters into their computers and then manipulate those images any way they wish—changing the color, twisting the viewpoint. Artist Lillian Schwartz sometimes incorporates her own face into the picture, or she layers one image on top of another, resulting in a picture that is both familiar and strange. Some of her images are painted directly onto the computer by using a pressure-sensitive screen and stylus. These images are often superimposed on top of scanned images, as when she merges her face with the faces of famous women, such as Nefertiti or Amelia Earhart. Would this computer art make Mona Lisa smile?

The first IBM was limited to 640K RAM (**conventional memory**). Instead of removing this limit when software outgrew conventional RAM requirements, IBM developed expanded memory and extended memory.

- **Expanded memory** commonly provides for 6 or more additional megabytes of RAM. It has a very precise set of rules for software using more than 640K RAM. There are also several versions of expanded memory available, and software developers have been left to decide which version to support. As a result, not all software supports expanded memory.
- **Extended memory** was designed more recently to provide up to 32 megabytes of additional memory without the conflicts associated with expanded memory. Extended memory is coming to be more commonly used than expanded memory because of the availability of a standardized version and more advanced techniques for providing additional memory.

As demands on RAM grow through larger programs requiring more than 640K of RAM, extended and expanded memory have become very important. Computers without these types of memory are not capable of using today's common, powerful software (Figure 2-5).

ROM Chips. **ROM** stands for **read-only memory**, meaning the computer can read its contents but cannot write to the contents of memory; that is, you cannot alter its contents. ROM chips store built-in permanent instructions called *firmware*. The firmware gives the CPU such instructions as what to do when the computer system is turned on.

The most common firmware is called **BIOS** (basic input/output system). When the computer is **booted up** (turned on), BIOS tests the memory, establishes connections to disk drives, keyboard, and monitor, and loads the operating system.

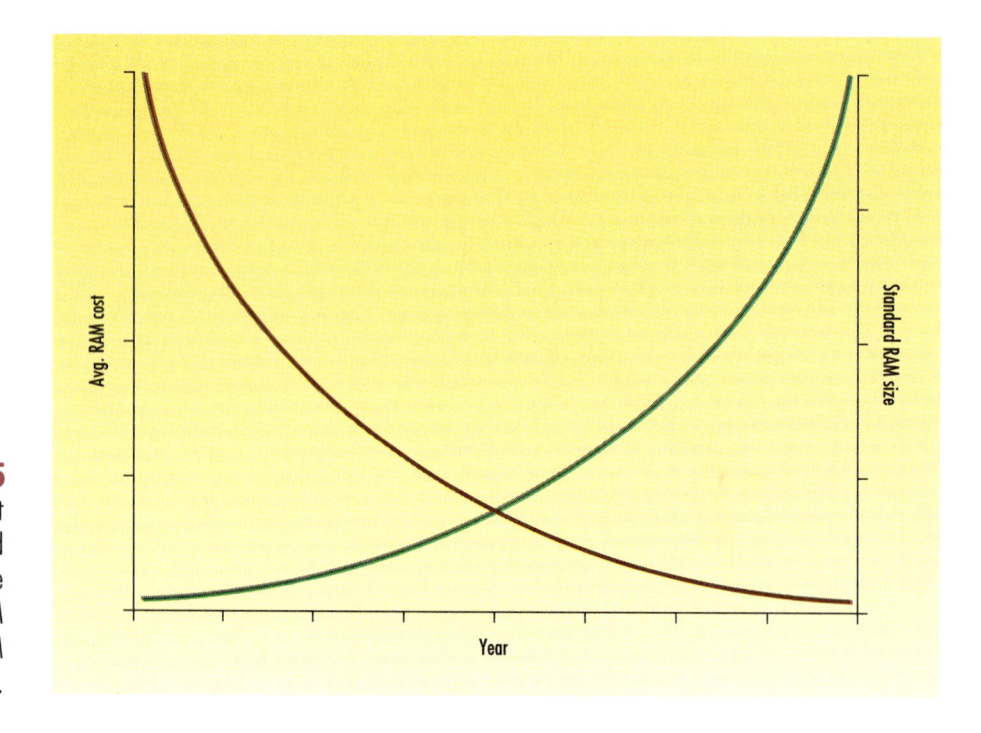

Figure 2-5
As the cost of RAM dramatically drops, it allows more sophisticated computers and software to be developed that require more RAM. Thus, the standard size of RAM supplied in microcomputers has risen as RAM cost has dropped.

ROM is used in many specialized computers in which instructions must be stored permanently, such as automobile computers that store instructions that control gasoline and air flow to the engine.

Additional Chips. What chips are there other than RAM, ROM, and CPU? Expansion boards typically contain chips that provide additional storage or memory and control monitors, printers, modems, and facsimile (fax) transmission.

Disk Drives

Typically microcomputer systems use magnetic disk storage; as the technology improves and prices decline, optical storage devices are becoming increasingly popular.

A magnetic disk is a direct-access storage device (DASD) that lets the computer directly locate a record of information. This differs from magnetic tape storage, in which records can be accessed only sequentially—one after the other. Thus, to access the last sequential record, the computer must first read all prior records.

The surface of a magnetic disk is read as concentric circles, called *tracks*, where data is stored as magnetic spots. The same amount of data is stored on each track, whether it is an inner or outer circle.

The disk drive is the device that allows data to be read from or written to a disk (Figure 2-6). It has an access arm equipped with read/write heads that move on the disk. The read/write head either reads (that is, obtains data from the disk and sends it to the CPU) or writes (that is, transfers data from the CPU to the disk). Reading makes a copy without altering the original data. Writing replaces—actually writes over—the original data, like recording a new song over an old one on a tape recorder or cassette player.

The typical microcomputer has one or two floppy disk drives and one hard disk drive.

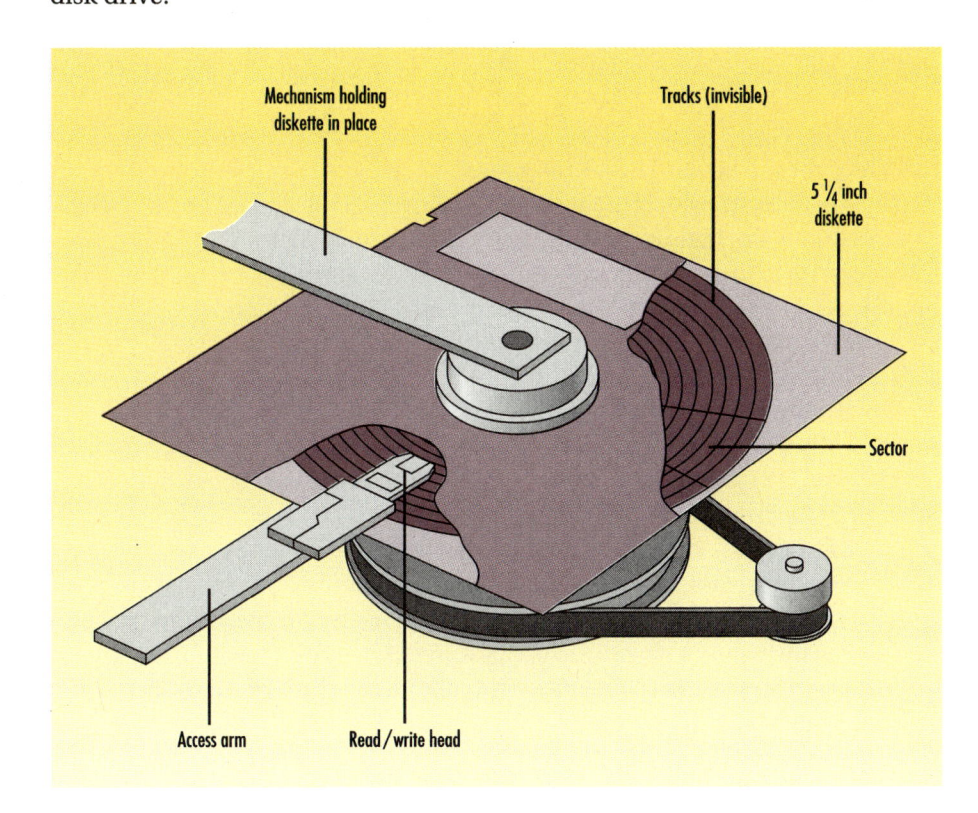

Multimedia's Pictures Are Worth How Many Words?

Thanks to CD-ROM and interactive video storage disks, huge amounts of information, especially visual information—photos, TV, and film, for instance—can now be stored on personal computers. A computerized book or catalog can now be more realistic, to say nothing of user-friendly. Taking advantage of this technology, Kodak has joined forces with L.L. Bean to scan its catalog onto disks that can be mailed to customers. By typing the words "red" and "dress" a customer can view all the red dresses in the catalogue. Encyclopedias on CD-ROM can include short animation segments to illustrate the functioning of a heart valve or the formulation of cumulus clouds, for instance. History texts can include newsreel footage of historical events, bringing a sense of immediacy to students.

Figure 2-6
The essential parts of a floppy disk drive: a motor to spin the drive, a mechanism to hold the disk in place, and a read/write head to transfer data to and from the disk. Data on the disk is organized into tracks (concentric circles) and sectors (pieces of each circle).

Figure 2-7
Two floppy disk types: 5.25″ and 3.5″. The 3.5″ format is considered superior, both because it stores more information and because it's more rugged: the 3.5″ disk's hard plastic case and sliding metal cover for the data window protect the disk better, and the locking write-protect tab is more durable and convenient than the stickers you must place over the write-protect notch of the 5.25″ disk.

Brushes for the Computer

Writers and musicians often feel immediately comfortable with a computer's keyboard, but traditional artists have a much more difficult time making the transition. A mouse and a paintbrush are just too different from each other. In fact, trying to draw with a mouse has been compared to drawing with a potato. So, even though a computer extends an artist's palette to literally millions of colors, until recently it was just too clumsy for most visual artists. However, now illustrators can take advantage of a pressure-sensitive 6-by-9-inch tablet and a cordless pen-like stylus that comes close to being a magical paintbrush. The tip of the stylus moves up and down in response to pressure, allowing the computer to simulate the pressure control of conventional artist's tools. In fact, the stylus acts like almost any medium, pencil, brush, watercolor, pastel, charcoal, gouache, crayon, or oil. The computer "paintbrush" even controls the "wetness" and dry-out speed of the stroke, and allows the artist to vary the density and width of the line. A lightbox feature allows user's to place drawings on top of each other like transparencies, creating collages. Given such "artist-friendly" technology, who knows what masterpieces will come from the computer?

Floppy Disk Drives. Floppy disks (also called *diskettes*) are magnetic storage media that are removable and easily transported from one computer to another (Figure 2-7). They are inserted into a floppy disk drive.

Floppy disk drives come in several sizes and storage capacities:

Family	Size (in inches)	Diskette Capacity (in bytes)
IBM	5.25	360K
IBM	5.25	1.2Mb
IBM	3.5	720K
IBM	3.5	1.44Mb
Mac	3.5	400K
Mac	3.5	800K
Mac	3.5	1.44Mb

Hard Disk Drives. The hard disk drives most often used in microcomputers are Winchester disks, in which the disk and its drive, including read/write heads, are sealed in a single unit, free from contamination (Figure 2-8). Removable disk packs are also available; with these, the access arm can be retracted and the disk pack removed from the drive. The sealed Winchester units are most often used because of their relatively low cost and increased reliability (more likely to be free of contamination).

The advantage of hard disks is that they provide greater storage capacity (from 20 Mb to several Gb of data) than floppy disks and operate at a much higher speed. They are also popular because they let the user access files easily rather than having to insert and remove diskettes. It is important, however, to include a floppy disk drive in a microcomputer system: Floppy disks are used to transport data from other sources and to store software for installation on the hard disk. Most important, floppy disks are useful for backup in case the hard disk malfunctions (crashes) and its stored data is destroyed. To avoid the loss of data, users periodically back up (copy) hard disk data to floppy disks stored outside the system.

Optical Storage Devices: CD-ROM and Interactive Video. One of the fastest-growing areas of data storage is the development of optical storage devices. These

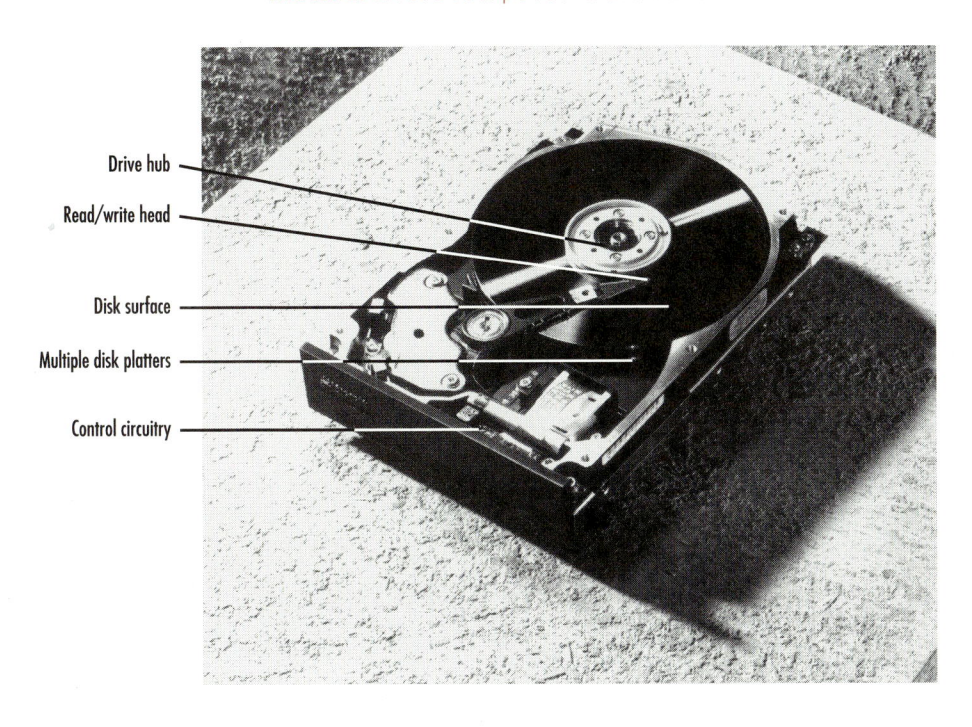

• CHAPTER 2: Microcomputer Hardware •

Drive hub
Read/write head
Disk surface
Multiple disk platters
Control circuitry

Figure 2-8
Although more detailed, the hard disk drive contains essentially the same parts as the floppy drive; the crucial difference is that by permanently encasing the disk itself, the drive ensures a sterile, clean environment that allows much greater storage capacity and data access speed.

devices use optical discs onto which a laser has encoded binary data (Figure 2-9). Another laser within the optical disk reader reads this data.

One advantage of optical storage devices is that they hold a great deal of information in a very small area. Several billion bits can fit on an optical disk smaller than a record album. Another advantage is that this stored data is actually burned into the disc, making it far more stable than magnetically stored data. Currently, most optical storage devices for microcomputers only read data. New types of optical discs, some combining optical and magnetic technology, allow both reading and writing of data, but these haven't yet replaced magnetic hard disks as primary storage devices. Magnetic disk technology is still faster at storing and transferring data.

Figure 2-9
Two standard optical disc formats: 5.25" CD-ROM and 12" laserdisc. CD-ROM is more often used for software, databases, and electronic art; laserdisc is more often used for interactive video.

Figure 2-10
Interactive video, and new expansion boards and software designed to receive and manipulate television pictures, allow you to see still video or active pictures on your computer screen.

There are two common uses of optical storage: CD-ROM and interactive video. CD-ROM (compact disc read-only memory) uses an optical disc of the same type as the compact discs commonly used for audio recordings. Interactive video uses a 12-inch optical disc to store video displays, including sound, text, and graphic images (Figure 2-10). Using interactive videodiscs and laser disk drives to read them, special computer monitors can display full motion pictures.

Ports

System units contain **ports**; these receptacles allow cables to be connected to **peripheral** (outside the system unit) **devices** (Figure 2-11).

- **Serial ports** are used for cables transmitting bits one after the other. They are frequently used for connecting modems or special input devices such as mice, light pens, graphics tablets, and joysticks.
- **Parallel ports** are used for cables transmitting several bits simultaneously, such as an entire 8-bit character. They are generally used with printers, although some printers use the serial port.
- Special ports include connections to networks and to peripherals such as keyboards, monitors, external disk drives, and scanners. These ports may work in either serial or parallel fashion, depending on the device for which they have been designed.

PERIPHERAL DEVICES

Peripheral devices can be classified generally as input devices, output devices, or both.

Input Devices

Keyboard. In addition to letters and numbers found on a typewriter, computer keyboards have a series of special keys to control sending information to the CPU. The use of these special keys is defined and controlled by the

Figure 2-11
This view of the back panel of a microcomputer shows some of the more common serial, parallel, and special ports used to connect peripheral devices to the system unit.

Figure 2-12
A typical keyboard and mouse.

software. For example, with word processing software, arrow keys move the cursor to any point in a document. The PgUp and PgDn keys let users move to different pages of text. The Home and End keys allow for movement to the beginning or end of text (Figure 2-12).

Mouse. A mouse is an input device that operates by controlling the position of the cursor (in the shape of an arrow) on the monitor. For example, with some programs, you can access a file by pointing the arrow at the file's name and clicking the mouse's button (Figure 2-13). This makes the mouse a quick, easy, and efficient way of controlling input.

Light pen. Light pens, often used in stores, are able to input a large amount of data quickly by moving a light beam across a bar code (Figure 2-14, p. 34). This converts the bar code into digital data that is usable by the computer. Other types of light pens are also used for computer-aided design (CAD) and

Figure 2-13
The mouse allows you to manipulate a pointer on screen to select items and commands.

MTV and PCs?

The video business just got a break. Just as desktop publishing programs made the printing business faster and easier, new broadcast-quality desktop video editing programs will be a boon to video production. One program (at $14,000) will allow the user to use a VCR and a Macintosh computer to transform a videotape into computer data and then store it on the disk where special effects, animation, titles, and instant editing can all take place. A $600 program does some of the same things, but its user needs about $6,000 in circuit boards to reach broadcast quality. A barrier has been the amount of memory video work takes: one second of broadcast-quality film is made of 32 frames (still pictures). Each one of those pictures can take up one megabyte of memory. These new video editing programs use image compression to save memory. Since more than half a dozen companies are planning to introduce versions of video editing software, prices should begin to decline, which means family videos of birthday parties and holiday gatherings will soon be up for sophisticated editing.

Figure 2-14
Light pens find most common use in business computing environments; however, their utility covers a wide range of applications.

Figure 2-15
Scanners come in both desktop (a) and hand-held (b) models; desktop models usually are more sophisticated and easier to use, but hand-held scanners can be very useful with portable computers in the field.

pen-based computers; the latter interpret and convert human writing into computer form.

Scanner. A scanner is an input device that acts like a miniature photocopy machine connected to a computer, copying graphic images into the computer and allowing typewritten pages to be entered without retyping (Figure 2-15). Scanners include both hand-held and desktop models. A scanner works by passing a beam of light across the original page or artwork and sensing the reflected light; it then assembles this information into a data file that describes the images as rows of tiny dots, each one noted for its color and brightness. That file is then passed on to the computer. To interpret an image of a text page into a word file, the computer uses software called **optical character recognition (OCR)**. To manipulate photos or art, the computer uses image-editing software.

Other Input Devices. Input devices can take many forms. For example, graphics tablets use a stylus and a special sensitive tablet to let users draw on the screen as they would on paper; this is very useful for graphics work and CAD. Trackballs allow the user the functionality of a mouse without a large flat surface to move around on. Touch-sensitive displays and touch pads are used in various businesses and industries to allow people to control the computer with the touch of a finger. Voice-recognition software allows the user to talk to the computer to give commands; this is finding a use in computer applications for the disabled.

Output Devices

Monitors. Monitors, which look like television sets, quickly display and redisplay the computer's output. They are often called *CRTs (cathode ray tubes)*, *VDTs (video display terminals)*, or simply *screens* (Figure 2-16). The image displayed on the screen is composed of many rows of tiny dots, called **pixels** (short for *picture element*). The number and size of pixels determine the resolution (sharpness and clarity) of the display. The more pixels, the higher the resolution. For example, a monitor having 300 × 200 pixels has a much lower resolution than one with 640 × 480 pixels (Figure 2-17).

a

b

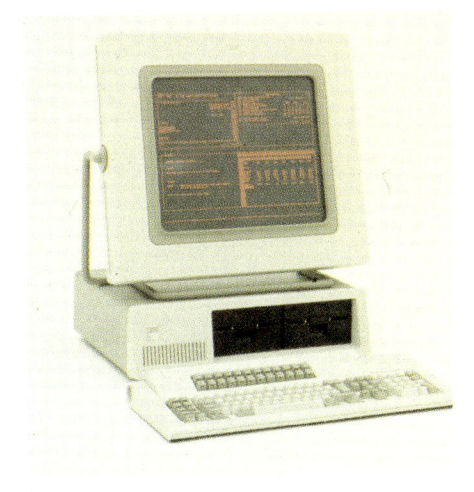

Figure 2-16
Various types of monitors: (a) CRTs are most common on the desktop. (b) Liquid crystal displays (LCD) are most common on laptop computers. (c) Gas-plasma displays generally find special-purpose uses.

Each type of monitor, such as monochrome or color graphics, requires a matching type of display adapter in the system unit. Some color graphics monitors, for example, generate 16-color displays; others generate 256-color displays. In both these cases, the monitor must match the graphics display adapter.

Desktop Monitors. CRTs are the desktop monitors that are built in the same way as television sets. They can be monochrome or color:

- **Monochrome monitors** show one color, generally white, green, or amber, on a dark background. They are relatively inexpensive and used principally for word processing or other applications where color is not needed.
- **Color monitors** (often called *graphics* monitors) display text characters and graphic images in color. They have advanced through various stages: CGA (color graphics adapter), EGA (enhanced graphics adapter), and VGA (video graphics array).

Color graphics adapters provide a color display for monochrome monitors. The four-color display's resolution (320 × 200) is lower than the monochrome's resolution (640 × 350), making text look grainier and harder to read than on the monochrome display. EGA supports 16 colors and offers resolution nearly that of the monochrome monitor.

VGA offers high resolution for text (720 × 400) and 16 colors with a resolution of 640 × 480. It also offers 256 colors with a resolution of 320 × 200 (Table 2-2). SVGA and extended VGA (XGA) offer even higher resolution, up to 1024 × 768 and more; and up to 16.8 million colors.

Portable Monitors. Portable, laptop, and notebook computers are microcomputers that have become smaller and smaller in size and weight. One

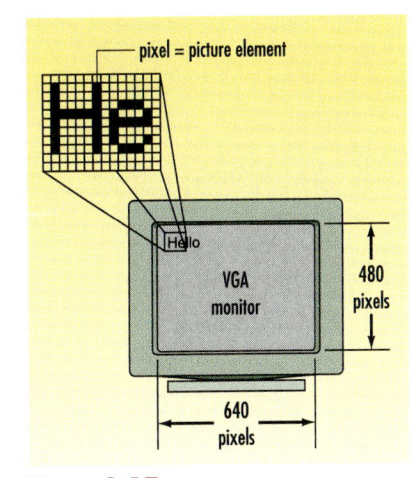

Figure 2-17
A computer monitor displays images by programming a rectangular array of dots; each dot is called a pixel. Text and images on the screen are each composed of particular patterns of pixels; the more pixels on the screen, the sharper and more detailed the image can be.

Table 2-2
Characteristics of Color Monitors

Monitor Type	Dimensions (in pixels)	Colors
CGA	320 × 200	4
EGA	640 × 350	16
VGA	640 × 480	16
	320 × 200	256
Super VGA	800 × 600, 1024 × 728	256
Extended VGA	1024 × 768 and above	256

Smart Printers

Portable laptop computers may soon include printers. IBM and Canon have announced a joint project using Canon's bubble-jet printing technology with a smaller cartridge, allowing it to be used in a laptop. Another smart printer is an ink-jet Braille printer that allows blind users to read hardcopy of their work. However, a portable version of the Braille printer is expected to take more time to hit the market.

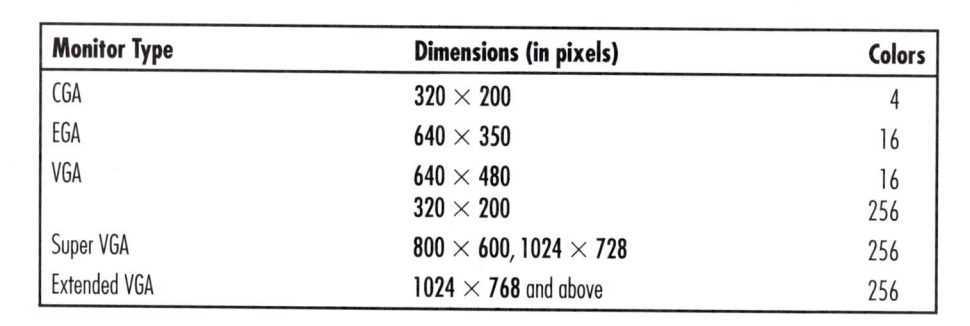

of the devices that has made their development possible is the flat-panel monitor. These compact devices consume little power, and their flat profile allows them to provide a full screen in a small folding unit. Early flat-panel displays were monochrome, but new technologies allow these screens to display color. They can be **LCD** (**liquid crystal display**), **EL** (**electroluminescent**), or **gas-plasma**:

- LCDs do not consume light of their own, but consist instead of crystal molecules. The backlit LCDs are easier to read than the original LCDs, which were difficult to read in strong light.
- EL screens are an improvement over LCDs because they actively emit light when electrically charged.
- Gas-plasma screens use a gas that emits light in the presence of an electric current. Unfortunately, gas-plasma displays cannot be battery-operated and must be plugged into a regular AC outlet. This limits their use in portable computers.

Printers. Printers create paper copies, called *hardcopies*, of information sent from the computer (Figure 2-18). Four types of printers are in common use:

- **Dot matrix printers** use a series of dots to form a character. They are fast and inexpensive, but the output quality can be relatively low. In near-letter-quality mode, dot matrix printers can produce hardcopy that is of very high quality.
- **Daisy-wheel**, or **letter-quality**, printers create print of the same quality as a typewriter. Letter-quality printers are slower and more expensive than dot matrix printers, but they produce a higher-quality print.

Figure 2-18
Common printers for microcomputer use. (a) Dot matrix printers are versatile and inexpensive, and some models produce very good quality printing. (b) Daisy-wheel printers produce output equivalent to a typewriter, but are slower than dot matrix printers and lack versatility. (c) Laser printers are more expensive, but produce the best quality output of the three, and are highly versatile.

a

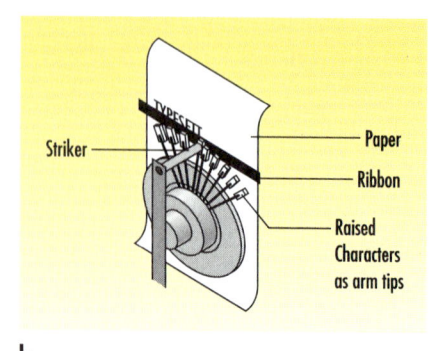

b

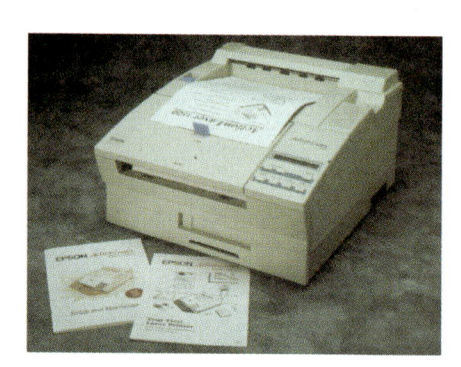

c

ActionLaser 1500

❏ 6 Pages Per Minute print speed

❏ HP III® / IIIsi® compatible

❏ RITech and MicroArt printing for outstanding print quality

❏ 27 internal fonts - including 13 that can be scaled to any size

❏ HP-compatible font cartridge slot

❏ 1 Mbyte standard memory, expandable to 5 Mbytes

❏ No memory upgrade board required

❏ Epson FX and LQ emulation

❏ Optional 250 sheet lower paper tray

Letter Quality Printing
Sharpest Ultra Letter Quality printing available at 360 dpi with optional film ribbon

Simple, Quiet Operation
A whisper quiet 46.5 dB(A) that's perfect for home or office

Fastest Print Speeds
337 characters per second in Draft and 112 cps in Letter Quality (rated at 15 cpi)

Wide Variety of Fonts
14 easily selectable typefaces, including four scalable from 8 to 32 point sizes

EPSON® LQ-570+
Dot Matrix Printer

Figure 2-19
A comparison of the output of a dot matrix printer against that of a laser printer shows the difference in quality.

- **Ink jet printers** spray small droplets of ink to create characters. These printers produce a fine-quality print at an extremely high speed; some print in color. Ink jet printers are usually expensive to purchase and operate.

- **Laser printers** are quickly taking the place of other printers for most uses. Laser printers produce an exceptionally high-quality print at a very high speed. They combine text and graphics to produce a page nearly equal in quality to traditional typesetting at a price that is becoming very affordable (Figure 2-19).

Laser printers work by passing a laser beam back and forth over a rotating drum, "drawing" the image on the drum by charging with static electricity the areas of the drum where the light hits. The charged areas pick up toner, which is deposited and fused onto the paper.

Plotters. A plotter is an output device that produces line drawings. These devices move a piece of paper under a series of moving pens. As the paper moves, the pens draw. Many plotters produce color output by drawing with several different-colored pens. Because it uses fine-point pens, the lines produced with a plotter can be very precise. Plotters are most often used to produce architectural drawings, maps, charts, and other technical types of line art (Figure 2-20).

Other Output Devices. While the most customary output devices are monitors and printers, not all such devices produce readable information. Computer-generated music and the movement of a robotic arm are just two items in a long list of different types of output from a variety of devices (Figure 2-21, p. 38).

Devices for both Input and Output

Some peripherals can be used for both input and output. Disk drives, tapes, and optical drives, while primarily thought of as storage devices, actually incorporated both input and output functions.

Figure 2-20
Plotters are invaluable for printing large-format images in color, such as architectural drawings and color charts.

One very important input/output device in common use is the **modem** (short for *modulator/demodulator*). A modem sends data from the computer out over telephone lines and accepts data over those same lines from other computers. It works by translating the electrical impulses of computer data into audible tones (modulation) and, at the other end, converting them back into electrical impulses (demodulation). A modem can be connected externally to the computer's serial port or mounted internally as an expansion board.

The availability of modems has opened up staggering opportunities for people to link their computers via phone, to access information from remote databases, and communicate in a variety of ways. For a fuller discussion of this topic, see the chapter on communications.

SUMMARY

In this chapter, we've described the various pieces of hardware—the physical devices—of a computer system that are used to input, process, and output data. Input devices, which range from keyboards and touch-sensitive screens to mice and light pens, translate the information into a series of on and off electrical signals. These signals, called *bits*, are combined in specific series to represent letters, numbers, and signals. Each series of 8 bits is called a *byte*.

Processing is controlled by the central processing unit (CPU), which consists of a control unit that directs the transfer of data and an arithmetic/logic unit (ALU) that performs mathematical and logical calculations. Once entered, data is moved to memory for processing—this is the information that appears on the screen—or written to the disk for permanent storage.

The system unit itself houses the processing devices, electronic circuits, and other components. Many of these devices are tiny silicon chips, also known as semiconductors or integrated circuits. These chips include the CPU, RAM (random access memory), and ROM (read-only memory); they are plugged into sockets on a printed circuit board (a board with electrical circuits printed on it). The board that contains the CPU is known as the system board (or motherboard); it provides several expansion slots that allow users to add memory and expansion boards for input and output devices (peripheral devices) such as mice, monitors, modems, and scanners.

Read-only memory contains the computer's built-in instructions; the computer can read but not alter the contents. Random access memory allows the manipulation of data; if the program is ended or the power turned off before the changes have been saved, all new material is lost.

Microcomputers typically include a hard disk and one or two floppy disk drives. The hard disk provides greater storage space and speed than a floppy disk provides; it is usually sealed within the unit (some removable drives are available) and contains the operating system and whatever programs and data you choose to write to it. Because hard disks can malfunction (crash), it is advisable to back up their data onto floppy disks (or tape) to be stored outside the system. Other storage devices include optical discs, where the data has been burned onto the disc by means of a laser, and interactive video.

Input and output devices, connected to the system unit through serial ports, parallel ports, and specialized ports, let the user interact with the system to input data and receive processed results. Common input devices include the

Figure 2-21
One of the newest uses of the microcomputer is in robotic control; the output of the computer is signals that the robot interprets as commands.

Computer Talk

Getting machines to talk to each other is not difficult when the machines are computers. Most computers can communicate if they are connected through telephone lines or through coaxial cable. Computers can also be connected by radio frequencies (like remote control) when wire connections are not practical. When a group of computers are connected it is called a *network*, and this greatly expands a computer's potential. Home computers have access to networks such as Prodigy, which has over 500,000 subscribers. There are hundreds of smaller networks for people with special interests: Deadheads, chefs, Go players—the list is endless. Networks were used to organize demonstrations against the Tiananmen Square crackdown in China, to help scientists across the globe track satellites, and to let physicians or gardeners trade information. In fact, about the only limit to networking via computer is that a day has only 24 hours.

keyboard, mouse, scanner, and light pen; common output devices include the monitor, printer, and plotter. The modem functions as both an input and output device.

KEY TERMS

arithmetic/logic unit (ALU)
binary system
BIOS
bit
boot up
bus
byte
card
central processing unit (CPU)
chip
control unit
conventional memory
daisy wheel
DIP (dual-inline package)
dot matrix printer
electroluminescent screen (EL)
expanded memory
extended memory
gas-plasma screen
ink jet printer
integrated circuits
laser printer
letter-quality printer
liquid crystal display (LCD)
memory
microprocessor
modem
motherboard
open architecture
optical character recognition (OCR)
output
parallel ports
peripheral devices
pixels
ports
printed circuit
random access memory (RAM)
read-only memory (ROM)
semiconductors
serial ports
storage
system board

REVIEW QUESTIONS

1. What does the term *CPU* mean?
2. What is the difference between RAM and ROM?
3. What is the function of storage?
4. What is the function of an input device?
5. What is the function of an output device?
6. What happens to information in RAM when the computer is turned off?
7. List three examples of an input device.
8. List three examples of an output device.
9. Why are binary numbers used to represent how a computer processes information?
10. What are a bit and a byte, and how they are related?
11. What is the purpose of extended and expanded memory?
12. What is the difference between 8-bit, 16-bit, and 32-bit computers?

3

Microcomputer Operating Systems

OBJECTIVES

After completing this chapter, you will be able to
- Name and describe common operating systems.
- Describe how to use character-based operating systems.
- Describe how to use a graphical user interface (GUI).
- Describe the functions of utility software.

FOCUS

An **operating system** is a group of computer programs that help manage the computer's resources. It acts as an interface between the computer and **application programs**.

The operating system is what turns the computer from an electronic zombie to an efficient machine with the ability to carry out instructions and perform intricate tasks. The operating system's job is to control the computer on the most fundamental level; it manages memory, controls access to peripheral devices, and serves as a translator between the user and the hardware, providing the means for the user and application programs to tell the hardware what to do. Its functions are frequently known as "housekeeping," in that they perform essential—but unseen—chores that allow application programs to work properly. Thus, while application programs perform such user tasks as word processing and spreadsheet calculations, the operating system performs such housekeeping tasks as creating files, keeping track of files, recovering damaged files, checking disks for errors, accessing peripheral devices, and running the application programs (Figure 3-1).

There are several different operating systems for microcomputers. The most common is known as MS-DOS, and it controls IBM PCs and compatibles; it uses a command-line interface. Other options for PC users include Windows and OS/2, two competing graphical user interfaces which offer multitasking capabilities, and UNIX, an operating system originally developed for mainframes. The Macintosh can run with Apple's System and its graphical user interface, Finder; or with UNIX.

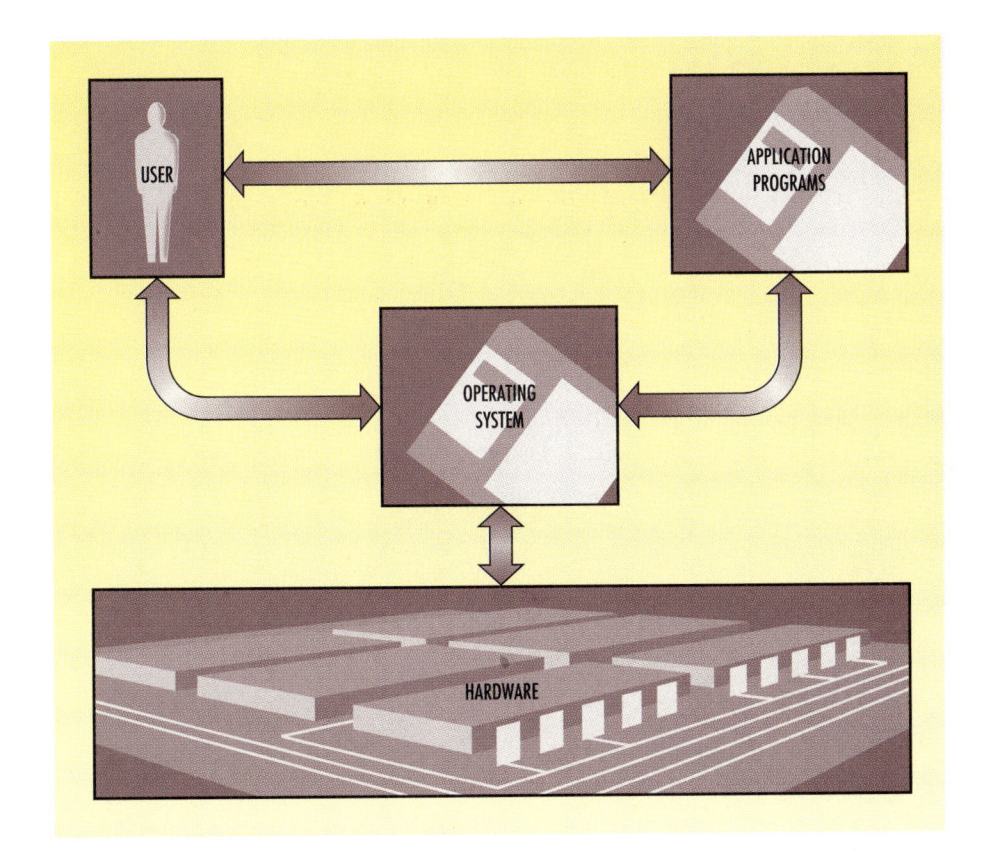

Figure 3-1
The operating system has direct communication with the hardware and interacts with both the user and application programs. It translates their commands to the hardware, manages the use of memory, and controls access to system devices, thus simplifying the task of running the computer.

COMMON OPERATING SYSTEMS

Operating systems are designed for specific microprocessors. For example, the operating system MS-DOS works with microprocessors manufactured by Intel; the Macintosh's operating system (called System) works with Motorola microprocessors. Similarly, an application program is designed for a specific operating system. For example, a word processor for use with MS-DOS will not run on a Macintosh computer.

MS-DOS

The majority of microcomputer software is written for Microsoft's MS-DOS (disk operating system; commonly called **DOS**), developed for IBM-compatible computers. PC-DOS is nearly a identical system developed for IBM Personal Computers (Figure 3-2, p. 44).

Loading DOS. When the power on an IBM-family computer is turned on, the ROM's BIOS (basic input/output system) begins instructing the computer in a precise sequence of steps that prepare the computer for use; this is called a **boot**, or booting up the computer (Figure 3-3, p. 45). After testing the hardware and establishing connections to disk drives and other peripherals, BIOS instructs the computer to load two hidden files, MSDOS.SYS and IO.SYS, from the boot disk (the disk on which the operating system is stored). These two files, together with COMMAND.COM (discussed later), form the core of MS-DOS.

BIOS next looks on the disk drives to find the files that complete the boot process. On a PC, the disk drives are labeled as follows: drive A is the first floppy disk drive, drive B is the second (if there is a second floppy), drive C is the first hard disk drive, and drives D and E are additional hard drives. If there is a disk in drive A, BIOS assumes that MSDOS.SYS and IO.SYS are stored on it; if they

Computers for the Blind

Recent advances in computer technology allow the blind to be more self-sufficient—thanks to programs that use voice recognition. By merely speaking to a computer, a person can operate appliances or dial the telephone. The computer can automatically dial a number every morning, upload the newspaper, and then read it back on demand. Even operating the computer has become easier with the addition of sound effects. For instance, storing a file can produce the sound of a cabinet drawer sliding shut, thereby verifying that the computer has done what it was told to do. Unfortunately, speech-recognition technology is still fairly crude, so the number of commands a computer can recognize is still limited. But the growth potential for such programs is staggering.

```
C:\> cd books

C:\BOOKS> dir \w

JOHNS    <dir>     JONES    <dir>     JOSEPH   <dir>
LINCOLN  <dir>     LOWLES   <dir>     MANESS   <dir>
INDEX    ASC       NEWBOOK  BAT       NEWBOOK  BAK

C:\BOOKS> cd lincoln

C:\BOOKS\LINCOLN> dir \w

CHAP01   WP        CHAP02   WP        CHAP03   WP
CHAP04   WP        CHAP05   WP        CHAP06   WP
CHAP07   WP        INDEX    TXT       PREF     TXT

C:\BOOKS\LINCOLN> rename pref.txt fm.txt

C:\BOOKS\LINCOLN> dir \w

CHAP01   WP        CHAP02   WP        CHAP03   WP
CHAP04   WP        CHAP05   WP        CHAP06   WP
CHAP07   WP        FM       TXT       INDEX    TXT
```

Figure 3-2
DOS is the most common example of a command line interface; commands are typed into the system by the user. While less convenient than later systems, DOS still provides a great deal of functionality for the proficient user, and its small size places fewer processing demands on the hardware; thus, applications can run more efficiently.

Speaking the Same Language

One of the problems with portable computers is that they often do not speak the same language, straitjacketing people when it comes to buying software and peripherals. One of the reasons Excel, a spreadsheet program from Microsoft, has become such a popular application is that its Macintosh and Windows versions operate using the same commands and share files from one machine to the other; Microsoft Word, a word processor, also works this way. To try and bridge the computer communication gap, more than 250 makers of computers and related products recently united behind a standard slot—or "bus"—for connecting add-on gear to portable computers. The PCMCIA (for Personal Computer Memory Card International Association) standard means that many PCs will be able to share programs, add-ons and peripherals by using interchangeable plastic-coated cards, each about as thick as a stack of four to six credit cards. Now if we can just get politicians to speak to each other...

are not found, BIOS will give the user an error message, as shown in Figure 3-4. If there is no disk in drive A, the computer will next search drive C, the hard disk (assuming your computer has a hard disk). Most microcomputers have hard disks set up to boot from drive C. Once MSDOS.SYS and IO.SYS are loaded, the system checks for CONFIG.SYS. This file is created by the user to customize the computer's setup by loading driver programs for special peripheral devices (such as a mouse), set certain system parameters, and load resident utility programs.

Finally, the system looks for a file named COMMAND.COM, which holds the instructions for interpreting most of the various DOS commands. For this reason it's known as the **command interpreter** or **command processor**. Without this file, DOS won't run; if the computer can't find COMMAND.COM (either on your boot disk or in another location specified in CONFIG.SYS), it will display an error message on the screen. Once COMMAND.COM has been loaded, it displays the DOS system prompt, like this:

C>

You'll see a blinking cursor next to the greater-than symbol (>); whatever you type will appear on the screen here. This is called the **command line**, because it's where you type commands to DOS.

The drive displayed in the system prompt is called the **default drive** (or current drive). Unless otherwise instructed, the default drive is the storage device where DOS searches for files to be loaded into memory; it moves files from memory to the default drive when it needs to store them. You can change the default drive by entering a different drive name (followed by a colon) on the command line.

One other option in the boot-up sequence is AUTOEXEC.BAT. This **batch file** (a file of ready-to-run commands) is created by the user to run certain programs or set up certain system parameters, similar to CONFIG.SYS. Because the contents of AUTOEXEC.BAT are DOS commands, it is loaded and run only after COMMAND.COM is loaded.

DOS File Structure. Before you look further at DOS commands, you need to understand the DOS file structure.

A computer file is similar to a paper document holding related information. For example, each computer program or document (word processing document, spreadsheet, or database) is stored in a separate file.

Each file is identified by a filename, such as

```
FILE1.WP
```

DOS filenames can be up to eight characters long—using letters, numbers, or certain symbols—plus a file extension that uses a period and up to three characters.

It is helpful to name data files in a meaningful, organized way. For example, .DOC might be the extension for all word processing files. A pharmacist might list files of prescriptions as .PRS files, and a teacher's lesson plans might be .LES files.

All files are stored in directories, much as a file folder is used to store individual files or documents. The directories are organized in an inverted tree structure where the top level is called the **root directory**.

Usually, only those files necessary to boot the computer should be placed in the root directory: MSDOS.SYS, IO.SYS, CONFIG.SYS, COMMAND.COM, and AUTOEXEC.BAT. Branching out from the root directory, users create their own directories (also called **subdirectories**) to organize their program files and data files. A program file contains an application program, such as a word processing or database program; a data file contains data entered by the user, such as a letter, spreadsheet, or other document. Other subdirectories should contain the rest of the DOS operating system, device-driver programs, user-created batch files, and utilities. Keeping the hard disk properly organized is the responsibility of the user.

In the example shown in Figure 3-5 (p. 46), a student created two subdirectories for her application software: one called WP for her word processing software and one called SS for her spreadsheet software.

For each application, the student created additional subdirectories for her data files. Thus, the ENGLISH subdirectory contains her English term papers;

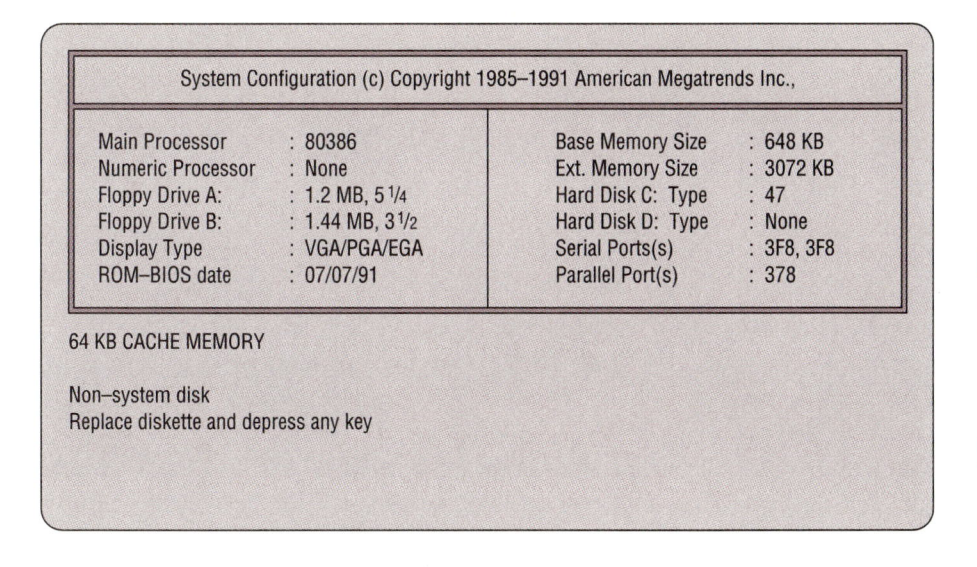

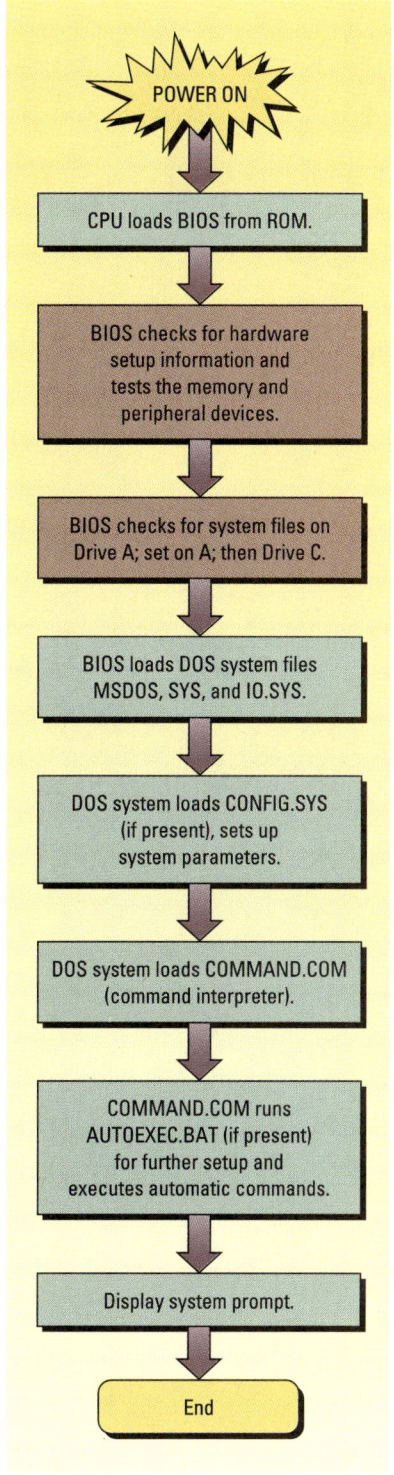

```
System Configuration (c) Copyright 1985–1991 American Megatrends Inc.,

Main Processor     : 80386         Base Memory Size  : 648 KB
Numeric Processor  : None          Ext. Memory Size  : 3072 KB
Floppy Drive A:    : 1.2 MB, 5 1/4 Hard Disk C: Type : 47
Floppy Drive B:    : 1.44 MB, 3 1/2 Hard Disk D: Type : None
Display Type       : VGA/PGA/EGA   Serial Ports(s)   : 3F8, 3F8
ROM–BIOS date      : 07/07/91      Parallel Port(s)  : 378

64 KB CACHE MEMORY

Non–system disk
Replace diskette and depress any key
```

Figure 3-3
A typical booting process for a DOS-based microcomputer.

(Flowchart: POWER ON → CPU loads BIOS from ROM. → BIOS checks for hardware setup information and tests the memory and peripheral devices. → BIOS checks for system files on Drive A; set on A; then Drive C. → BIOS loads DOS system files MSDOS.SYS, and IO.SYS. → DOS system loads CONFIG.SYS (if present), sets up system parameters. → DOS system loads COMMAND.COM (command interpreter). → COMMAND.COM runs AUTOEXEC.BAT (if present) for further setup and executes automatic commands. → Display system prompt. → End)

Figure 3-4
This error message displays if BIOS cannot find the system files.

46 • CHAPTER 3: Microcomputer Operating Systems •

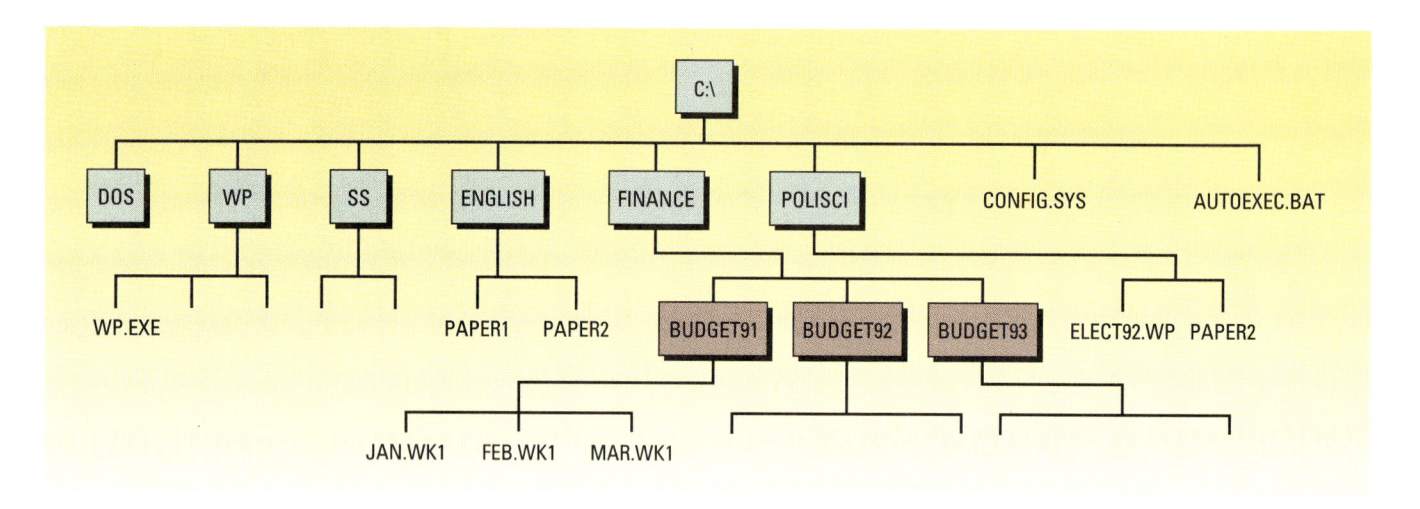

Figure 3-5
This tree diagram (directories are boxed) shows the structure DOS uses to organize files. The root directory, C:\, is at the top; each level beneath can store both files and subdirectories.

the POLISCI subdirectory contains Political Science term papers; and the FINANCE subdirectory contains her financial planning information. To see the structure of your subdirectories, you can use the TREE command (Figure 3-6). MS-DOS does not require the use of capital letters; you can enter commands in either upper- or lowercase.

Suppose the student writes a paper about the 1992 presidential election. She names the document ELECT92.WP and stores it in the POLISCI subdirectory. The document's complete name is now

```
C:\POLISCI\ELECT92.WP
```

To completely identify a DOS file, you must include its name and path to the root directory; the path includes all the subdirectories between the file and the root. A colon (:) must be placed after the disk drive name; a backslash (\) must be placed in front of each subdirectory and filename.

Entering DOS Commands. Once you understand DOS file structure, it's easy to enter a DOS command. On the command line, type the command, followed by the required drive, directory, and/or filename.

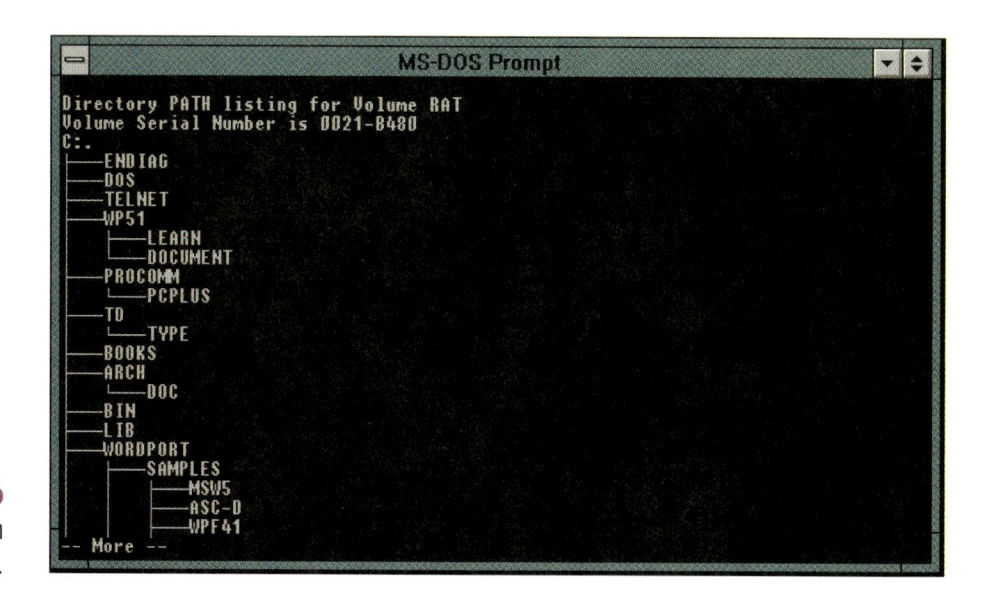

Figure 3-6
The TREE command displays a tree diagram of a disk's files and directories.

> HISTORY

Birth of DOS

The story of MS-DOS, and its acceptance as the premier operating system for personal computers, has become legendary.

Before MS-DOS, the best-selling operating system was CP/M, manufactured by Digital Research. Invented by Gary Kildall, CP/M was first sold through the mail for $75 by Kildall and his partner and wife, Dorothy McEwen. CP/M became the preferred operating system, thanks, in part, to a friend of Kildall's, Bill Gates, whose company, Microsoft, provided microcomputer languages. It was simpler for Microsoft to support its product on a limited number of operating systems, so Gates referred clients who needed operating systems to Kildall, who returned the favor when Digital Research was approached by clients for language software.

In July 1980, IBM approached Gates and Microsoft about providing the languages it wanted in a new personal computer. This top-secret undertaking was on an astonishingly tight deadline—12 months from the decision to enter the personal computer market to introduction of a finished product—and IBM had not yet made up its mind what to do about

> Before MS-DOS, the best-selling operating system was CP/M... Gates and Microsoft desperately needed to either buy, lease, or develop an operating system

the necessary operating system.

As was his custom, Gates picked up the phone, called Kildall, and said he was sending Digital some important customers. Kildall and the IBM representative, Jack Sams, made an appointment for the following day.

IBM arrived at Digital to find that Kildall was out flying his personal plane. (Kildall maintains he was on a business trip, though he had made the appointment with IBM.) Kildall's wife and the company lawyer balked at signing the standard nondisclosure agreement that IBM insisted on before proceeding with the meeting. Apparently things went downhill from there.

Whether or not Kildall ever arrived to talk with IBM (and that varies with the version of the tale being told), IBM returned to Microsoft the next day and asked Gates to see what he could do about getting a commitment for the 16-bit operating system IBM needed.

Kildall and his wife flew off to the Caribbean on vacation—ironically, on the same San Francisco-to-Miami flight with the committee from IBM, so the parties talked business during the flight.

Meanwhile, Gates and Microsoft desperately needed to either buy, lease, or develop an operating system, without which the entire IBM PC project was in jeopardy.

As luck would have it, they found what they needed just a 20-minute drive from Microsoft's offices. At a small company called Seattle Computer Products, Tim Paterson had developed an operating system to support the company's 8086 CPU boards. Seattle Computer had repeatedly tried to get Digital Research to develop a 16-bit version of CP/M, and the continued delay was beginning to cost the smaller company money. In desperation, Paterson had taken Digital's printed documentation and come up with his own operating system which he called 86-QDOS—or "quick and dirty operating system." Among the differences between Digital's operating system and Paterson's was the way QDOS stored data on a disk and the way it organized files.

Once Paterson had 86-QDOS running, he contacted Microsoft to ask if the company wanted to adapt any of its software for his new operating system. The timing could not have been more perfect. A few days later, Microsoft contacted Seattle Computer and said it had a potential OEM (original equipment manufacturer) customer who might be interested in 86-QDOS but they could not reveal any more details. Would the company allow Microsoft to act as licensing agent? Seattle Computer agreed.

While IBM completed development on the PC, Microsoft developed Seattle Computer's 86-QDOS into MS-DOS; two weeks before IBM triumphantly announced the PC in August 1981, Microsoft bought the rights to the original code outright from Seattle Computer for $50,000. Today Microsoft is one of the world's largest companies based on Tim Paterson's "quick and dirty operating system." ■

Portable Assistants

Want to know what the weather is across the country, what time the next plane leaves for your destination, or what's the best way to get around a traffic jam—but you're not by your telephone or computer? No problem! Just make sure you have your Personal Digital Assistant. At six by nine inches, the device easily fits into a coat pocket, purse, or briefcase. And it can do just about anything. One program allows the user to type in a word in English and a digitized voice will respond in a foreign language. By using PDAs, New York City policemen can find out the history of any license plate on the Eastern seaboard in ten seconds. Some of Chicago's commodities traders, who traditionally transacted business by screaming and waving their hands, are now using PDAs. And just in case you didn't get through the traffic jam in time to catch your airplane, it's nice to know your PDA can also play video games!

For example, typing DIR (the Directory command) displays all files in the designated drive and directory. Typing

```
DIR C:\POLISCI
```

displays all files in the POLISCI directory on the C drive.

You can shorten the command by eliminating default information. For example, if C:\POLISCI is the current directory, you need only type

```
DIR
```

to display the same information.

When you command DOS to perform an action on a file, you include the pathname and filename(s):

```
COMMAND pathname filename
```

The Rename command, for example, changes a file's name. Thus, typing on the command line

```
RENAME C:\POLISCI\ELECT92.WP PRESELEC.WP
```

changes the ELECT92.WP (election '92) paper in the POLISCI subdirectory on the C disk to the name PRESELEC.WP (presidential election). This looks like a lot of typing, but remember, you can eliminate default information. In this example, if you issue the command from the C:\POLISCI directory, you need type only

```
RENAME ELECT92.WP PRESELEC.WP
```

DOS provides other ways of shortening commands as well. RENAME, for example, can be entered as REN. Because the DOS environment is text (or character) based, commands must be typed in on the command line.

Other commonly used DOS commands include

FORMAT drive: Formats a disk; that is, DOS prepares the disk so that it can accept data in a format compatible with the operating system (Figure 3-7).

Figure 3-7
To prepare a new disk for data storage, you must insert it into the disk drive and give the FORMAT command. Formatting a disk will destroy all data; however, with DOS 5.0 you can recover the lost information with the UNFORMAT command.

```
C:\format a: /F:360
Insert new diskette for drive a:
and press ENTER when ready...

Formatting 360
Percent Complete .

Volume Label (11 characters, ENTER for none)?

    360952 bytes total disk space
    360952 bytes available on disk

       512 bytes in each allocation unit
       703 allocation units available on disk

Volume Serial Number is 1521-0990

Format another (Y/N)? y


Insert new diskette for drive a:
and press ENTER when ready...

Formatting 360
```

• CHAPTER 3: Microcomputer Operating Systems • 49

MD (Make Directory):	Creates a new subdirectory.
CD (Change Directory):	Moves the current subdirectory to another subdirectory.
COPY (Copy):	Copies a file from one area to another.
DEL (Delete):	Erases a file from disk storage.

Windows

As noted, in a character-based environment, commands must be keyed in on the command line. New versions of DOS provide different types of operating environments (also called **shells**) that provide an interface between the operating system and the user. Instead of memorizing commands to type, you need only select from available choices.

The most popular shell program for DOS is called **Windows**. This environment provides a **graphical user interface** (GUI) for PCs to eliminate the need to type in commands. With a GUI, you can command the computer by using a mouse to manipulate a pointer on screen, clicking the mouse button when the pointer is on the file you want to open or the program you want to run. With different combinations of the mouse button; special keys on the keyboard; commands accessible through menus; **icons** (pictures) representing disk drives, files, and programs; and windows (functional areas of the monitor screen) to organize your access to data, applications, and commands, you can run the operating system without typing cryptic commands.

Windows presents the user with the Program Manager (Figure 3-8), which organizes all the programs and system utilities into groups; clicking on a programs icon loads and runs the program. For managing files and disks,

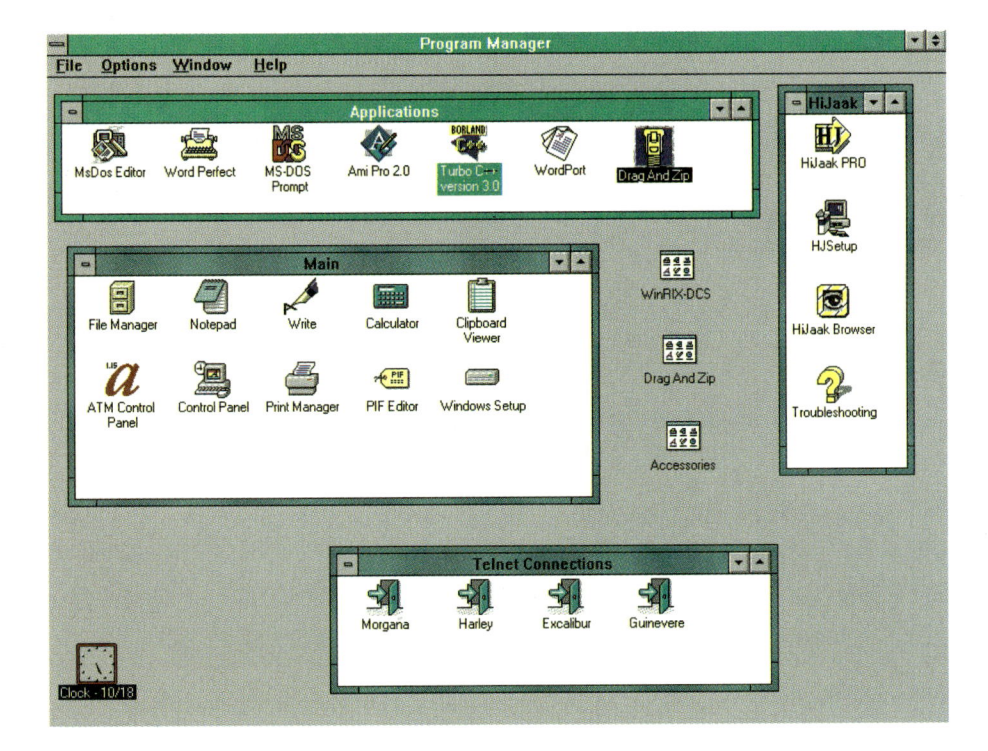

Figure 3-8
Windows' Program Manager organizes applications and utilities into groups, allowing you to load and run an application simply by opening its group and clicking on its icon with the mouse. System commands are given by clicking on menus to open them, then clicking on the command desired.

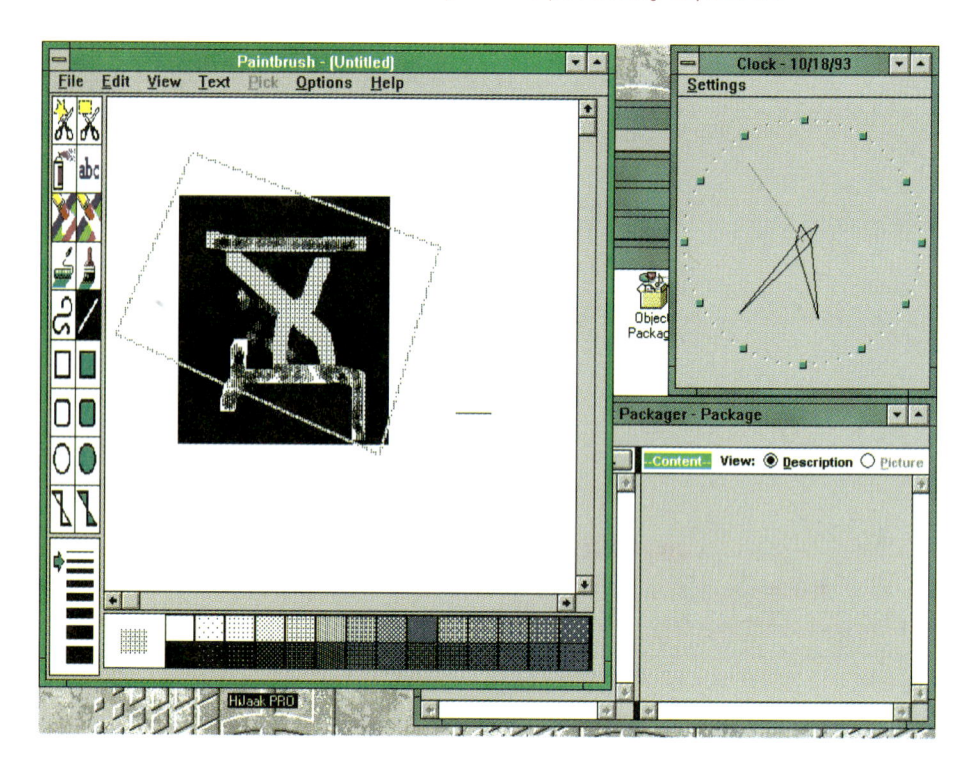

Figure 3-9
Windows' multitasking capability allows you to run several programs at once and control how they share processing time. OS/2, UNIX, and the Macintosh System provide similar capabilities.

Windows provides the File Manager (accessed from the Program Manager), which shows the disks and DOS directories on the system and provides menus of commands for managing files, directories, and disks. Other Windows utilities control system devices and allow the user to customize the look of the screen.

A major advantage of Windows is its **multitasking** capability (Figure 3-9). This means that more than one application can run at the same time. To be practical, however, Windows requires a minimum of 2Mb of memory and at least the speed of an 80386SX microprocessor.

Macintosh System

The Macintosh family of computers has been based on the Motorola 68000 line of processors. The Power PC microprocessor is used in more recent Macintosh computers. The Macintosh operating system, referred to as System (for example, System 7), and its GUI operating environment, Finder, are inseparable. You cannot access the Macintosh operating system without Finder (Figure 3-10).

The Macintosh operating system, System 7, supports multitasking; it is quite similar to Windows. Unlike the IBM environment, however, the Macintosh environment was originally designed for a standard graphical interface. Rather than the separate modules Windows provides for managing programs and data files, the Macintosh system and Finder integrate the two functions, using the desktop as a metaphor for organizing the system. The Finder shows on-screen a "desktop" consisting of a menu bar at the top of the screen where commands are accessed; icons showing the disk drives; and an icon labeled "Trash," into which you drag files you want to delete. When you double-click on a disk's icon, a window opens to show you the disk's contents of files and programs, which are themselves

• CHAPTER 3: Microcomputer Operating Systems •

Figure 3-10
The Macintosh System uses Finder as a GUI, providing a visual "desktop" on which icons for drives, folders, and documents are located. Multifinder will switch between several programs, changing the menus at the top of the screen to match each program you have running.

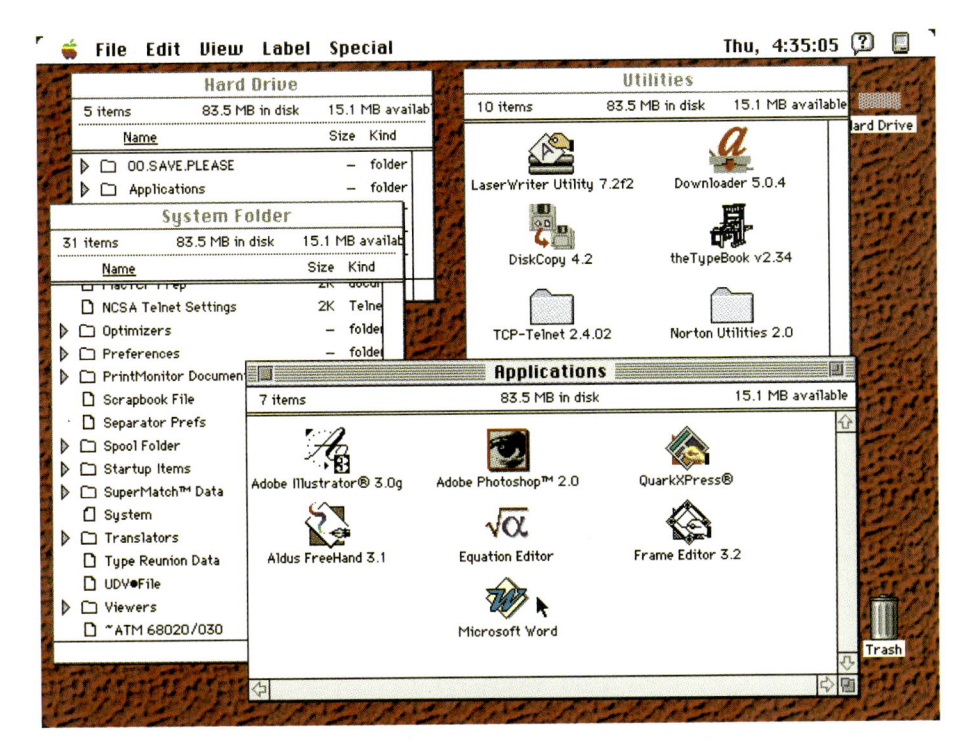

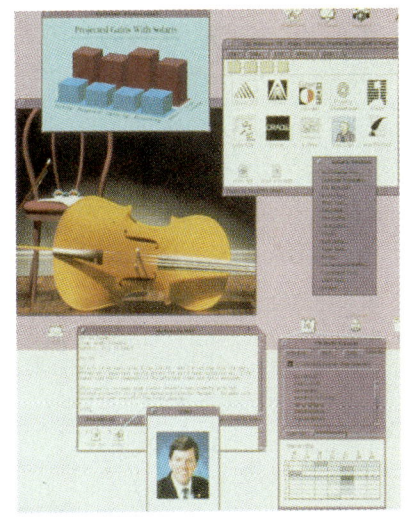

represented by icons, as well as folders (equal to DOS directories) in which more files and programs can be stored. Clicking with the mouse on a document's name or icon loads the program used to create the document and opens the document for viewing or editing; clicking on a program icon loads the programs directly. To delete files, simply use the mouse to select and drag them to the Trash. For many people, the Mac's consistency and integration of functions make it the easiest operating system to use.

UNIX

The **UNIX** operating system was created in the early 1970s for minicomputers, and was later adapted for mainframes and microcomputers. UNIX was an early supporter of multitasking, which made it popular for networking and multiuser communications environments.

UNIX has kept pace with microcomputer advances and now runs on both Macintosh and the IBM family of microcomputers. It is the leading operating system for powerful workstation computers, such as those by Sun Microsystems and NeXT.

UNIX generally operates in a character-based environment, but GUI environments, including XWindows and OpenLook, are also available (Figure 3-11).

UNIX provides additional features:

- Multitasking among multiple users is possible; that is, simultaneous programs can be shared by several users at one time.
- UNIX can run on many different computer systems. Unfortunately, the many versions are not standardized, and not all are compatible with others.
- Advanced networking capabilities allow sharing of files over networks that have several different kinds of equipment.

Figure 3-11
UNIX is a command line operating system, like DOS, but GUIs such as OpenLook can make this sophisticated operating system easier and more convenient to run. However, UNIX places the greatest demands on the hardware of any microcomputer operating system.

Science Fiction? Hardly—Try Reality

Plunging into a different dimension by donning gloves, goggles, and a helmet and staring at a screen was a device often used in pulp fiction to describe amusement parks in space. But virtual reality (the term coined in the 1980s to describe such programs) is very much here today, and is being used to train people in a wide variety of ways. The gloves (or an entire suit that one wears) act as an input device for the computer; the helmets (which can also have stereos in them) are output devices. Virtual reality is so effective as a training device because it totally immerses the person in a task. For example, medical students can train on virtual patients; students can experience a distant land rather than just reading about it. Sportsmen can use virtual reality to train more effectively. One researcher put a glove on two Red Sox pitchers and had them throw the ball while the glove sent a computer information on speed, position, and flex. The computer analyzed all the data, and the results helped the pitchers correct what was not working.

Figure 3-12
OS/2 was created to replace DOS and incorporates a GUI, the Workplace Shell. OS/2 was designed to implement the fullest capabilities of today's advanced microprocessors, and can run applications designed for both DOS and Windows.

OS/2

In 1987, IBM and Microsoft Corporations introduced Operating System/2 (**OS/2**). OS/2 was developed for powerful microcomputers, such as the IBM PS/2 line. Because it can access up to 18 Mb of memory, it can simultaneously run powerful programs that access huge amounts of data. Each program is protected so that if one crashes, the others do not lose data.

OS/2 is compatible with and can run application programs written for DOS. It also provides a graphical environment compatible with Windows so it can run Windows applications as well (Figure 3-12).

UTILITY PROGRAMS

Utility programs perform operating system tasks. A number of these programs have been developed by independent manufacturers to enhance existing operating systems (Table 3-1). The programs are not inherent in the operating system itself, but are loaded separately into the computer. For example, early versions of DOS did not include antivirus programs (see Issues and Ethics); you had to load a separate DOS utility for this purpose.

Utility programs can also do the following:

- Provide an easier way of managing files.
- Optimize use of available RAM.
- Optimize disk storage.
- Monitor the system's use of memory and storage space resources.
- Recover lost data or, as with antivirus software, prevent the loss of data.
- Compress large files so they require less storage space.
- Terminate an application before it crashes the whole system.

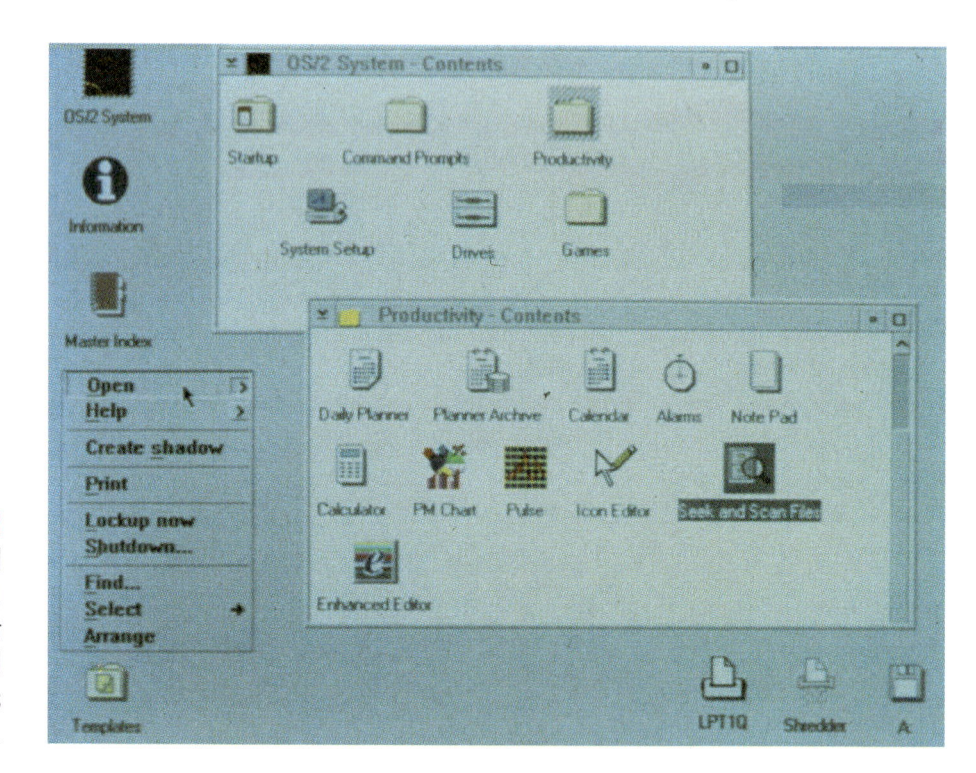

Table 3-1
Some Microcomputer Utility Programs

Program	Publisher	Description
DOS/Windows:		
Norton Utilities	Symantec	Disk optimization, formatting and backup, file and disk recovery, DOS command shell
PC Tools Deluxe	Central Point	Disk optimization, formatting, backup and recovery; DOS command shell; calculator and notepad; virus protection
Xtree Gold	Xtree	Utilities for maintaining DOS files and directories; copying, deleting, and moving files
SpinRite II	Gibson Research	Hard disk diagnostics, optimization, and formatting
LapLink III	Traveling Software	File transfer and communication
PKZIP	PKWare, Inc.	File compression and decompression
QEMM	Quarterdeck	Manages extended and expanded memory; optimizes conventional DOS memory
Virex-PC	Microcom	Virus protection
Norton Desktop for Windows	Symantec	Streamlines the functions of Windows Program Manager and File Manager
Adobe Type Manager	Adobe Systems	Coordinates PostScript font usage; creates optimized screen fonts as needed by Windows applications
Macintosh:		
Norton Utilities	Symantec	Disk optimization, file and disk recovery, desktop customization
MacTools Deluxe	Central Point	Disk optimization, file and disk recovery, backup, file compression
Stuffit Deluxe	Alladin Systems	File compression and decompression, archives
SAM	Symantec	Virus protection
Suitcase II	Fifth Generation	Coordinates desk accessories, fonts, and sounds
After Dark	Berkeley Systems	Screen saver
QuicKeys	CE Software	Keyboard macros
Adobe Type Manager	Adobe Systems	Coordinates PostScript font usage; creates optimized fonts as needed by applications

- Protect your data from other users by denying access to your system and/or directories without a password.
- Protect your monitor when it is on for long periods of time.

SUMMARY

An operating system is a group of computer programs that help manage the computer's resources, acting as an interface between the computer and application programs. It performs such housekeeping tasks as creating and keeping track of files, recovering damaged files, checking disks for errors, accessing peripheral devices, and running application programs.

Mirror, Mirror in the Computer

One of the most common fears new computer users have is, "If I just touch the wrong button by mistake I'll lose all my work." Actually, the computer can be rather forgiving; hence the "undelete" function. A file consists of three things: the name of the file, the physical location of the file, and a pointer from the name to the location. When a file is deleted, the name is lost. Using the undelete function recovers a file by renaming it. There are even recovery tools, such as Mirror, that can rescue materials after that most dreaded of all computer malfunctions, a hard disk crash. And that's pretty forgiving.

Every Day Can Be April Fool's

The computer often seems to be a dull, even dehumanizing invention. But it has given rise to some awfully goofy humor and bizarre practical jokes. Sound effects can be programmed to play when a particular command is given: deleting a file can be accompanied by a loud "kaboom" or a more gentle "bonk"; scanning a disk can elicit a character from Monty Python's Flying Circus hollering "I didn't expect the Spanish Inquisition." When turning on your computer in the morning you can be greeted by Robin Williams screaming, "Good morning Vietnam!!" (Guaranteed to let the rest of the office know you're in.) Or if you prefer music, another program plays the Bugs Bunny cartoon's "That's All Folks" theme as you shut down. The DRAIN.COM program for DOS allows you to flummox an unsuspecting co-worker. Once a person hits any key after the C> prompt, the message "System error: water detected in disk drive A:" appears, followed by the shushing noise of water flowing down a drain. The computer then announces "Spin Dry in Progress" and lets the disk drive whir for a few minutes. If only washing clothes were that simple.

The major operating systems for microcomputers are MS-DOS, PC-DOS, the Macintosh System, UNIX, and OS/2. Each is designed for specific microprocessors. Application programs, such as word processing and spreadsheet programs, are designed for specific operating systems.

DOS runs on the IBM family of computers using Intel microprocessors. It is a character-based system that requires the entry of commands on a command line. The Windows operating environment provides a graphical user interface (GUI) that lets users select from icons that show the available choices. Windows also provides multitasking, allowing several application programs to run simultaneously.

The Macintosh System runs on the Motorola 68000 line of processors. It provides multitasking and a graphical environment, Finder; you cannot access the operating system without the graphical environment.

Although UNIX can work with different microprocessors, each requires a different version, and the versions are incompatible. UNIX generally operates in a character-based environment, but GUI environments exist as well.

UNIX provides multitasking, which allows simultaneous programs to be shared by several users at one time. Its networking capabilities allow sharing of files over networks with several different kinds of equipment.

OS/2, developed for such powerful microcomputers as the IBM PS/2 line, is compatible with DOS. It can thus run application programs written for DOS, and it provides a graphical environment. Its multitasking ability allows it to run several large programs simultaneously. If one program crashes, the others do not lose data.

Utility programs enhance existing operating systems. Although many of these programs must be purchased separately, there appears to be one for virtually every operating system function.

KEY TERMS

application programs	default drive	OS/2
batch file	DOS	root directory
boot	graphical user interface (GUI)	shell
command interpreter	icons	subdirectories
command line	multitasking	UNIX
command processor	operating system	Windows

REVIEW QUESTIONS

1. What functions do operating systems perform?
2. Describe four common operating systems.
3. What is a default drive? Give an example.
4. What is multitasking? Which operating systems offer it?

5. Describe the difference between a character-based operating environment and a graphical user interface.
6. Define DOS. How are files organized and named? What are five common commands? What do these commands do?
7. Describe a graphical user interface.
8. Describe three kinds of utilities for microcomputers.

Selecting Software and Hardware

4

OBJECTIVES

After completing this chapter, you will be able to

- Distinguish between computer families and decide which is best for you.
- State what features are most important when buying software.
- Explain how various components affect a computer's usefulness.
- Explain where to buy a computer and get the best value for your money.

FOCUS

Which is the best computer for you? What software will you need? Where should you buy it? Which popular features are the most important? The answers to these questions depend on how you plan to use your computer. Will you use it primarily for term papers and correspondence, or do you foresee using it to create four-color newsletters? Will you use your computer to balance your checkbook or for complex financial modeling? Will you create an electronic address book, or will you need to analyze the 1990 census data?

In this chapter we will step you through the process of selecting microcomputer software and hardware. This process involves evaluating your computing needs, deciding on a computer family and operating system, selecting software applications that meet your computing needs, and finally, selecting hardware that best supports the software you've chosen.

EVALUATING YOUR NEEDS

A microcomputer system is a significant investment. Before you decide to purchase one, you need to think seriously about what you want to do. Do you plan to write the next Great American Novel? Publish a newsletter? Or just write occasional correspondence? Do you want to keep the books for your new business? Track your local softball team's batting averages? Or do your own household budget? There are innumerable tasks you can do with a computer; assessing your needs carefully can make the difference between owning a highly useful tool and watching your computer gather dust.

But even knowing what you want to do with the computer, how do you find out what fits your needs? Experience is best; possibilities include your school's computer lab, friends who can show you the ropes, computer rental agencies, and computer dealers. You should also do some research; popular computer magazines provide a wealth of information, including reviews of software and hardware.

SELECTING A FAMILY

Selecting a **computer family** is the broadest decision you face. A family is a group of similar computers built around a common standard. The **IBM PC** (and **IBM-compatible computers**) and the **Apple Macintosh** (Mac) are both families. Because each family uses a different method for controlling software, different types of programs tend to operate better on computers in one family than on those of another. The Mac has built a reputation around manipulating graphics. The Macintosh is therefore popular with people, such as graphic designers and desktop publishers, who produce material that is highly visual. Apple has expanded this niche by designing Macs to be very easy to use; they require very little setup and are nearly ready to run right out of the box. This "plug and play" aspect of the Macintosh has been one of its major selling points.

The PC is known for its flexibility and ability to manipulate data. This is one of the reasons for its use by financial analysts and database managers. A few years ago the differences between IBM and Macintosh were much more pronounced. Today, the gap is narrowing with the growing popularity of **Windows** and OS/2, as PCs become more graphics oriented. It has also become much easier to get the kind of computer system you want preconfigured to your needs, so that getting started with a PC is nearly as simple as with the Mac. The bewildering variety of choices being offered makes the buying decision more complex, however, and requires you to know enough about microcomputers to make an intelligent choice.

Ultimately, though, the most important factor in a buying decision is making sure it will handle the job(s) you have in mind. This means that the computer family you need will depend on the specific software you choose and the hardware needed to run it. However, you should keep the differences between computer families in mind as you try out software and hardware.

CHOOSING SOFTWARE FIRST

Software, more than anything else, determines how easily and productively you will work. Because it is the bridge between you and the computer that lets

---

For the Wee Ones

Amanda is two years old and can barely pronounce the word "computer," but she is getting one this Christmas. Why? As a salesperson at the famous toy store FAO Schwartz put it, "Kids like to push a button and make something happen." A growing amount of software is designed to take advantage of this natural curiosity, and, in the process, to help preschoolers learn numbers, letters, and simple words. Amanda can press the number 4 on her computer keyboard and watch four joggers sprint across the screen to the "Chariots of Fire" theme. An extra benefit is that these toys will acquaint children with computers early on, giving them an edge in later life when they have to use computers for more than playing.

Communicating by Computer

In Scottsdale, Arizona, students not only learn about science and history, they actively participate in them, thanks to their computers. When the Berlin Wall fell, sixth graders used the Global Education Network to link up with their contemporaries in Munich to ask how they felt about the events. "Imagine, the younger generation in the East and West have never had a chance so far to see their neighbors," replied the German students. Some of the students are helping a student in Chicago conduct an acid rain study by collecting and analyzing their own rain for comparison. Others are exchanging information on local animal and plant life with a school in Martha's Vineyard. The goal is for students to be independent thinkers who use the computer as a tool, rather than being passive receivers of information.

the computer do the tasks you want done, first choose the software that best fits your needs—then select the computer that best runs this software.

When choosing software, keep several criteria in mind:

- *How easy the program is for you to use.* Does the program's interface suit your style of work? Can you master its functions quickly?
- *Compatibility.* Will the program allow you to share data with the people with whom you work? How important is data sharing to you?
- *Marketable skills.* Will learning how to use this software give you a competitive advantage in the job market?

The best way to find out whether a piece of software meets these criteria is to use it. Find a dealer who will let you try the software before you buy. Try the software installed in your school's computer lab, on your friends' computers, or on rental computers as well. In addition to your current needs, consider your future needs. How do you see yourself using the computer in six months? A year? Once you have become accustomed to the software, you will probably begin using the computer for things you never dreamed of when you first bought it.

Operating Environment: DOS or GUI?

The most basic software decision is which operating environment you will work in. DOS, as we saw in the operating systems chapter, is a command-line interface. Software applications designed to work under DOS each have their own interface, learning each one is different. GUIs such as Windows, Finder, and OS/2 Workplace Shell (Figure 4-1) provide a common interface for software applications, so similar functions in different programs are executed the same way; this makes learning several applications quicker and easier. GUIs also provide easier ways of commanding the computer

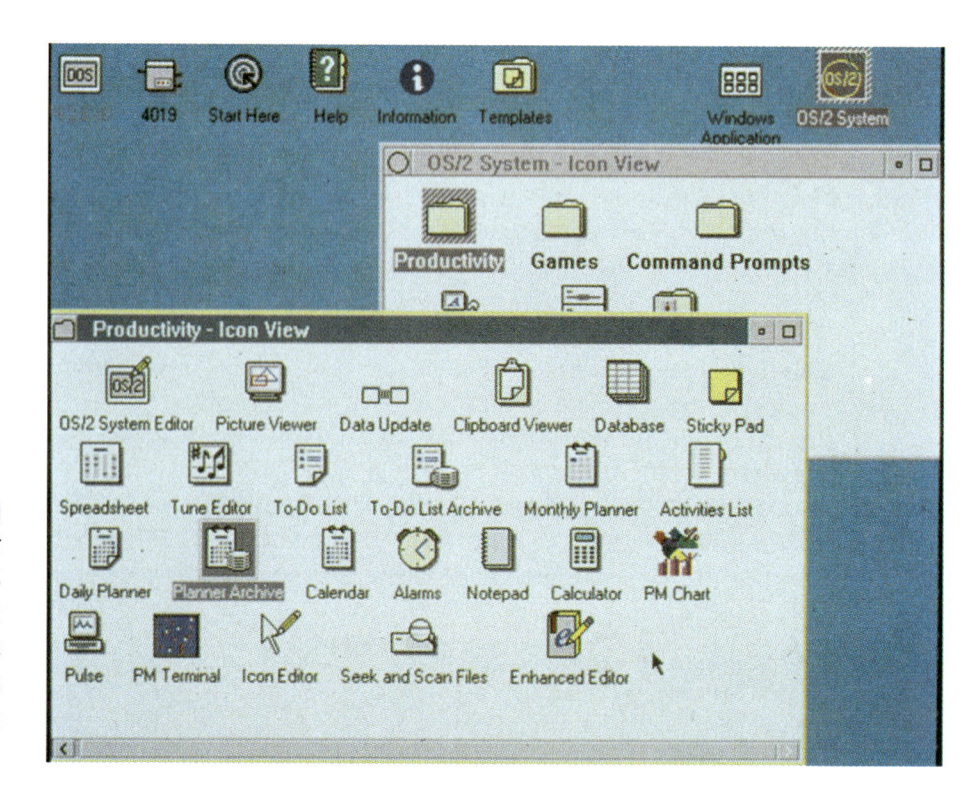

Figure 4-1
IBM's OS/2 is an example of an operating system with a graphical user interface; it competes directly with Windows and DOS for PCs and compatibles. While OS/2 provides greater functionality, it also requires more sophisticated hardware. Compare its features to Windows and the Macintosh System.

to perform operating system tasks such as copy, move, or delete files and directories.

Because DOS requires less computing power, it is better for meeting simpler computing needs on less-expensive PCs than Windows or OS/2. DOS applications can typically run on cheaper 8086- or 80286-based PCs. Windows and OS/2 need a more powerful microprocessor (80386-, 80486-, and beyond) or with more memory than DOS applications require, to be of any practical use. Comparing DOS with the Macintosh System is difficult, but new versions of System also require more expensive hardware.

The trade-off comes with the sophistication of your computing needs. If you need to run only a few simple applications, such as everyday uses for word processing and spreadsheets, a DOS-based computer system will suit you well. If your needs are more demanding, and if you need to use more complex applications, you will find the common interface provided by GUIs to be convenient and efficient. You also need to consider your future needs here as well; if your use of the computer is likely to become more sophisticated (which is often the case), you should invest in an operating environment that will not only meet your present needs but those you will have in the future.

The Big Six and Integrated Packages

Applications are programs that make the computer process text, manipulate numeric data, store and locate sets of data, connect to other computers, generate graphics, produce high-quality documents, and more. It is these applications that make computers valuable to users. In this section, we review the big six application packages—word processing, graphics, desktop publishing, spreadsheet, database, and communications—and integrated packages, single pieces of software that combine the basic tools of several applications.

Word Processing. A word processor makes writing and editing everything, from a brief memo to a novel, much easier and faster. The real strength of word processors is their ability to edit and format documents, and they vary in the strength and variety of these functions. Word processors range from simple programs to sophisticated packages that include many tools and features usually found only in desktop publishing programs (Figure 4-2, p. 63).

At one end of the spectrum are programs that are designed primarily for memos and short correspondence and that focus on ease of use through the use of menus. These programs are appropriate for people with limited budgets and for those who plan to use their word processors to edit rather than format text. More advanced packages focus on longer, more complex documents and offer far more options for formatting and automating work. Most can even systematically create the table of contents and index and update them as pages change. When buying a word processor, look for a package that supports your printer, lets you have several files open at once—a must if you plan to cut and paste between documents—and includes a built-in spelling checker.

Graphics. Graphics software is any application that helps you manipulate nontext elements, ranging from charts created by a spreadsheet to special

> HISTORY

Apple Computer

The story of Apple Computer combines all the legends of the industry—only in this case, they are all true.

In 1976, Steve Jobs, then not quite 21 years old, proposed the idea of a personal computer to Nolan Bushnell, visionary head of Atari, where Jobs was working. Bushnell nixed the idea. Jobs's good friend and fellow member of the Homebrew Computing Club, Steve Wozniak, tried to persuade his bosses at Hewlett-Packard that the time had come to build personal computers. They, too, said no.

So Jobs and Wozniak promptly formed Apple Computer and set out to build a personal computer on their own. Or rather, Woz built the computer—in his spare time, in a couple of months—bullied and goaded by Jobs.

At first, Apple operated out of the bedroom of Jobs's sister, until their father cleared the garage for the two entrepreneurs, both of whom were college dropouts. Jobs sold his Volkswagen van and Wozniak parted with his progammable calculator, which netted them all of $1,300. A fellow member of the Homebrew Club had started one of the first personal computer stores, and he ordered 50 of the machines, which sold for $666.66.

Woz built the Apple I to impress his fellow club members and to prove it could be done. But Jobs had higher plans, and he nagged, bullied, pleaded, and generally coerced his five-years-older friend until Woz came up with a computer that reflected Jobs's vision of what a personal computer could be: the Apple II.

Jobs was convinced—and remains convinced to this day—that computers can literally change the world, making it a better place, and making the people who own them happier, more satisfied individuals. One of the reasons Jobs called the company "Apple" is that he thought of the apple as a perfect fruit: it comes in a nice package, is not damaged easily, and has a high nutritional content. Jobs wanted the company to be the perfect company, the computer to be the perfect machine.

Introduced in late 1976, the Apple II ignited the personal computer revolution. It was the first microcomputer that was also a major commercial success. People could buy the Apple II from a dealer who would fix it if something went wrong, and who could also probably teach them how to use it. It did not require a separate video terminal or a teletype machine; it had a floppy disk drive for storing data; and it also had a color monitor that displayed graphics as well as text. Besides, the whole thing looked like a consumer electronics product, not like a refugee from a scientific laboratory.

At $3,000, the Apple II was hardly priced to be the home computer Jobs was touting it to be. But through sheer force of will, the often scruffy-looking, unwashed, bearded, sandal-wearing Jobs convinced thousands of others at local computer shows that they had to have his "insanely great" machine.

Wozniak's floppy disk controller used less than a quarter of the number of integrated circuits required by other controllers at the time. This meant the Apple II could be used to run accounting programs and store financial data, a fact that quickly became evident to tens of thousands of small business owners and middle managers of large corporations, especially after the software package VisiCalc was introduced.

Other computer companies sold their wares to hobbyists; Jobs took out full-page, four-color ads in *Playboy* and *Scientific American*, convincing doctors, lawyers, and corporate executives the way they could ensure they were part of a changing world was by owning an Apple II.

Jobs has been accused by detractors of having more style than substance. But for 15 years he has forced the computer industry to follow his direction. ■

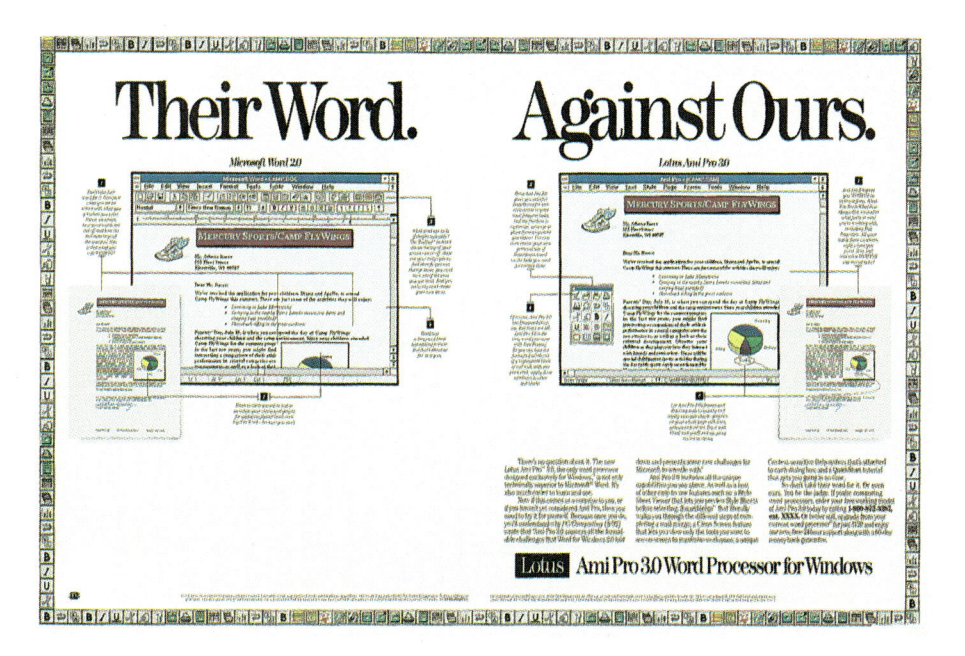

Figure 4-2
This ad for Ami Pro gives important points of comparison between word processors. Are they the ones you're concerned about? Also, consider opinions of ease of use, productivity, and ease of learning carefully; these questions you can answer only from personal experience.

effects for films and movies. Graphics programs fall into three broad categories: charting and representation graphics, paint and draw programs, and image-editing software (Figure 4-3).

Charting and presentation programs allow you to transform information from spreadsheets and databases into easily understandable graphs. Nearly all programs let you create standard bar, column, pie, and scatter charts. Some of the more powerful packages enable you to plot data in three dimensions and add color. When examining presentation software, look for programs that not only read data from your favorite applications, but that also let you easily add text, such as titles and captions.

Paint and draw programs enable you to do just that—create images with an electronic stylus (controlled by a mouse). Unlike charting software that uses imported data to create graphics, this approach lets you create original images freehand. You can vary the effects by using different tools. When choosing a paint or draw program, look for one that contains several different drawing tools; at least basic text formatting, such as control of fonts and type styles; and a wide range of special effects, such as the ability to edit individual pixels.

The final and most powerful graphics application is image-editing software. Image editors give you almost total control over any graphic image, particularly scanned photographs such as, for example, a black-and-white family photo. With image processing software, you can colorize it, remove the family dog and replace it with a scanned image of the neighbor's cat, and change the background so it looks as though you took the picture on a tropical beach.

Such power does not come without cost, however. To use this software effectively, you need very high quality hardware, including a compatible scanner. You will want a package that supports a wide variety of graphic formats, and as with draw and paint programs, you will want as many special effects as possible so you can achieve the desired results.

Which type of software you should buy—charting and presentation, paint and draw, or image editing—depends on your needs. If you plan to use graphics to convey data and don't plan to use your computer as an artist's tool, look at stand-alone presentation software or the charting programs that come with

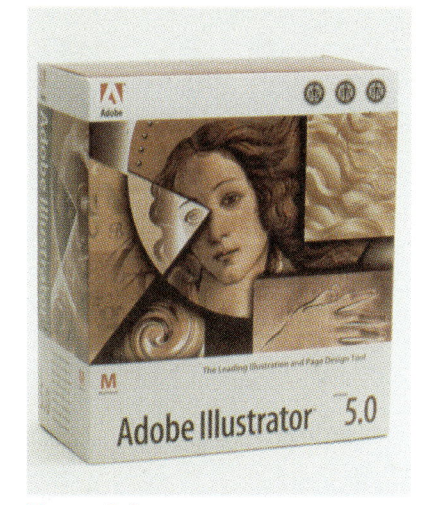

Figure 4-3
How much need do you have for a presentation graphics package? Make sure your needs can't be met by other software, such as the built-in graphics features of spreadsheets, before you invest in presentation graphics. Top-of-the-line software includes some highly specialized features you may not use.

many popular spreadsheets and databases. If you plan to use individualized graphics, your choice depends on whether you plan to create your own works or modify other images. If you plan to start from scratch, go with a draw or paint program; to manipulate other images, stick with image-editing software.

Desktop Publishing. Desktop publishing (DTP) once was easy to describe: any program that combined text and graphics and created a new publication was a desktop publishing program. Nowadays most word processors, and even many spreadsheets and database programs, fit this description. With the functional differences blurring between high-end word processors and DTP programs, the distinction comes down more to approach than to features. Word processing programs tend to deal with content; they look at all the text in a document as a single piece placed on the page. DTP programs, on the other hand, focus on style; they look at a document as a series of stories (and graphics) placed as separate elements on a page. With a word processor, you manipulate the text; with a DTP program, you manipulate the elements.

Desktop publishing programs fall into two categories: those that focus on short, unstructured documents, and those designed for longer, highly structured ones (Figure 4-4). PageMaker exemplifies the former; Ventura Publisher, the latter. When using this type of program, you usually define the style first, then import the text and graphics into the frames in the document. This approach works very well for highly complex documents such as technical reports, where structure is crucial.

For short, creative pieces, such as flyers and brochures, PageMaker's unstructured approach fares much better. PageMaker uses a paste-up board analogy. Rather than create styles first, the user simply places an element on the electronic paste-up board and moves it to the desired location. From there, you can make adjustments as you wish.

In both these categories, programs range from the simple to the sophisticated. Whether you need an entry-level or a high-end package depends on the extent of your use. If you only occasionally need to produce a brochure or flyer, an entry-level package will fit the bill, particularly if you have a good

Figure 4-4
PageMaker is one of the leading software packages for desktop publishing. Deciding between DTP packages is a matter of working style and the types of documents you do. Also, make sure your needs aren't already met by the capabilities of your word processor.

word processor. In this case, look at programs with the greatest number of features *not* included in your word processor. If you plan to do extensive DTP, only a full-fledged program will work. If you fall into this latter category, focus more on approach than on features.

Spreadsheets. In addition to their use in the financial community, spreadsheets are commonly used for everything from producing household budgets to tracking sports statistics. A spreadsheet is essentially an electronic ledger that performs all the calculations any time you change a number (Figure 4-5). This lets you tap your spreadsheet's most powerful function—*what-if?* analysis. Suppose you use your spreadsheet to track your household budget. By changing a few numbers, you can analyze the impact of buying a new car, getting a raise, or using your savings to go on vacation.

Although most spreadsheets work on the same principle, there are significant differences in power and ease of use among the various products, involving the following features:

- The number of functions; this provides a good indication of the program's overall power.
- The option to incorporate specially designed functions.
- The ability to open several worksheets at once and link separate worksheets together.
- The ease of integrating charts and data.
- Compatibility, particularly with Lotus 1-2-3, whose files use a standard format.

If you plan to use a spreadsheet for home budgeting, either a basic model or one that comes as part of an integrated package will be sufficient. If you plan to develop applications for others, however, look for a more sophisticated product with a flexible macro language.

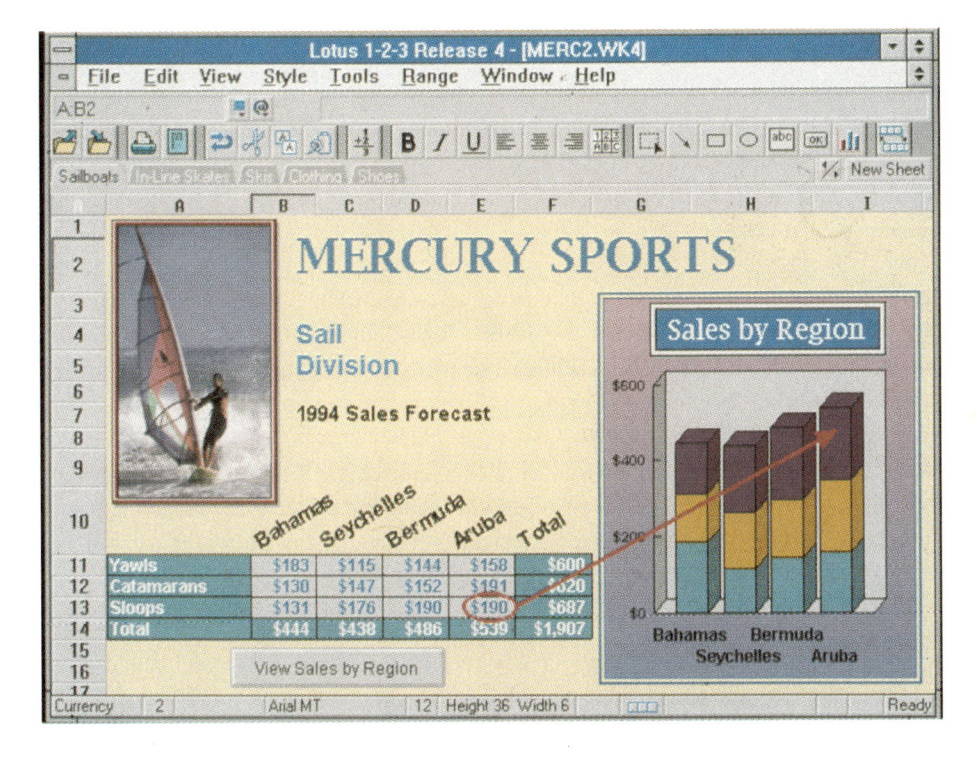

Figure 4-5
Lotus's entry into the Windows market offers compatibility with its own DOS program, long an industry standard. But if you don't already have a large investment in Lotus spreadsheets, is Lotus compatibility really important? An objective buying decision means comparing features with competitors such as Microsoft Excel. Can you find an Excel ad that responds to Lotus's claims?

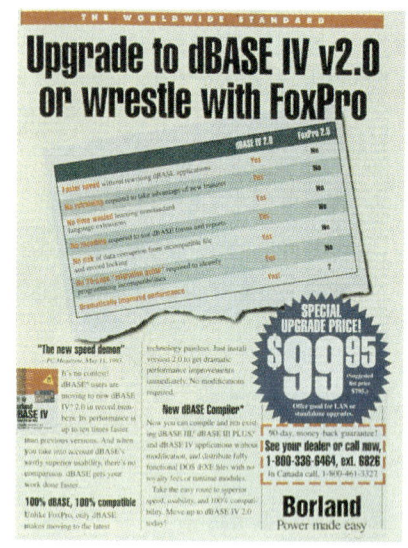

Figure 4-6
Ads for dBASE IV compare against FoxPro, but not against Paradox, which is also a Borland product. Do you believe the productivity claims in this ad? Would they apply to your situation? And do you need all the features of a major database?

"That's Entertainment..."

Hollywood has never been slow to cash in on the newest fad, and a growing number of Tinsel Town inhabitants are exploring ways to combine their pet projects with interactive video and CD-ROM. George Lucas, no less, has been digitizing all of the "Young Indiana Jones" series for a possible series of games aimed at students and history buffs. Actress Shelley Duvall has developed a game to teach children about birds and their habitats. When a child touches the picture of a parrot, the rainforest where the parrot lives appears on screen and a voice tells how the bird traveled to its home. Fans of MTV will be able to develop their own music video, thanks to a game developed by the groups C& C Music Factory and Kriss Kross. How many of these projects will be successful is anybody's guess, but one thing is for sure: with Hollywood supporting the technology, a lot of people will hear about it.

Databases. Word processors are essentially limited to storing text and spreadsheets to numeric information, but databases can store almost any type of data (Figure 4-6). The real power of databases comes from their ability to sort through large volumes of information and produce reports that highlight the desired information. For example, by searching the Census Bureau's databases, you could generate a report ranking the counties in each state by the income levels of single-parent families of four.

There are several types of database structures; the two most common are flat-file and relational. An address book is an example of a flat-file database, where each record contains the same number of the same type of information: name, address, phone number, and so on.

What if you wanted to compare your holiday card list with your address file? You would of course want to link these files. To do so, you would need a relational database. A relational database lets you work with several files simultaneously and establish relations, or cross-references, between them. In addition to allowing for a more complex file structure, the real power of relational databases lies in letting you design very complex applications using the data.

The type of database you need depends on your intended uses. If you have a fairly simple use in mind where each record will have exactly the same structure, a flat file will meet your needs. If you plan to track many pieces of complex data where all the data will not fit into a single, well-defined structure, you should probably opt for a more expensive relational database. When comparing relational databases, look for packages that maintain compatibility with the Xbase (based on dBase III+) and structured query language (SQL) standards. This will give you access to the vast library of applications already written in this language. If you need a database designed to your specific needs, menu-driven packages will guide you through the process.

Communications. With a modem and communications software, you can transform a computer normally limited to the data on its hard disk to a machine capable of accessing millions of files ranging from tomorrow's weather report to debates of current events to the latest in virtual-reality demos. Before your modem places a single call, of course, you need communications software. When purchasing a communications program, ease of use is most important. To exchange messages with people, to send and receive data and documents, you will want a program that has a good built-in editor or that is compatible with your word processor.

Because of the vast number of communications options available, menus are essential. At the very least, a program should let you create a dialing directory of frequently called numbers. This way, you need to enter the parameters for your favorite bulletin board only once; after that you simply make your choice from a menu and the software remembers the settings. Better programs are preset to log you on to the most popular services. Also, look for a variety of file transfer protocols. All communications programs support the basic protocols, and most provide status reports and error checking and correcting. The best programs let you transfer files in the background so that you can do other work during long file transfers.

Integrated Packages. Until recently, the biggest advantage of **integrated packages**, which combine several applications in one (typically word processing, spreadsheet, database, graphics, and communications), was their common interface and ability to exchange data between the different applications (Figure 4-7). The latest features of GUIs have largely minimized this advantage, however. Not only do all GUIs provide a common interface for applications, but the latest versions of the Macintosh System, Windows, and OS/2 all include features for data exchange.

Where integrated packages do stand out is value. The applications they include are those that nearly everyone needs, and the features, while somewhat limited compared to the best stand-alone software packages, are robust enough to handle most ordinary computing needs; and the cost of integrated packages is far less than purchasing stand-alone software. When evaluating an integrated package, make sure that the application you plan to use the most is powerful enough; you may also want an integrated package that will install only those applications you actually use, if you need to conserve storage space on your hard drive.

The first thing to look at when choosing integrated software is which application you plan to use most. This is important because each package tends to have its home application, its strongest program around which the rest of the package was built. Other features to look for include a communications module that will let you retrieve data from your home or office. Business travellers often use integrated packages because their laptop computers do not have enough hard disk space to load several stand alone applications. If this is true for you, look for a package that will let you install only the modules you want and thus conserve disk space.

Figure 4-7
Integrated packages such as LotusWorks promise a cheaper alternative to stand-alone application software, with ability to integrate different kinds of data. Are their features adequate to your needs? Would you benefit from the power of stand-alone applications?

SELECTING HARDWARE

Unlike purchasing software, in which qualitative factors such as look and feel are every bit as important as performance, most hardware purchases revolve around easily quantifiable specifications. Although this makes it easier to compare two products, a major difficulty lies in discerning the importance of a given specification (see Figure 4-8). In this section, we cover the major components in a computer system and help you determine your needs.

Figure 4-8
Comparing advertising for computer systems is complex. More than just the price, check specific features: how much RAM? What size cache? What type of monitor? What type of video graphics card? What size hard disk? One floppy drive, or two—and what size? What ports and how many? What software comes installed? In addition, look for guarantees, shipping, technical support policies, and small-print caveats. Finally, check computer magazines for objective reviews.

The Electronic Cadaver

It's not exactly Frankenstein, but now medical students can interact with the computer to learn anatomy. Called The Electronic Cadaver, the multimedia program runs on a Mac II, a laserdisc player, and HyperCard, and it combines graphics, text, and images into a unique teaching tool. For instance, a student studying the nerves in the human hand can ask the computer, "Does it hurt here?" while clicking the mouse on the thumb. "Ouch!" replies the computer if the nerve in question is where the student pointed. Students can watch short animations that demonstrate how muscles and tendons move the fingers, or see the bone development of a hand as it ages from infancy to nineteen years old. They can scan images of the muscles and internal organs. Students can also create their own playlists, ordering stacks of images and text as they need to, creating their own textbook.

Apple Macintosh Computers

Apple Computer, Inc.'s commitment to ease of use makes choosing a Macintosh very straightforward. Apple produces several lines of Macintosh computers, including the Macintosh Classic, the Macintosh LC, the Macintosh Performa, the Macintosh Quadra, the Powerbook, and Power Macs. The Macintosh Classic comes with enough memory and speed to run most types of software; however, its performance tends to lag when using high-end applications. Because the Classic comes with a built-in monitor, plugging it in is essentially the only setup required. The Macintosh Classic is appropriate for people who want to move to a Macintosh interface but who do not plan to do extensive work with graphics.

The Macintosh Performa line is intended for first-time and at-home computer users who want a simple choice of hardware, software, and peripherals to suit the various computer needs of their family members. One Macintosh Performa model is all-in-one, whereas other models include monitors that are not built in. This flexibility allows you to add color to the system and choose the size of the monitor—both essential if you plan to use your computer for graphics applications or DTP. This line also allows you to add a much greater amount of memory than the Macintosh Classic, making the Macintosh Performa appropriate for more complex applications.

The Macintosh LC line of personal computers is ideal for the education market because of its low cost, versatility, and color capabilities. The Macintosh LCs come complete with many built-in features such as large monitor support, networking, and memory expansion. Like the Macintosh Performa line, one Macintosh LC model is an all-in-one design, while other models allow you to choose your monitor size.

The Macintosh Quadras are designed for entry-level and mainstream professional users. Based on a faster CPU, the Macintosh Quadras include other enhancements for increasing performance and flexibility. If you expect to use your computer for extensive image editing or multimedia presentations, a Quadra will perform significantly better than the others.

The Powerbooks are notebook-sized computers that contain all the power and function of any of the other Macintosh computers. The main advantage of Powerbooks is that they are portable. You can keep a Powerbook in your briefcase, take it to class, and even work with it on an airplane.

Once you decide on the product line, the rest is relatively easy. For each line, Apple produces a few models with different memory and hard disk configurations. Because of the vast requirements of Macintosh computer applications, the best rule of thumb to follow is to purchase as much memory and hard disk space as you can afford—and more than you think you need.

IBM and IBM-Compatible Computers

Because so many companies produce IBM-compatible computers, there are many possible configurations—which makes purchasing a PC more complex than buying a Mac. When you look at an ad, you examine it in terms of the configuration that will meet your needs and provide the best performance for the lowest price. To determine which computer will best do this, you need to understand the major options available. These options fall into three broad categories:

- The *system board,* which includes the motherboard, or circuitry, and the amount of memory
- *Storage,* consisting of the floppy and hard disks
- *Video,* the monitor and the video card

The System Board

The CPU. The most important consideration is the microprocessor, or central processing unit (CPU)—the brains of the system. There are currently several groups of microprocessors: 8086/8088, 80286, 80386, 80486, the Pentium, the Power PC, and more being developed every year. The processors vary in the number of bits they process simultaneously and the size of their data bus. As you learned in the chapter on hardware, the number of bits a CPU processes determines how powerful it is; the more bits, the more powerful the computer. The size of the data bus determines how quickly information can get into the CPU; the larger the bus, the faster the microprocessor.

How powerful a CPU you need depends on the software you will use. For simple word processing tasks, a 386 (maybe even a 286) will be sufficient. Complex applications, such as Windows programs, require more speed, and a 286 can be agonizingly slow (this type of application usually requires at least a 386). If you plan to use CAD (computer-aided design) software or do complex engineering and statistical analysis, you would probably appreciate a Pentium or Power PC.

The 386SX, the minimum processor needed to run most Windows applications effectively, remains a very popular processor, offering enough speed to run most applications at an affordable price. As software becomes more complex, however, the 386SX is falling behind in its ability to provide acceptable performance. And as CPU prices continue to drop, many people are starting to consider the 486SX an even more cost-effective computer system.

After selecting the type of microprocessor, look at the clock speed, which has the next greatest effect on the computer speed. The clock speed of the processor is generally included with the processor name. For example, an advertisement listing a 4865X-25 refers to a computer with a 486SX processor operating at 25 MHz.

RAM. The amount of primary memory, or random access memory (RAM), a computer contains also affects the speed of a computer system (Figure 4-9). The more memory, the faster a computer system can perform. When you increase the amount of RAM in your computer, you will increase its performance because it can then store more information in RAM rather than on the disks, which are much slower in retrieving data.

Almost all computers come with at least 1 megabyte of memory. While this might suffice for a simple word processing program, most programs today require at least 4Mb—and many require 16Mb. Because memory prices have decreased, you can often realize a significant improvement in performance for a relatively small investment. Therefore, you should look at computers with at least 8Mb of RAM.

In some computer systems, particularly those with faster processors, such as the 486 and Pentium, the CPU must wait for data it requests from memory. This is called a **wait state.** As you might expect, this makes the computer slower; the best way to avoid wait states is with a **RAM cache,** which moves the

IBM		
PS/1 286, 386SX	2MB	$99
PS/2 90, 95 and P75	4MB	$135
	8MB	$289
Expansion Boards for	2-8MB	$269
50, 50Z, 555X, 60	2-16MB	$309
65SX		

COMPAQ		
Deskpro 386-20, 20E	4MB Module	$159
and 25	4MB Broad	$219
Deskpro 386-33, 486-33	2MB	$99
and System Pro	8MB	$328

ZENITH		
Zenith Z-386/20, 25	1MB	$49
33 and 33E		
Zenith Z-386SX	2MB	$99
286PL+, Z-LS		

HEWLETT-PACKARD		
Vectra 386/16N, 386/20N	2MB	$99
	8MB	$319
Vectra 486 PC	7MB	$109
	8MB	$349

Figure 4-9
Buying RAM upgrades can be simple or complex. If you trust yourself to understand an ad like this one, and are comfortable opening up the computer yourself, you can get very good prices; however, many users will prefer to bring their computer in to a dealer for installation.

> SECOND OPINION

The Rapid Rate of Technological Change and the End User

As I write this, in 1993, the minimum standard requirements for IBM PCs and their clones are a high-speed 486 microprocessor, lots of internal memory, a high-capacity hard disk, and a high-resolution color monitor. The first PC I bought, back in 1984, had an 8088 processor, less than one-tenth the memory of today's PCs, no hard drive, and a monochrome monitor. I paid a lot of money for that PC. It was not leading-edge technology, as IBM had just introduced the AT, but my old PC was what I needed at the time.

Anyone who buys a PC today that meets the minimum standard requirements for 1993 is already behind. Soon Intel's Pentium chip will be standard in PCs and their clones, and such novel capabilities as reliable voice recognition will eventually become standard, too. The marching advance of technology continues unabated. And it isn't just hardware—new, improved releases of software packages appear on the market almost as soon as users have mastered the prior releases.

What's driving this continual march? There is no doubt that users want more powerful, easier-to-use technology. There is also no doubt computer firms want to turn out more product to generate more profits. In one sense, a new release of a software package is no different than a new, improved box of laundry detergent. Both are improvements over their predecessors, both breathe new life into dying product lines, and both will soon be the only version of that product on the market. So what if users want to stay with what they have now? Staying with the old software is possible. You can still use the software to do what you've always done, but you risk being left behind by the fast-moving train of technological advance. Because your software isn't the only package that's been upgraded, all PC software gets upgraded, and the hardware gets upgraded, too. The entire computing milieu changes. Today's personal computing world is very different from the world of only 10 years ago. The changes are seductive—it's tough to say no. No one wants to be left behind, watching everyone else move up to the new technology standards.

So there are risks to standing still. But are there also risks to forever riding the wave of technological advance? Absolutely. Staying on the leading edge can be expensive. You have to be willing to throw out perfectly good hardware and software and purchase the latest available. You have to ride a learning curve on your new equipment, just to get to the same level of productivity you had before you upgraded. But once you reach your former level of productivity, your new computing equipment should help you become even more productive. But what do you do when the next software release comes out, or when the next microprocessor hits the market? When should you upgrade again? Unfortunately, there are no easy answers to these questions, just a wide range of opinions. ∎

Joey F. George,
Florida State University

> There is also no doubt computer firms want to turn out more product to generate more profits. In one sense, a new release of a software package is no different than a new, improved box of laundry detergent.

most commonly accessed data, such as program menus, to a location where it can be retrieved very quickly. A memory cache is a small amount of very fast memory placed between the CPU and the slower primary memory. While the CPU performs one operation, the cache controller fills fast memory with the information it anticipates the CPU will need next. If the prediction is correct, the required information is passed directly to the CPU without any delay.

Storage

As discussed in the chapter on hardware, there are two basic types of disk drives: those that use removable floppy disks and those that use fixed hard disks.

Floppy Disk Drives. Floppy disk drives are needed to place software on your computer and exchange data with other people. There are currently two sizes of floppy disks: 5 1/4-inch and 3 1/2-inch.

Most computer manufacturers and software publishers have standardized by adopting the 3 1/2-inch disk. Many computers that are just a few years old, however, contain only 5 1/4-inch disk drives. If you want to exchange data with someone who uses such a machine, you will need a 5 1/4-inch drive. The best configuration, then, is to have both high-density 3 1/2- and 5 1/4-inch floppy drives, allowing the computer system to use either type of floppy disk.

Hard Disk Drives. In addition to the floppy drives, most software requires a hard disk. A hard disk is a very fast, high-capacity disk that is usually permanently installed in your computer, and most computers come with at least a 100Mb hard drive. Because some programs require over 30Mb of storage space, many people opt for much larger hard disks. If your budget allows, a good rule of thumb to follow is to select a hard drive twice as large as you think you will need. This leaves room for next year's programs, which will require even more free disk space.

The speed of a hard drive also affects your computer's performance. Hard drives are rated according to the average time (measured in milliseconds) it takes to locate a particular piece of information. For acceptable performance, look for a hard drive with an access time of 16 milliseconds or so. You can further increase the performance of your hard drive by installing a disk cache. Just like a memory cache, a disk cache moves frequently accessed data from the disk into RAM. Installing a hard drive cache can increase your hard drive's performance ten to twenty times. Caches come as either hardware or software. Software caches usually cost less and give performance superior to that offered by a hardware cache. The only drawback of a software cache is that it requires you to set aside 1 or 2 megabytes of RAM. Because the cost of RAM is low, stick with a software cache and add more memory as needed.

Video

The video subsystem has two basic components: the video graphics adapter, or graphics card, which plugs into your computer; and the monitor.

Graphics Card. In selecting a graphics card, consider the number of colors available and the resolution. First, do you need a color display or will a single-color (monochrome) display suffice? Most people prefer color because it makes the computer easier to use and can help reduce eyestrain.

Go Ahead, Take God's Job for a Day

Think you could do a better job of running your city than the politicans? Do you fantasize about being in control of the Earth so you could fix things once and for all? Well, take heart. A variety of computer games gives you your chance to be in charge. You can even build your own world and set up things correctly from the start—but beware of the consequences. SimEarth lets the player start primitive life on its evolutionary path, but once goaded into intelligence, the computer characters have minds of their own. Global Effect directs a city's development while a graph at the side of the screen shows the environmental effect of this growth. How do you balance the need for reliable energy against a worsening ecology? That's your problem, er job. In Balance of the Planet, the players must untangle interlocking problems like overpopulation, disease, hunger, and pollution as they seek utopia. And if you completely mess up your world, don't worry. The computer gives you the chance to start all over again.

Getting the Most for Your Hardware Buck

Buying the best computer hardware depends not only on the computer manufacturers, but also on your own priorities. Is it important to you to have a name-brand computer like IBM or Apple? Or do you want a rock-bottom price from a no-name company that might be out of business in six months? Big-name compatible makers like Dell and Compaq have lowered their prices to compete with the no-name clones. IBM released a new line of low-cost computers to try and regain some of its market share. Even Apple lowered its prices to compete with the IBM clones. But, while taking advantage of this boon in pricing, consumers still need to know some facts. There may be more than pricing differentiating today's less expensive computers from yesterday's pricier models. When you are shopping for the best price, find out *exactly* what the difference is between machines. If the company has cut costs by using fewer layers in the motherboards, find out if there have been any problems with delamination. If they are using a less expensive disk drive, find out what the life expectancy of that drive is compared to the more expensive model. You might get exactly what you pay for.

The next question involves the level of resolution. The term *resolution* refers to the number of pixels, or dots, on your screen. The higher the resolution, the crisper and more defined the graphics will be. There are five types of color graphics adapters that provide various levels of resolution:

CGA (color graphics adapter)	320×200
EGA (enhanced graphics adapter)	640×350
VGA (video graphics array)	640×480
SVGA (super VGA)	$1,024 \times 768$
XVGA (extended VGA)	$1,024 \times 768$

At the very least, you should look for VGA. Nearly all software supports the VGA standard, and many applications now require it. If you expect to be using Windows applications or working extensively with graphics programs, also consider a graphics card with an accelerator, which will substantially improve the performance of your PC. With a standard graphics card, the CPU must create the graphics; the graphics card simply transfers the data to the monitor. A graphics accelerator, however, reduces the work the CPU does (thus freeing it to do other things) by drawing some of the more common images itself. This reduced workload allows a 386-20 to run Windows applications faster than a 486-33 can without an accelerator card.

Monitor

The final issue is the size of the monitor (Figure 4-10). The standard size is 12 inches for monochrome and 14 inches for color. The standard size is generally adequate for most work, but some people, particularly those working extensively with graphics, prefer larger monitors. Whatever size you decide on, however, make sure you buy a **noninterlaced monitor** because it greatly reduces any perceived flicker. To reduce flicker further, look for a monitor with a vertical refresh rate—the number of times it redraws the screen—of at least 72Hz.

WHERE TO BUY YOUR COMPUTER

Now that you understand the hardware options that are available, you need to decide which brand of computer you will purchase and from whom

Figure 4-10
With monitors, make sure the one you're buying is noninterlaced for the resolution you plan to use and compatible with the video format (VGA, SVGA, XGA) your video graphics card generates. If you use a GUI, try for the greatest resolution and largest size monitor you can afford; it's worth the money. Finally, a monitor that can handle several different video formats may be important to running certain applications.

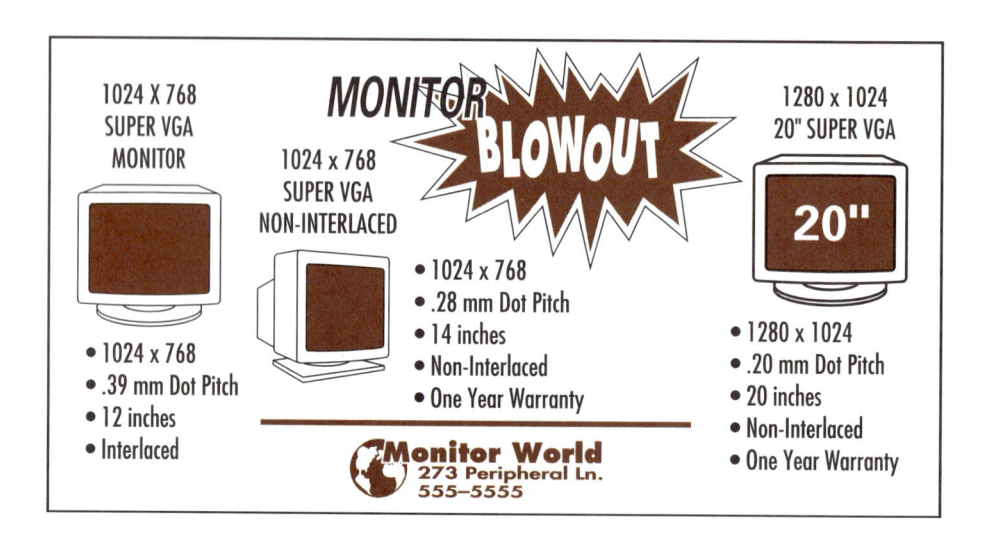

will buy it. Will you choose a Macintosh or a PC? If you choose a PC, will you purchase an IBM, a name-brand compatible, or a no-name clone? Will you buy your computer from a computer speciality shop, a mass-market chain, or a mail-order house?

With Macintosh, the decision of which brand to buy is trivial; only Apple makes them. With PCs, you have a wide variety of choices. IBM-brand PCs usually cost more than other PCs. For this extra cost, IBMs offer a product backed by the reputation of one of America's largest companies. Name-brand compatibles, such as Dell, Compaq, AST, NCR, Digital, Zeos, Gateway 2000, and Northgate, are produced by major manufacturing companies that design, build, and test the machines themselves. These machines often cost less than IBM PCs and offer reliability that rivals them. No-name clones are assembled by smaller—often local—companies who buy parts from all over the world. These companies tend to compete solely on price, so it is not uncommon for the appearance and contents of no-name clones to change frequently as new, less-expensive suppliers are found.

Opinions vary on where one gets the best value for the money. IBMs and name-brand compatibles may prove to be more reliable, but no-name clones are usually less expensive. The cost of a microcomputer system does not always reflect its value, however. Some local companies can produce high-quality machines at lower prices because they do not have the overhead that the larger, national companies have.

When selecting the brand of PC, there is no easy decision, but there are a few tips. You are buying the company and its dealers just as much as you are buying the computer. The manufacturers of IBM microcomputers and name-brand compatibles usually require their dealers to meet a series of requirements before they can become dealers; this is not usually the case with no-name clones. Your first step, therefore, is to look at the company's reputation and how long it has been in business. Will it be around in two years to support its products? Ask your friends about their computers; don't buy a computer that has caused problems for others. Consider your own expertise; you may need it since no-name clones usually do not provide the same level of after-sale technical support provided by IBM or many of the name-brand companies. And consider the configuration of the microcomputer. IBM and many name-brand clones offer fixed models; no-name companies will generally build a computer to your exact specifications.

Once you have chosen the brand of computer, the decision of where to buy is fairly easy—it becomes a trade-off between purchase price and service. Although buying from authorized dealers will almost always cost the most, they generally give you all the support you need. Service and support vary widely with mail-order houses; check the manufacturer's service and support policies as well as the service and support ratings in computer magazines. Mass marketers usually offer competitive prices and provide limited support until you get the computer up and running. Which avenue is best for you depends on your level of technical expertise and your purchasing priorities; many people feel that the mass marketers offer the best balance between service and price. (See Figure 4-11, p. 74.)

	COMPUTER 1	COMPUTER 2	COMPUTER 3
Brand name			
Microprocessor			
Clock speed (MHz)			
RAM			
Installed size			
Maximum size			
Memory cache (Y/N; size)			
Disk drives			
Floppy disk A Size/type			
Floppy disk B Size/type			
Hard disk size/speed			
Monitor			
Color/monochrome			
Size			
VGA/SVGA adaptor			
Noninterlaced (Y/N)			
Warranty			
Free on-site service?			
Free software?			
Total Price			

Figure 4-11
Use a checklist like this one to track the characteristics of the computer you want. As you research options, record the features each one has and compare them across the board to determine the real value of what you're being offered.

SUMMARY

The broadest decision in purchasing a computer system is deciding which computer family is best for you. Macintoshes are popular with people who work mainly with graphics; people who analyze data often prefer PCs. Today, the differences between these families are not as great as they used to be, with Macs being used more as business tools and PCs being used more for graphics. You then need to decide between DOS and a graphical user interface (GUI). The latter provides a common command structure based on icons, but it requires a more powerful computer.

Application software determines what your computer will do. Because you will interact directly with the software far more often than with the hardware, select the software first and then choose the computer that best runs that software. There are six major types of application programs: word processing, graphics, desktop publishing, spreadsheet, database, and communications. In addition to these stand-alone programs, you can buy packages that integrate these functions.

After you've chosen the software, you can consider the computer itself. Macs offer several product lines, including the Classic, the Mac II/Performa, the Quadra, the Powerbook laptops, and Power Macs. With PCs, you can choose the best configuration of system board, storage, and video for your needs. The system board contains the CPU and RAM; the two main types of storage devices are floppy disks and fixed hard disks; and the video subsystem consists of the video controller card and the monitor. If you are buying a PC, you must also decide whether to purchase an IBM, a brand-name IBM-compatible, or a no-name clone.

You can buy your computer from an authorized dealer, a mail-order house, or a mass marketer. Authorized dealers offer the best service, but they can charge higher prices for their goods. Mail-order firms vary widely in the service and support they offer; mass marketers generally offer a balance of price and service.

KEY TERMS

Apple Macintosh
clone
computer family
IBM-compatible computers
IBM PC
integrated packages
noninterlaced monitor
RAM cache
wait state
Windows

REVIEW QUESTIONS

1. In general, does a software or a hardware disk cache give better performance?
2. How do draw and paint programs differ from charting programs? From image-editing programs?
3. What are the major differences between word processing and desktop publishing? What kind of work makes these differences significant?
4. What is the difference between VGA and Super VGA?
5. How does a graphics accelerator work, and when would buying one be a good investment?
6. What is the minimum hardware requirement to run Windows or OS/2 effectively?
7. What is compatibility? Why is it important?
8. What advantages do integrated packages offer over stand-alone GUI applications?
9. How does the IBM PC family differ from the Mac family?
10. When is a DOS environment better than a GUI? When is a GUI better?

Working with Word Processing

5

OBJECTIVES

After completing this chapter, you will be able to

- Define a word processor.
- Describe some of the uses for word processing.
- Identify the ways the text may be entered.
- Describe document setup, editing, and formatting procedures.
- Identify special features of word processors.
- Explain why saving and backing up your work is important.
- Discuss document printing options.

FOCUS

Word processing—using the computer as a writing tool—is for many people the most important reason for buying and learning to use a microcomputer. Whether you need to write a letter, a term paper, or the Great American Novel, a word processor can ease the process, allowing you to concentrate on what to say and how to say it, rather than on the physical effort of writing (Figure 5-1).

But what is a word processor? A word processor is software that enables you to type and edit text on a computer. It lets you enter text into the computer using the keyboard, change words or their order, and add or delete sentences or paragraphs—all without retyping the entire document. It lets you determine how the words should appear, print one or many copies of those words, and save them for another time.

TYPES OF WORD PROCESSORS

Microcomputer word processing software isn't the only type of word processor. If we think of the central idea here—a tool for processing words—then we can call a typewriter, a pencil, a piece of chalk, or even the rocks primitive humans used to mark cave walls word processors. What word processing tool you use is a matter of choice; no software, no matter how sophisticated, will make you any better a writer than you can be using pen and paper. However, the great advantage of word processing software is efficiency: no writing tool gives you more power to quickly express yourself, organize and edit your words and ideas, and present your expression to others. In the larger sense, all computer software is designed to help you express your ideas; but as more people have need to express themselves in words than in any other way, word processing is the most universal of microcomputer applications.

The universal need for word processing capability has inspired many different word processors, ranging from the simple to the sophisticated. Deciding which word processor to use is a choice that should be based on your specific needs as a writer. In fact, if word processing is all you need from a computer, you might consider a dedicated word processing machine: essentially a microcomputer with only one kind of software built in, dedicated word processors often include printers as well, functioning as an enhanced electronic typewriter (Figure 5-2). However, by far the majority of computer users have other computing needs as well, which is why microcomputer word processing software is the most common choice as a word processing tool.

Figure 5-1
More people use microcomputers for word processing than for any other type of application. Word processing is still the primary reason most individuals purchase a microcomputer.

Figure 5-2
An option between the typewriter and the microcomputer is the dedicated word processing machine. Such machines are actually single-purpose microcomputers with built-in printers. Some can store documents in formats compatible with common microcomputer word processing programs.

Teacher's Pet

Teachers of the MTV generation have a challenge. How to capture—and keep—the attention of students who are used to a change in picture every three seconds? One answer to which many schools are turning is multimedia. Laserdiscs, computers, and CD-ROM offer an astonishing number of ways to present information to students while getting students to participate in the process. For instance, one school uses multimedia in an Italian language lab. Students watch a popular Italian television show, choosing a simultaneous running text in Italian or English, and also have access to a program that gives a cultural commentary on the program. In a medical school, students learn how to read the rather unclear video images of hearts created by an ultrasound machine by juxtaposing an animated version with a video clip of an actual heart. By clicking a mouse next to the name of a heart disease, students can hear the sound a heart makes when suffering from that disease, as well as see a picture of the diseased heart.

Despite all the different features of competing word processors, most word processing programs share the same set of core functions. All word processors let you enter text, edit it, format it, save it to a file on disk, and—with a printer—print it. Nearly all include a spelling checker, and many include grammar-checking programs that point out problems in wording and suggest improvements. Other common features include headers and footers, automatic page numbering, automatic hyphenation, multicolumn text, a thesaurus, indexing and tables of contents, footnotes and references, form letters, special typefaces and character sets, ability to import data from other applications, graphics, and macros.

CHOOSING A WORD PROCESSOR: USES AND USERS

As the use of microcomputers has grown, no application has become more universal, and yet as specialized, as word processing. At one time, it was fairly easy to categorize word processing uses and programs as either home- or business-oriented. Now, with the pervasive use of microcomputers throughout business and academia, word processing uses have become so varied as to defy easy categorization. Whether used at home for letters, journals, and personal records; at school for essays, reports, and teaching materials; at the office for reports, correspondence, and contracts; in academia and science for research, opinion and argument; in civics for regulations, legal documents, and public records; or for literature, art, and criticism, word processors have gone beyond easy categorization to embrace a nearly limitless range of fields.

Some professions have specialized word processing needs that can be met with specialized word processors. Teachers can use dedicated word processors for lesson plans and syllabi; legal firms can use dedicated word processors to prepare briefs, forms, and other legal documents; playwrights can use specialized word processors to to prepare scripts. Some software companies market specialized spelling dictionaries and **thesauruses** for these and other professions, including medical and scientific disciplines. Major dictionary publishers are now offering their dictionaries in electronic form, available to the writer at the touch of a key or click of a mouse.

Your choice of a word processing program should be based primarily on what use you will have for it. Most people have fairly straightforward uses in mind for word processing software: letters, memos, school papers, and such. For these users, almost any word processor has the features necessary to meet their needs; deciding which to use is then a matter of finding one that works in a way you find easy and comfortable. If your needs are more extensive, however, you will need to evaluate specific features of word processors to determine which is best for you. Are you going to produce highly formatted text, such as newsletters and brochures? Will you be printing form letters? Will you be handling large volumes of information from databases? Do you need to produce one highly specialized type of document? Do you need help with spelling and grammar? Word processors today have specific features designed to meet all these needs; examine the features of the most popular programs to determine how well they will work for you.

USING A WORD PROCESSOR

Learning to use a word processor involves learning to enter text, set up documents the way you want, edit your work, format text, take advantage of special features, and finally, save and print your document.

Entering Text

The first thing to learn about entering text in a word processor is the **cursor**. This is a blinking vertical bar, rectangle, or underline on the screen that shows where the text you type will be entered into your document. As you type, characters appear on the screen, and the cursor will move to the right. You can move the cursor with the arrow keys on the keyboard, or by using the mouse to point and click at the location in the document where you want to enter text. The backspace key (labeled delete on Macintosh keyboards) moves the cursor to the left, backing up and erasing your recent typing.

The Keyboard. Although word processors have displaced most typewriters, typing skills are far from obsolete; in fact, computer keyboards have made the need for typing skills more acute, because a computer keyboard is a more versatile input device than a typewriter keyboard. You type text into a word processing document the way you would with a typewriter, but there are many special functions a microcomputer keyboard performs beyond that of a typewriter. Let's look at some more specialized keys (Figure 5-3):

- **The Enter Key.** The Enter key is most often compared to the carriage return on a typewriter, but its function is a little different. On a typewriter you press the carriage return at the end of every line, but on a word

---

Word Processing: It's a Home Business

One of the jobs created by the computer is word processing. For the entrepreneur, word processing can offer the possibility for self-employment. All that is needed to become a word processor is a computer, a printer, good keyboarding skills, a good word processing program—and a way to attract customers. Some entrepreneurs find it helpful to begin by targeting a particular type of business—attorneys, perhaps, or the medical profession. With a few hundred dollars of equipment and a catchy advertisement in a local paper, people can stop commuting across town to their job. Instead, they can commute across their house and work at home.

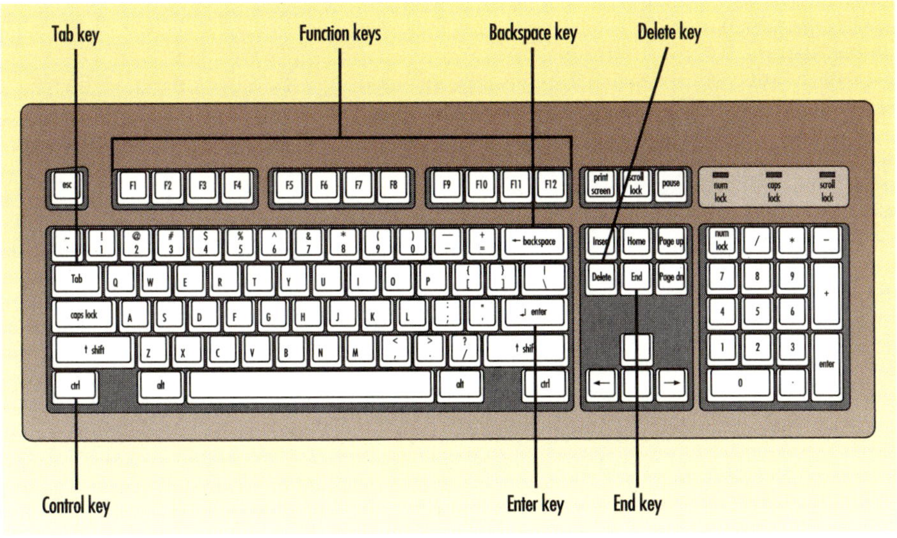

Figure 5-3
A typical microcomputer keyboard. Note the function keys, Ctrl and Alt keys, and other specialized keys for editing documents, issuing commands to the computer, and moving the cursor. Each word processing program (indeed, each software program of any kind) uses the function keys and other special keys in its own way.

> HISTORY

WordStar

The single most popular program in the early days of microcomputers was WordStar, which allowed early PC users to turn their computers into word processors. Introduced in 1979 about the same time as VisiCalc, WordStar took the computer world by storm. It also showed software developers there was a potentially vast and lucrative market for their wares, and in doing so helped spawn what is now a multibillion-dollar-per-year industry.

WordStar's developer and seller, Seymour Rubinstein, is a scrappy, tough-driving guy who clawed his way from the streets of Brooklyn to being a multimillionaire.

Rubinstein was born during the Great Depression. His father (a pinball machine distributor) died when Seymour was seven years old. While growing up, the boy worked at a variety of odd jobs, including repairing televisions back when they were still a novelty. Perhaps because of that experience, he first entered City College of New York as an engineering student but dropped out after flunking most of his courses.

> **Rubinstein spoke to software dealers daily about exactly what their customers wanted in a word processing program. It was an instant success.**

Getting involved with the Institute of Applied Psychology turned Rubinstein around. "I was letting the world pass me by," he later recalled, "but the world was prepared to give me anything I wanted if I worked for it."

Entering Brooklyn College as a psychology major, he completed all the graduation requirements except for a German course, which he arranged to take as a crash summer course at Long Island University. As fate would have it, Rubinstein was stopped for speeding while hurrying to take the final exam. Since no make-ups were allowed, he had to retake the class that fall at Brooklyn College. But he thought it made no sense to take only one class, so he signed up for the only computer science class Brooklyn College offered in 1964, Computer I. Only a third of the students finished the course, but Rubinstein was one of them.

After graduation, the new computer enthusiast got a job with Sanders Associates, a firm that supplied electronic equipment to the military. There Rubinstein programmed IBM mainframe computers, learning how to take the machines apart and rebuild them.

Over the next few years, Rubinstein variously worked for himself as a computer consultant and for a variety of firms on both the East and West coasts, including a jaunt in Switzerland where he set up a branch banking system using data management system software he had developed. He returned to California in 1977 and bought a kit for $700, from which he built a microcomputer. The company that made the kit, IMSAI, was headed by an old friend of Rubinstein's for whom he had worked in the past, Bill Millard. Rubinstein became director of marketing for IMSAI and soon pushed sales from $300,000 a month to $1.2 million a month.

But within months Rubinstein left IMSAI to form his own company, MicroPro, and one of the first things he did was hire programmer Rob Barnaby, who had left IMSAI two weeks before Rubinstein. Together the two men developed a data management program (SuperSort) and a video text editor (WordMaster), which soon became a new program, WordStar.

Always the consummate salesman, Rubinstein spoke to software dealers daily about exactly what their customers wanted in a word processing program. He then specified to Barnaby what the end product should look like and precisely what it should do. When WordStar was released in the middle of 1979, it was an instant success, even priced at $495. By the time Rubinstein took MicroPro public in 1984, sales had topped $100 million. ■

processor you only press the Enter key at the end of the paragraph (this is sometimes called a **hard return**). The word processor automatically inserts a **soft return** to start a new line when you reach the end of the current line of text; this feature is called **word wrap**.

- **The Home and End Keys.** In most word processing programs, pressing End moves the cursor to the end of the line; pressing Home may take it to the left margin or the top of the page—or you may need to press another key as well, before the cursor moves.

- **Function Keys.** Word processors set up the function keys for you to execute commands such as text formatting, printing, saving, or accessing special features. Often, function keys will be used together with the Shift, Alt or Control keys to provide more useful features; but since each word processor sets up the function keys differently, you need to check your word processor's manual to understand how to use them.

- **The Control and Alt keys.** The Control key (usually called Ctrl) is used in combination with other keys to execute specific commands. Used with a right or left arrow key, for example, it will (in some programs) move the cursor to the next or the previous word. The Alt (alternate) key is also used in combination with other keys—either to issue specific commands, or, frequently, to call up macros (see discussion later).

Typing Modes. Most word processors allow you to enter text using one of two typing modes: insert mode or typeover mode. In insert mode (which most word processors assume you want), the text you type at the cursor will be inserted between any text before and after the cursor; the text after the cursor will simply be pushed to the right to make room for what you type. If you switch to typeover mode, however, the text you type will replace any text to the right of the cursor, thereby erasing it. Make sure you know which typing mode is active when you edit text.

Setting Up

Margins and Justification. The left and right margins can be set to make narrow or wide text columns; the top and bottom margins can be set to center text, to print at the top of the page or at the bottom. You can have a justified right margin so that it is as straight as the left margin, or the text can have a ragged right edge, with the lines ending unevenly. You can also leave the left edge of the text ragged while justifying the right edge, or center every line (Figure 5-4, p. 84).

Automatic Hyphenation. When you reach the end of a line and there's no room to fit a word like sesquipedalian, you don't have to worry about how to hyphenate it. Many word processors feature automatic **hyphenation**, which will hyphenate the word for you at the appropriate place. With most word processors, you can set the program to hyphenate automatically, or with direction from you on where to hyphenate words (Figure 5-5, p. 84).

Spacing. Letters are generally single-spaced; manuscripts are generally double-spaced. The default setting is normally single-spaced text; the setting can be changed at the beginning of the document or at any point after that. Spacing commands take effect differently with different word processors. With some,

Watching Spot Run on Screen

Generations of students learned to read by following the adventures of Dick and Jane and Spot in large-print primers. Now some students are learning to read by learning to write at the same time. "Writing to Read" is a computer program that shows pictures and speaks the name of the object slowly, so students can break down words into their phonetic parts. When prompted by a picture, they type these parts into the computer, eventually assembling the parts into sentences. Since students are learning phonetically, their own spellings are not corrected as long as they are consistent and phonetically accurate. So "Mki ms wz n t b" would be considered correct, though conventional spelling would be "Mickey Mouse was on the beach." An added advantage to learning this way is that very young students find using a keyboard much easier than holding a pencil. And as any teacher will tell you, lowering a student's frustration level is a big boost to learning.

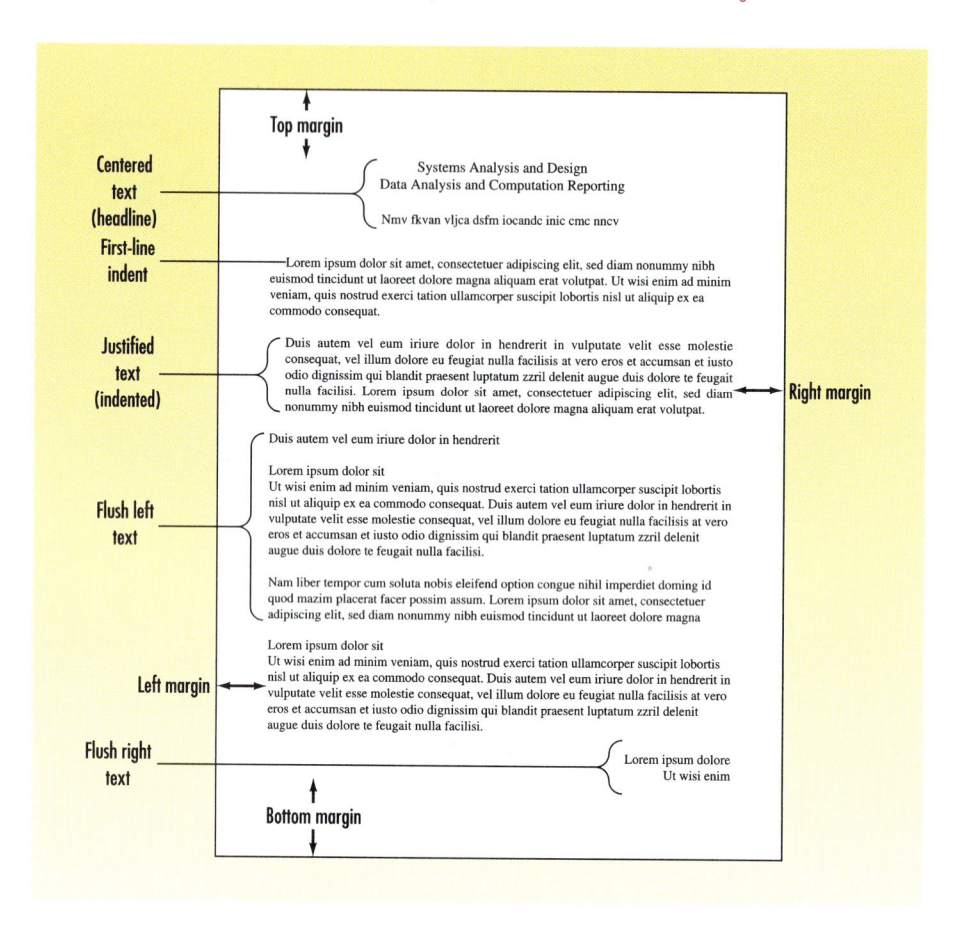

Figure 5-4
A sample document showing the top, bottom, and side margins, and the various ways text can be aligned.

the spacing command affects all text after the cursor; with others, you must select the text you want to change first (or the whole document, if that's what you want), then give the spacing command.

Tabs. The Tab key is useful for **indenting** the first line of a paragraph, for aligning columnar material, and for moving the cursor a present number

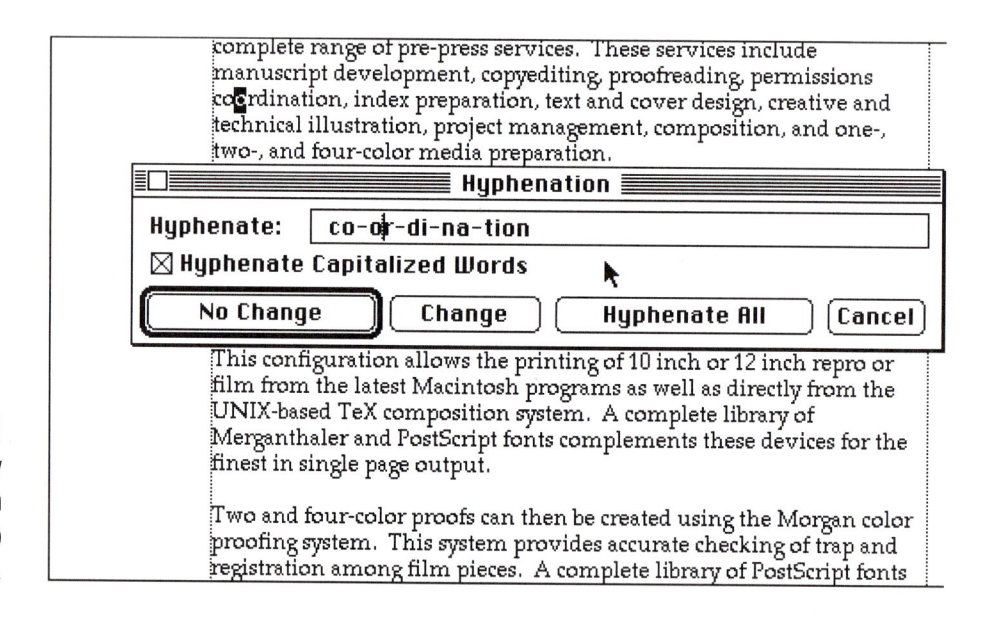

Figure 5-5
The automatic hyphenation feature in many word processors allows you to control in general how words are hyphenated and to hyphenate specific words as you wish.

of spaces. For many word processors, the default setting is 5 spaces or the equivalent fraction of an inch (this number can be changed as desired). Pressing Tab rather than the spacebar avoids the possibility of an uneven look when the work is printed.

Columns. Many word processors allow text to be placed in columns. The columns can be parallel even though the information is not; that is, they can contain information about hedgehogs in one column and a mathematical formula in the other. The columns can also be set up in newspaper style, with text being cut off at the bottom of the page and continuing at the top of the next column automatically (Figure 5-6).

Headers and Footers. A **header** is text placed at the top of every page in a document; it is usually used to indicate chapters (such as the headers in this book), page numbers, or other identifying or organizing information. A **footer** is text placed at the bottom of every page; it is used much the same way as a header.

Most word processors have special features for placing headers and footers, allowing you to format the text as you want, and place it in the center or at either margin. Some let you alternate headers and footers on even- and odd-numbered pages, or different headers or footers in different parts of the document.

Page Numbers. Page numbering can be part of the header or footer; in either case, the user can specify whether it is to be roman or arabic and at the right, left, or center of either the top or bottom of the page. Most word processors also include a separate page-numbering feature, so you can number pages the way you like without dealing with headers or footers.

Editing and Manipulating Text

Although the newly entered text may be filled with errors, once the text has been entered a prudent first move is to name and save the file. This important step allows you to change the words and move text around—to edit—without losing the original work.

Inserting and Deleting Text. Inserting and deleting text at the cursor location is simple; as we've previously discussed, you can erase something you've just typed by pressing the backspace key, and insert and typeover modes take care of most small edits. Just move the cursor to where you want, and insert or replace text as you wish.

Working with Text Blocks. When you need to change larger portions of your document, working with text blocks is more efficient than retyping and erasing text at the cursor. All word processors let you select a group of text (a single character, a word, a sentence, a paragraph, or as much text as you want) and treat it as a single entity, called a text block. How you select a block of text varies from one word processor to the next. Those that support a mouse allow you to click the mouse pointer at the beginning of the text you want, and drag a highlight over the text; most programs also let you use combinations of function keys, arrow keys, and/or the Control or Alt keys to select the text

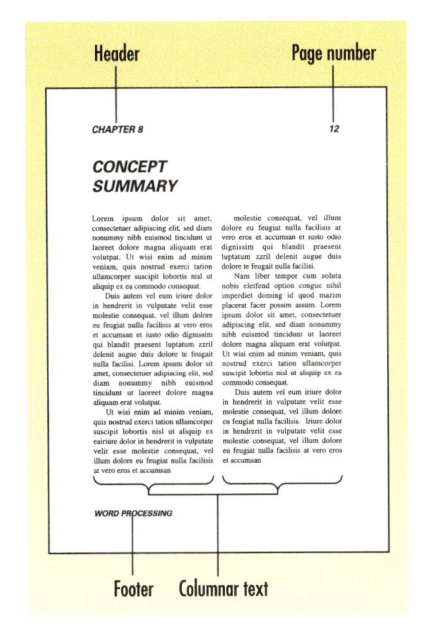

Figure 5-6
This sample page shows how headers, footers, and page numbers are placed on the page, as well as an example of newspaper-style columns.

Tell It to the Fax

Despite all the labor saving uses of computers, integrating the technology can sometimes be an effort. Consider the author who has just discovered that a crucial paragraph is missing from the final proof of her new book. Since the paragraph is on her computer's internal hard disk, she prints it out and faxes it to the publisher, who must retype the text into the appropriate computer, print the change, and then fax the new copy back to the author. Now there is a piece of hardware called a scanner that can automatically integrate the fax into the text. Scanners read many forms of typeface and can increase the background brightness to improve image quality. Some scanners can even convert handwritten notes into text, but the notes must be printed in all capital letters and evenly spaced.

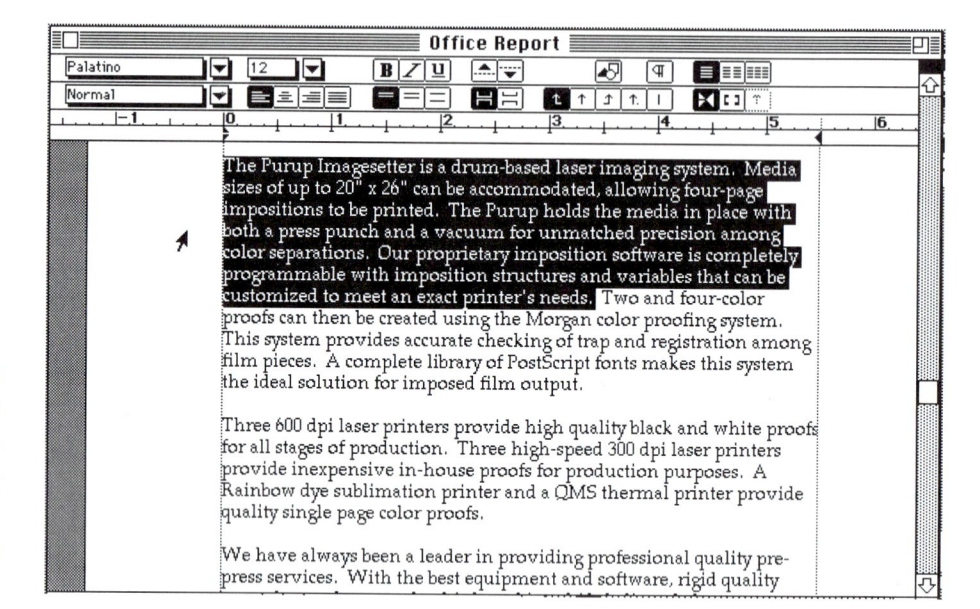

Figure 5-7a
Marking text for editing: to mark a block of text, most programs let you highlight it by clicking the mouse pointer and dragging over the text you want, or by using a combination of control or function keys and arrow keys.

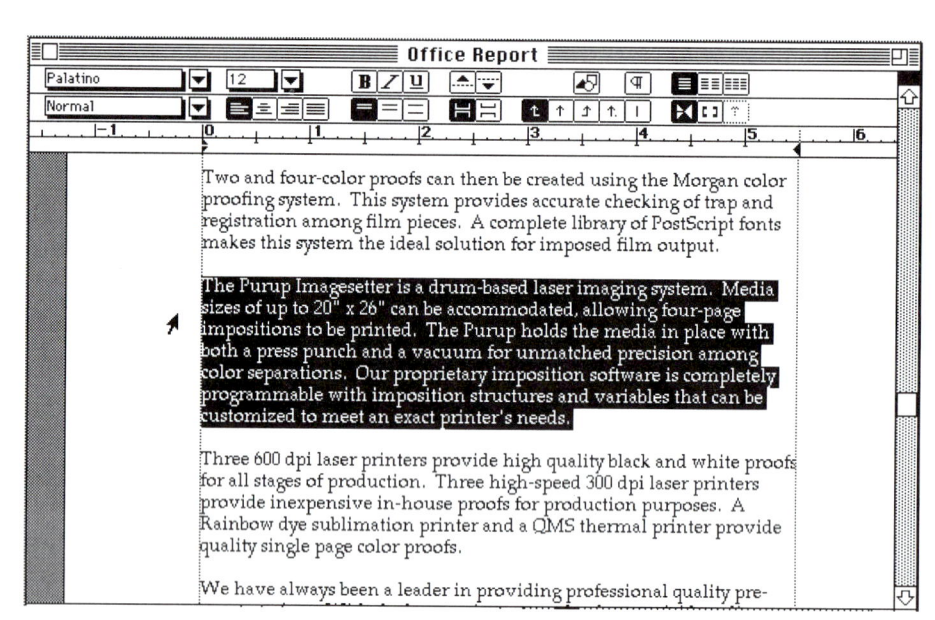

Figure 5-7b
The marked text can be easily moved with the cut and paste feature, or copied in a similar fashion.

you want. The block of text, once selected, can be moved, copied, deleted, or formatted (Figure 5-7a,b).

Searching and Replacing. When a word needs to be changed or its applicability checked, looking for it through an entire multipage document can be both time-consuming and fruitless. The search capability of most word processors will go through all the text and move the cursor to the word, allowing it to be seen in context. This search can be repeated as many times as the word appears in the document.

Authors who decide to change the name of the hero from Ralph to Thor in the middle of the novel can use **Search and Replace** to find every Ralph and change it to Thor. This is more efficient than reading every line and trying to do it manually. If the word processor allows the option, the user can also

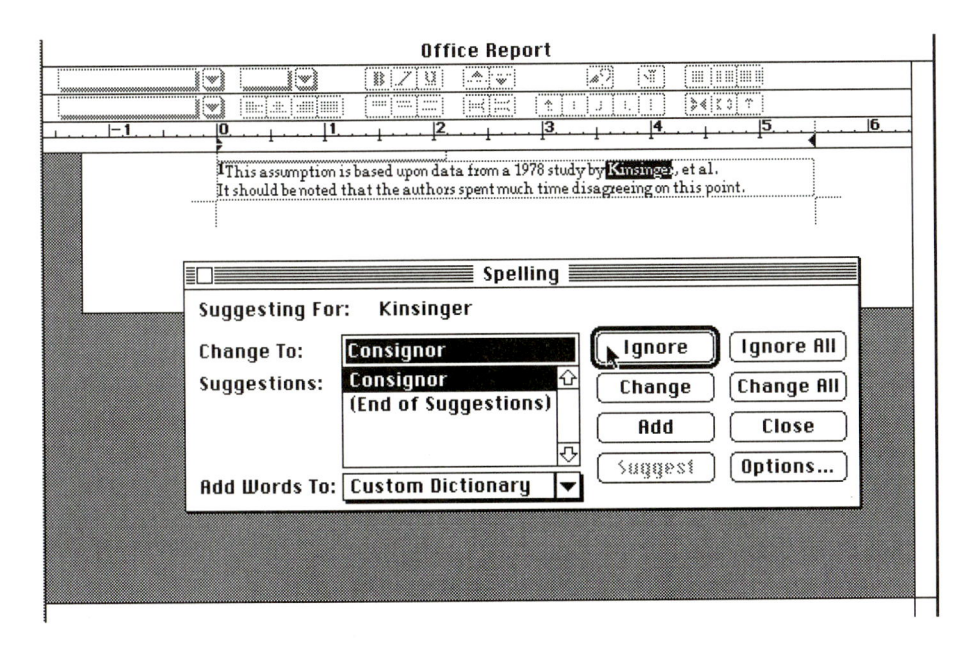

Figure 5-8
The spelling checkers in most word processors can find and correct thousands of everyday words, and let you add any specialized words you like, such as technical terms or proper names.

choose when *not* to make the change, for example, deciding when a comma before the word *and* would be unnecessary.

The Spelling Checker. Using only a few keystrokes, you can get the **spelling checker** in most word processors to compare the words in the document with those in the dictionary. Those that don't match are flagged for correction; some programs highlight each misspelled word and provide a list of possible correct spellings and may allow you to edit the word, skip it, or add it to the dictionary (Figure 5-8).

What spelling checkers cannot do is to catch incorrect usage. Saying **urbane** for **urban** or **it's** for **its** will go unnoticed because, although these are the wrong words for your meaning, they are correctly spelled; the program is not looking at them in context. To catch these errors you must read the document carefully. Using a grammar checking program that does point them out helps. Such a program can be used in conjunction with the spelling checker. Also note that while spelling checkers normally work very efficiently, there is always the possibility (albeit remote) that they will miss a word. In addition, because impact printers can (infrequently) skip letters, documents should be reread both before and after printing.

Formatting

Left, Right, and Center. Word processors, like typewriters, typically start each line at the left margin, and no special command is needed. Hanging indents (the terminology and commands vary with the program) have a flush left first line and indent the rest of the paragraph.

The date and the writer's address often appear at the right margin of a letter; using the Flush Right command will place them there with no need to count or estimate the spaces needed.

Centering a headline can be done without counting spaces; a single command will center the line between the margins. Paragraphs and pages can also be centered, but it should be understood that the center of the screen is not

Checks and Balances

Clear, concise writing is almost impossible to find in the tangle of government tax forms, even when it is the law. In 1988 Maine passed a taxpayer's bill of rights which required all tax forms to be written in plain English. This was the result of a study that found many people simply did not understand the language used in their tax forms, which were written in "bureaucratese." To make sure forms were written in plain English, the government began to use a computer program that checked both style and grammar in the rewritten forms. Terms such as "claimant" were changed to the simpler "homeowners." It will still hurt when you have to pay the taxes, but at least now you can understand the forms.

always the center of the printed page: if the margins are uneven, the text will be off-center.

Boldface, Italics, and Underline. Print enhancements add emphasis to text. You can use **boldface** on headlines and **italics** (this becomes an underline with some word processors and printers) or underline within the text to emphasize words or publication names. These enhancements should be used sparingly; too many will destroy the desired effect.

Other Text Enhancements. Many word processors let you format text in other special ways: as superscripts, subscripts, all caps, small caps, strikethrough, and double-underline; these, like boldface, italics, and underline, should be used sparingly and only where appropriate. Some word processors even let you specify text to print in color, if you have a color printer.

Fonts. Most word processors can now use special software that lets you print your text in various typefaces, called **fonts** (see the chapter on desktop publishing). Fonts give your text the appearance of professionally typeset copy, and print at any size and scale. Fonts come in several formats: PostScript, TrueType, and Laserjet (Hewlett-Packard); which kind you use, or whether you use fonts, depends on the kind of printer you have. Dot matrix and daisywheel printers can't use font software (with some dot matrix models being the exception), so to use fonts, you generally need a laser printer.

Finding and Using Special Characters. Some word processors (WordPerfect, for example) have a large number of special characters that can be accessed. A lawyer writing a brief may want to use §, or an author may want to tell the editor to leave ¶3 alone—but neither of these symbols appears on the keyboard. Some word processors allow access to these special characters with a particular key (such as Alt) and the symbol's ASCII (American Standard Code for Information Interchange) code entered on the keypad. Depending on the program, such symbols as ♡, ©, Æ, ¥, and ∞ can be found; any word processor and printer that can use PostScript or other interchangeable fonts can use special character sets to print a great variety of special characters.

Special Features

Macros. A **macro** is a shortcut, a command to the computer to perform a series of tasks or to insert a string of letters or words, without the need to type the commands or words each time. Many word processors allow users to define a macro—to type the commands or words once—and assign a key or word (sometimes called a *token*) that will recall the information or perform the function each time. An author working with two documents (as can be done with some word processors), for example, might write a macro that would save the current document and switch to the second one, using only a two-key combination. Macros can indent paragraphs and perform formatting functions; they can be used to set text attributes, insert paragraphs of text, and save hundreds of keystrokes.

Job Hunting

Anyone who has laboriously typed and re-typed cover letters and resumes while hunting for a job can appreciate how much simpler that process is with a computer. But now there are computer programs to help job seekers in other ways. Some programs provide a database of potential employers organized by region of the country, or by job type. Some programs, such as Peterson's Career Options, also provide extensive assessment questionnaires designed to produce a list of career possibilities. Yet another possibility is the job kiosk, which uses an ATM-like screen to provide job listings, including necessary skills required, in multiple languages. Looking for a job is still work, but at least the computer can help.

Indexes and Tables of Contents, Footnotes and References. A number of sophisticated word processors have the capability of generating indexes and tables of contents. The words to be included in the index are marked while writing or editing the text, and the program will compile the marked words into a listing that reflects the latest page number. Headings can also be marked for the table of contents, which will include the specified levels of headings and the appropriate page numbers.

Footnotes and endnotes (or references) are an easy-to-use feature of many word processors (Figure 5-9). Footnote numbers can start with 1 on each page or be numbered sequentially throughout the document. Notes can instead be placed at the end of the document and numbered automatically, greatly simplifying the writing of reference listings.

Drawing Lines, Working with Numbers. Some word processors have rudimentary drawing programs that draw lines and boxes; there may also be some limited arithmetic manipulations. Depending on the compatibility of the word processor and other programs, it may be possible to import and print graphics and spreadsheet data.

Importing Graphics and Spreadsheets. If your word processor is part of an integrated package (one example is Microsoft Works for either the Macintosh or PC) that includes a database program, graphics, and spreadsheet, it should be a simple matter to incorporate data from these into a document. If, however, the programs are from a variety of vendors, importing data and graphics may be more difficult, depending upon the word processor's ability to understand files created by other applications. Saving the spreadsheet or the database data as an ASCII file may allow the word processor to access it.

The leading word processors support importing art in a variety of graphic file formats. Keep in mind, however, that the word processing program must be able to understand the format of the graphic file you wish to use. Both the

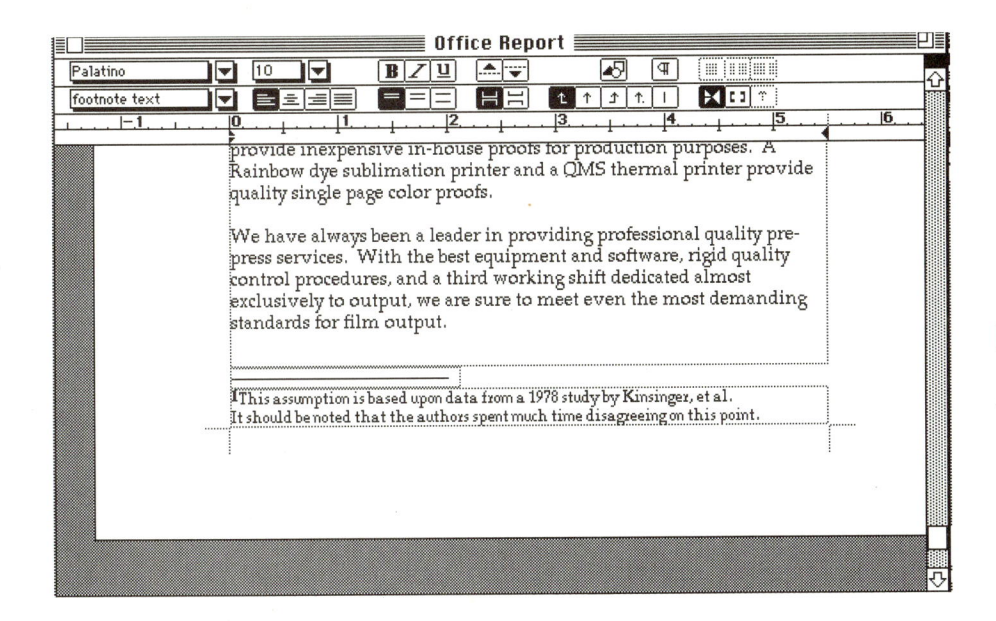

Figure 5-9
Many programs, such as Microsoft Word for Windows, bring up a special window where you type in the text of your footnote. The footnote is keyed to the location in the text where it's referenced, and will be automatically placed at the bottom of the same page as its reference.

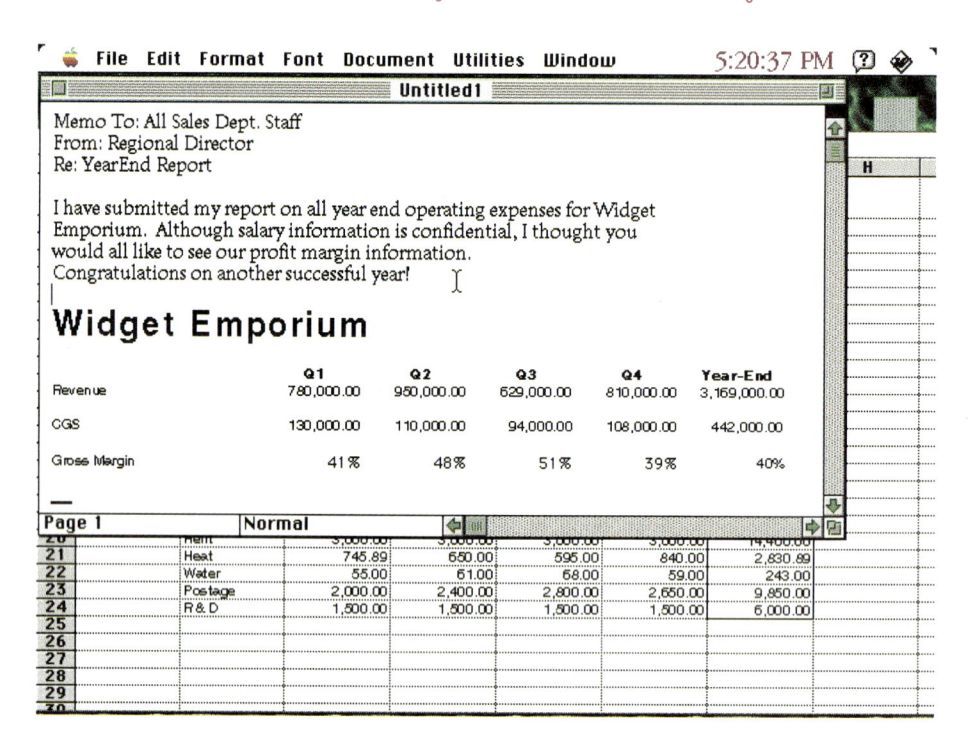

Figure 5-10
Importing spreadsheet data can be very simple. In GUIs such as Windows or Macintosh Finder, you can load your spreadsheet, select the data you wish to import, switch to your word processing document, and paste the data right in. Once it's there, you can format it as you like.

Figure 5-11
Files for creating form letters. (a) This letter written in WordPerfect contains codes for inserting the addressee's name and address, and a salutation. (b) The names, addresses, and salutations are stored in a special file, which is read by the computer when you give the Merge command. The computer inserts the information.

ability to import data from other programs and the printed quality of that data depend on the specific programs used.

Importing data and graphics from other programs gives you a way to integrate your information and coordinate its presentation (Figure 5-10). For example, a psychology student writing a report on a personality survey may tabulate the data and produce charts in a spreadsheet program, and then import the data and charts into a word processor to be included as illustrations in the report. Thus, the graphics and other data you import into your word processor can be used to make your document communicate more effectively.

Personalizing Form Letters. Everyone with a listed name, address, or phone number has surely received one of these: what is obviously a form letter with your own name and address at the top and your name sprinkled through the text—sometimes in red or green (or both).

```
Jerry Woolrich
Frequent Flyers Program
Apollo Airlines, Inc.
Beverly Hills, CA  90210

{FIELD}1 ~ {FIELD}2 ~ {FIELD}3 ~
{FIELD}4 ~

Dear {FIELD}1 ~ {FIELD}3 ~,

I would like to take this opportunity to welcome you to our frequent flyers
program.  We know that you will be enjoying your service and benefits
with Apollo Airlines.

Please take a moment to review the enclosed information package.  It
contains all the facts you need to know to get the most from the program.
I will be calling you in a few days to make sure that you received this letter.

Happy Flying,
        Jerry Woolrich
```
a

```
Mrs. {END FIELD}
Ellen {END FIELD}
Argyle {END FIELD}
34 Lakewood Road
Jacksonville, FL  32243 {END FIELD}
{END RECORD}
=============================================
Mr. {END FIELD}
John {END FIELD}
Hopkins {END FIELD}
63 Sanderson Drive
Dalls, TX 75217 {END FIELD}
{END RECORD}
=============================================
Mrs. Cynthia {END FIELD}
Quan-Lee {END FIELD}
19 So. Berkshire
Lexington, KY  40507 {END FIELD}
{END RECORD}
```
b

There is no mysterious process involved, and anyone can send out personalized form letters using the Merge function of the word processor. All it takes is a data file containing a list of names, addresses, salutations, and personalized messages for the intended recipients and a form letter keyed for each of those insertions (Figure 5-11a,b). The two files are merged and printed, producing personalized, individually typed letters.

Saving Your Work

Don't leave the computer without saving your work to a file. In fact, it's good practice to save your work every five or ten minutes—or however long you are willing to spend retyping the work you may lose should something unexpected happen. Should the power be cut off—which can happen by any cause from lightning to accidentally kicking the computer's power cord—everything you've typed since the last time you saved your work will be lost permanently. This rule applies for any computer work you do.

Many word processors offer an automatic save feature. You can set the time interval, and the program will do the rest. To ensure that the original text remains intact, it can be copied (or **saved**) to a file with a different name. The original file will remain "Cookbook," for example; the new version can be called "Cookbk2."

Giving files appropriate names is important if they are to be found again without scanning every file on the disk. Term papers can be identified by names that indicate their contents—"Hist1" or "Econ3" or "Eng201"—rather than such generic names as "Paper1" and "Paper2."

Backing It Up

This is another area where even the most experienced computer user can fail. Saving data files to the hard disk does not guarantee against their loss; neither does saving them to a floppy disk that is stored away from—but near—the computer. A fire that destroys the computer will probably also burn the floppy disk case stored next to it.

When you save your files at the end of each working session, back them up by saving them to another floppy disk. Store that backup disk in another room; backup disks stored with or next to the original disks provide no safety at all.

Printing the Document

The chapter is finished; the Christmas letter has been written and personalized; the term paper is annotated and pages properly numbered. It is time to print—to produce **hardcopy**.

Most word processing programs support a number of printers. If the printer is supported and has been installed correctly, there should be few problems in having the printer do what the word processor specifies. Many programs show on the screen how the printed text will appear on paper; some allow the document to be previewed before printing (Figure 5-12, p. 92). (If the appearance is unsatisfactory, it can be redone.)

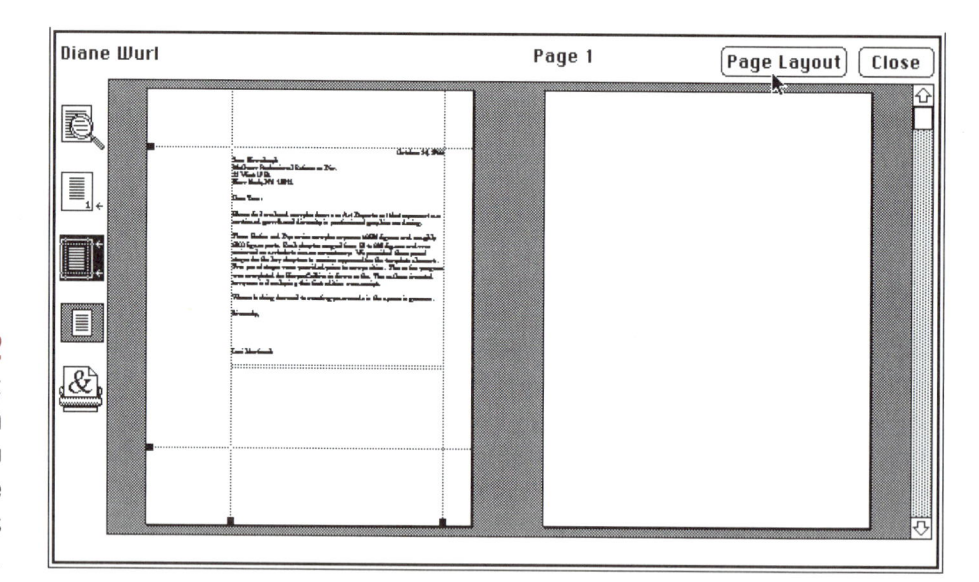

Figure 5-12
The print preview feature is important; looking at your document on the screen before printing can let you see problems you need to fix, thereby saving paper and the time you'd otherwise spend printing copies with errors.

The Right Printer for the Job. Some word processors let you define more than one set of printer specifications in terms of type style, pitch, paper size, and so on. Taking advantage of this will let you use Printer A for $8\frac{1}{2}$-by-11-inch paper with 12 characters to the inch; Printer B for notepaper with proportional spacing; Printer C for invoices—and so on. These are, of course, all the same printer; the word processor will simply send different instructions to the printer in each case.

Draft Versus Letter Quality. The default setting for many dot matrix printers is draft quality (daisy wheels provide letter-quality printing); some offer near-letter-quality printing at a slower speed. Draft quality is faster than letter-quality printing, but it is obviously poorer quality; many users are willing to sacrifice speed for professional-looking hardcopy, using draft quality for preliminary editing and proofreading.

All or Some—And How Many? Most word processors can print all or part of a document. This flexibility allows printing the entire document, a selected

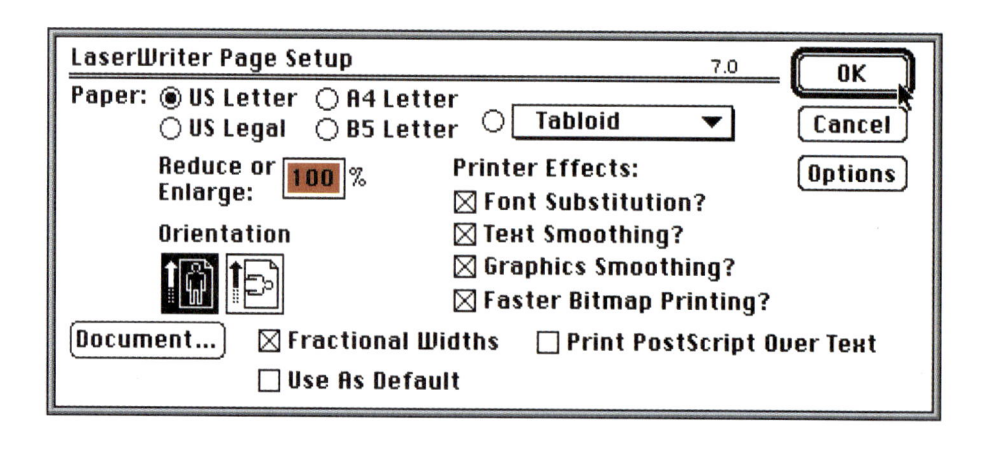

Figure 5-13
This Macintosh print setup screen lets you specify many details of how you want to print your document.

Figure 5-14
Portrait orientation (printing across a vertical page) is more common; but landscape orientation (turning the paper sideways) can make it easier to print large tables, signs, banners, and wide columns of text.

page in the middle of a long document, or a group of consecutive or single, nonconsecutive pages (Figure 5-13).

The number of copies can also be controlled through the word processor. If a dozen copies of a long paper are to be printed, however, be sure there is an adequate supply of paper and enough ribbon or ink to finish the job.

Up and Down and Sideways. Laser and dot matrix printers can print horizontally or vertically (Figure 5-14); which they do depends on the instructions coming from the word processor. Letters and most other documents are printed on a vertically aligned page (**portrait** orientation). If your word processor and printer have the capability, you can create banners or similar material (**landscape** orientation).

SUMMARY

As you have learned in this chapter, a word processor is an automated writing tool—a program that lets users enter and edit text quickly and efficiently.

Word processing is the most universal of all microcomputer applications, and the one that justifies buying the computer for many people. Those who use word processing programs range from students to lawyers to corporate executives to scholars to scientists to writers and artists. Choosing which word processing program is right for you depends on the type of documents you're likely to create.

Word processors vary in specific features and working styles, but all share a core of common functions. They all let you enter text, edit it, format it, save it to disk, and print it.

Entering text is done through the keyboard; the text you type shows up at the cursor. Computer keyboards have many specialized keys, which are programmed to perform different functions.

Setting up your document consists of specifying its margins and justification, hyphenation, spacing, tabs, columns, headers and footers, and/or page numbers.

Although text can be edited easily at the cursor using the backspace or delete keys, and insert or typeover mode, the real editing power of a word processor lies in manipulating text blocks. Once a group of text is selected as a block, it can be deleted, moved, copied, or formatted as you wish. Spelling and grammar checkers are useful utilities for catching typing errors and grammatical mistakes.

Word processors offer many choices for formatting text: paragraphs can be aligned left, right, or centered within the margins; characters can be boldface, italic, underlined, or set in other special formats. Using fonts can give your document a professional look. Special character sets let you type symbolic and other special characters.

Many word processors offer special features to improve the utility of the software, including macros, indexes, and tables of contents, footnotes, and references, and the ability to work with graphics and data imported from other programs. The merge function of many word processors lets you print form letters and other documents based on database information.

Saving your work is of paramount importance. Save often to avoid losing your data, and keep your information organized by using meaningful file names. Keep backup copies of all your work.

There are many options for printing your document. Most word processors let you print any portion or all of your document, and any number of copies; the quality of your printout depends on the quality of your printer.

KEY TERMS

boldface	hardcopy	macro
cursor	hard return	portrait
delete	header	save
edit	Home	Search and Replace
End	hyphenation	soft return
Enter	indent	spelling checker
font	insert mode	Tab
footer	italics	Thesaurus
format	justify	typeover mode
Function	landscape	word wrap

REVIEW QUESTIONS

1. How does a word processor differ from a typewriter?
2. What are the advantages of a spelling checker?
4. Why should you read a document after it is printed?
5. What is a hard return? A soft return?
6. Should you use the spacebar or Tab key to indent a paragraph?
7. Why is it important to back up your files?

8. Where should backup disks be stored?
9. What are the two types of columns?
10. How can macros save time?
11. How can you move text?
12. How can you move the cursor?

Working with Graphics

6

OBJECTIVES

After completing this chapter, you will be able to

- Understand the difference between an object-oriented and a bit-mapped graphic.
- Identify different graphic file formats.
- Describe data-generated graphics and how they are created.
- Describe device-generated graphics and how they are created.
- Describe user-generated graphics and how they are created.
- Explain how draw and paint applications differ.
- Tell how different professions use graphics software.
- Discuss presentation applications.
- Discuss multimedia applications.
- Discuss utility graphics software applications.

FOCUS

Images generated on a microcomputer help present information in a form that is easy to understand. Posters, signs, and billboards often contain computer-generated art, and so do newsletters, brochures, and advertisements. Microcomputer graphics create titles and special effects for both film and television (Figure 6-1).

With a microcomputer and graphics software, you can create a variety of high-quality graphics. For example, manually drawing a circle—even with special equipment—takes a steady hand and precision. Drawing a circle with graphics software is as simple as picking the size and location and telling the software to do it.

This chapter discusses the different types of graphics programs and applications and the basic procedures for using most graphics software. Because the concepts presented here are shared by most graphics programs, learning them will help you learn how to use specific graphics applications.

• CHAPTER 6: Working with Graphics •   99

WHAT ARE GRAPHICS?

In the world of microcomputers, the term **graphics** describes a variety of concepts. Some use the term to mean drawings, photos, and similar types of images. Others use it to refer to charts and graphs. Still others use it in describing microcomputer games. In fact, *graphics* is an all-encompassing term that refers to any nontext image generated by a computer (Figure 6-2).

Computer graphics can be categorized in several ways: by the type of image (object-oriented or bit-mapped); by their file format (TIFF, PCX, EPS, and so on); and by their use of color. These categories are briefly discussed in the following section; the remainder of the chapter categorizes images and graphics applications by who or what originates the image: data-generated graphics, device-generated graphics, and user-generated graphics.

Image Types

Microcomputer-generated images can be object-oriented images or bit-mapped images. **Object-oriented images,** sometimes called *vector* images, are pictures made up of specific lines and shapes. They combine several distinct lines, rectangles, squares, circles, or other shapes created with the application's set of drawing tools.

An easy way to think of object-oriented graphics is to consider a drawing of a kitchen table standing on a rug. As an object-oriented graphic, the kitchen table can be made up of a rectangle representing the tabletop, with a polygon for each leg, and an oval for the rug. Each shape or object remains independent of all other objects or shapes; the computer file for such an image is made up of mathematical descriptions of the shapes that compose the image. Each object in the total graphic image can be moved independently, or various objects can be grouped into a single object and manipulated that way (Figure 6-3, p. 100). Draw programs are used to produce object-oriented images.

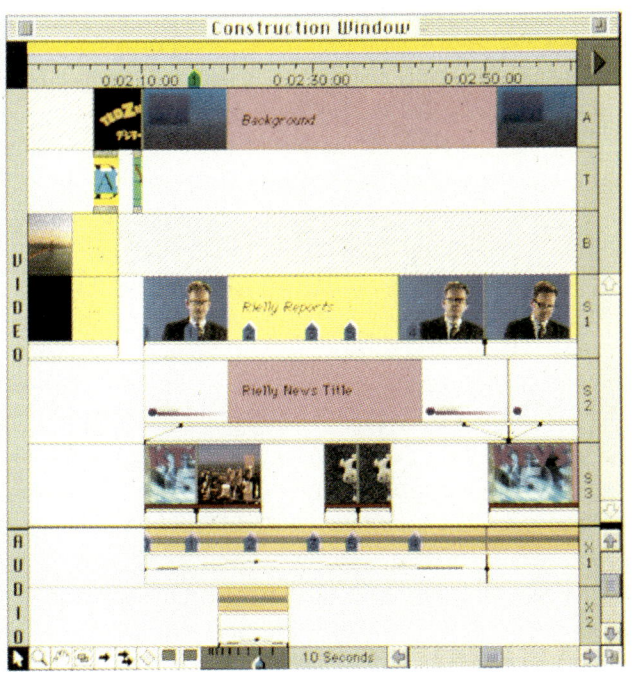

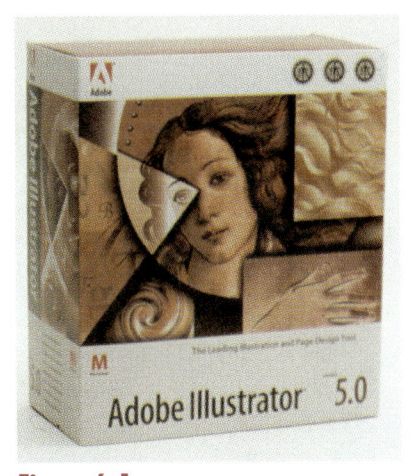

Figure 6-1
Graphics software for microcomputers is capable of an astonishing variety of images, printed and displayed in many ways. Computer graphics have revolutionized publishing, advertising, and many other industries.

Animating Commercials

Advertisers are constantly searching for ways to intrigue television viewers. And one of their latest tricks is using computer animation in their commercials: a bottle of Listerine knocks out gingivitis in a boxing ring, a Bud Light delivery truck suddenly turns into a racing car, a sheet blows off a Lexus car and then the car's skin blows off to reveal a newer Lexus underneath. Match Light charcoal, Volkswagen, Alcoa, Amtrak, and 7-Up also have all taken advantage of the latest in computer graphic technology. The sophistication of the new tools means computers are better at making animated motion more fluid, and at controlling shadow and light. The resulting hard-edged, clean look of the image is somewhere between traditional animation's cartoony feel and stop-action photography's realistic, but choppy images.

Figure 6-2
In the broadest sense, the term *graphics* can mean any computer-generated image, such as this multimedia presentation screen.

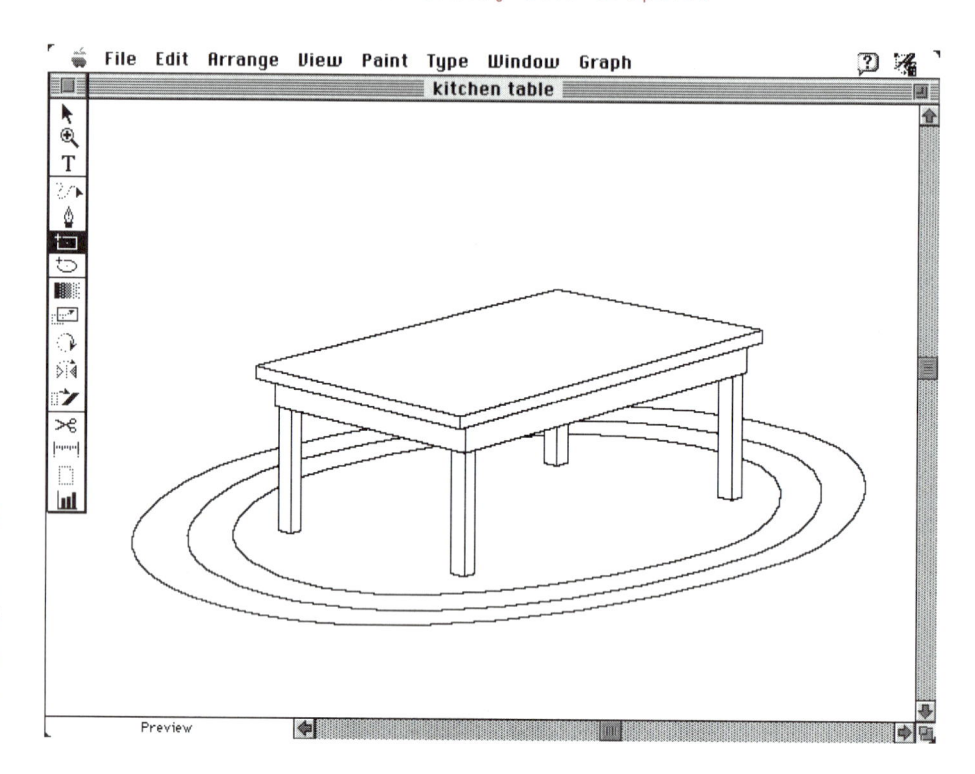

Figure 6-3
An object-oriented graphic, such as this one, can be manipulated as such; you can stretch or shrink it, rotate it, or do any number of things and the object will remain intact and separate from any other element of the image.

A Priceless Fax? Or, Yes, But Is It Art?

Artists have been using computers, still video cameras, and other high-tech equipment in their art for more than a generation. But consider artist Roz Dimon, who creates a painting on a video screen, then stores it. The data file is used to produce 25 transparencies. However, one of her patrons owns the "electronics rights" to some of her works, which are stored on a hard disk in the patron's safe-deposit box. British artist David Hockey has taken to faxing some of his work to friends, once going so far as to fax an entire exhibition to São Paulo, Brazil. All of which raises an interesting question for serious art collectors. If the art is only the string of electronic zeros and ones that tells a computer's screen how to light up, how can the art be worth anything? Apparently this doesn't bother some collectors. Three years ago Roz Dimon's computer works went for $800 to $1,000 per transparency. Now those same works are selling for $4,000 to $7,000.

A **bit-mapped image** is actually a complete pattern of the pixels on the screen. You may recall from our hardware chapter that the picture you see on your monitor is made up of thousands of dots and that each dot is called a *pixel* (short for *picture element*). Bits are binary digits (0s and 1s), so a bit-mapped image is the binary record of the bit values of each pixel making up the image. The record includes location and color information for each pixel in the bit map.

With bit-mapped graphics, the computer doesn't keep track of the image of a kitchen table as an object; it merely understands the location and color of the pixels that form the table. Therefore, when editing a bit-mapped image, you don't manipulate objects; instead, you change the color values of the pixels in the part of the image you want to edit. Paint programs and image processors typically produce bit-mapped images; they include appropriate tools for editing the images (Figure 6-4).

Many people consider object-oriented graphics superior to bit-mapped graphics because of the crispness of straight lines. The designer of a city street map, for example, needs very precise straight lines that can be moved and changed easily. Object-oriented graphics work very well for this type of image. These images can also be more easily resized and printed on any scale, whereas resizing a bit-mapped image either sacrifices detail (if scaled down) or makes the image look coarse and jagged (if scaled up). On the other hand, bit-mapped graphics are considered superior to object-oriented graphics for highly complex and detailed designs that are not based on straight lines. For example, a portrait of a person has far more detail and intricacies than a city map does. Bit-mapped software provides more visual control by letting users change each pixel or dot. In addition, since object-oriented graphics are a series of individual lines, many such programs provide only a few tools for editing the graphic. Bit-mapped graphics software offers a greater variety of tools for freehand drawing, to produce very detailed graphic designs and to let the artist work with the computer in a way very similar to working on paper.

Figure 6-4
A bit-mapped graphic, such as this image of a flower, isn't composed of distinct objects, but simply a map of all the pixels in the photo. You can't manipulate parts of the graphic as objects, but you can do other kinds of editing, such as erasing regions of the image.

This makes it easier to translate traditional artistic skills into computer graphic skills.

Image File Formats

An image file format is the method used to record a microcomputer generated image on disk. Each file format is associated with a unique image file extension name.

The three most widely used image file formats are **TIFF (tagged image file format)**, **PCX/PCC (Paintbrush)**, and **EPS (encapsulated PostScript)**. CAD users know the DFX extension, and Windows users are familiar with the BMP (bit-map) file format (which differs from the OS/2 BMP format). They will also recognize the CLP (ClipBoard) format. Almost every draw and paint program has a variation of these with its own file extension, but most support the first three. Macintosh applications also usually support MAC and PICT, and Macintosh users will know the MAC format from MacPrint and the PICT format from MacDraw.

TIFF, PCX/PCC, BMP, and MAC are bit-mapped image formats. PCX/PCC and BMP are indigenous to the PC microcomputer; each has a unique way of saving the bit values of each pixel in an image. While the TIFF format is generally standardized, there are several versions produced by different software companies and some applications save what they call a TIFF—but it cannot be displayed except by the original application. TIFFs on the Macintosh differ from TIFFs on the PC. Some software can read both Mac and PC TIFFs; some can save a file as either. Although MAC images are generally used only on the Macintosh, some PC programs can import and display them.

EPS stands for encapsulated PostScript and is used on all microcomputers. PostScript is a page description language—a way to describe an image or page using mathematical formulas that define the shapes that make up the page (Figure 6-5, p. 103); therefore, it is used for object-oriented graphic files. The

HISTORY

AutoCAD

In late 1981, while on a business trip to Los Angeles, John Walker, one of the partners of a San Francisco Bay area computer company called Marinchip Systems Ltd., decided the time was right to form a software-only company. He foresaw a "tidal wave" of "popular mass-market computer systems" coming from large companies and realized all these machines would need software to run on them.

Marinchip Systems was a full-service computer company that Walker had founded in 1977, back when, as he puts it, "This business was fun. The sellers and buyers were hotshot techies like us, everybody spoke the same language and knew what was going on, and technical excellence was recognized and rewarded." But by the end of 1981 Walker decided Marinchip Systems did not have a bright future. To succeed in a full-service company would require too much venture capital and an organization much larger than he felt able to run. Besides, by then "the microcomputer business was run by middle manager types who know far more about profit and loss statements than they do about RAM organization."

However, Walker was sure that a software-only company had several things going for it. First of all, a software package could be produced out of pure effort, with very little capital needed—only enough to finance the computer and to pay the programmer. Software manufacturing is as easy as copying disks. He saw that the huge companies making computer hardware seemed fairly ignorant about providing software, and, in addition, there were a number of independent software marketing channels a new company could use to distribute its product.

He knew that using the assets of Marinchip Systems to fund such a company would be labeled "high risk," but felt such a venture could succeed.

The new company, initially called Marin Software Partners (later, Autodesk, Inc.) was formed January 30, 1982 as a limited partnership of 16 people, most of whom lived in the San Francisco Bay area and most of whom also had other full-time jobs. "We wanted a venture that would in three years be one of the top five names in the microcomputer software business," Walker once wrote. "We'd be crazy to aim lower or limit our sights."

One of the software products the new company decided to market was a graphics program called Interact, which was to become the basis of AutoCAD, one the most successful computer-aided design programs ever. Written by Mike Riddle, one of the few partners who lived outside of California, Interact required a lot of memory to run, which meant it was outside the range of most of the desktop mass-market computers at the time, but Walker thought it was "a superb product in a virgin market."

By March, Interact had been renamed MicroCAD and a "cobbled up" version—targeted to IBM personal computers—was exhibited at the West Coast Computer Faire. It enabled computer systems costing from 10 to 15 thousand dollars to do much the same thing as systems costing $70 thousand, namely to draw two- and three-dimensional objects using the computer rather than T-squares, rulers, pencils, and pens.

This was a boon for architecture and engineering offices (among others), since it meant tremendous savings in labor. For instance, a drawing could be rotated along any axis, or parts of it could be magnified; changes could be made in part of a project and then seamlessly incorporated into the drawing of the whole; and the entire schematic—or any part of it—could be printed out as often as necessary, incorporating any necessary revisions.

In August 1982, the first version of MicroCAD was shipped, and in November 1982, only 11 months after the company was formed, a renamed AutoCAD was displayed at fall COMDEX. It was an immediate hit. Today, AutoCAD remains the industry standard in computer-aided design software. ■

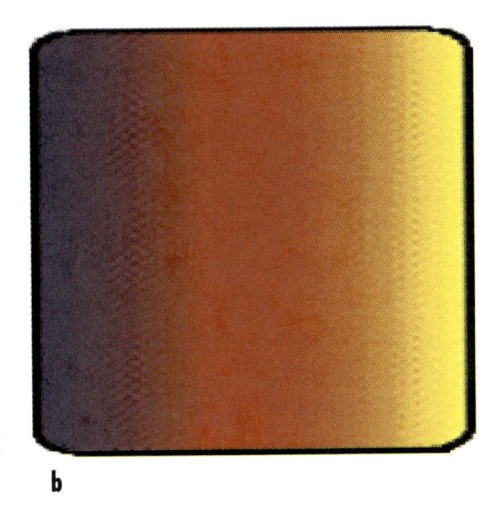

```
%IPS-Adobe-3.0 EPSF-3.0
%%Creator: Photoshop Version 2.0
%%Title: new.06.05b.eps
%%CreationDate: 10/28/93 5:43 PM
%%BoundingBox: 0 0 115 173
%%SuppressDotGainCompensation
%%DocumentProcessColors: Cyan Magenta Yellow Black
%%EndComments
%ImageData: 115 173 8 4 1 115 2 "beginimage"
40 dict begin
/_image systemdict /image get def
/_setgray systemdict /setgray get def
/_currentgray systemdict /currentgray get def
/_settransfer systemdict /settransfer get def
/_currenttransfer systemdict /currenttransfer get def
/blank 0 _currenttransfer exec
1 _currenttransfer exec eq def
/negative blank
{0 _currenttransfer exec 0.5 lt}
{0 _currenttransfer exec 1 _currenttransfer exec gt}
ifelse def
/inverted? negative def
/level2 systemdict /languagelevel known
{languagelevel 2 ge} {false} ifelse def
```

a   b

Figure 6-5
A Postscript file: the excerpts shown in (a) describe the shaded box shown in (b).

PostScript language was developed by Adobe Systems to print microcomputer images and create fonts that would print in different sizes (dicussed in the chapter on desktop publishing). A PostScript laser printer can print out the image the EPS file describes by *rasterizing* the image, that is, by calculating the shapes and converting them into a bit-mapped image that the laser can create on the printer's drum (see the chapter on hardware). The EPS format can also be used to store bit-mapped images; in this case, PostScript merely defines the size of the image and forwards the bit map to the printer's image processor. Graphics and desktop publishing applications take advantage of this capability by storing a bit-mapped image (called a *header*) along with the object-oriented image in the EPS file, and using the bit-mapped image on-screen while sending the object-oriented image on the printer.

Draw programs, including **CAD (computer-aided design)** sofware, save their files in their own object-oriented formats. The information saved is not a record of each pixel but a collection of formulas for each object and what color fills each object. You usually need the original application to make changes to these images. To use these images in other applications usually requires that they be converted into bit-mapped images or saved as EPS files. Some graphics applications, however, now understand CAD file formats and can use them directly.

Use of Color

An image generated on a microcomputer can be black and white, shades of gray, green, or amber, or up to 16.8 million colors. The colors available to you are determined by the micrcomputer's monitor and the ability of your graphics application to use the colors available; the monitor's graphic display format (CGA, EGA, VGA, SVGA, and so on) determines how many colors you can see on screen, and the capabilities of the graphics application determine how many colors you can actually use. Black, white, and the shades of gray are considered colors, just as are red, green, blue, aquamarine, violet, and so on.

Object-oriented and bit-mapped images approach the issue of color differently. With object-oriented images, for each object in the image, you specify the color of the image's outline and the color of the space filling the image. Then a color printer converts these colors into values that can be printed.

With bit-mapped images, the number of colors available to you is determined by how many bits are used to describe the color of each pixel.

Hard Evidence

Computer animation re-created the shooting of porn king Artie Mitchell when his brother Jim was tried for the murder in 1991. The jury was shown an animated film of a walking figure hit with the same number of bullets (8) in the same amount of time (1 minute.) Ballistics experts used software and a UNIX system to find the bullet trajectories, the angle height, and the time of each shot, as well as exactly where the bullets landed. Jim Mitchell was found guilty of manslaughter, but his defense is appealing on the grounds that the film prejudiced the jury by showing Artie as a passive victim.

Figure 6-6
Clip art comes in a variety of formats for a multitude of subjects.

The simplest case, 1 bit per pixel, describes black and white only (also called monochrome). The other two standard formats are 8 bits per pixel, which gives you either 256 (2^8) colors or 256 shades of gray, ranging from black to white; and 24 bits per pixel, which gives you about 16.8 million (2^{24}) colors—more than the eye can see. The number of colors in the image has a drastic effect on file size. Storing an image in 8-bit format results in a file eight times the size of the same image stored in 1-bit format; a 24-bit image is three times larger still.

The other major factor in graphic file size is **resolution**; that is, the number of pixels per inch. An image stored at 300 pixels per inch (typical laser printer resolution) occupies a file considerably larger than does the same image strored at 72 pixels per inch (typical monitor resolution).

All these factors should be taken into account when you use graphic images; because of the effect of color and resolution on file size, how big and how fine an image you can use depends on how much memory and storage space your computer has. It's also a major consideration to take into account when using clip art. **Clip art** are images that have already been created and stored on disk or CD-ROM for your use. Clip art can be object-oriented (line art) or bit-mapped drawings or photos and is available in black and white, grayscale (shades of gray), and color (Figure 6-6 and 6-7). These images can be brought into graphics applications and edited; they can be imported into desktop publishing, presentation graphics, and multimedia applications.

Image Origination

In addition to image type, file format, and color use, you can describe the images generated on microcomputers and their software applications by the origin of the image: whether the image is generated from preexisting data created by an input device or created by the user.

Data-generated graphics use numeric data to create graphics such as pie, bar, and line graphs. Spreadsheet software often includes the ability to generate data-generated graphics (Figure 6-8). Other software that accepts numeric data creates data-generated graghics with greater options than is usually available with spreadsheet software alone; these are usually bit-mapped images.

Device-generated graphics are produced by scanners or other input devices. Scanners, as we learned earlier, digitize an image. The user then applies software to alter or enhance the scanned image or simply to change its format for use with other applications. Computerized cameras can now take a digitized picture and write it directly to disk; this picture can be manipulated in the image processing software just like a scanned image (Figure 6-9). Video can also be edited with special graphics programs; frames of the video can be isolated, or "grabbed," and manipulated just like a scanned image. Screen capture software can record or capture the monitor screen at your command; the resulting image can then be edited.

Users create all graphics, in one way or another. The term **user-generated graphics,** however, refers specifically to art created with special draw-and-paint software. These images begin in the imagination of the user and are constructed on a microcomputer with a mouse, graphics tablet, or light pen (Figure 6-10).

Many graphics programs allow for the creation of two—or all three—major types of graphics. We will break down these three categories further as we discuss graphics applications.

Figure 6-7
Whether grayscale or color, there are photographs available in electronic form to cover nearly any subject.

• **CHAPTER 6:** Working with Graphics •

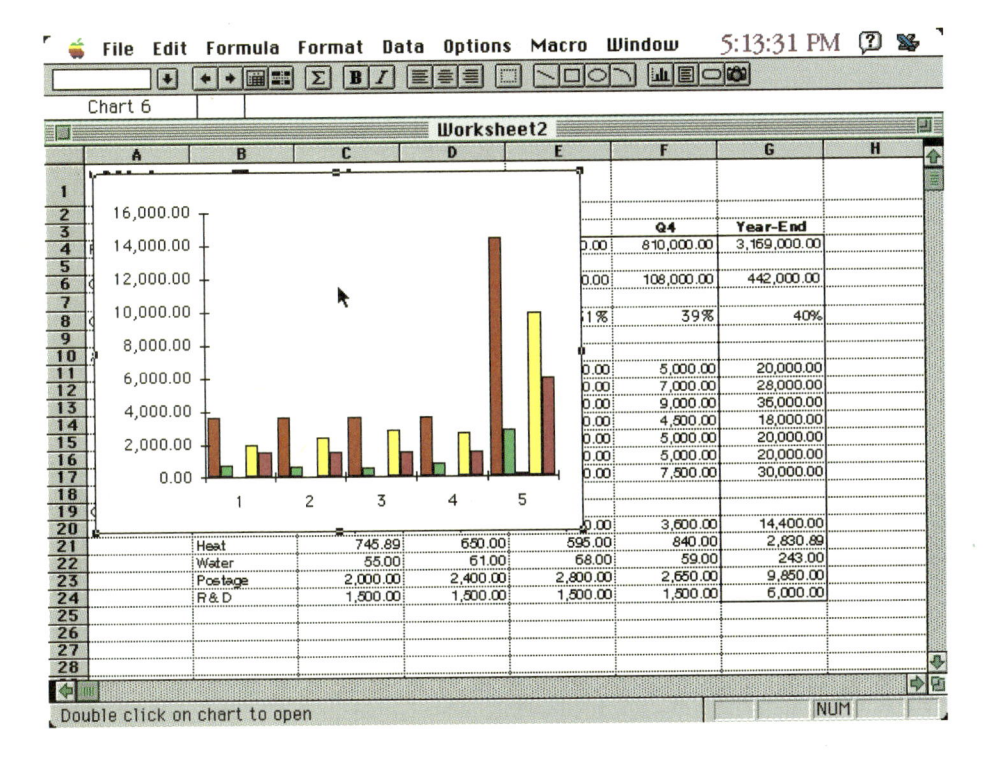

Figure 6-8
A spreadsheet package such as Microsoft Excel is capable of generating a large variety of charts and graphs from available data.

Figure 6-9
A digital camera may look similar to a normal 35mm SLR, but it stores images on a small disk instead of exposed film. These images can then be imported to the computer and used like any other electronic image.

Figure 6-10
Graphics tablets, especially those designed for use with a pressure-sensitive stylus, can make creating images on the computer feel almost as natural as paint, brush, and canvas.

Have You Seen This Child?

When a child has been missing for a number of years, outdated photos can no longer be used to identify him or her. Now computer graphics can create new images that "age" the child, resulting in more up-to-date photos that help find missing children better. Artist Nancy Burson was doing photo merging of celebrities for *People* magazine when she was approached by the mother of a missing child and asked to do an age progression of the child. Burson and programmer David Kramlich developed the software, which is now being used by the FBI. Using a scanner and a PC, the artist can merge photos of the child and other members of the family, creating overlays and sketches. Distinguishing marks are kept in, and visual information from the family serves as a guide to aging the photo. The computer-aged photos have been credited with finding a number of children, some of whom had been missing for almost a decade.

DATA-GENERATED GRAPHICS

As mentioned earlier, graphics can be generated from data sets stored in spreadsheet, database, or word processing files. Most graphing and charting software falls into this category, producing bit-mapped images.

Graphing and Charting Software

People disagree on definitions of graphs and charts. For our purposes, a *graph* is the image drawn on a grid with a horizontal x-axis and vertical y-axis; a chart—which may include a graph—can also include labels, a title, and explanatory notes.

Spreadsheet software, such as Lotus 1-2-3 or Excel, give users built-in graphing and charting options. Creating a graph or chart can be as simple as selecting the data you want to use, then clicking the mouse on an icon showing the type of graph or chart you want (Figure 6-11). These features aren't built into all spreadsheet programs, however, and you may need to create charts that are beyond the scope of the spreadsheet program or from data generated in software that lacks graphing and charting features. Special-purpose graphing and charting software allows you to take data from spreadsheets, databases, or text files, enter it directly, and create a wide variety of graphs and charts. You can also change imported data. Remember that with linked data, any change to the original data changes the graph. Presentation graphics packages also offer sophisticated features that produce professional-looking graphs and charts.

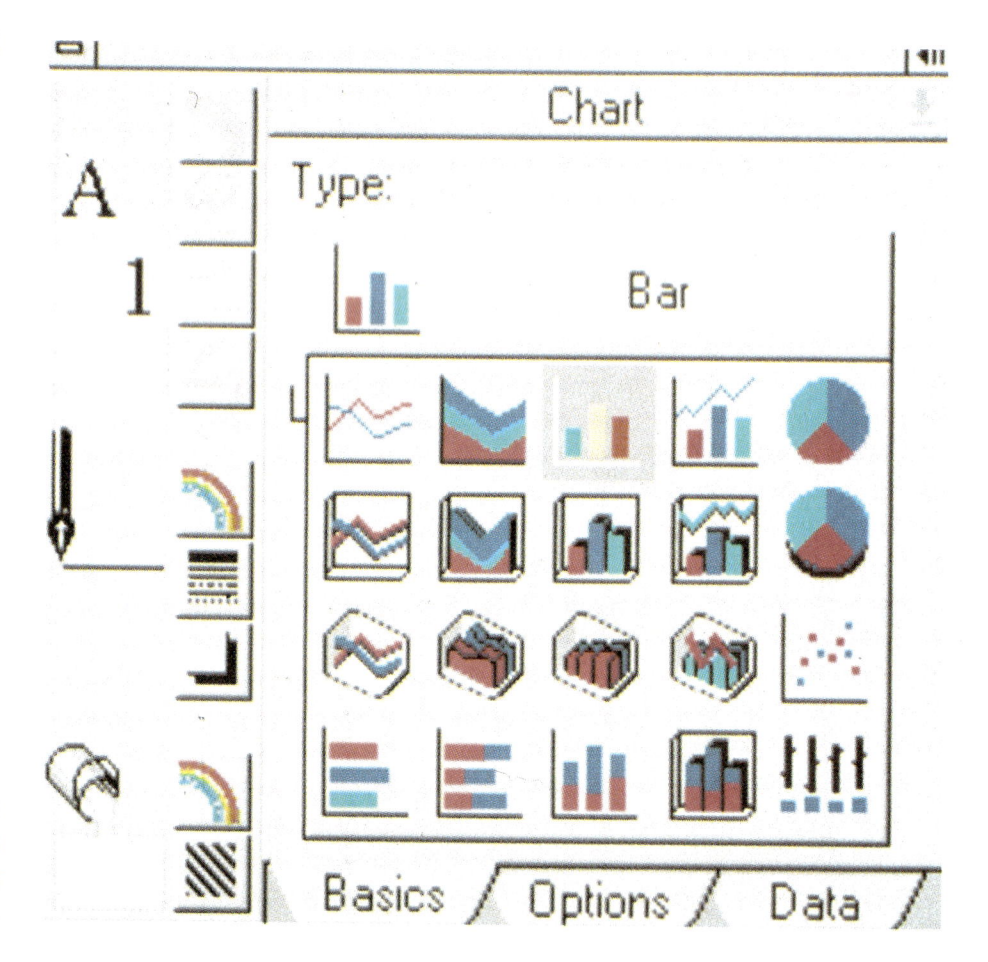

Figure 6-11
Some of the many types of charts you can print from spreadsheet software. Having a color printer expands your capabilities greatly.

> SECOND OPINION

Multimedia: A Bandwagon or a BMW?

Multimedia presentations! The words conjure the image: smooth, glamorous, and very, very effective. I used to have a coffee mug with the motto, "Nothing is as easy as it looks."

It's not as easy as it looks, and it's not simple in any way, to produce glamorous, smooth presentations, or tell when it's worth it. We in the computer field are all too prone to fall in love with our own technical capabilities, producing solutions in search of a problem. Is multimedia just the next techno-fad, a bandwagon to be abandoned in a couple of years, or something more? And how do we tell?

First, let's look at the downside. There are hard technical problems to be solved in order to put together a multimedia device. The computer has to operate fast enough, it has to have enough storage, it has to have the right kind of peripheral devices (like high-quality stereo speakers), and so on. That much good hardware costs more than a bare-bones PC.

> Is multimedia just the next techno-fad, a bandwagon to be abandoned in a couple of years, or something more? And how do we tell?

Also, producing a good multimedia product is very much like producing a motion picture. It is a specialty in its own right, involving a great deal of knowledge and skill that you simply do not have if you are an accountant, a fashion designer, a programmer, a computer scientist, or even a multimedia systems expert. Making a movie is trivial; making a good movie is very hard; making a good movie that works together with everything else happening on the screen of a multimedia workstation is harder yet. There isn't a program available that can turn an amateur into a professional producer.

A third problem involves a different kind of technical issue. A frequent claim for multimedia is that it allows for highly interactive products. Well, sometimes. Think of it this way: It's easy for us to interact with a computer; it's very hard for the computer to interact with us. It knows only what keys you're hitting, and perhaps the pauses between keys. It's tremendously difficult to interpret such limited data.

Okay, there are obstacles. But aren't there benefits too? Absolutely! If you're trying to decide on a multimedia project or system, you have to balance the costs against the benefits. The catch is this: to estimate the benefits, you have to use some imagination, some skill, and some old-fashioned intuition. You have to have a vision of how things would be improved for you and your audience by developing a multimedia product. Maybe in spite of all those difficulties mentioned earlier your multimedia product can do a much better job that really needs doing.

In determining the merit of multimedia, concreteness and technical details are marvelous things, but not if you leave out the vision. ■

H. Joel Jefferey, Ph.D.,
Northern Illinois University

Flowchart Applications

Flowcharts are a special type of chart designed to show a process or structure; they use boxes of various shapes to show stages of the process or elements of the stucture, with lines linking the boxes to show relationships between elements. Two of the more common programs used to produce flowcharts are project management software and group organization software.

Project management software uses dates and times as well as the goals and objectives of a person or group of people to illustrate how a project should progress from beginning to end. It uses a particular shape for each event and, since one event may depend on another event's completion, displays them in the order in which they should occur (Figure 6-12). For example, when producing a book, each task in the process (writing, copyediting, typesetting, page composition, proofreading, and printing) must be completed in sequence; starting any of them depends on completing the tasks that come before.

Group organization software uses the names and ranks of people in an organization to create an organizational flowchart. Group members' names and titles as well as other pertinent information may appear in or around their boxes. The names of officers and supervisors may be shown larger and above the names of rank-and-file members. Arrows show levels of hierarchy and how the members of the group interact.

Flowcharts created by project management and group organization software are usually object-oriented images, allowing the shapes and lines to be moved around as needed. In some project management applications, moving events causes the data to be automatically changed.

Other Data-Generated Graphics Sources

It's hard to imagine any professional using numeric data to make decisions who would not benefit from data-generated graphics, but some depend on

Figure 6-12
Project management software, besides being an effective management tool, produces graphics that can clarify the complexities of a project.

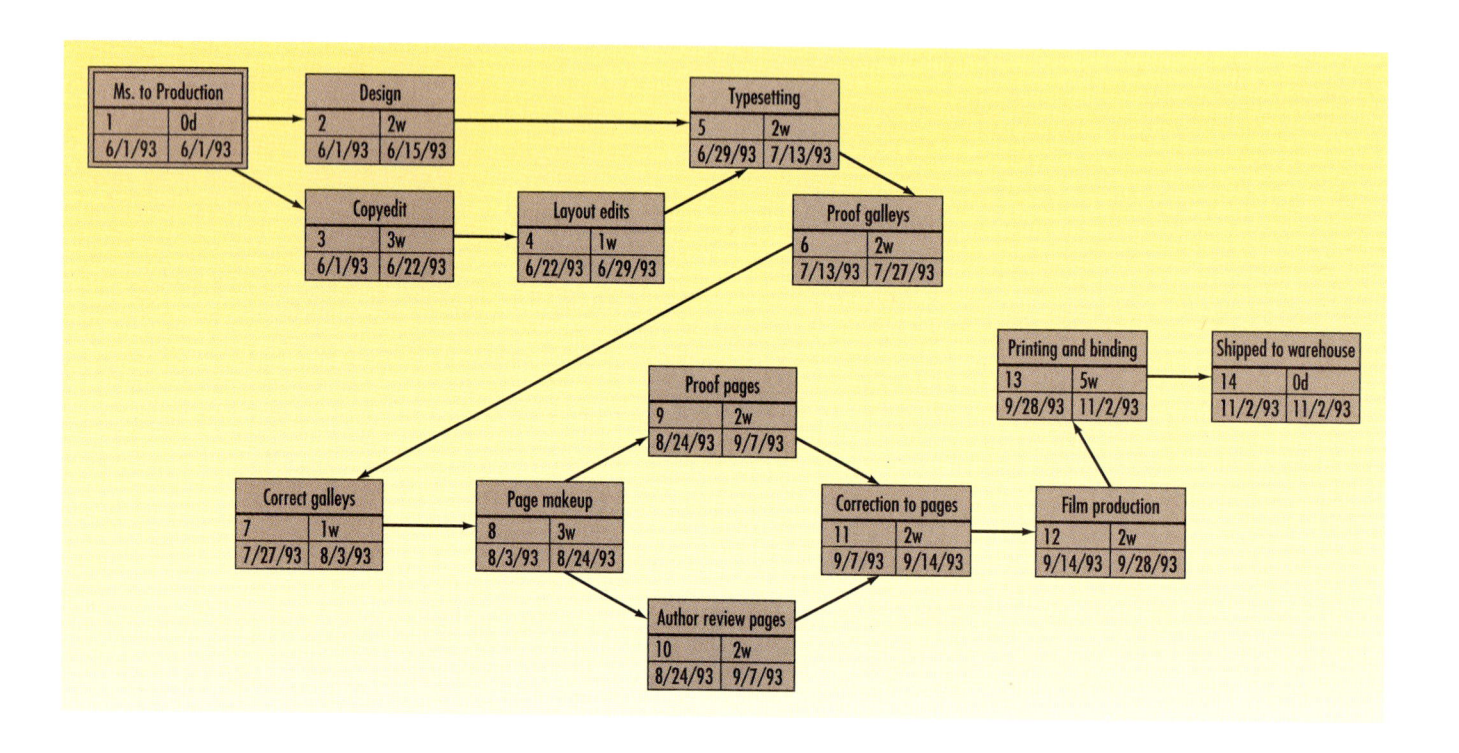

• **CHAPTER 6:** Working with Graphics •

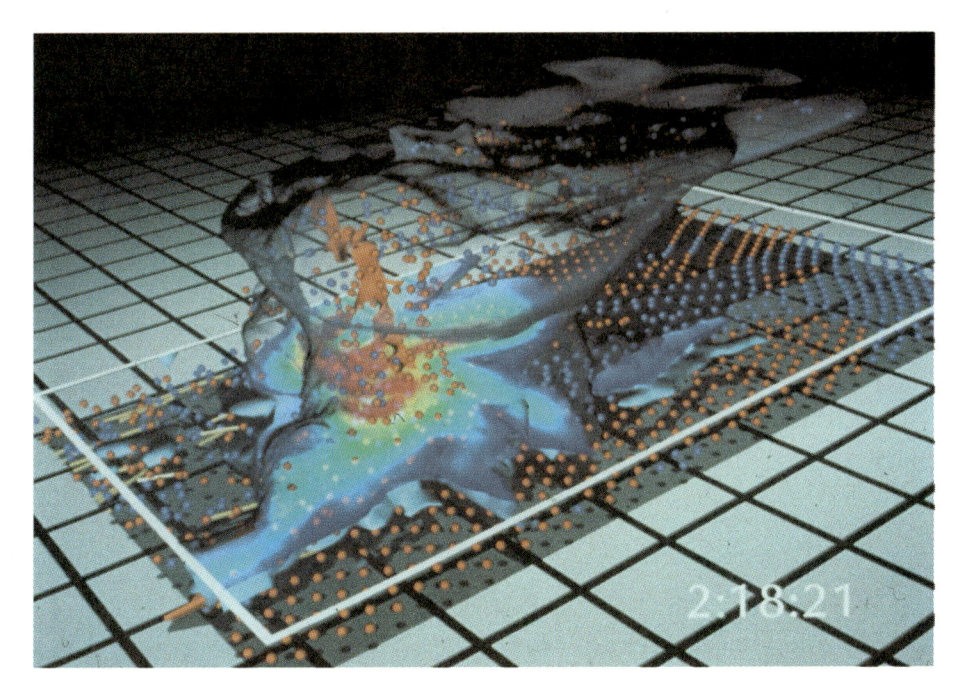

Figure 6-13
Weather reporters are the most visible everyday users of computer-generated graphics. Weather information can be processed by supercomputers to create graphics such as this representation of a storm front.

them more than others do. Graphics software enables geologists to generate highly detailed visual displays of rock formations and visual estimates of oil-resource information. A television weather reporter may use computer graphics to convey weather information. Data-generated graphics show the location of weather fronts, display weather patterns, and provide other detailed visual information for weather forcasts (Figure 6-13). Geographers employ data-generated graphics, such as pictures created from satellite data, to create highly detailed maps for a variety of applications. Both topographical and political maps are produced by these specialized graphics programs.

DEVICE-GENERATED GRAPHICS

Scanners can input bit-mapped images (including 24-bit images) with a great degree of detail. Other device-generated graphics, from camera, video, or your monitor's screen, also provide unique images that are not easily created by data or users. Scanning software and image processing software allow you to manipulate and use the images created by these devices in a variety of applications.

Scanning Software

Scanning software gives you the ability to control the scanner. The software usually lets you preview the image before scanning it. You can see how the entire image would look and select only the area you want. You can then crop the image, eliminating its unnecessary or unwanted parts and thereby saving both disk space and memory.

Most scanning software also lets you control the lightness and darkness of the original scanned image as well as color intensities. You also choose how to

Museum Tech

Computer graphics can now predict the changes in color as a painting ages, the effect a cleaning might have on the painting, and to what degree a painting might crack if it were transported to another museum. London's National Gallery has started to scan its pictures each year to determine how the color will change over time. The museum hopes to use the knowledge as an aid to storing paintings so the colors will remain vivid longer. A museum in Munich used computer technology in an experiment on "craquelure," the hairline cracks on a painting's surface. Officials electronically scanned the surface of a worthless painting before and after it went for a 250-mile ride in the back of a car. The results will help museums pack paintings more securely when they are loaned out for exhibitions.

Figure 6-14
The scanner has made it easy to incorporate any printed graphic into an electronic document; image editing software lets you manipulate the graphic as you see fit.

scan the image—as black and white, grayscale, or color; the pixel resolution at which to scan it, and for photos, the halftone screen frequency to use (Figure 6-14). Be aware that control of the scanning process, especially with color images, in terms of resolution and lighting, takes a great deal of practice; the first step is to get the clearest possible image.

Image Processing Software

Once you have the image on disk, **image processing software** gives you the tools, which vary in number and quality, to edit the image and enhance it. Some widely used products are, for the Macintosh, Adobe Photoshop and Letraset's ColorStudio, and for Windows, Picture Publisher and Aldus Corporation's PhotoStyler.

Image processors let you zoom into any section of the picture to edit and improve the image. For example, you can copy the surrounding pixels to damaged areas and cover up scratches or other marks scanned from the original. You can lighten or darken the picture, adjust the color, add lines, stretch or compress the image, and add many other special effects (Figure 6-15). You can also further crop the image by selecting the cropping tool, creating a rectangle over the area of the image you want to preserve, and then cutting away everything else.

Image processing programs also serve as file conversion tools. Since they specialize in image manipulation, they must be able to accept, or read and save, many image file formats. Thus they can be used to change an image's file format to a format that the target DTP, word processing, or other application will be able to incorporate into its documents.

Other Uses and Devices

Desktop publishing industries are probably the greatest users of device-generated graphics. Advertisers, newspapers, magazines, and book publishers depend on the scanner to reduce the cost of putting pictures into publications. A cartographer may scan aerial photographs of roads or other terrain and then

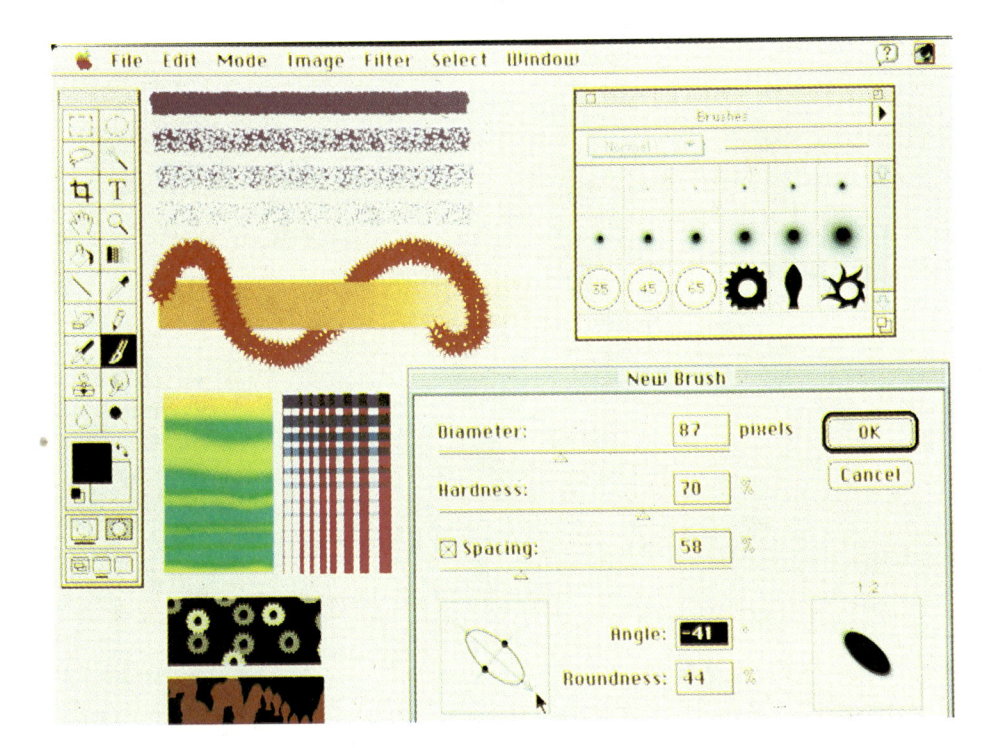

Figure 6-15
Processing a photo in PhotoShop: one click can turn your mouse into a wide variety of brushes for applying paint.

trace the roads in perfect scale to make a new map. Electrical engineers may scan a schematic to be **vectorized** (changed into an object-oriented image) and altered for correction or redesign.

Earlier in the chapter we mentioned video grabbing, screen captures, and the digital camera. Many image processors have a screen capture feature; some specialize in this. The Windows environment, for example, allows sceen captures by pressing the Print Scrn key and pasting the image from its clipboard.

Device-generated graphics are also produced by devices other than the scanners discussed here. Medical scans of the body produce diagnostic maps. Radio telescopes can be used to produce a picture of another planet's surface.

USER-GENERATED GRAPHICS

Before user-generated graphics programs were available, graphic artists working in commercial art, advertising, and related fields spent most of their time at drawing tables producing images by hand. User-generated graphics software has replaced much of this work with features that allow the graphic artist to work on a computer the way he or she once worked at the drawing table. These applications offer the advantages of easy editing, easy recovery from errors, and easy reproduction.

Draw and Paint Programs

As stated, user-generated graphics software includes draw and paint programs that support a creative, freestyle approach to creating images that is similar to using an artist's canvas, pencils, pens, paintbrush, and paint. You are given a blank screen area (canvas), several drawing tools (paintbrushes, pen, spray, and so on), and several color options (paint and ink). **Draw programs** create object-oriented images; **paint programs** create bit-mapped images.

Painting a Picture by Math?

People have been using Paint By Number kits for years, but new mapping programs for computers have put an electronic twist on this old hobby. By using sets of numerical data—for instance, scientific information sent back via satellites—the programs can create visual images of an unseen object. NASA scientists recently used computer mapping to give us our first look at the actual surface of cloud-covered Venus. Other scientists have used similar programs to map the ocean's bottom. One dedicated scholar took measurements of the Sphinx in Egypt, which he combined with historical accounts and other ruins near the Sphinx, to produce a model of the Sphinx when it was first built.

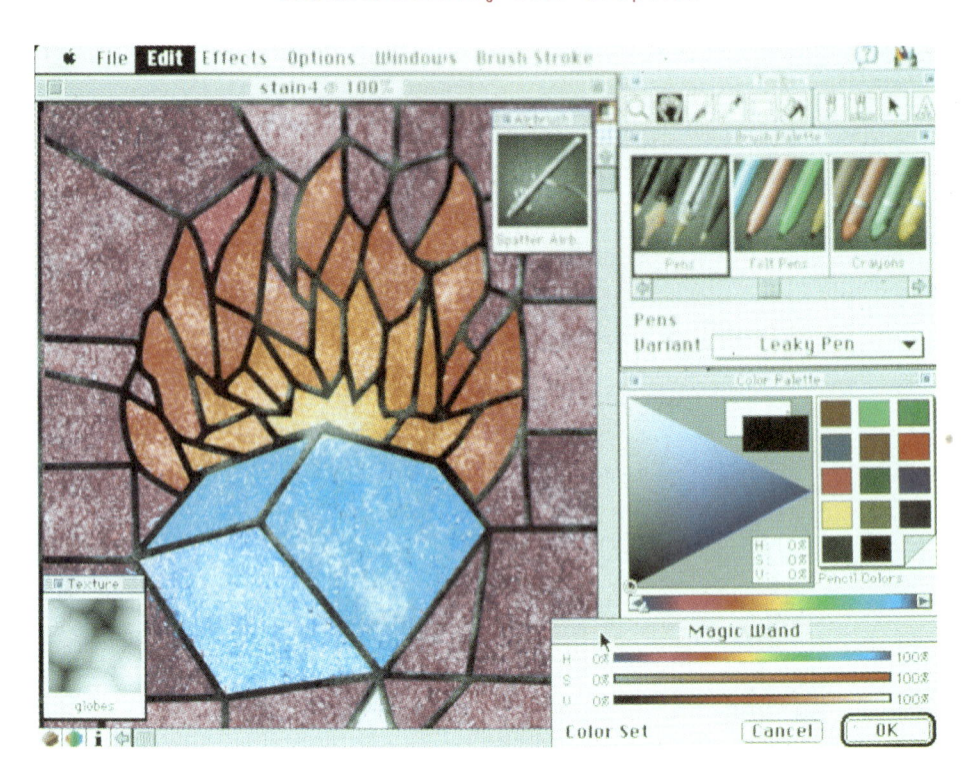

Figure 6-16
Paint programs include a wide variety of tools for creating bit-mapped graphics.

Most draw and paint programs (of all types) provide graphic tools in the form of **icons** accessible with a mouse. Pointing to an icon and clicking on it activates the graphic tool, in essence letting you use the mouse as that tool (Figure 6-16). For example, clicking on the straight line tool lets you use the mouse to draw perfectly straight lines. If you click on the box tool, you can create rectangles and squares of various sizes. In addition, you can erase (paint

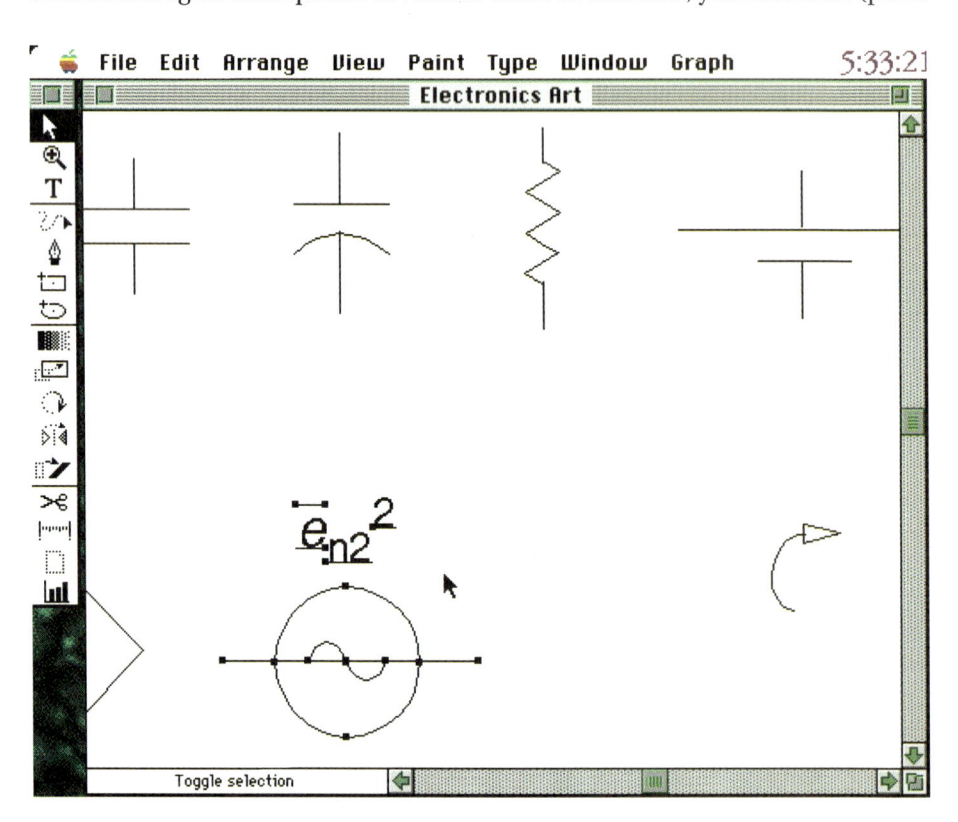

Figure 6-17
Draw-programs produce object-oriented images; they're more often used than paint programs when precision is required.

• **CHAPTER 6:** Working with Graphics •

programs) or delete (draw programs) unwanted materials, select colors from a color palette, and automatically fill areas with different patterns or colors. The text tool provides text in a variety of fonts that you can then change to create unique letters (for example, a T that looks like a tree).

Several draw programs, including CorelDRAW!, Adobe Illustrator, and Aldus Freehand, are available for both the Macintosh and the PC Windows environments. Paint programs such as PC Paintbrush, Fractal Design Painter, and Windows Paintbrush (a Windows accessory) for the PC, and Oasis, Canvas, and SuperPaint for the Macintosh are common examples of software based on bit-mapped graphics (Figure 6-17). Paint programs may also double as image processing programs, because they can work with many of the same file formats.

Computer-Aided Design

CAD (computer-aided design) programs are also object-oriented, but they include many specialized features required by professional drafters, engineers, architects, and technical designers. Draw programs may provide 10 to 15 drawing tools, but most high-end CAD software, such as AutoCAD (Figure 6-18), provides as many as 100 specialized drawing tools. Draw software is often easy to learn and use, but learning all the features of CAD software may require a great deal of time—in fact, many colleges offer full courses on just its basic operations.

Engineers use CAD to help them design and create a wide range of products. Electrical engineers, for example, use CAD to design complex circuits and circuit boards. Automotive engineers design cars, structural engineers design the structure of buildings, civil engineers design bridges and other structures, and they can all use CAD to do so. CAD gives them the flexibility to change designs easily. For example, automotive engineers may want to change the design of the front of a car to improve fuel efficiency by decreasing wind resistance. Instead of hand-building a model to see the effects of a design change, they can create a detailed visual representation on a monitor screen.

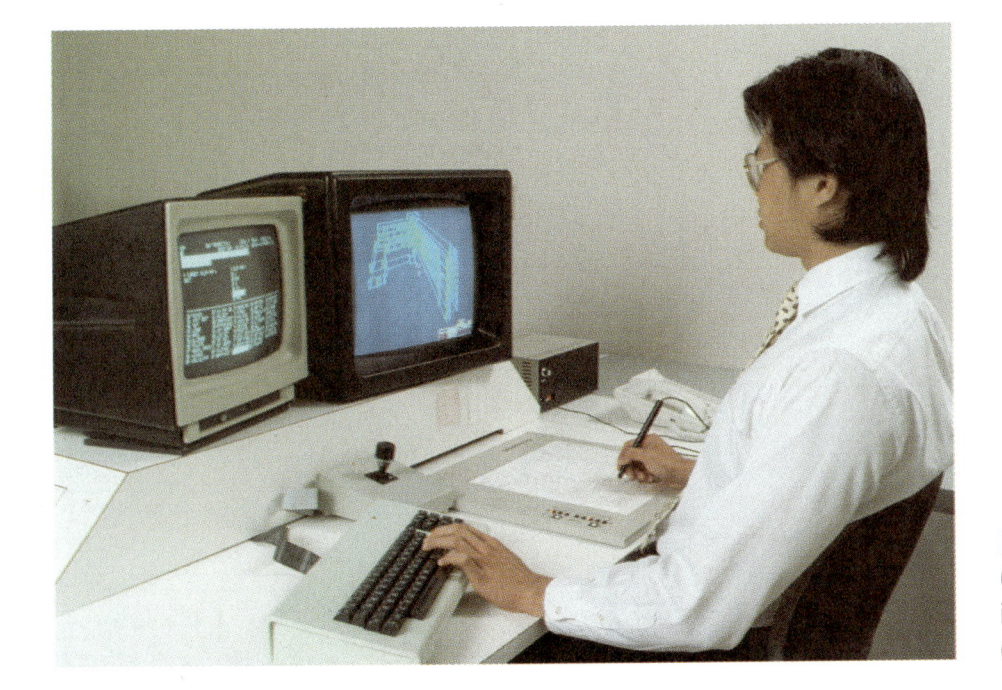

CAD

Computer-aided design programs are showing up in some rather unusual places these days—like in the jungles of South America. Archeologists set up computer stations at the site of an ancient Mayan city that was being excavated. They hoped that re-creating Mayan palaces using CAD programs could give them a better idea of what they were looking for. Since CAD can create models in three dimensions and can offer the viewer different perspectives instantly, the program is invaluable to almost anyone who deals with design. A fashion designer can lengthen the skirt he or she has just designed, decide it looked better short, add more fullness at the hip—all with just a few commands. Designers of waterslides for an amusement park can use CAD to visualize the velocity and effects of friction from bathing suits— and all without ever using a pencil.

Figure 6-18
CAD programs let you create working drawings on-screen for architectural and industrial applications.

Figure 6-19
Presentation graphics software lets you create custom charts, graphs, and other images, and some packages also coordinate the presentation for you.

Architects can change a number for the length of one wall, changing a whole skyscraper's measurements automatically. Aerospace engineers can "walk through" a model of a space station and put the design under stress tolerance tests without anyone having to leave the ground.

Presentation, Multimedia, and Utility Graphics Applications

Once images are generated, they can be used to communicate a message. Applications that use images for this purpose include desktop publishing (DTP), presentation, multimedia, and utility graphics. DTP applications are covered extensively in the chapter on desktop publishing, where the principles for combining text and images are presented. These principles also apply to presentation, multimedia and utility graphics productions.

Presentation applications use software that combines text and images in a series of pictures. These pictures are like slides, and the presentation is much like a slide show (Figure 6-19). The pictures can be saved as bit-mapped images, sent to a service bureau, and made into photographic slides. When presenting pictures on a micocomputer monitor, you set the length of time for each slide display, the order of display, and the special effects such as dissolving from one slide to the next. Popular presentation programs include Microsoft's PowerPoint, Aldus Persuasion, Lotus's Freelance Graphics, and Harvard Graphics.

Related to presentation graphics is **multimedia** software which incorporates video, animation, and sound into presentation graphics. These programs let users create a full range of graphics and import sound, music, animation, and video images from other sources, combining them into a cohesive presentation. For the novice and expert alike, programs such as Macromedia Director (Figure 6-20) yield the style and quality of professional television and other video productions. Making full use of the capabilities of multimedia software requires a variety of specialized peripheral devices and additions to the computer; this has resulted in a profusion of products

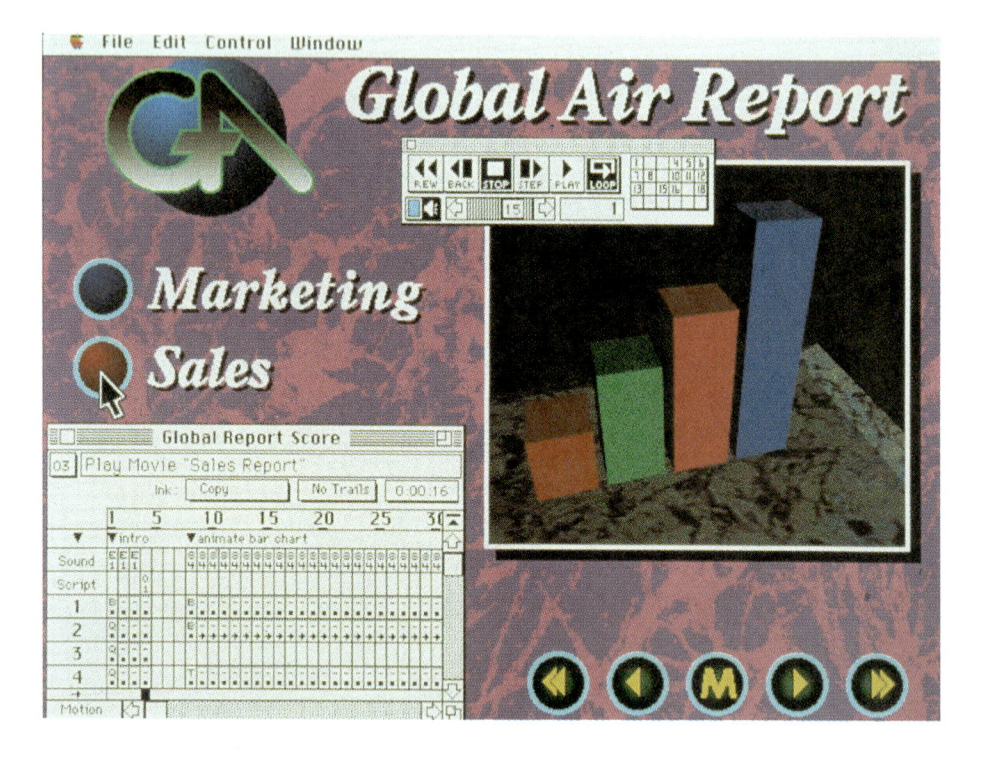

Figure 6-20
Multimedia requires a variety of equipment, depending on how sophisticated you get. Macromedia Director allows you to produce multimedia documents of professional quality.

that are sometimes incompatible with each other. New multimedia standards for microcomputers, including Quick Time on the Macintosh and the Multimedia PC, promise to coordinate the working of the various multimedia components.

Utility graphics software is a general class of graphics software designed for specific and limited functions. It lacks the flexibility of popular draw and paint programs but provides a very easy method for generating one or two specific types of graphics. Some of these programs allow users to create calendars, generate signs, produce greeting cards, and create awards and certificates, for example. While these can be created with draw and paint and DTP programs, specific utility software makes creating these unique types of graphics easier. Some popular utility programs include The Print Shop for posters, signs, cards, and letterheads; Create-A-Calendar; Certificate Maker; and, for appealing newsletters, The Newsroom.

SUMMARY

Graphics are any nontext image generated by a computer. They can be categorized by image qualities, file format, or by who or what originates the image.

Object-oriented images are made up of independent shapes. Bit-mapped images are single entities—patterns of the pixels shown on the screen. These two image types also distinguish many graphics file formats.

TIFF (tagged image file format) files are commonly used bit-mapped records of images; the Macintosh and PC versions differ. PCX/PCC and BMP are also bit-mapped PC formats; EPS files use mathematical formulas to describe images but can also incorporate bit-mapped images.

Microcomputer images can be black and white (monochrome), grayscale, or full-colored pictures, depending on your equipment and the software used. The resolution and the number of colors in the file greatly affect file size; the quality and size of the image therefore depend on the computer's memory and disk space.

Data-generated graphics are bit-mapped images produced by a program using numeric information. The values usually come from spreadsheets but can also come from database, text files, and direct input. The graphs and charts produced by data-generated software includes maps, flowcharts, and weather-forecasting graphics.

Device-generated graphics are most commonly the digitized images from scanner imput. The bit-mapped images can then be modified by image-processing software. Image processors also perform file conversion and screen capture functions. Images can also be created from data supplied by cameras, medical equipment, and radio telescopes.

User-generated graphics include draw programs and paint programs. Draw programs produce object-oriented images and provide the most precise user control over every object that makes up the image. Paint programs create bit-mapped images. Graphics programs provide the tools that let you use your mouse for different jobs (for example, the text tool lets you place text, the line tool draws a straight line, and so on). Draw and paint programs are used in a great variety of professions to produce and edit graphic images for many purposes. CAD (computer-aided design) applications are specialized draw programs for drafting, engineering, and technical illustration.

An Imaginary Tour

Architects can now "walk" clients through a new building long before the foundation is even poured—thanks to new computer-aided design programs. Clients have the opportunity to make changes and to see the results almost instantly. Want three windows rather than two? Wonder what the room would look like if the door was a little to the left? How would the room "feel" if the walls were brick rather than wood? Today it's no problem.

The process of building a model of a room on a computer has several stages. First the architect sets the objects in space and defines their characteristics, such as shape or surface finish. Then a perspective on the room is chosen so the computer can orient the view it will create. What can and cannot be seen must be calculated, as well as the angle, reflections, color, and intensity of light. The result can either be viewed on a computer screen, printed, or put directly onto a color slide. The program can also let people "walk" through famous buildings on the other side of the world.

Presentation and multimedia applications use the images created in other programs, mixing images with text, sound, or video to produce an animated slide show that can be very impressive. Utility graphics software provides an easy method of producing greeting cards, posters, calendars, and many other products with microcomputer-generated images.

KEY TERMS

bit-mapped images
CAD (computer-aided design)
clip art
data-generated graphics
device-generated graphics
draw programs
EPS (encapsulated PostScript)
file conversion
flowchart
graphics
group organization software
icon
image processing software
multimedia
object-oriented images
paint programs
PCX/PCC (Paintbrush)
presentation application
project management software
resolution
scanning software
TIFF (tagged image file format)
user-generated graphics
utility graphics software
vectorized

REVIEW QUESTIONS

1. What is the difference between an object-oriented and a bit-mapped graphic?
2. What are the three most common graphic file formats? Describe each.
3. What are data-generated graphics, and how are they created?
4. What other kinds of graphics originate in the same way?
5. What are device-generated graphics, and how were they created?
6. What kind of file is produced by an image processor? What is the advantage of an image processor that reads and creates files with many different file formats?
7. What are user-generated graphics, and how are they created?
8. What are the uses of a draw program and a paint program?
9. Name three professions that would make use of graphic images.
10. How might you use a presentation application?
11. How would a multimedia application help you?
12. What special products could you produce with utility graphics software?

Working with Desktop Publishing

7

OBJECTIVES

After completing this chapter, you will be able to

- Define desktop publishing software.
- Identify controls for text attributes.
- Describe the major types of desktop publishing software.
- Identify the major page layout features of desktop publishing software.
- List the major types of typographical controls.
- Describe several different special effects and how they can be used in a document.
- Identify four major types of spacing controls common to desktop publishing software.
- Describe the major graphic controlling features found in many desktop publishing programs.
- Name different types of documents created with desktop publishing software.
- Explain how desktop publishing software is a tool for expression.
- Explain several design principles used in desktop publishing.

FOCUS

Communicating is important, and communicating effectively is even more important. Effective written communication involves two basic issues: *content*—what is written—and *style*—the way in which it is presented; this includes both the writing technique and the appearance of the document. An attractively typed letter may look good, but if the content makes no sense, it will not be effective. A well-written business letter that is scribbled on ruled paper also lacks effectiveness. Newspaper style books, for example, address not only such issues as grammar and punctuation but the correct use of headlines and type faces and the sizing and placement of photographs.

Some microcomputer software, such as word processors, spelling checkers, and grammar analysis programs, may enhance the content of written communication, but they do not fully address this issue of style. Some word processors help users produce visually appealing documents, but desktop publishing software has the design tools necessary to produce an almost complete range of publications. It cannot improve the content of a document, but it does provide the tools to make it visually appealing—to give it style (Figure 7-1).

Figure 7-1
Desktop publishing software has put into the hands of the everyday user the tools to produce just about any kind of printed document.

WHAT IS DESKTOP PUBLISHING SOFTWARE?

Desktop publishing (DTP) software provides a microcomputer with typesetting and page-layout capabilities. Typesetting (controlling the appearance of text on a page) and page layout (determining the location of and coordinating the various text and graphic elements of a publication) have traditionally been complex, time-consuming, and expensive tasks. By combining sophisticated typesetting and page-layout controls, desktop publishing has replaced traditional methods, simplifying and speeding up the process significantly (Figure 7-2).

Figure 7-2
Traditional publishing methods involve a large number of complex steps: typesetting (accomplished through metal type or phototypesetting), manually creating the art, and assembling all the pieces of the document by hand on the pasteup board.

> **I Write What I Please**

Once upon a time, publishing a book, pamphlet, newsletter, or advertising brochure was a job for professionals. If an individual or a small group of people wanted to put out a printed piece, they either had to come up with enough money to have someone else do it (often a prohibitive undertaking, which was also time-consuming) or do it themselves with a mimeograph (which produced a distinctly amateurish-looking product).

Unlike word processors with desktop publishing features, these programs are not designed to add and edit large segments of text; their unique role is to combine text, graphics, and page layout.

With computer desktop publishing programs the line between "professional" and "nonprofessional" publishing has just about disappeared. DTP programs allow users to incorporate color, graphics, and a wide variety of type styles and sizes in their work. Text can be "wrapped" around graphic elements that users can design themselves rather than relying on graphic artists. Anyone with a computer and the right software, plus access to a high-quality printer, can produce top-notch printed material almost instantly.

Schools can contact parents about events, political activists can advertise meetings and demonstrations, fan clubs can stay up-to-date with their favorite idol—all by using their personal computer.

DTP software combines text files generated with a word processor and other applications and graphics files generated with scanners, draw and paint software, and other graphics applications to produce a new publication (Figure 7-3).

DTP Types

There are two basic types of DTP software. The first is **command-driven,** in which the user enters commands into the document itself to control its appearance. In LePrint, for example, commands specifying both the kind and height of text are placed at the beginning of the document as well as at any other point where the user wants the text appearance to change. The results of the commands are not displayed on the monitor. The user sees what the document looks like only after it is printed.

The other major type of software is known as **WYSIWYG,** short for "what you see is what you get." Such software—QuarkXPress or PageMaker, for example—lets people set and change specifications for text and graphics and see the effects immediately on the monitor (Figure 7-4). The monitor displays exactly (or almost exactly) what the document will look like on paper.

These two categories of software include a range of desktop publishing programs and processes. Some programs are little more than word processors with features to control text and graphics. More sophisticated—"high end"—programs provide a more complete range of text and graphics control.

A Tool of Expression

Desktop publishing is a tool of expression: it provides a medium for expressing ideas through the design and style of text and graphics on a page. Publication

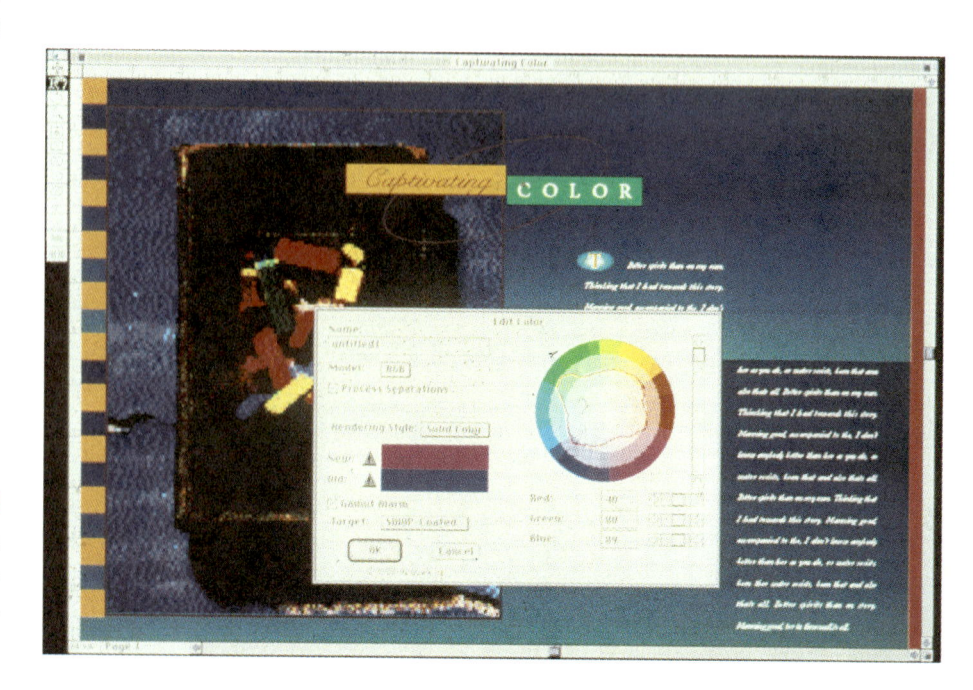

Figure 7-3
Desktop publishing places the whole typesetting and pasteup process on the computer, giving one person on a micro control of type, graphics, and layout.

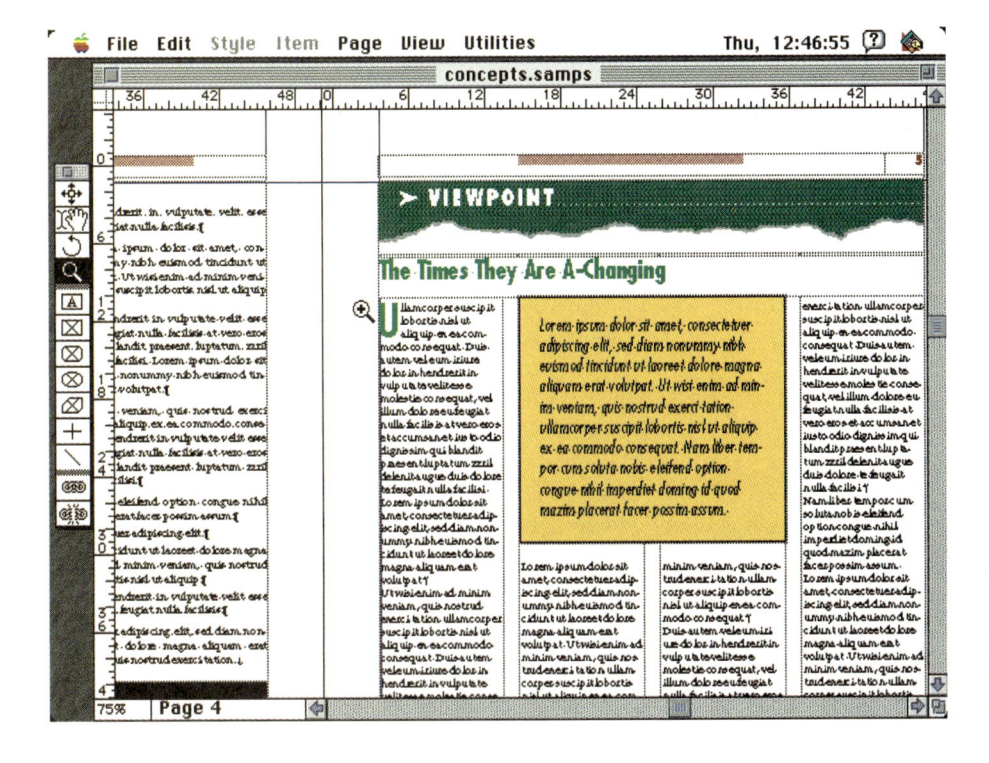

Figure 7-4
With WYSIWYG DTP software, you can see on screen what the printed document will look like, allowing you to directly manipulate its appearance.

design is both an art and a craft. It's an art because a publication's design can not only help express the meaning of the content, but can also enhance that expresion in new and original ways. And it's a craft because the practical application of standard design principles is used to make the effect of the design suit the purpose of the publication. Desktop publishing applications give the designer or page layout artist the tools to implement the design ideas that determine the look and effect of the finished document, controlling page layout, type, and graphics.

PAGE LAYOUT

A desktop publishing program uses the tools and processes of **page layout** to control the page size, orientation, margins, and columns (where text appears in columns) and how graphic elements are integrated. In short, page layout determines the overall appearance of the document by organizing the text, graphics, and white space. **White space** is the area on the page without text or image, and the design must take into account the effect of white space on the appearance of the publication.

Page Size

The term **page size** refers to the dimensions of the printed document. Most programs support several page sizes, including $8\frac{1}{2} \times 11$, $8\frac{1}{2} \times 14$, and 11×17 inches. A good range for a DTP application runs from the size of a business card (commonly 3×2 inches) to 17×22 inches (a small poster). Anything smaller or larger requires a specialty application.

Playing the Time Zone Game

In publishing, a writer, editor, graphic artist, and production manager must all work together to produce the finished product. Traditionally this could be a time-consuming process, since each person had to have physical possession of the material to work on it. For instance, unless the graphic artist strolled into the editor's office while the editor was working on a piece, the two could not work together. Thanks to computer networks, people can now work on documents at the same time, even while being physically separated from each other. Improved telecommunications and image compression allow a graphic artist in Milan, a printer in Tokyo, an editor in New York, and a writer in Santa Fe to share their ideas instantly and to see what the others think—instantly and in color. Assuming, that is, they can all be awake at the same time.

> HISTORY

Aldus, PageMaker, and Paul Brainerd

It was inevitable that someone would develop a software program that allowed the user to "set type" on a computer. It was also logical that the program would have some graphic capabilities. What surprised the computer world about PageMaker, the first true desktop publishing program, was that it was targeted to the general user rather than to professional typesetters. But this brilliant marketing scheme was what made the program such an astonishing success.

When Aldus introduced PageMaker, the company's original strategy was to show dealers that the software package could help them sell hardware—specifically Apple's Macintosh computer (which desperately needed a boost) and LaserWriter. The MS-DOS world had nothing like PageMaker, and small businesses flocked to the product. PageMaker let them produce top-quality newsletters, brochures, and other printing jobs without going to outside typesetting firms (which traditionally did not pay much attention to customer's needs) or having their own in-house graphic art staff (which most could not afford). With only a Macintosh computer, LaserWriter printer, and PageMaker software, people could save time and money, and get total control over their printing needs.

It was not surprising that Aldus came up with a desktop publishing program, because the company was an offshoot of Atex, a maker of minicomputer-based publishing systems for newspapers and magazines. When the Massachusetts-based Atex decided to close its branch in Redmond, Washington, Paul Brainerd, the local manager, got together with five engineers and started a new company specifically to invent what has become known as desktop publishing.

The five engineers agreed to work for half of what they made at Atex; Brainerd contributed his time and $100,000. The money lasted six months, which was just long enough to come up with a prototype program and a business plan. Brainerd took to the streets, knocking on the doors of venture capitalists, desperate to raise the $1 million his business plan required. But venture capitalists were leery of investing in software; in fact, most of them were so unimpressed that they had not even bothered to read his business plan. After 49 unsuccessful pitches, Brainerd finally found one taker who invested $846,000. It was (barely) enough.

When PageMaker was released, it was full of bugs. There had been talk within Aldus of delaying the release while the problems were ironed out, but the company was out of money. Fortunately for Aldus, early users were patient with the groundbreaking program.

With PageMaker, the page appearing on the computer screen is virtually the page that will be printed (this has come to be known as WYSIWYG, "what you see is what you get"). By using a mouse or other pointer, the user clicks on "master icons" at the bottom of the screen to specify the page's general characteristics: page size, margins, number of pages, and so on. Once these characteristics have been determined, a blank page built to the specifications appears on screen.

Text can then be imported and, after the desired part of the text is highlighted, can be manipulated as the user wishes using over 100 combinations of typeface sizes and styles. A "tool box" lets the user create simple graphics (charts, graphs, boxes) or import graphics from other programs. Once the graphics are placed on the page, the program adjusts text accordingly.

PageMaker made the Macintosh computer a success. And it made Paul Brainerd—who had incorporated Aldus by giving himself 90 percent of the stock for his $100,000 investment—a multimillionaire. ■

Page Orientation

The term **page orientation** refers to the direction of the page in relation to the text. Two orientations are available: **portrait** and **landscape.** In *portrait* orientation, text and graphics are printed across an upright page; on an $8\frac{1}{2} \times 11$-inch piece of paper, the $8\frac{1}{2}$-inch edges are at the top and bottom. *Landscape* orientation turns the paper sideways, placing the 11-inch edges at top and bottom.

Margins and Columns

Margin settings control the amount of space along the edges of the paper, and most programs allow margins to be set at virtually any location. WYSIWYG software usually displays a line, called a *margin guide,* showing the location of the margin. Text and graphics stay within these margins unless you deliberately move text and graphics outside the margin guides.

Columns are vertical spaces that contain text or graphics within the margins. Columns can vary by their number, their width, and the width of the gutters (the white space between the columns).

Number of Pages, Double-Sided Pages, and Facing Pages

The number of pages in a document is part of the page design. The user may set this number before entering text and graphics. You can change the number of pages at any time, however, or have the software create the pages automatically when the text is first entered.

Pages can be set to print as **single-sided** (printed on only one side), **double-sided** (printed on both sides), or double-sided and facing (printed on both sides, with alternately wider left and right margins to provide room for binding the book).

Ruling Lines

Lines used to set off, or draw attention to, various elements in a document are **ruling lines,** or rules (Figure 7-5). Ruling lines can be vertical or horizontal, thin or heavy. They can separate headings from text or columns from each other. Placing rules all the way around text or graphics creates a box, commonly used by newspapers and magazines to draw attention to particular articles.

Headers, Footers, and Page Numbers

Headers, footers, and page numbers make it easy to locate information. *Headers* are a few words placed at the top of every page of a section, chapter, or document, often with the purpose of grouping similar pages. Books frequently use headers to identify chapters: for example, the headers of this book. *Footers* are like headers but appear at the bottom of the page.

Headers and footers may appear on every page at the same location, or they may alternate from the left to the right side to accommodate facing pages. Automatically generated page numbers can combine chapter and section numbers, and they can appear on different sides of facing pages as either part of or independent of a header or footer.

Holy Microchips

The first comic book ever produced entirely on computer has Batman battling—what else?—a computer. In creator Pepe Moreno's offering, "Digital Justice," Gotham City is trapped in a computer network that has fallen into evil hands; a deadly virus is decimating the population. Though intrepid Bruce Wayne is dead, he has left a computer that recruits another human Caped Crusader to take his place and save the citizens of Gotham. Moreno created the backgrounds using computer modeling programs and then scanned in the hand-drawn figures. He then used the computer to manipulate the images—for instance, placing the text balloons in different places. In the future Moreno plans to come out with a CD-ROM version of the comic book that would eliminate entirely the need for paper. "Readers" would scan through the images on their computers, which would speak the text. Holy Microchips indeed!

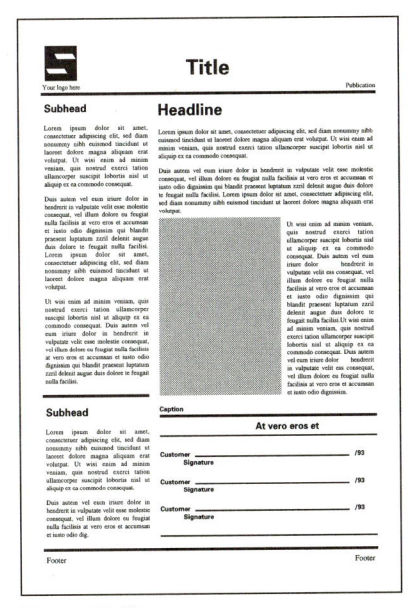

Figure 7-5
Using ruling lines effectively can add style to your document and emphasize important elements in the design.

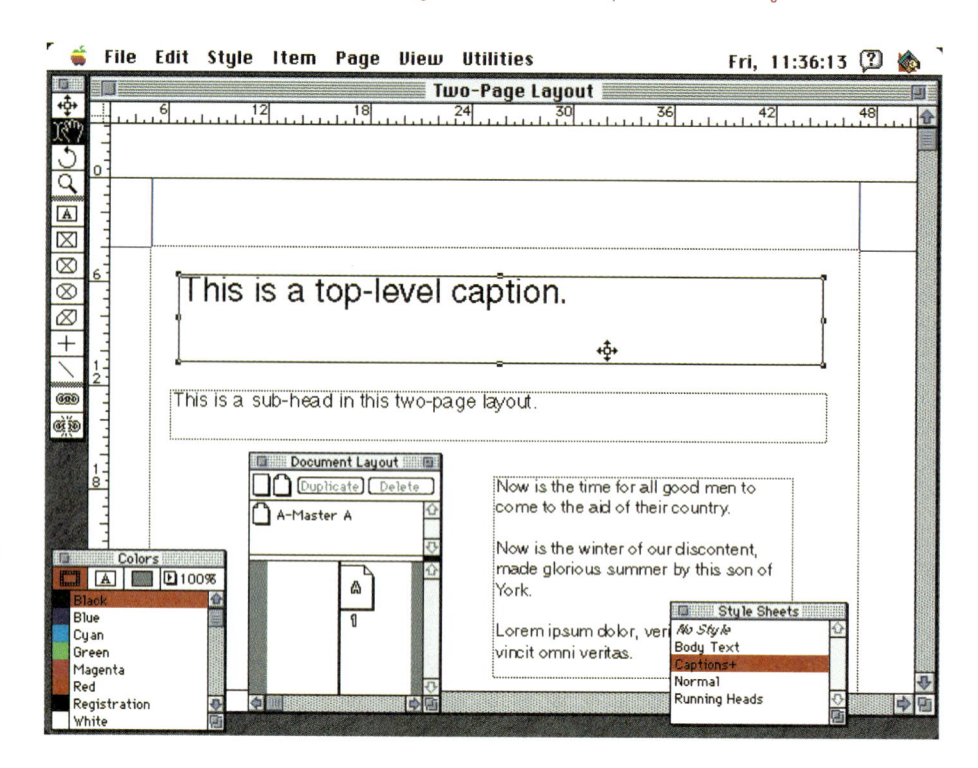

Figure 7-6
You can create standard types of documents using the templates provided by DTP software, such as this brochure template showing placeholders for text and heads, and style tags already created.

Page Setup

Desktop publishing applications provide two ways to set the page layout. First you define the margins, and so on, in a page setup **dialog box** (an on-screen menu of choices that appears in a box). Then you create the ruling lines and other elements that will be duplicated throughout the publication, either on master pages, as in PageMaker, or as elements on the base page, as in Ventura Publisher. To give the novice user ideas of what kinds of layouts are appropriate for different types of publications, these and other DTP applications come with *templates* (DTP files with already-created layouts; Figure 7-6). All you need to do is add the text and graphics.

Life Imitates Art Imitates...

In the 1960s a fictitious rock band was created for a television program called "The Monkees"—only the band became very successful on its own. Now Davy Jones, pop music star and Monkee, has created a book called *Monkees Memories and Media Madness* in which the book's medium is very much the message. Using the latest in computer desktop color technology, Jones manipulated the 300 photos, which tell the twenty-five-year story of the rock group. The book will include anecdotal essays and the story of post-Monkees life—all created on computer.

Figure 7-7
This type specifications dialog box in QuarkXPress lets you select the font, size, and other typographical effects all at once.

TYPOGRAPHICAL CONTROLS

Typographical controls determine the appearance of individual text characters by designating the type attributes (Figure 7-7). They also control the space between letters and lines of type. These and other controls contribute to the appearance of text within paragraphs.

Type Attributes

The three major type attributes—typeface, type style, and type size—are collectively known as *fonts*.

Typeface. One **typeface** is a single design of a set of letters, numbers, and symbol characters. Each typeface includes all the letters, numbers, and symbols used in most written communication, and each is a unique design for the shape and overall look of these characters. The two major kinds of typefaces, serif and sans serif, include many individual typefaces within each category (Table 7-1).

Serif typefaces are those with short lines, called *serifs*, projecting from the ends of the main strokes of the letters and characters. As cursive writing helps a reader's eye flow smoothly from one letter to the next, typefaces that use serifs make reading easier; therefore, most texts are set in serif typefaces.

Sans serif typefaces use no serifs, giving the printed words a block appearance that causes them to stand out. This makes sans serif typefaces useful for display type, such as headlines and captions.

Type Style. Variations in a typeface are known as type style. The most common type styles include **boldface** (the type appears thick and dark), *italics* (the type appears to be almost handwritten), and underlined (the type has a line drawn under it).

Type Size. **Type size** is the height of text characters, numbers, and symbols, measured in points. A **point** is about $1/72$ of an inch, so 10-point type measures about $10/72$ inch, 36-point type measures about $1/2$ inch, and 72-point type measures about 1 inch in height. Typically, sizes should vary for different types of text within a document. For example, 10- or 12-point type is the size most often used for the major body of text, with 18-, 20-, and 24-point type common for headings (Table 7-2). Larger sizes are often used for banner headlines.

Fonts

All the possible combinations of typeface style and size are included in a single *font*. In traditional printing, a font was a set of characters cast in one particular typeface, style, and size. An electronic font, however, includes all the styles and sizes available for a given typeface. Font software thus provides the wide variety of fonts needed to create interesting and varied DTP, word processing, spreadsheet, and other documents.

Fonts are used in two forms. **Outline fonts** are equivalent to object-oriented images and can be scaled to any size; **bit-mapped fonts** are equivalent to bit-mapped graphics (see the chapter on graphics). Outline fonts are for use by the printer; most laser printers come with a standard set of basic fonts

Table 7-1
Common Serif and Sans Serif Typefaces

Serif
Times
Palatino
New Century Schoolbook
Courier
Bookman
Sans Serif
Helvetica
Futura
Frutiger
Avant Garde
Franklin Gothic

Table 7-2
Common Type Sizes in Serif and Sans Serif Type

7pt. Palatino
10pt. Palatino
12pt. Patatino
14pt. Palatino
18pt. Palatino
24pt. Palatino

7pt. Futura
10pt. Futura
12pt. Futura
14pt. Futura
18pt. Futura
24pt. Futura

stored in ROM, and additional fonts can be stored on your hard disk and downloaded to the printer as desired. Bit-mapped fonts, which are made for the monitor, are stored on the hard disk. When you purchase a font, you copy the outline font to your hard disk, and you generate bit-mapped fonts for your applications. The application software will show the bit-mapped fonts on-screen and send the outline fonts to the printer. The most popular format for outline fonts is PostScript; thousands of fonts are available in this form. A more recent format called **TrueType** also provides outline and bit-mapped fonts.

Special Effects

Special typographical effects can add interest to any document. Some of the commonly used special effects include drop caps, raised caps, reverse type, deviant text, and rotated text (Figure 7-8).

The **drop cap** is larger than the body text. It starts at the top of the first line of a paragraph and extends to the bottom of the letters in the second or third line. The **raised cap** is similar, but it extends above the first line of the paragraph and does not go below it.

Reverse type attracts a reader's attention by placing white text on a darkened or black background. The term **deviant text** refers to a typeface that is changed from the original shape to create a unique presentation. The most common use of deviant text is in a masthead or logo.

Other special effects include **rotated text** that is set sideways, upside down, or upside down and sideways on the page. Desktop publishing applications vary greatly in the degrees of rotation the text can be turned and the amount of text that can be rotated.

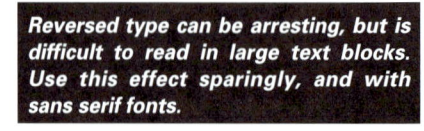

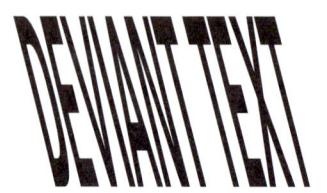

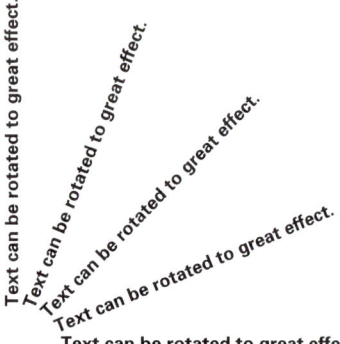

Figure 7-8
Special typographical effects: raised cap (upper left), drop cap (upper right), reversed type (middle left), rotated text (lower right), and deviant text (lower left).

Spacing Controls

Controlling the spacing between letters and lines within a paragraph as well as the spacing between paragraphs is an important part of controlling a document's appearance.

The basic level of letter-spacing control is the choice between using a monospaced or proportionally spaced font. In a **monospaced** font, such as Courier, each letter occupies the same amount of space; thus, a narrow letter, an *i* or *l* for instance, occupies the same space as a wide letter, such as an *m* or *w*. This often makes the type look as though there were too much space around the narrow letters and too little space around wide letters. **Proportionally spaced** fonts, such as Utopia (the typeface you are reading now), solve this problem by assigning each letter an amount of space proportional to its actual width; thus, the spacing looks consistent for all letters. Proportionally spaced fonts generally fit more text on a page and are easier to read than monospaced fonts are (Figure 7-9).

For a few letter pairs, the standard spacing between the letters also gives the appearance of too much or too little space. Consider the letter pair *Yo*. Even with proportional spacing, without reducing the space between them the *o* would look too far from the *Y*. **Kerning,** the process of adjusting the space between the individual letters, moves these two letters closer together to improve their appearance. Kerning on common letter pairs needing less space is automatic in most DTP applications, but you can also manually adjust the space for any letter pair. Some DTP programs also let you make a general setting for the spacing between all letters; this is called **tracking.** Tight tracking draws the letters closer and fits more type in a given space; loose tracking spaces the letters farther apart.

Leading (rhymes with *heading*) is the distance in points from the baseline of one row of type to the baseline of the next. The text's baseline is an imaginary straight line along the bottom of all characters except the descender letters (*g, j, p, q,* and *y*). If the size of text in a paragraph is 10 points and the leading is also 10 points, then the descenders of one line in many typefaces will touch the top of the ascenders (*b, d, f, h, k, l,* and *t*) in the next. Using 10-point text with a 20-point leading, on the other hand, creates a double-spaced effect. In general, less leading produces a darker, denser appearance; more leading makes the type look more open, lighter, and usually more readable (Figure 7-10, p. 128). Depending on the typeface, a rule of thumb is leading equal to 120 percent of the type size for what is to be single-spaced lines of text.

Most DTP software lets users add extra space above and below entire paragraphs. This is commonly known as **interparagraph spacing.** Headlines are usually followed by extra interparagraph spacing to separate them from the body of text. Extra interparagraph spacing placed above a paragraph is useful when starting new articles in a newsletter.

Paragraph Controls

Paragraphs differ by how the first letter and last letter in a row of text align within the columns and margins. Paragraphs can be aligned flush left, flush

---

Monospaced fonts, such as Courier, give each letter the same amount of space; this creates gaps around narrow letters such as i and l, and squeezes wide letters such as m and w.

Proportionally spaced fonts, such as Garamond, assign an appropriate space to each letter according to its width, conserving space and improving readability.

WATER

Unkerned: the A is surrounded by large spaces, while the E is squeezed between the T and R.

WATER

Kerned: dropping space aound the A and adding space around the E balances the spacing visually.

Figure 7-9
Spacing and kerning effects.

Underground Savings

The New York City Transit Authority moves millions of people every day through the city's five boroughs. Updating maps, schedules, and signs is somewhat mind-boggling, but thanks to computer technology, the Transit Authority saves $200,000 a year by doing the job in-house rather than relying on outside typesetters. Using 12 Macintosh workstations, an image processor, and laser image setter, the TA's graphic artists have complete control over letter spacing, leading, and kerning. Now if there were just a way they could get the subways to run more frequently....

right, or centered; they can have justified or ragged margins. A **flush left** paragraph starts with the first word in a line of text even with the left margin. A **flush right** paragraph has the last word in each line ending at the right margin. A **centered** paragraph has each line equidistant from the left and right margins. In a **justified** paragraph, each line stretches from the left to the right margin. Justified paragraphs require increasing or decreasing space between words and letters, another automatic control in most DTP applications. **Ragged margins,** where the line begins or ends unevenly along a margin, have a less formal appearance.

Desktop publishing software also lets you set indents and tabs and rules for hyphenation. You can instruct the software to hyphenate words automatically within a certain number of characters next to the right margin; this is called the *hyphenation zone*. You can instruct the software not to hyphenate at all, leaving the decision up to you.

Tags

Paragraph **tags,** or **styles,** are sets of text, spacing, and paragraph controls you can assign to a block of text. A tag is based on a series of text attribute settings; this set of attributes is then named for easy recall (Figure 7-11) and tag names are usually provided in a list for easy access. You can designate paragraphs for inclusion in the table of contents, and the DTP software will generate the table of contents text from this and from the page-numbering information. Individual words can be tagged for inclusion in an automatically generated index.

GRAPHICS CONTROLS

Desktop publishing software also provides graphics controls that manage how and where graphics appear within a document. These controls include sizing

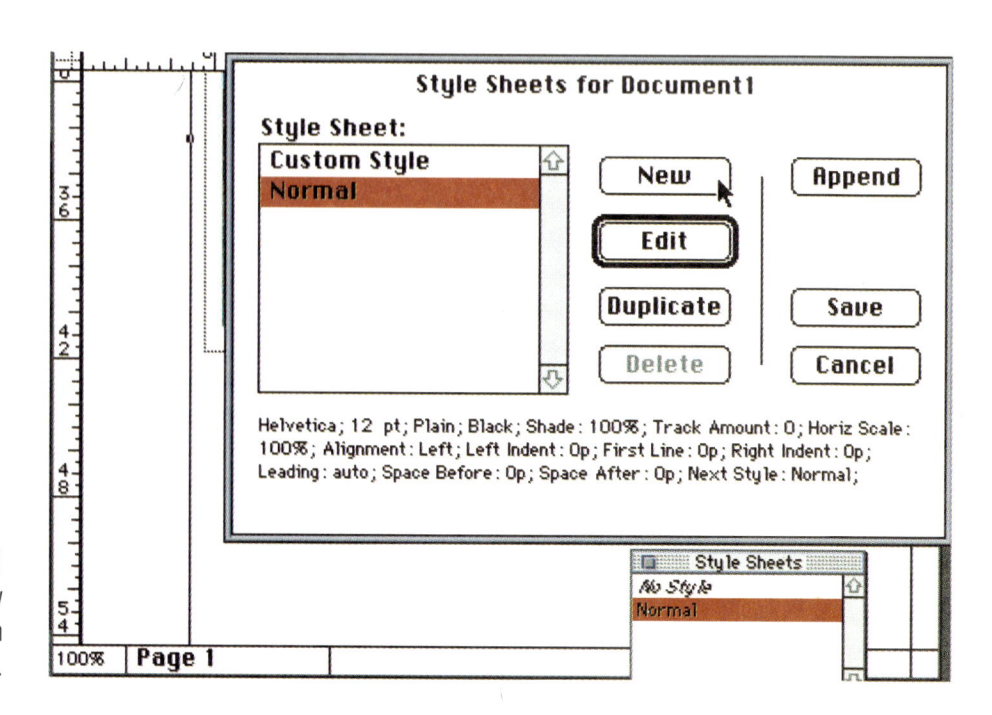

Figure 7-10
Changing the leading on a paragraph affects how much type fits in a given space and how it looks on the page. The 9/11 type occupies a shorter column, and looks darker and denser than the 9/13 type.

Figure 7-11
QuarkXPress allows you to create a new type style or edit an existing one, then name it for later use.

Figure 7-12
You can easily reduce or enlarge an image in QuarkXpress, or stretch or squeeze it as you like.

and scaling, cropping, creating simple line art, contouring the flow of text around images, and determining image appearance.

Sizing and Scaling

Sizing and scaling controls let users fit imported graphics into a specific space. The **sizing** control allows you to specify the actual size of a graphic on a document page (Figure 7-12). The original size of the graphic is of little concern because the sizing control lets users take any graphic and enlarge or reduce it as needed. While this is especially true of draw-type graphics, it is less true of paint-type or bit-mapped graphics, where enlarging the graphic too much decreases the quality of the printed image.

Scaling controls determine how a reduced or enlarged graphic will appear on a page. Proportional scaling prevents the distortion of the image by maintaining the original image's ratio between height and width. As either the horizontal or vertical side changes, the opposite side changes automatically. A graphic can also be scaled without maintaining its proportional image. For example, it is possible to stretch a graphic vertically without changing the horizontal size to produce a unique graphic effect.

Cropping

You can also **crop,** or trim, a graphic so that only a specified portion of it is visible. Unlike image processing software, no part of the actual image is ever removed in DTP applications; all that changes is the portion of the image displayed. Desktop publishing cropping is easily changed, which makes it easy to experiment with several sizes and views (Figure 7-13).

Line Art

It is common to use a variety of graphic drawing tools to enhance the appearance of a document. In most DTP software, the only type of art that can be created directly is line art.

Figure 7-13
A cropping tool (note the highlighted icon in the Toolbox) lets you hide part of the image, thus selecting only the part you want to show.

News in the Coup

During the attempted military coup in the Soviet Union in 1991, the official Soviet newspaper *Pravda* was shut down, as was the news agency TASS, which had long been the official mouthpiece of the government. But this did not stop Russian president Boris Yeltsin and his staff. While he was barricaded in the Parliament building, his staff used a microcomputer to publish a newspaper that carried news of the street protests, plans that Yeltsin's government had to resist the coup, and the use of military force against the protesters. Thanks to computers, Yeltsin was able to disseminate information while official sources were mute.

The four most common line art tools are simple lines, ovals, boxes, and rounded-corner boxes that are used to draw attention to text or to frame an image. As noted earlier, placing a box around an article on a newsletter page separates it from the rest of the text and draws attention to the text inside.

Other forms of line art can be imported as graphics. Clip art is predrawn art that is available for public use; nowadays, there are large libraries of clip art stored on disk in formats that DTP applications can import. Photo libraries similarly provide a wide variety of stock photos, converted to electronic form and available for use.

Graphics and Text

How much space separates the text from a graphic and how the text fits around a graphic are important considerations. Many DTP applications automatically control the space around a graphic; the **text wrap** control allows users to customize this spacing.

The text wrap control lets you designate whether text will produce a finer image. It also can wrap text in an irregular shape, possibly following the shape of a single object in the image (Figure 7-14).

Other Graphics Controls

High-end DTP applications also let you affect the lightness of an image, increase or decrease the contrast, and make changes to its screen pattern (Figure 7-15). The **screen pattern** control affects the quality of the image when printed; using a screen pattern with more dots per inch (dpi) will produce a finer image. Other graphics controls, including image rotation, vary with each

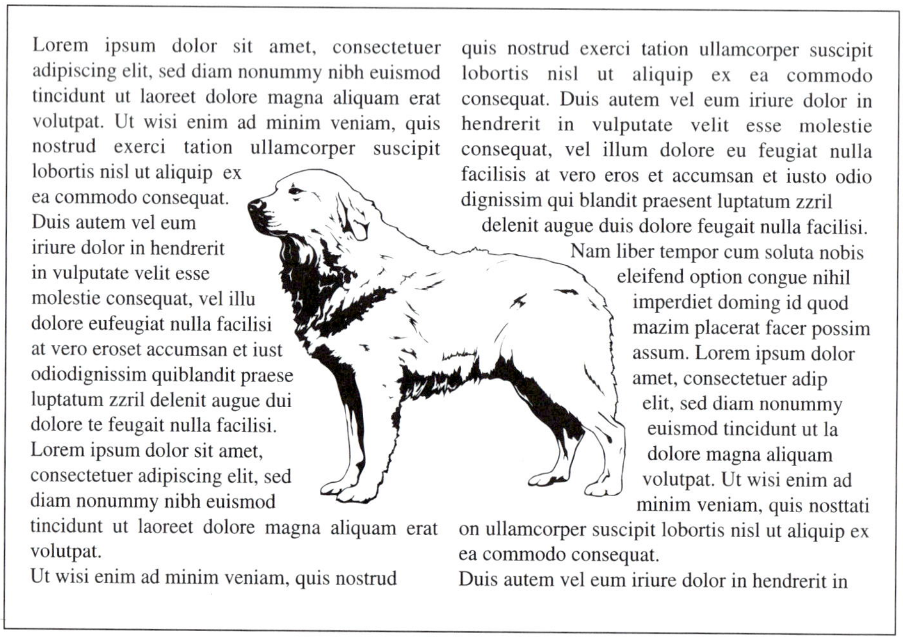

Figure 7-14
Text wrap controls can be used imaginatively; wrapping text around a graphic can add dramatic effect to your document.

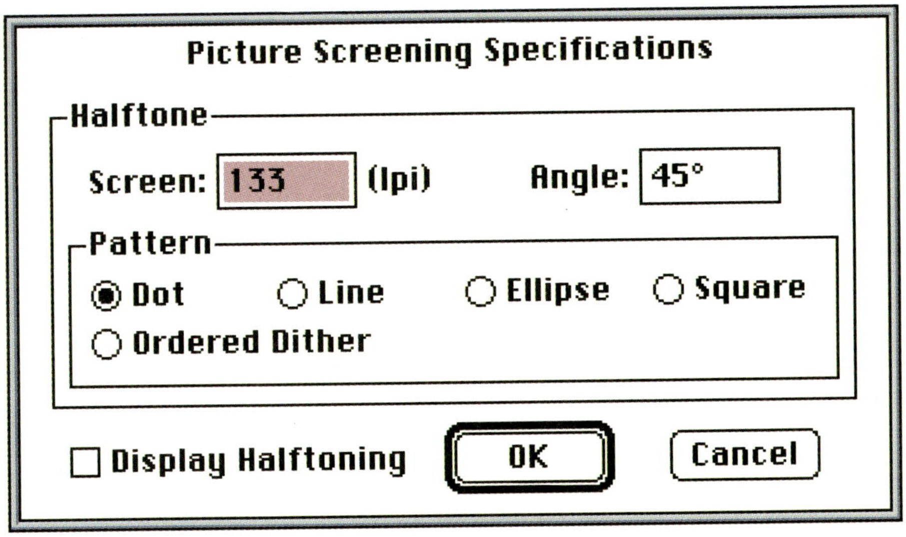

Figure 7-15
The screen controls in QuarkXPress let you adjust settings for photographs to print at the proper resolution, screen pattern, and halftoning.

application (depending on each one's specialty), but the ones mentioned here are the most common.

DESKTOP PUBLISHING OUTPUT

Output from a DTP application ultimately results in a printed product, but there are many ways of getting that final product. You can send the output directly to a laser or ink jet black-and-white or color printer, to a digital imagesetter to make positives (black on white paper or film) or negatives (film), or to disk for later publication. A digital imagesetter uses a laser to print directly onto a photosensitive print medium; it produces very high resolution.

Much of the DTP done in marketing and public relations departments is put out directly from laser printers with additional copies produced on photocopy machines. Color publishing in this manner is in its infancy, but is growing rapidly as color copiers become more sophisticated and less costly.

To get a high-quality product with very high resolution (1,000 dpi or more) you can use a digital imagesetter and take the film to a printshop for offset printing. A less costly process would be to output to a 300-dpi or better laser printer, mount the page on a paste-up board, and have the printshop photograph and print it; or take the output of the laser printer and simply photocopy as many copies as needed (as mentioned earlier).

Sending your DTP output directly to a digital imagesetter gives you a great deal of control over the results. For many desktop publishers, the cost of the imagesetter is prohibitive, however, and they use service bureaus, which provide a wide range of DTP services and equipment for hire. The pages (or the entire publication) are printed to disk first, and the service bureau makes the film from these files. Just as with word processing or graphics files, printing to disk means that the files created by the application are saved to a disk or other permanent storage medium. They can then be sent to a service bureau

Morning Fix

It's a journalistic cliché that the most important stories happen just as the newspaper begins to be printed. Morning papers with large circulations usually must be printed by 3 or 4 A.M., but that is no longer the problem it once was—thanks to the computer. Journalists use their desktop computers to add late-breaking stories at the very last minute. A page's layout can be altered electronically to accommodate the story, photo, or graphic—all of which means newspapers can be even more timely. How long will it be before the morning "paper" isn't even printed on paper, but is sent electronically to subscribers' computer screens?

A Gold-Medal Paper

During the summer 1992 Olympics in Barcelona, a legion of journalism students from the University of Navarro published a daily newspaper for the Olympic Committee that was distributed to the Olympic family. From their headquarters at the Barcelona Trade Fair, they used PCs and Aldus's PageMaker to create the paper in English, French, Spanish, and Catalan, the dialect of Barcelona. They built their own spell-checking dictionary for the articles in Catalan using the provided spell-checkers for the other languages. Once that hurdle had been cleared, the biggest problem was layout: each article, translated from the original three times, had four different lengths. Again computers came to the rescue and the paper made every deadline.

or printshop, or they can be used later to print the publication on film or paper on-site.

A TOOL OF EXPRESSION

Because DTP is both a set of technical typesetting tools and a tool of expression, learning to use this software is more than simply learning the procedures for selecting a typeface or placing a graphic image. It also requires learning how to use these tools to communicate effectively.

Athough there are many design principles that have evolved over more than 500 years of publishing (see the following section on designing with desktop publishing software), there still remains an unlimited area for creativity. Following these principles creatively involves balancing text, graphics, and the empty space on a page in an attractive and pleasing way, in a manner that invites the reader to read the publication and that reflects the publication's content.

Types of Publications

One of the strengths of desktop publishing software is its ability to create a wide range of publications, from flyers, newsletters, brochures, and manuscripts to business cards and catalogs. Flyers are most often single-page documents that convey a single message. Creating newsletters typically involves using different types of headlines, generating tables of contents and indexes, using a number of different text columns, drawing lines to separate articles and boxes to highlight information, and using other special effects. Desktop publishing applications can produce two-, three-, and four-fold brochures of different

Figure 7-16
DTP software has found uses in nearly every corner of the microcomputing world, as businesses, organizations, educators, and everyday users discover the power to publish their own documents quickly and inexpensively.

sizes. Desktop publishing software can also generate long manuscripts and can produce camera-ready pages for books and magazines of virtually any length and size. Many other publications, such as advertisements, letterheads, business cards, and catalogs, can also be created with DTP software.

Users of DTP Software

Desktop publishing applications have found homes in all kinds of industries. In addition to the book and periodical publishing industries, the marketing needs of business are one of DTP's biggest niches. Newsletters for all kinds of organizations and industries have sprung up in the wake of DTP availability. Educators find that professional-looking materials enhance student learning and students find that professional-looking schoolwork gets higher grades. The publishing industry as a whole has greatly expanded since the coming of desktop publishing. More publications are produced in a single day now than we could ever possibly see produced 15 or 20 years ago. A good deal of this production is done in small offices or by people working at home (Figure 7-16).

DESIGNING WITH DESKTOP PUBLISHING SOFTWARE

A publication's design is the overall plan for the arrangement of components—text, images, and white space—on each page. As we have said, the objectives for a design are to enhance the content and make the publication appealing to its audience. Achieving these objectives requires a design that balances consistency and variety.

Consistency

Consistency in publication design means that the pages are similar, with headlines, body text, images, and the distribution of white space following a constant pattern throughout. The design must also be consistent with the expectations of the publication's audience. There are a number of principles that provide consistency.

- *Plan the document first.* Outline how the document will appear. Begin with a specification sheet that includes details about the type of document, the intended audience, page-layout characteristics, body text size and leading, normal paragraph alignment, and so on.
- *Use standard designs.* Readers expect a brochure to look like a brochure, a newsletter to look like a newsletter, and a book to look like a book. This does not preclude variety (discussed later); it merely means that readers should not have to guess what they are reading.
- *Consider the audience.* The design of a document should focus on the target audience. If the document is intended for parents of schoolchildren, make it look like a school bulletin, not a corporate financial statement.
- *Use the design to focus attention.* The design of a document should call the reader's attention to the important information it contains.

A Muckraking Computer?

Getting inside an investigative journalist's mind might seem an impossible (and thankless) task, but that's exactly what a new computer program called Muckraker aims to do. Based on the premise that everything is documented somehow, the program divides up sources into people trails and paper trails, guiding a journalist through the steps of finding sources, conducting interviews, getting past secretaries and, ultimately, bringing reluctant sources on the record. Muckraker runs on a PC and is structured by questions and answers, making a dialogue between the user and the computer. More information can always be requested, and a user can switch back and forth between the paper and people trails. Muckraker is similar to other programs that assist doctors to diagnose infectious disease or geologists to analyze data on mineral resource locations.

- *Limit the amount of new information.* Good design helps readers remember information by limiting the important new items to from five to nine pieces per page.
- *Make information easy to find.* Use a table of contents, an index, and page numbers whenever appropriate. Titles should use larger type than the body of the article, and sections should stand out from other sections.
- *Follow a logical sequence.* The most important information in a document should be at the top of the page. The least important information should be in a lower corner. Items that are too long for one column should move to the top of the next column to the right.
- *Use column and page balance.* Facing pages and columns should begin and end at the same point.
- *Consider proportion.* Proportion in page design is the relationship in size among the components on a page and across facing pages. The size of a component is relative to its surrounding components. A single component should neither overpower others nor be too small.
- *Avoid odd-shaped paragraphs.* Odd-shaped paragraphs (such as diamond-shaped) are difficult to read; use them very sparingly. Don't specifically create designs with lengthy text (a paragraph or longer).
- *Avoid widows and orphans.* Paragraphs that end with less than a full line at the top of a page or column (widow) or begin with a single line at the bottom of a page or column (orphan) should be avoided. In addition, a paragraph should not end with a single short word (or part of a word) on the last line.
- *Avoid excesses.* Good design does not draw attention to itself. Use all the special features of the software in moderation.
- *Limit the number of fonts.* Do not overuse bold, italic, and uppercase letters, and limit the number of different fonts on a page to three or less.
- *Create appropriate white space.* Adding white space to a page not only makes information easy to read, it allows the reader to focus attention on what is most important. Too much white space, however, can lead to a document that appears disjointed and fragmented. Be judicious in its use.
- *Use appropriate margins.* Documents with wide margins are considered "airy" because they give a sense of openness. Documents with narrow margins are considered "heavy" because they convey a dense feeling. Although margins do not have to be equal on all sides, they should present a balanced image.
- *Use appropriate columns.* Columns wider than 5 inches make it difficult for the reader's eyes to return accurately to the beginning of the next line down. Columns narrower than 2 inches cause the reader's eyes to move down too frequently. Too many columns crowd the page and make it hard to read.

Variety

A boring design makes boring reading; variety prevents boredom. An inviting document helps convey the message by enticing the reader.

- *Use contrast.* This term refers to the use of light and dark areas on a page. There is nothing in a low-contrast document that draws the reader's attention. High-contrast documents use light areas to emphasize dark areas (and vice versa). If the leading is too tight between lines of text, the publication looks dark and foreboding. If the leading is too wide, the pages are too bright.
- *Surprise the reader.* Suprise keeps readers curious. Although the element of suprise seems to contradict the notion of consistency, it does not; an occasional suprise provides an added dimension to a document.
- *Use text wrap features.* Letting text flow around a graphic's shape increases the impact of the graphic. Although it does create odd-shaped text, it adds interest; use it carefully.
- *Try different paragraph alignments.* Drawing attention to one or two paragraphs within a document can be accomplished by aligning them differently.
- *Use different-sized columns.* To provide some variety in a publication, you can use different-sized columns on the same page and place graphics and headlines across columns. Again, don't overdo it.

Learning How to Design

To learn how to create document designs, get a book on the basic elements of graphic design. Many bookstores and libraries carry such books in their art, printing, and computer software sections. Another source of ideas is the design of other documents. Look at several and ask youself what makes them effective. Does the design enhance or detract from the message? Is the document easy to read?

SUMMARY

Desktop publishing software provides the tools and controls to combine text and graphics files into publications. These controls provide manipulation of the page layout, typography, and graphics. Whether it is command-driven or WYSIWYG-oriented, DTP software is always a tool for expression.

Page layout controls the page size and orientation, margins and column sizes and their placement on the page, and the placement of graphics and their relation to the text. It also controls the number of pages and whether these pages are double-sided or single-sided. You also use page layout controls to place ruling lines, headers, footers, and page numbers, and, in some programs, to define a master page or base page on which to model the rest of the publication.

Typographical controls determine the appearance of type, which can vary according to typeface, type style, and type size; these three factors make up a font. Type can be manipulated to create special effects, such as drop caps and reverse type. Controlling the spacing makes the text attractive and easy to read. Paragraphs can be flush left, centered, flush right, or justified. All text attributes can be set in user-defined paragraph tags.

Graphics controls start with the sizing and scaling of original images. Proportional sizing preserves the original ratio of height to width of an image, but this ratio can be altered for a special effect. Images can be cropped, and line art can be drawn on the page to make lines, boxes, ovals, and round-cornered boxes. Text wrap controls can flow text over an image or space it equally around the image or irregularly to conform to the image's shape. The appearance of the image can be adjusted for lightness, contrast, and screen pattern, but the original image is never changed by DTP software.

Desktop publishing software output is sent to disk, to a laser or other printer, or to a digital imagesetter. The product from an imagesetter or printer can be reproduced by photocopier or in a printshop. These and disk files can also be handled by service bureaus.

Following established design principles, DTP software can be used to create an unlimited variety of publications. Flyers, brochures, business cards, books—virtually anything printable—can be produced for a wide variety of uses.

KEY TERMS

bit-mapped font	landscape	sans serif
centered	leading	scaling
columns	margin	screen pattern
command-driven software	monospaced	serif
crop	outline font	single-sided
desktop publishing (DTP)	page layout	sizing
deviant text	page orientation	styles
dialog box	page size	tags
double-sided	point	text wrap
drop cap	portrait	tracking
facing pages	proportionally spaced	TrueType
flush left	ragged margins	typeface
flush right	raised cap	type size
interparagraph spacing	reverse type	type style
justified	rotated text	white space
kerning	ruling lines	WYSIWYG

REVIEW QUESTIONS

1. What is desktop publishing software? How is it used?
2. What is page layout? What is the function of a master page? List the elements involved in page setup.
3. Describe the common typographical controls available in most DTP applications.
4. What comprises a font? Define each component of a font. How do fonts differ?

5. How do DTP applications control the space between letters, words, and lines?
6. What are paragraph tags?
7. In what four ways can text be aligned relative to the margin?
8. Describe the graphics controls common to most DTP applications.
9. What special effects can you perform on text and graphics with DTP applications?
10. What are the different output options for a DTP publication?

8

Working with Spreadsheets

OBJECTIVES

After completing this chapter, you will be able to

- Define a spreadsheet.
- Identify the three types of data to be entered in a spreadsheet.
- Describe the uses of formulas and functions.
- Describe how to make and use a template.
- List spreadsheet applications for different professions.
- Know when to use absolute and relative references.
- Identify the typical graphics available through spreadsheets.
- Describe how to add worksheet data to a word processing file.
- Discuss the importance of the recalculation feature when asking *What if?* questions.

FOCUS

Just as word processors make working with words more efficient, spreadsheet programs make working with numbers more efficient (Figure 8-1). A spreadsheet is essentially an electronic ledger sheet that lets you enter, edit, and manipulate numeric data. A word processor allows you to enter text as you please in the document, but spreadsheets require that you place data in precise locations: cells that are created at the intersections of rows and columns (as on the grid of a paper ledger sheet). Spreadsheet data can be labels (names assigned to entries), numbers, or formulas.

Figure 8-1

Spreadsheets have become an almost universal business tool for financial analysis and forecasting.

SPREADSHEET FUNCTIONS

A spreadsheet's built-in mathematical formulas and functions manipulate the numbers for us: adding, subtracting, multiplying, dividing, finding square roots and averages, recalculating the answers when we change the values, and—for the statisticians among us—finding variances and deviations. These common functions make spreadsheets powerful tools for a very broad range of users (Figure 8-2).

- Keeping accurate financial records is agony for many people. The paper-and-pencil routine of listing and categorizing income and expenditures, then adding each column and comparing the results with the total income and outgo, can be more than frustrating (Figure 8-3a, p. 142). A single transposed number means finding the error (unfortunately, this part of the task will never change), erasing it, and manually recalculating the answer.

- Entering the data on an electronic spreadsheet allows you to recalculate the results automatically (Figure 8-3b, p. 142). It also allows you to ask *What if?*: What happens if you get a raise? If you need a new car? If you want to save for a vacation? Changing the values—net income, discretionary income, savings—on the spreadsheet will provide the answers quickly and accurately (Figure 8-4, p. 142), so you can evaluate the results of your changes and make decisions.

- School administrators and teachers—at all levels—use spreadsheets to track expenses, current and projected enrollment, income from taxes and fund-raisers, classroom attendance and performance records, test scores and grades. Here too, administrators can play *What if?*; for example, changing values on expected revenues to plan next year's budget more accurately.

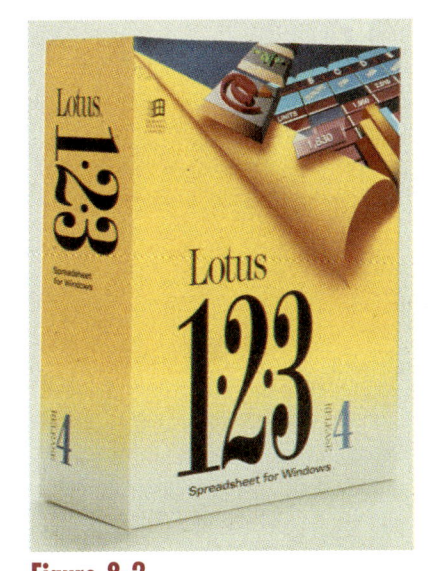

Figure 8-2

There are many different spreadsheet packages on the market, designed for DOS, Windows, the Macintosh, and other systems.

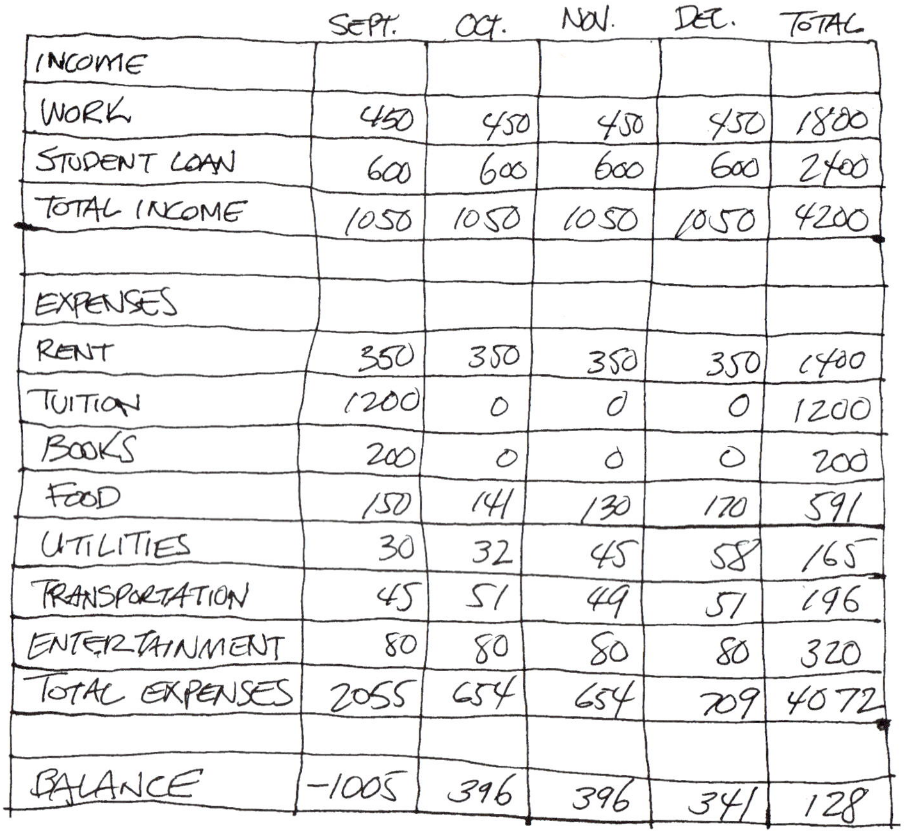

CHAPTER 8: Working with Spreadsheets

	SEPT.	OCT.	NOV.	DEC.	TOTAL
INCOME					
WORK	450	450	450	450	1800
STUDENT LOAN	600	600	600	600	2400
TOTAL INCOME	1050	1050	1050	1050	4200
EXPENSES					
RENT	350	350	350	350	1400
TUITION	1200	0	0	0	1200
BOOKS	200	0	0	0	200
FOOD	150	141	130	170	591
UTILITIES	30	32	45	58	165
TRANSPORTATION	45	51	49	51	196
ENTERTAINMENT	80	80	80	80	320
TOTAL EXPENSES	2055	654	654	709	4072
BALANCE	-1005	396	396	341	128

Figure 8-3a
Doing budgeting by hand is a messy, tedious task; it's easy to make mistakes that take a long time to correct.

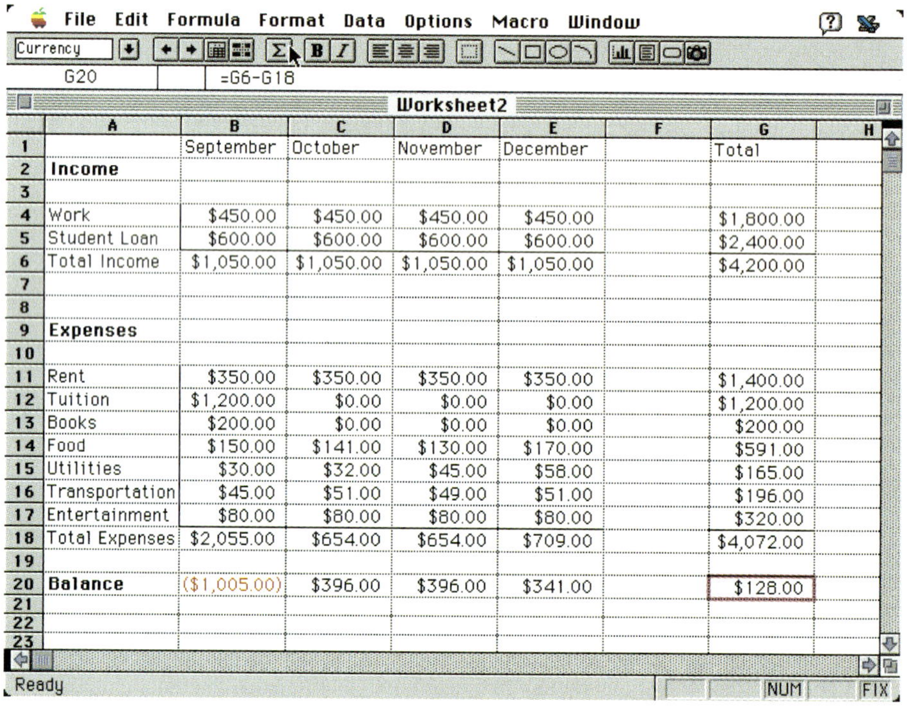

```
 File  Edit  Formula  Format  Data  Options  Macro  Window
Currency
 G20          =G6-G18
                              Worksheet2
    A          B          C          D          E       F       G          H
1              September  October    November   December         Total
2   Income
3
4   Work       $450.00    $450.00    $450.00    $450.00          $1,800.00
5   Student Loan $600.00  $600.00    $600.00    $600.00          $2,400.00
6   Total Income $1,050.00 $1,050.00 $1,050.00  $1,050.00        $4,200.00
7
8
9   Expenses
10
11  Rent       $350.00    $350.00    $350.00    $350.00          $1,400.00
12  Tuition    $1,200.00  $0.00      $0.00      $0.00            $1,200.00
13  Books      $200.00    $0.00      $0.00      $0.00            $200.00
14  Food       $150.00    $141.00    $130.00    $170.00          $591.00
15  Utilities  $30.00     $32.00     $45.00     $58.00           $165.00
16  Transportation $45.00 $51.00     $49.00     $51.00           $196.00
17  Entertainment $80.00  $80.00     $80.00     $80.00           $320.00
18  Total Expenses $2,055.00 $654.00 $654.00    $709.00          $4,072.00
19
20  Balance    ($1,005.00) $396.00   $396.00    $341.00          $128.00
21
22
23
Ready                                                       NUM   FIX
```

Figure 8-3b
Budgeting using the spreadsheet is far more neat, easy, and convenient: just type in data and formulas, and the program calculates everything for you.

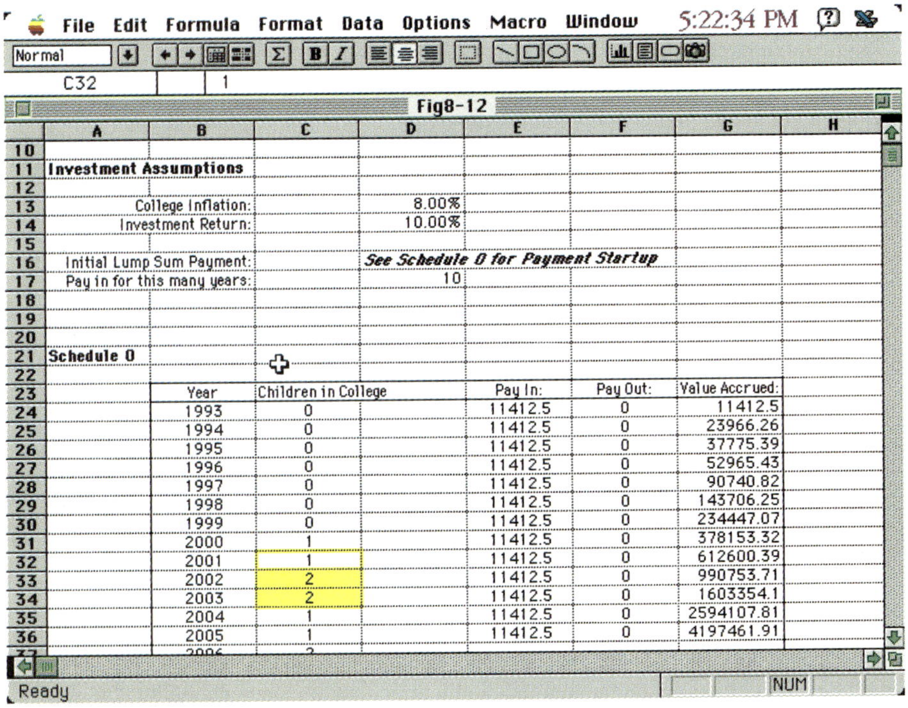

• CHAPTER 8: Working with Spreadsheets •

[Spreadsheet showing Investment Assumptions with Schedule 0 table containing Year, Children in College, Pay In, Pay Out, and Value Accrued columns for years 1993-2006]

Figure 8-4
To play *What if?*, just select an item you're interested in, and change its value to see what effect it will have on the spreadsheet's calculations.

- Sports statistics are often calculated to decimal points—and argued about heatedly (Figure 8-5). Batting averages, winning percentages, and other data can be updated and calculated much more conveniently than by hand, making it possible for teams to analyze player performance more completely; this affects trades and contract negotiations.

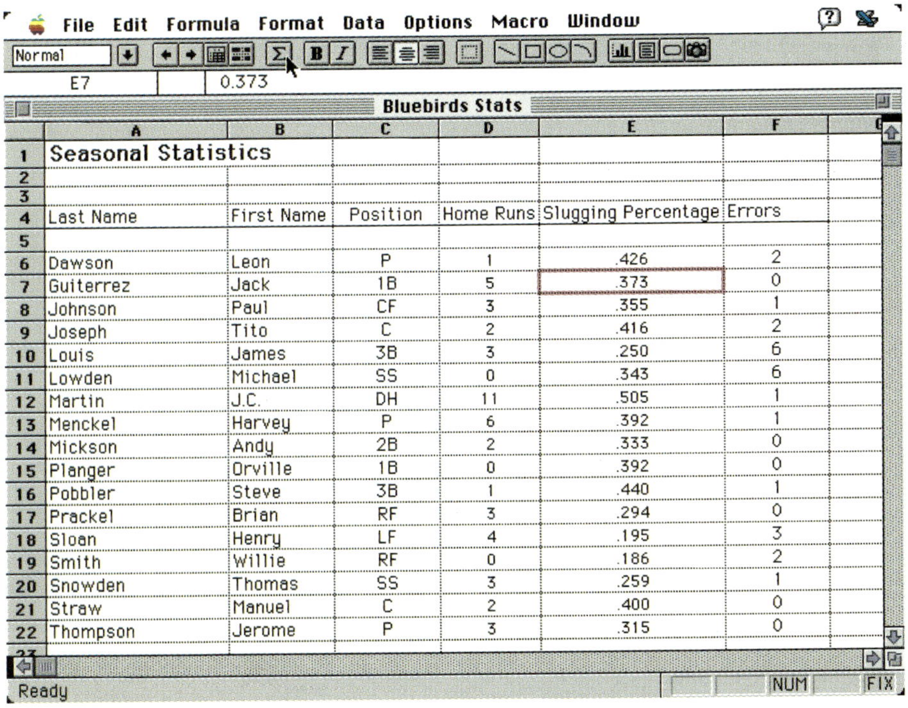

[Spreadsheet titled "Bluebirds Stats" showing Seasonal Statistics]

Last Name	First Name	Position	Home Runs	Slugging Percentage	Errors
Dawson	Leon	P	1	.426	2
Guiterrez	Jack	1B	5	.373	0
Johnson	Paul	CF	3	.355	1
Joseph	Tito	C	2	.416	2
Louis	James	3B	3	.250	6
Lowden	Michael	SS	0	.343	6
Martin	J.C.	DH	11	.505	1
Menckel	Harvey	P	6	.392	1
Mickson	Andy	2B	2	.333	0
Planger	Orville	1B	0	.392	0
Pobbler	Steve	3B	1	.440	1
Prackel	Brian	RF	3	.294	0
Sloan	Henry	LF	4	.195	3
Smith	Willie	RF	0	.186	2
Snowden	Thomas	SS	3	.259	1
Straw	Manuel	C	2	.400	0
Thompson	Jerome	P	3	.315	0

Figure 8-5
Professional and recreational sports teams have used spreadsheets to track player performance in fine detail in a wide variety of situations, affecting both strategy on the field and trades and negotiations off the field.

Home Spreadsheets

Some people have the mistaken idea that a home computer is really just a calculator in a box. Although a computer does crunch numbers (and crunch them very well), home versions of spreadsheet programs can harness this power in much more creative ways, turning a home computer into a real labor-saving device. Programs are available to do everything from balance your checkbook, calculate mortgage payments and car payments, and record travel expenses, to predicting changes in property values or what stock would be the best investment over a period of years. Some spreadsheet programs can also produce graphs, flowcharts, and other visual aids to help interpret information. And—oh yes—the computer can help figure out your taxes, too!

- Business and government uses of spreadsheets are almost endless. Most of these programs are specialized and highly sophisticated, offering functions and formulas beyond the needs of the average user. Accountants, for example, may use specific programs to track daily income and expenditures, to prepare quarterly and yearly tax returns, or to analyze the worth of a business. A marketing department can use spreadsheets to analyze current and potential sales; the personnel department can use spreadsheets to track the costs of personnel or health care; managers can use spreadsheets to develop budgets and track inventory.

  Government uses spreadsheets at almost all levels, from planning to taxing. City planners can project growth—and its costs—by asking *What if?*. What if the city grows by 5 percent over the next year? Over the next two years? Or five years? What would the projected costs be? How many new schools would be needed? How many service personnel would be needed? What, on the other hand, would happen if the city population decreased?

  Such projections are important to taxing authorities also. How much would a 0.1 percent tax increase on industry bring in? Would this amount be enough to cover the projected expenditures? What would happen if industry left the area? Would an increase in real estate taxes curtail sales? The spreadsheet allows planners and taxing authorities to write best-case/worst-case scenarios and project the monetary results.

  In these examples, use has been made not only of the routine mathematical functions but also of the spreadsheet's easy ability to recalculate results based on changes in the values entered—to play *What if?*.

- And, as mentioned earlier, spreadsheets can also be used to keep inventories: what's in the shop, the warehouse, the classroom, the office, the house, or the freezer (Figure 8-6).

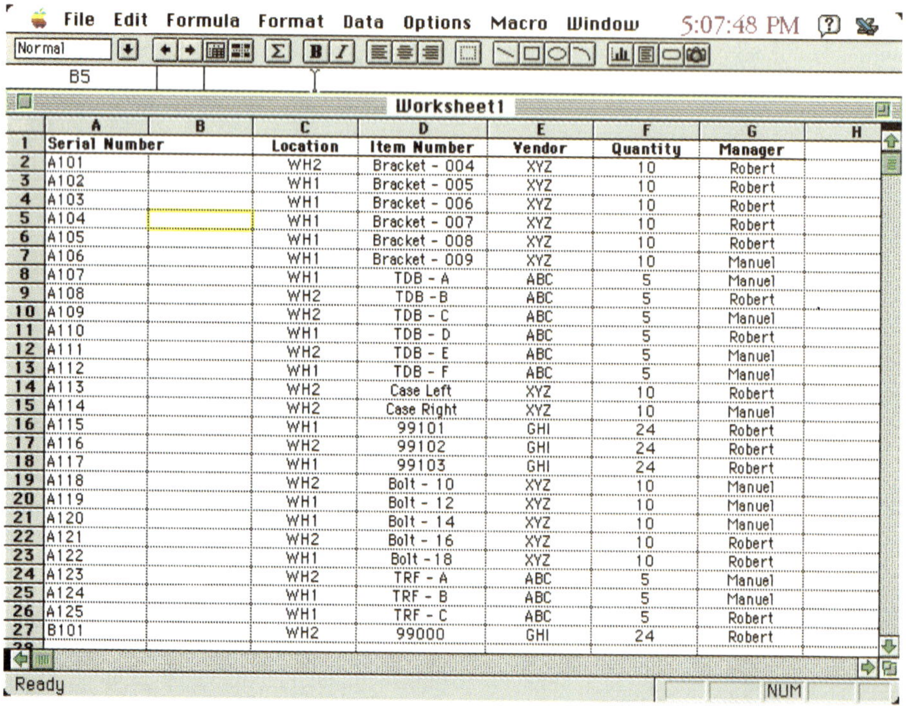

	A	B	C	D	E	F	G	H
1	Serial Number		Location	Item Number	Vendor	Quantity	Manager	
2	A101		WH2	Bracket - 004	XYZ	10	Robert	
3	A102		WH1	Bracket - 005	XYZ	10	Robert	
4	A103		WH1	Bracket - 006	XYZ	10	Robert	
5	A104		WH1	Bracket - 007	XYZ	10	Robert	
6	A105		WH1	Bracket - 008	XYZ	10	Robert	
7	A106		WH1	Bracket - 009	XYZ	10	Manuel	
8	A107		WH1	TDB - A	ABC	5	Manuel	
9	A108		WH2	TDB - B	ABC	5	Robert	
10	A109		WH2	TDB - C	ABC	5	Manuel	
11	A110		WH1	TDB - D	ABC	5	Robert	
12	A111		WH2	TDB - E	ABC	5	Manuel	
13	A112		WH1	TDB - F	ABC	5	Manuel	
14	A113		WH2	Case Left	XYZ	10	Robert	
15	A114		WH2	Case Right	XYZ	10	Manuel	
16	A115		WH1	99101	GHI	24	Robert	
17	A116		WH2	99102	GHI	24	Robert	
18	A117		WH1	99103	GHI	24	Robert	
19	A118		WH2	Bolt - 10	XYZ	10	Manuel	
20	A119		WH1	Bolt - 12	XYZ	10	Manuel	
21	A120		WH1	Bolt - 14	XYZ	10	Manuel	
22	A121		WH2	Bolt - 16	XYZ	10	Robert	
23	A122		WH1	Bolt -18	XYZ	10	Robert	
24	A123		WH2	TRF - A	ABC	5	Manuel	
25	A124		WH1	TRF - B	ABC	5	Manuel	
26	A125		WH1	TRF - C	ABC	5	Robert	
27	B101		WH2	99000	GHI	24	Robert	

Figure 8-6

Using color and type enhancements can make your worksheet more readable and useful; be careful, however, that you don't clutter the screen with too much formatting.

• **CHAPTER 8:** Working with Spreadsheets •   **145**

SETTING UP THE WORKSHEET

Whether it is called a *spreadsheet* or a *worksheet,* the basic concept is the same: a grid of **columns** (usually identified by letters) and **rows** (usually identified by numbers). To distinguish between a spreadsheet program and the spreadsheet on which the work is performed, we'll use the word **worksheet** throughout this chapter to denote the latter. Unlike the paper ledger sheet, the gridlines of an electronic worksheet are usually invisible (although some programs let you display them on screen and print them as well). Although programs differ in their specifics, the basic concepts, capabilities, commands, and terms are very similar.

- **The Cell.** The intersection of a row and column, the cell, is identified by the column letter and row number; for example, A1 (Figure 8-7). This is called a **cell address.** Sequential cells—for example, cells A3 through A10, or cells A4 through Z4—are a **range,** usually indicated by a colon or two dots, as in A3:A10 or A3..A10 and A4:Z4 or A4..Z4.

- **The Cursor.** The cursor indicates the cell in use, typically highlighting the entire cell. It is moved by the arrow keys, the Tab key, or (if the program supports it) a mouse. Many programs have a line at the top or bottom of the screen that indicates the cursor's location; this—or watching the cursor's movement carefully—helps prevent you from entering data in the wrong cell.

- **The Grid.** A worksheet can contain several hundred columns and several thousand rows—far more than can be shown on the screen, which can display only a small section of the work area at a time. The arrow keys, Tab, or mouse can move the cursor to the desired location, with the worksheet scrolling through the screen.

Community Spreadsheets

Big projects are always easier when you have a little help from your friends, and spreadsheets are no exception. By using computer networks and telephone connections, people in different locations can now work on the same spreadsheet at the same time—an ideal way for a community charity, for instance, to finalize a fund-raising drive. Without leaving home, workers can give immediate feedback to each other, fill in gaps of knowledge, comment on each other's work, and approve changes made. Just the thing for a cold, rainy night!

	A	B	C	D	E	F
1						
2		Sept.	Oct.	Nov.	Dec.	TOTAL
3						
4	INCOME					
5	Work	450	450	450	450	1800
6	Student Loan	600	600	600	600	2400
7	TOTAL INCOME	1050	1050	1050	1050	4200
8						
9	EXPENSES					
10	Rent	350	350	350	350	1400
11	Tuition	1200	0	0	0	1200
12	Books	200	0	0	0	200
13	Food	150	141	130	170	591
14	Utilities	30	32	45	58	165
15	Transportation	45	51	49	51	196
16	Entertainment	80	80	80	80	320
17	TOTAL EXPENSES	2055	654	654	709	4072
18						
19	BALANCE	1005	396	396	341	128

Figure 8-7

A typical spreadsheet screen. Note that columns are labeled with letters, rows with numbers. Any intersection of a column and row is called a cell; the highlighted cell is the cursor, where anything you type will be entered on the worksheet.

Talking Spreadsheets

It's late and you are working on a spreadsheet, when suddenly you realize there is an easier way to analyze all the data. The only problem is that it will take a long time to write a memo explaining your idea to your boss. No problem. A recently introduced computer program allows users the option of recording verbal remarks with their spreadsheets. By merely clicking on a cell, a second person can play back the verbal annotation. Obviously, this merging of voice and data technology could make working with spreadsheets a lot easier.

A blank worksheet has default column widths, generally nine characters. This space is often too narrow to display all the desired data—or it may be wider than necessary. In either case, the width can be easily adjusted, either for a single column or multiple columns at once, to accommodate the display of data. Most spreadsheets allow alignment of data within the cell—right, left, center, or along the decimal point.

In addition to adjusting the width of a column, you can specify the way you want the worksheet to appear. You can choose the format for numbers (discussed later), and you can indicate boldface or italics for both labels and values (Figure 8-8). These enhancements are particularly effective on a color screen, where the column might appear in red. Too much of a good thing however, will clutter both the screen and the eventual printout.

ENTERING DATA

Labels

Simply put, **labels** are the words used to name columns or rows or to explain or identify a formula or numeric entry (Table 8-1). A budget worksheet, for example, might categorize such expenses as Food, Medical, Entertainment, Auto, Debts, and so on. The text is entered by typing it; the program recognizes the letters as text.

The first column in the budget worksheet might include all the expense categories, with the months of the year entered across the page. Note that labels may contain numbers, such as dates, zip codes, or Social Security numbers, but, these numbers cannot be manipulated mathematically. A journal or ledger spreadsheet might include transaction dates, which are treated as text

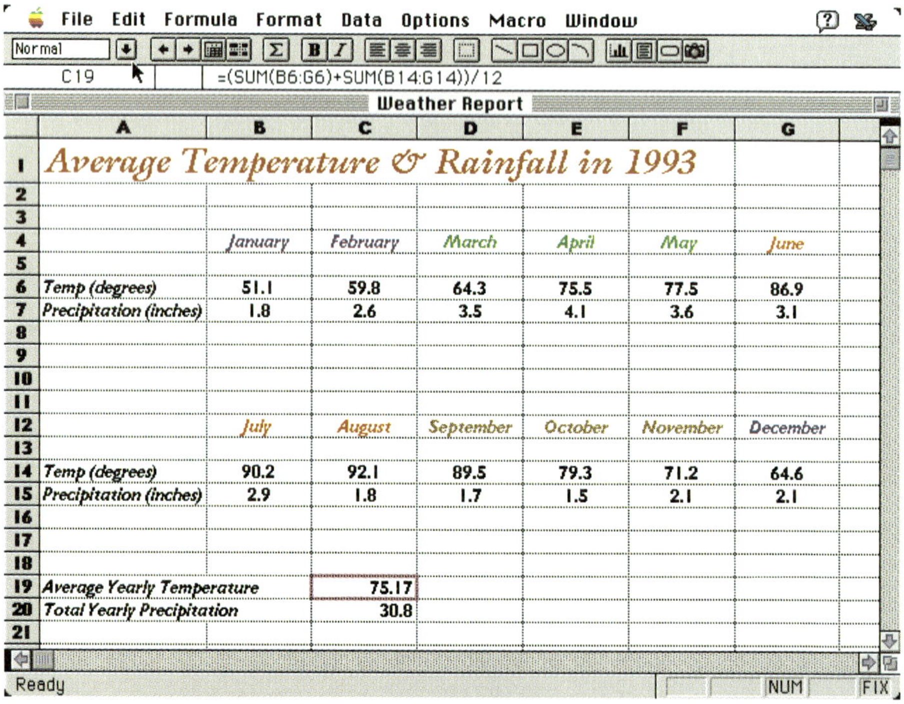

Figure 8-8
Using color and type enhancements can make your worksheet more readable and useful; be careful, however, that you don't clutter the screen with too much formatting.

by the program when a space or other character is entered first. Unless the program is told to treat the number as a label, entering 7/30 might produce .23 instead.

Values

Values are the numbers that are available for mathematical manipulation. A $150 car payment in cell E12 (the transaction date might be in cell A12, the bank's name in B12) can be added, subtracted, multiplied, or otherwise manipulated with other numbers.

Although the values are often dollars and cents, it is not necessary to enter these symbols. Most spreadsheets offer a choice of formats: scientific, percentage, currency, and so on, as well as the number of decimal places to be shown.

Formulas and Functions

Formulas are the means for manipulating the numeric values in the cells. Rather than use the numbers themselves, you can instruct the program to add, for example, the values in cells E4, E5, E6, and so on, through E15. As noted earlier, most spreadsheets assume that letters are labels and numbers are values. To let the program know you are using a formula, it is necessary to begin with a special symbol such as +, @, or = (these indicate that the entry will be a formula). The formula (Table 8-2a) might read

@E4+E5+E6+E7+E8+E9+E10+E11+E12+E13+E14+E15

Once entered, the formula automatically performs its operation on the numeric contents of the cells specified, no matter how the values are changed. This capability allows you to ask *What If?* and to see, for example, how an increase in the car payment to $178 would affect the total budget.

Functions are mathematical shortcuts that allow you to manipulate data—especially long strings of information—with very little effort (Table 8-2b). Even if you are willing to enter a long formula, most spreadsheets will not accept formulas longer than about 250 characters. The preceding formula can be rewritten using a range (E4:E15) and the SUM function: @SUM(E4:E15). It will total the values and display the result at the cursor position.

Note the use of parentheses in formulas. Just as we use parentheses to show the order in which to calculate figures with paper and pencil, so do spreadsheet programs. For example, (5 × 3) + 4 equals 19, while 5 × (3 + 4) equals 35.

Spreadsheets typically offer a number of other functions. @AVG (C12:C38) will average the values in cells C12 through C38; @SQRT(n) will find the

Table 8-1
Examples of Valid Labels and Values in Lotus 1-2-3

Labels	Values
Johnson	3,234
NAME:	−34
October	$1,352,345
Net Income	(3 * 150) + 50
R. Smith	.0075
Score 1	−89.6

Table 8-2a
Examples of Simple Spreadsheet Formulas

Formula	Explanation
A1+A2	The value of cell A1 added to the value of cell A2.
A1−A2	The value of cell A2 subtracted from the value of cell A1.
A2*B2	The value of cell A2 multiplied by the value of cell B2.
B1/A1	The value of cell B1 divided by the value of cell A1.
(A1+B1)/2	The sum of cells A1 and B1 divided by 2.
(A1−B1)*(A2−B2)	The difference of cells B1 and A1 multiplied by the difference of cells B2 and A2.

Table 8-2b
Common Functions in Lotus 1-2-3

Functions	Explanation
`@AVG (range)`	Calculates the average of a range of values
`@COUNT (range)`	Counts the number of filled cells in a range of values
`@MAX (range)`	Determines the largest of a range of values
`@SQRT (number)`	Calculates the square root of a number
`@SUM (range)`	Calculates the sum of a range of values
`@IF (condition, value, or formula)`	Chooses between two possible values or formulas based on results of test

positive square root of (n); @RAND generates a random number between 0 and 1. Standard deviations can be found with @STD and population variances with @VAR.

RANGES IN FORMULAS AND FUNCTIONS

Ranges are extremely useful in formulas and functions. A range can represent all or part of any column or row, or several adjacent columns or rows. In fact, any rectangular section of cells in a spreadsheet can be described as a range or block. This gives you great convenience and flexibility when composing formulas and using functions. Most spreadsheet programs also let you name a range of cells. The row in which the budget spreadsheet calculates monthly totals can be specified (as B22:M22, for example) and named Totals. Then you can use the names instead of the cell designations when writing formulas. This makes the formulas far more readable. It is especially useful if you're modifying a spreadsheet you created long ago, and you're trying to remember what all those formulas you created back then mean.

In many spreadsheet programs, giving a name to a range of cells also allows you to link that range to another worksheet, thereby automatically transferring the data. For example, if you're the statistician for your local softball or Little League team, you can keep individual worksheets for each player's statistics, and name the range of cells that represents that player's statistical totals. By linking all these named ranges to the master sheet that includes all the players, you can print totals for the team and all the players on one sheet. These named ranges can be dynamically linked; that is, every time the master sheet is opened, it retrieves updated information from the linked ranges in all the other worksheets, automatically keeping your master sheet information current. These techniques of naming and linking ranges apply to many other fields as well.

MANIPULATING DATA
Editing

Changing the contents of a cell before pressing the Enter key is as simple as editing with a word processor. Use the Delete or Backspace key to erase the numbers or letters, type in the correct data, and press the Enter key. Edit existing data by moving the cursor to the cell and retyping the information. Many spreadsheets let you edit part of a cell (there may be a function key that allows this) rather than making you retype the contents completely.

Copying and Moving

The value in cell B26 may also be needed in cell XX26; rather than retype it, you can copy the value and enter it where desired. Using the spreadsheet's ability to copy single or multiple cells lets you move all or part of the data to another area or another worksheet (Figure 8-9). Once the headings for a budget worksheet have been entered, for example, you can copy the entire row of labels to the worksheet for the next month. You can copy formulas as well: when the expenditures for the month have been totaled (using @SUM, for example) in one column, you can copy the formula to each of the columns for the other months. Also, you can move the data and formulas, leaving the original cells blank.

An important consideration in copying formulas from one location to another is that of **absolute reference** or **relative reference.** For example, copying cell A44 containing the formula @SUM(A3:A43) to cell B44 as an absolute (unchanging) reference causes B44 to display the sum of cells A3 through A43. This can be a problem if the sum of cells B3 through B43 is desired; in this case, copy the formula as a relative (variable) reference, which will then change the formula to fit the data in the new column, @SUM(B3:B43). Note that relative references are assumed when copying formulas. To use an absolute formula, you generally have to specify that with a symbol; for example, @SUM($A3:$A43) instead of @SUM(A3:A43).

Inserting and Deleting Rows and Columns. Most spreadsheets allow you to add columns and rows to an existing worksheet. Although some programs automatically adjust the formulas to reflect the change, others may require the insertion of values into specific cells. Columns and rows can also be deleted; again, formulas are often adjusted automatically. Beware when deleting columns or rows, however. Deleting a column or row in the middle of a range won't damage

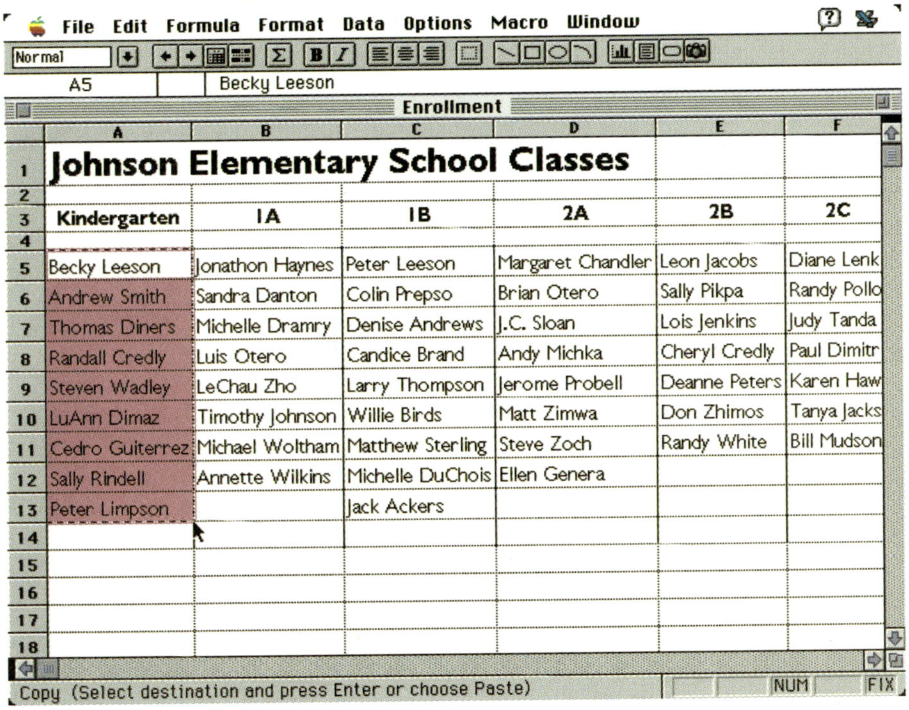

	A	B	C	D	E	F
1	Johnson Elementary School Classes					
2						
3	Kindergarten	1A	1B	2A	2B	2C
4						
5	Becky Leeson	Jonathon Haynes	Peter Leeson	Margaret Chandler	Leon Jacobs	Diane Lenk
6	Andrew Smith	Sandra Danton	Colin Prepso	Brian Otero	Sally Pikpa	Randy Pollo
7	Thomas Diners	Michelle Dramry	Denise Andrews	J.C. Sloan	Lois Jenkins	Judy Tanda
8	Randall Credly	Luis Otero	Candice Brand	Andy Michka	Cheryl Credly	Paul Dimitr
9	Steven Wadley	LeChau Zho	Larry Thompson	Jerome Probell	Deanne Peters	Karen Haw
10	LuAnn Dimaz	Timothy Johnson	Willie Birds	Matt Zimwa	Don Zhimos	Tanya Jacks
11	Cedro Guiterrez	Michael Woltham	Matthew Sterling	Steve Zoch	Randy White	Bill Mudson
12	Sally Rindell	Annette Wilkins	Michelle DuChois	Ellen Genera		
13	Peter Limpson		Jack Ackers			
14						
15						
16						
17						
18						

Figure 8-9
By highlighting the cells you want and using the Copy command, you can copy an entire row of cells.

a formula, but if you delete data specifically used in a formula you will have to adjust the formula yourself—or the spreadsheet won't calculate properly.

Recalculating

Automatic **recalculation** is a time-saver for the typical spreadsheet user: insert a new value in a cell and watch all the totals change. Large worksheets—those with hundreds of formulas that require multiple calculations—are another story. Adding new values may require that the program recalculate every one of those hundred formulas. This process can take several seconds—or several minutes—and will be repeated for each new value.

Manual recalculation, which means you control when the worksheet will be recalculated, can save time. Many spreadsheets offer this option, allowing you to make all the necessary value changes and then recalculate the entire worksheet at one time.

Determining the order of recalculation—that is, which formula is calculated first—is another choice offered by most spreadsheets. The typical choices are by column, by row, or what is called *natural calculation.*

The column-first method calculates the contents of columns before rows; the row-first method calculates rows first. Problems arise when a formula at the top of a column or the beginning of a row requires the results of a formula at the bottom of the column or the end of the row. Recalculating the top or beginning formula first will cause an error: the information on which it depends has not yet been calculated. Natural calculation (often the default setting) checks each formula in the worksheet to determine whether it requires information from another formula; if it does, the necessary formula is calculated first.

Sorting

A standard spreadsheet capability is the **sorting** of information numerically or alphabetically. Suppose you have a worksheet that lists your clients in one

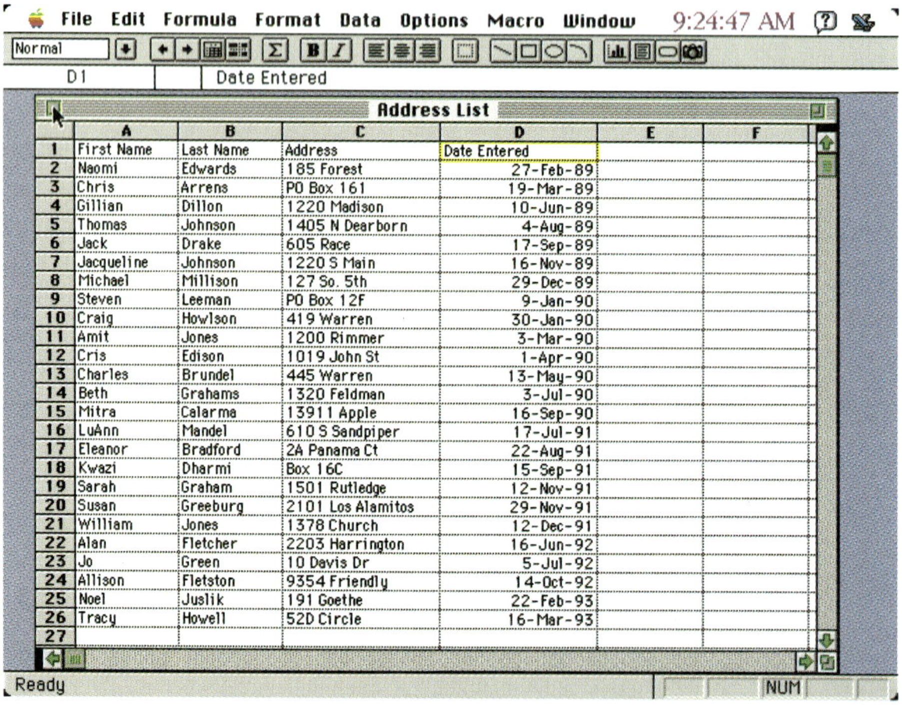

	A	B	C	D	E	F
1	First Name	Last Name	Address	Date Entered		
2	Naomi	Edwards	185 Forest	27-Feb-89		
3	Chris	Arrens	PO Box 161	19-Mar-89		
4	Gillian	Dillon	1220 Madison	10-Jun-89		
5	Thomas	Johnson	1405 N Dearborn	4-Aug-89		
6	Jack	Drake	605 Race	17-Sep-89		
7	Jacqueline	Johnson	1220 S Main	16-Nov-89		
8	Michael	Millison	127 So. 5th	29-Dec-89		
9	Steven	Leeman	PO Box 12F	9-Jan-90		
10	Craig	Howlson	419 Warren	30-Jan-90		
11	Amit	Jones	1200 Rimmer	3-Mar-90		
12	Cris	Edison	1019 John St	1-Apr-90		
13	Charles	Brundel	445 Warren	13-May-90		
14	Beth	Grahams	1320 Feldman	3-Jul-90		
15	Mitra	Calarma	13911 Apple	16-Sep-90		
16	LuAnn	Mandel	610 S Sandpiper	17-Jul-91		
17	Eleanor	Bradford	2A Panama Ct	22-Aug-91		
18	Kwazi	Dharmi	Box 16C	15-Sep-91		
19	Sarah	Graham	1501 Rutledge	12-Nov-91		
20	Susan	Greeburg	2101 Los Alamitos	29-Nov-91		
21	William	Jones	1378 Church	12-Dec-91		
22	Alan	Fletcher	2203 Harrington	16-Jun-92		
23	Jo	Green	10 Davis Dr	5-Jul-92		
24	Allison	Fletston	9354 Friendly	14-Oct-92		
25	Noel	Juslik	191 Goethe	22-Feb-93		
26	Tracy	Howell	52D Circle	16-Mar-93		
27						

Figure 8-10a
A spreadsheet's sorting capabilities are flexible. Here, a spreadsheet is sorted by date.

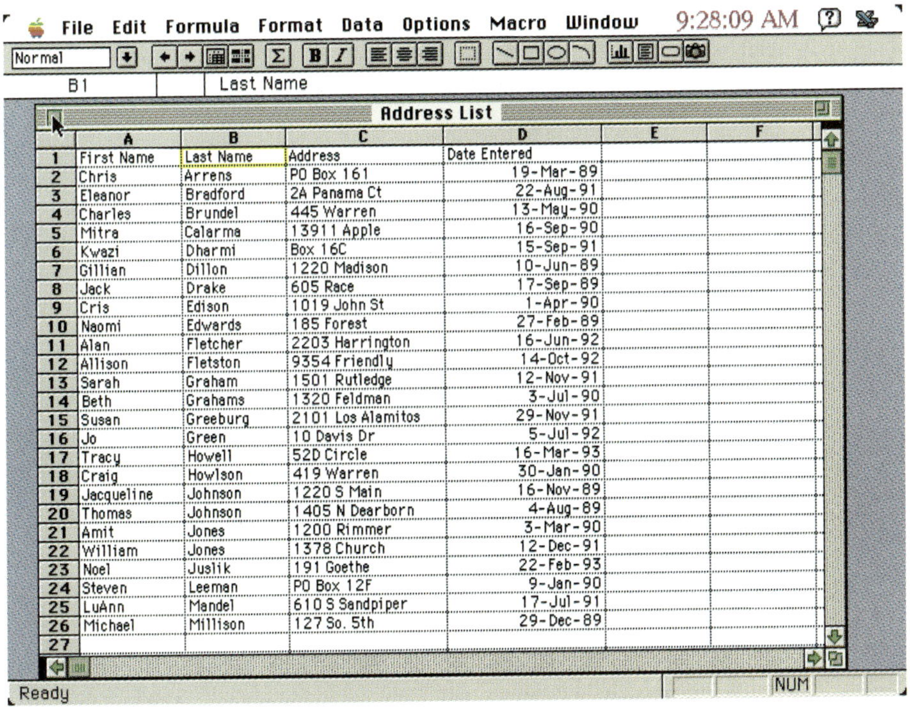

CHAPTER 8: Working with Spreadsheets

Figure 8-10b
You can take the same spreadsheet and sort it according to last name instead.

column, the items each client purchased in a second column, the amount billed in the third, and the purchase date in the fourth. You can sort this information by client name, by item name or number (this number would be entered as a label), by the dollar amount, or by the date(s) (Figure 8-10a, b).

SPECIAL FUNCTIONS

Graphs

Let us suppose the worksheet has been sorted, and the information, although complete, is very dull. Or perhaps there is so much that it is confusing. The graphics capability of many spreadsheets lets you display the data as a **graph:** a bar graph, a line graph, a pie chart, and so on. Creating a graph or chart is often as simple as choosing the data to display and the type of graph or chart, and entering the x- and y-axes (Figure 8-11, p. 152). The process is repeated for each group of cells to be displayed, and the graph can usually be enhanced with x and y labels, headlines, captions, legends, and distinguishing patterns (for example, cross-hatched, striped, or solid).

Displaying the completed graph on the screen allows it to be previewed and changed as necessary. It can be printed (depending on the capabilities of the printer) and saved to file for later use—possibly as a slide or viewgraph.

Macros

Macros are predefined sequences of commands and keystrokes. Spreadsheet users—like word processor users—frequently use the same sequence of commands repetitively. Rather than type a long string of instructions every time you need to do something, you can write them once, define them as a macro, and use them over and over. Invoke the macro function, enter the desired sequence of commands, choose the key or keys that will recall the sequence, and

Figure 8-11
Creating a graph or chart in most spreadsheets is as simple as selecting the data you wish to use and clicking on the type of graph or chart you want.

Spreadsheet Graphics

Traditional spreadsheets can look intimidating with all those rows and columns of numbers. A new program called Walden can help the computer deal with this information in a more intuitive way—which also, incidentally, makes manipulating the data easier and faster. This is accomplished by building a spreadsheet that is completely graphical. Data is moved by pointing and clicking the mouse at various icons and tool bars. The main icon is an InfoBox. Objects such as graphs and forms are organized in Books or Documents with their related data so that materials can be grouped together. Users can even create scripts that will record a series of commands that are performed repeatedly.

save the macro (Figure 8-12). Once stored in the program library, the macro can be called up again as needed with a one- or two-keystroke command. This saves time and makes your spreadsheet use more efficient.

Templates

What a macro is to a sequence of commands, a **template** is to a frequently used worksheet. Using the template function, you can create a basic design with labels, functions, formulas, and other constant information. Once saved,

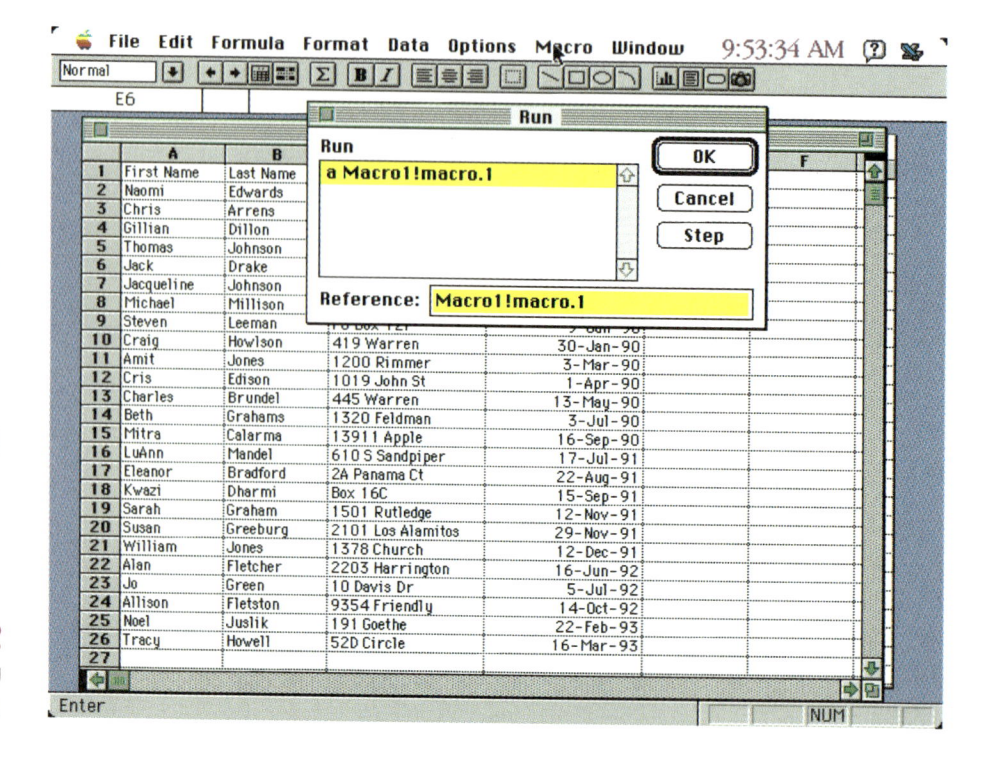

Figure 8-12
Microsoft Excel's menu commands allow you to record and run macros easily.

HISTORY

VisiCalc

On May 11, 1979, the first commercial program designed for an inexperienced user on a personal computer was introduced at the West Coast Computer Fair. Called VisiCalc (short for *visual calculator*), the program was not only the first spreadsheet program for microcomputers, it made Apple II *the* computer of choice for American business. This event also widely credited with finally turning the microcomputer from a hobbyist's plaything into a business machine.

One reason VisiCalc was so successful was that it provided immediate, significant benefits to business users, allowing them to ask "What if?" kinds of questions about a project, and then calculating the answers quickly: What if the cost of labor goes up 5 percent? What if we can get the material more cheaply? What will happen to profits?

It is not surprising that VisiCalc provided those tools, since it was developed by a 26-year-old student at Harvard Business School named Dan Bricklin. Always fascinated by computers and programming, Bricklin and some friends had once broken into their high school computer room, dismantled the door, and persuaded a local locksmith to make them keys.

After graduating from MIT, Bricklin had worked as a programmer for Digital Equipment Corporation, but he thought he would soon be out of a job because writing computer programs was becoming so simple "anyone could do it." So he entered business school in 1977.

One of Bricklin's professors mentioned that most corporations were still doing financial planning on blackboards, which occasionally stretched for room after room, each blackboard segmented in rows and columns, many of which were interconnected. As the number in one cell changed, all related cells had to have their numbers changed accordingly, and financial planners lived in fear that in the process of erasing and recalculating their numbers by hand, a cell might be overlooked.

Intrigued, over a weekend Bricklin pieced together a simple spreadsheet program in BASIC. It was slow and small, but it worked.

To help him write the code, Bricklin turned to a friend from MIT, Bob Frankston. On the advice of a professor, the two entrepreneurs then approached a recent Harvard Business School graduate named Dan Fylstra about marketing their program. Fylstra was selling application software—primarily a microcomputer chess program—out of his back bedroom. He agreed to handle their program and loaned them an Apple II for their work. Since there was no precedent for what later became known as software publishing, the three entrepreneurs came up with a royalty rate for Bricklin and Frankston of between 37.5 and 50 percent depending on the type of sale. (Fifteen percent is usual today.) Thanks to this generous agreement, VisiCalc made its inventors nearly $12 million in 1983 alone.

Bricklin and Frankston formed a company called Software Arts and set up in a refurbished chocolate factory in a Boston suburb. VisiCalc finally hit the market in October 1979, priced at $100.

Sales were slow at first. But soon middle managers who were tired of waiting for time on their company's computer—or of waiting six months for the computer department to generate a report—caught on to what a life saver the program could be. The $3,000 necessary for an Apple II (the only computer on which VisiCalc would run at the time) could be scrounged from petty cash, bypassing the data-processing managers who sneered at microcomputers. In 1979 Apple sold about 50,000 machines. With the success of VisiCalc, the next year Apple sold 125,000. ■

Spreadsheet Movies

Working with a spreadsheet program can be intimidating, especially for a first-time user. But help is on the way, thanks to multimedia. A CD-ROM device now adds sound and images to illustrate basic spreadsheet functions. Need help figuring out how to go from one column to the next? Just click on "help" and an animated film example shows the way.

the template can be used with different sets of values and by different users. A real estate firm may design a worksheet for customer analysis: the client's name, type of house wanted, desired price range, down payment available, and so on.

This template can be used by every agent in the firm—with one important warning. The original should be named appropriately—for example, "Analysis," and each data-filled worksheet created from it should be saved and named separately. Calling the new worksheet "Jones1" or "Farber2" will prevent overwriting the template on the disk—but you *did* save a copy of the template on a backup disk, didn't you?

SAVE, SAVE, SAVE

Just as a power failure can erase all your word processing or graphics data, so can it wipe out your worksheet and all the data on it. And, as in the example just given, saving a new worksheet under an old filename destroys the original data.

Save your work frequently; if you are updating a file, save it under the same name. If you need both the original and the new files, save the new one under a different name, changing "Farber2" to "Farber3," for example. At the end of the working session, back up the file and store the backup disk away from the original.

Many spreadsheet programs allow files to be written to disk (saved) in either ASCII or a generic word processing format. This lets you add the worksheet data to a word processing file where it can be edited and formatted as text. Saving the worksheet in this way does not affect the worksheet itself, which should then be saved in the regular manner.

It is also sometimes possible to import data from other spreadsheets, database programs, or word processors. Shell programs make this process particularly easy.

PRINTING THE WORKSHEET

Most spreadsheets offer a range of printing options; some, such as horizontal (or sideways) printing, depend on the capabilities of the printer (Figure 8-13).

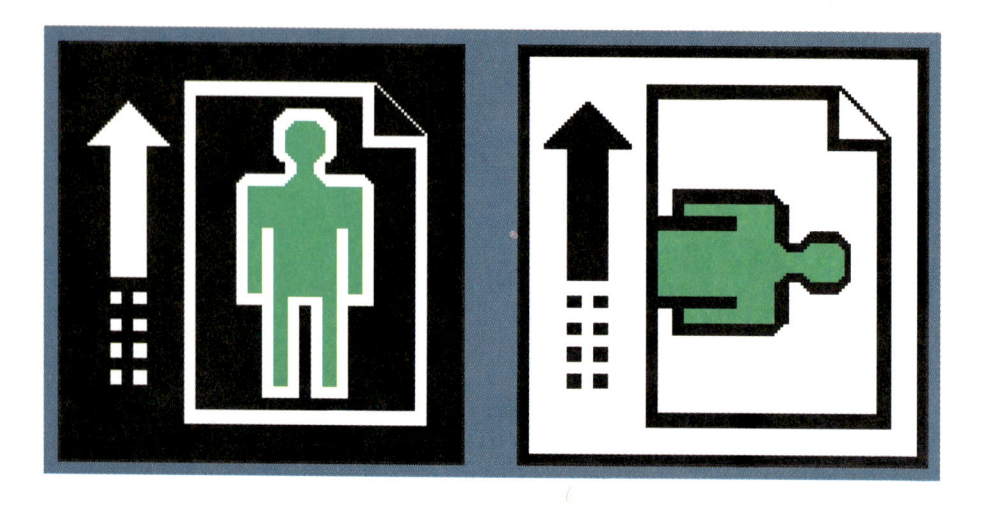

Figure 8-13
Worksheets can be printed in either portrait (vertical) or landscape (sideways) format.

Generally, users can choose the default settings or change them to suit the content. The **default settings** are typically for standard 8-1/2-by-11-inch paper and include top, bottom, and side margins; type size and style; headers; and page numbering.

With most programs, each of these settings can be changed to accommodate more or fewer columns, to compress more lines onto the page, to format the page so that it more closely fits in with those produced by the word processor, to change the type style and size. Unless you have a color printer, the aqua italics and fuchsia boldface that distinguished the worksheet on the screen will translate to italic (or underlined) and simple boldface type.

And remember to save your work first. In some circumstances, a printer error can cause your computer to malfunction, and any unsaved work will be lost.

SUMMARY

A spreadsheet program is essentially an electronic ledger sheet that performs mathematical manipulations on numeric information. Its ability to perform complex operations quickly and accurately makes it an ideal tool for accountants, government agencies, schools, businesses, industry—in short, anyone who must work with numbers. Teachers can keep classroom attendance and performance records; sports fans can record scores and batting averages; city planners and taxing authorities can project growth and revenues; business users can track inventory, personnel, the customer base, and so on.

Like a paper ledger sheet, the worksheet organizes data by row and column, forming cells into which labels, values, or formulas are placed. The data is manipulated by functions and formulas, providing prompt answers to complex operations. The program's recalculating ability allows users to ask *What If?* questions about changes in income, expenditures, and growth.

Macros, templates, built-in functions, and graphics capabilities add to the usefulness of most spreadsheets. Although spreadsheets vary in complexity, they provide the capability to enter, edit, and manipulate data—from basic arithmetic functions to the highly sophisticated offerings designed for the professional user.

KEY TERMS

@ sign	default settings	relative reference
+ sign	formula	row
= sign	function	sorting
absolute reference	graph	template
cell	label	values
cell address	range	what if?
column	recalculation	worksheet

REVIEW QUESTIONS

1. Define a cell.
2. What are the three types of data that can be placed in a cell?

3. Differentiate between absolute and relative reference.
4. Define a template.
5. How does the spreadsheet cursor move?
6. List three typical spreadsheet users.
7. How should you enter a formula?
8. How should you enter text?
9. How should you enter numeric data?
10. How would you add the values in cells A43 through A89?
11. Why is the order of recalculation important?
12. How often should you save your work?
13. What are the typical graphs available though the spreadsheet program?
14. What is the first step to take when you enter data?
15. What is the purpose of a label?

9

Working with Databases

OBJECTIVES

After completing this chapter, you will be able to

- Identify some major uses of database software.
- Differentiate database software from other types of application software.
- Identify the components of a database.
- Identify four common data types.
- Describe the role of planning in creating a database.
- Differentiate between indexing and sorting.
- Describe a data query.
- Describe the basic processes of the structured query language (SQL).
- Identify the six major types of database organization.

FOCUS

Before the advent of the computer, maintaining large collections of data was, at best, awkward. People stuffed documents into paper folders, stuffed the documents into file cabinets, stacked the file cabinets and stuffed them into a room—and then couldn't find the information they needed. The Office of the Registrar at any college was a good example: When a student enrolled, his or her name, address, and other pertinent data were typed or written on a form that was inserted into a file folder. Each semester, course information was added to the folder; at the end of the semester, the folder was manually pulled from the file drawer and grade information was entered. The grade-point average was calculated and entered, the information was manually entered on the transcript (possibly several days or weeks later), and the folder was put away—until the next semester (Figure 9-1). Mistakes were common. Folders were easy to misfile, and a graduate student applying for an assistantship might wait forever if her application went into the wrong folder or file drawer.

Computers—and computerized databases—have solved many of those problems. Mistakes can still be made, but the ease of both entry and access and the ability to scan many files (for that elusive assistantship, for example) can provide correct data almost instantly. The electronic database cannot really replace paper and pencil (and the hand-held calculator), but it can be used to compile and calculate and generate reports on a very wide range of topics with a few keystrokes. Database software allows the search committee to find and list the grade-point averages of all math majors or to locate all students who entered as sophomores or who have made the dean's list more than three times. And it can do these tasks in minutes rather than hours or days.

ELECTRONIC DATABASES

Word processors store primarily text; spreadsheets store primarily numbers. **Database software** can store virtually any form of data—documents from a word processor, mailing lists, accounting information, personnel records, salary schedules, Social Security numbers, places of birth, credit histories, military service records, high school and college grades, and political party affiliations (Figure 9-2). Anyone who needs to store and use large amounts of data will find database software useful.

Law Enforcement Databases

Police departments keep track of outstanding local warrants, stolen cars, criminal records, and missing persons. A police officer who stops someone for a traffic violation enters that person's name directly into a database or calls it in to police headquarters where a dispatcher checks the name against the police database (Figure 9-3, p. 160). Within a few seconds, the information is reported back to the police officer. Many police departments also have access to national law enforcement databases to help identify and locate criminals and missing persons throughout the country.

General Business Databases

The number of business database applications is almost endless, from customer data, research and development, product ideas, and marketing results to order entry and corporate personnel directories.

One typical use of a customer database is the creation of mailing lists. If you purchase a set of golf clubs at a sporting goods store, data about you and your purchase is entered into a customer database. The sporting goods store can then notify you when golf shoes or shirts go on sale.

Businesses also develop market research data with database software. A list of items purchased can help identify which products are selling faster, which need to be removed from inventory, and which need to go on sale. Databases can be used to identify market trends and help businesses make better decisions.

Government Databases

Government agencies collect and store data on individual citizens. The IRS keeps data on salaries paid by employers. Individual tax returns can be checked against these records to show whether people are claiming all their earnings. The FBI database maintains information about crimes and criminals. In investigating a crime, the FBI can compare aspects of the crime with details about other crimes stored in the database, and can generate a profile of the perpetrator as well as a list of suspects.

Bank Databases

Banks store data about customers' checking accounts, savings accounts, indebtedness, and credit history. If a customer requests a loan, the bank can use this information to help determine the likelihood of repayment. Bank

Figure 9-1
Traditional methods of filing can be overwhelming when trying to maintain a large database. Just finding a file amid all the folders, drawers, and cabinets is a significant task, and maintaining many different individual files requires a tremendous amount of effort.

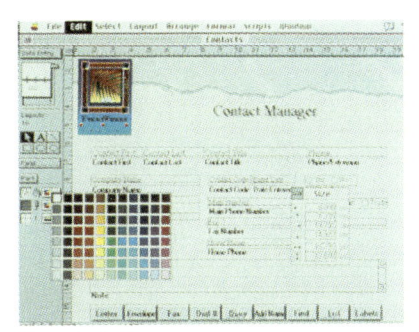

Figure 9-2
The database programs available for microcomputers can eliminate the need for an endless variety of printed records.

Figure 9-3
Law enforcement agencies make extensive use of databases for criminal records, car registration, and existing warrants.

examiners use databases to locate illegal loans, fraud, embezzlement, and unethical banking practices.

Home Databases

Students can use database software on their home computers to store and access research notes for assignments, from term papers to dissertations. A home database can contain phone numbers and addresses of friends and relatives. Because additions and changes are simple to make, the directory can easily be kept current. Using one field to identify persons who should receive Christmas cards, it is easy to produce an accurate and current Christmas card list.

Database software is useful for even the simple organization of tape and album collections, books, travel logs, and lists of household goods for insurance.

Communications with Databases

Through communications links, users at one location can access a computer and database at another location. For example, it is possible to connect a home computer to a database containing current airline flight schedules and prices. A bank loan officer can use the bank's computer to access a credit bureau's database to determine whether the bank should lend an applicant money. And the credit bureau's computer can receive data on the bank's credit customers. Although data transferred in the credit bureau's database is often shared with other banks or credit-giving organizations, federal regulations offer some protection against unauthorized access to these records (see the discussion on privacy later in this book).

DATABASE DESIGN

Databases have three levels of organization: files, records, and fields (Figure 9-4).

Figure 9-4
When viewed in list format, a typical database file looks like a table, with each record occupying a row, and field names listed across the top; each column, then, represents a field, and the cells (like those in a spreadsheet) contain data items. This format works best with relational and flat-file databases.

Last Name	First Name	City	State	ZIP
Rogers	Mark	San Francisco	CA	94914
Seaver	Laura	Baton Rouge	LA	34169
James	Frances	Tumwater	WA	74761
Rhodes	Joe	New York	NY	65165
Stone	Kerry	Miami	FL	77137
Towers	Alan	Tempe	AZ	87842

Files

A **file** is similar to a physical file cabinet; it consists of a group of records. For example, the university's student history file contains each student's academic record. A student file contains each student's personal record, including name, address, and date of birth; date of enrollment; courses taken; and so on. A course file contains a record of each course that the university offers.

Records

A **record** is similar to a paper file folder containing one student's data. A record stores a group of data relating to a single specification such as a person, place, or thing; each item is stored in a separate field.

Fields

Each **field** in a record stores specific data. For example, each student's record in the university's student file contains a name field, an address field, and an identifier field (a unique name or number). Each field is further assigned a field type, field name, and field size.

A **field name** describes the field; for example, LASTNAME. The name typically can consist of a limited number of characters, including digits and underlines, and must start with a character.

The **field type** tells the computer whether the field data is to be manipulated mathematically, sorted alphabetically, compared to other dates, or used for making IF-THEN comparisons. Field types are numeric, alphanumeric, logical, or date (Figure 9-5).

- **Alphanumeric data** includes any alphabetical character, number, or symbol entered from a keyboard. The numbers in this case are treated as descriptive characters rather than those with a mathematical quality. That is, they cannot be added, subtracted, or subjected to any other mathematical operation. For example, we would classify zip codes, driver's license numbers, Social Security numbers, and credit card numbers

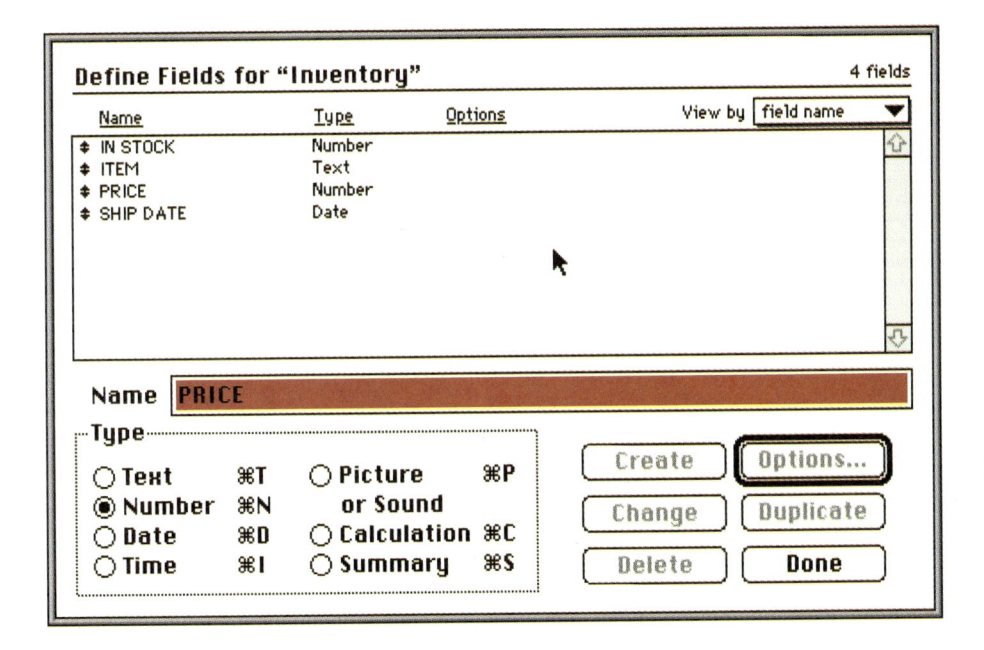

The Résumé Bank/Database

All job-seekers wonder if anyone really reads their résumé, but frustrations run high on both sides of the interviewing process. One of the nation's largest companies, Johnson & Johnson, is using computer software to help cope with the problem. "We know we have a gold mine of people out there," says Catherine King, Johnson & Johnson's manager of employment, "but finding the right person has been darn near impossible." Now a computer program that reads and files résumés has created an in-house database of prospective employees. Candidates are called up by words used on their résumés that match the description of the job being filled. Another side of the process is résumé job banks, such as Banc One Corporation in Columbus, Ohio, which has an employment kiosk where people can fill out applications on screen. Employment manager Greg Burk points out, "Every time a search is done, everyone in the database is considered equally and consistently based on their qualifications. Even though you apply for a specific job, you might be considered for vice president strictly based on what you say your skills are."

Figure 9-5

The fields ITEM, PRICE, SHIP_DATE, and IN_STOCK each hold different types of data items, such as alphanumeric text, numbers, or dates.

Tracking Clients

Every salesman knows how vital it is to keep in contact with clients. Thanks to computer database programs, nothing could be easier. No more frantic racking of the brain to remember the names of the client's children, or what baseball team he or she prefers. It's all in the computer. If Donald Trump sells a casino to a new customer, one Madaas Mussuh, he could enter the following information into his client database. Interests: casinos, racehorses, almond M&Ms. Also fond of toy poodles and late-17th-century artwork. May be looking for a condo in Miami for next Spring. Financial: Casino negotiated at 450. Final deal on 9/26. Last contact: 8/3/92. Trump could set up any categories he pleased and add new information to the existing file on Madaas. To call up the information, he could enter the date they last spoke, the casino name, or the name Mussuh. By pressing autodial, the computer could even dial the phone for him. In addition, to mail out his Christmas letter, Trump could have the database fill in the blanks with each client's name and address.

as alphanumeric because we do not add or subtract them. They can, however, be sorted alphabetically or numerically.

- **Numeric data** are numbers used in mathematical operations. Numbers in an alphanumeric field cannot be subjected to mathematical operations; numbers in the numeric field can. For example, a student's grade is entered as a number in a numeric field so that the grade-point average can be calculated.

- **Logical data** entries identify one of two alternatives—true or false (yes or no). Logical data are used to make IF-THEN comparisons for decision making. For example, a logical field named CHRISTMAS may contain a Y(yes) or an N(no). The user can generate a Christmas card list based on CHRISTMAS fields containing a Y. If a Y is in the CHRISTMAS field, then send a Christmas card.

- A **date field** indicates to the software that the numbers used are a date. This lets the software make comparisons and calculations based on the occurence of an event. It can compare a target date with the date field in every record, producing a list of customers based on when each purchased a given product. Six months after purchasing a product, the customer can be sent a letter inquiring about product satisfaction.

Field Size specifies the maximum number of characters allowed in the field. To decrease processing time, assign the smallest possible size to each field; the computer requires less time to read a 15-character field than a 30-character field.

Planning A Database

Planning is the single most important step in creating a successful database. A poor plan and design can make manipulating and controlling data difficult or impossible.

Let's look at a plan for a university registrar's database. Figure 9-6 shows a sketched layout that describes the fields for each record in the registrar's student file. For each field, the sketch displays the field type and field size. When data is entered into this database, the records appear as shown in Figure 9-7.

Figure 9-6
This plan for a school registrar's database shows the thinking that must go into database design. The table shows what information is to be stored, how it will be labeled as fields, what type of data each field is to contain, and what size the fields should be.

Description	Field Name	Field Type	Field Size
Student Number	ID	Numeric	5
Last Name	L_NAME	Alphanumeric	20
First Name	F_NAME	Alphanumeric	10
Street Address	STREET	Alphanumeric	20
City	CITY	Alphanumeric	20
Zipcode	ZIP	Numeric	5
Date of Birth	DOB	Data	8
Minority Status	Min	Logical	1

• CHAPTER 9: Working with Databases •

ID	L_NAME	F_NAME	STREET	STATE	CITY	ZIP	DOB	MIN
01	Bender	Jane	221	NY	NY	11026	090	.T.

Figure 9-7
Implementing the database plan from Figure 9-6, we can see a sample record in list format, showing how the information we need to store fits into the database we've planned.

An essential step in the planning process is determining precise search factors. If a field called NAME contains both the first and last names, for example, it will be difficult to search for records based on just the last name. In this case, designating two fields—F_NAME (first name) and L_NAME (last name)—in the initial design makes it possible to search for records based on either a first or last name.

It is also important in planning a database to determine all the fields needed (Figure 9-8). For example, including a TITLE field allows you to indicate whether a person is to be addressed as Mr., Mrs., or Ms. This is useful for such greetings on letters as "Dear Mr. Smith" or "Dear Ms. Smith." Without the TITLE field, the greeting might say "Dear Joe Smith" or "Dear Jane Smith."

If, after the database is established, you realize you've forgotten an essential field, you can add it quite easily with some types of software, but other programs present major difficulties. In any case, an added field generally means adding new data to every record in the file.

When all the fields are defined, the next step is to assign each record to a file. With most databases, it is more efficient to group a small number of

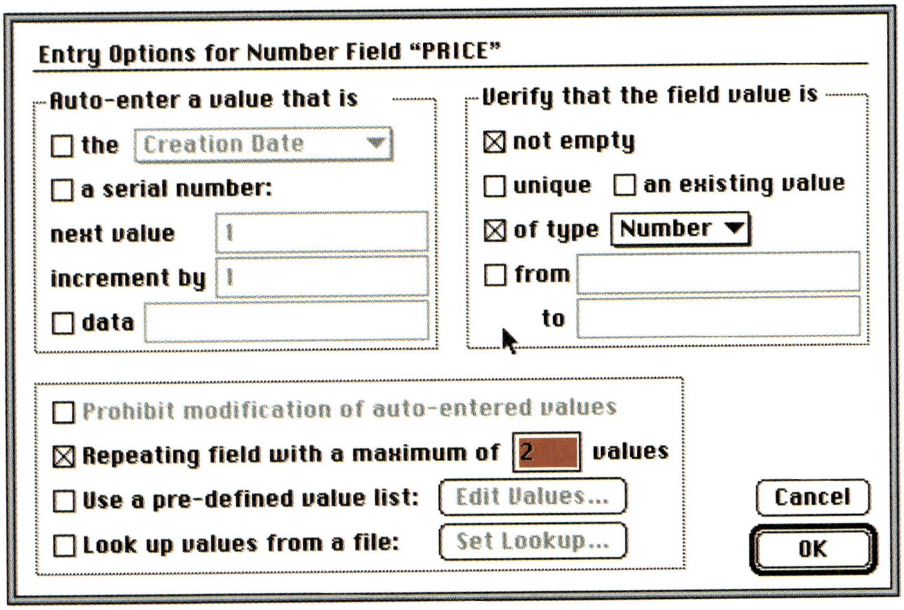

Figure 9-8
The field definition screen, a crucial part of all microcomputer database programs, lets you implement your database plan by giving the computer the specifications for each field you want in the database.

Changing Junkmail?

Computers have certainly contributed to the growth of junk mail, thanks to swelling databases of mailing lists that companies swap or sell to each other. But Phil Herring, a direct mail marketer, suggests that computers can also help solve the problem of annoying junk mail by properly using database technology. These databases would only contain the names of people who want to be on it, who bought specific products in the past, or who contacted the company for information. To help companies further target their mailings (and thereby get more return for their money), Herring says the databases should also include consumers' buying patterns and changes in income. Since more than 600 legislative bills were pending in 1992 that addressed direct mail marketing, Herring thinks it's a good idea for the industry to regulate itself before the government steps in. For starters, companies can use recycled paper and mention that fact prominently on the mailing. Who knows? Maybe junk mail could become something people would like to see in their mailboxes!

---

related fields in each record and to assign a manageable number of records to a file. For example, the registrar's database needs all students' course grades as well as their names, addresses, dates of birth, and so on. Rather than placing all this information in one huge file, it is better to break up the course history information and the personal data into two separate files such as a student file and student history file. Using a common field name—for example STUDENT_ID—in each file allows the software to look up data for that student in both files.

After the hard work of creating a detailed plan for the database structure, the actual process of creating a database is easy. Depending on the software, once the structure has been defined, building the database is as simple as entering the record name, each of its field names, and each field name's field type and field size. The rest is data entry.

DATA ENTRY

Data entry is generally the simplest part of using a database. Once you've planned your database and defined all the fields, the software will provide you with an on-screen data entry form to directly type in data. You can move from one data field to the next, generally with the Tab key or the arrow keys. Some database software packages provide a list view that shows several records at once. This view generally places each record in a row, with fields in columns (as Figure 9-4 demonstrated). This way you can compare data in several records and modify the information as needed.

Data is also entered in a database by reading a data file. To do this, the file must be organized according to the fields you've defined in your database. The data file is usually plain text (although some databases understand other file formats), with information for each record in one paragraph and the fields separated by tabs or commas. If the data file is properly formatted, it can be imported to the database quickly, giving you immediate access to a large amount of information.

SORTING AND INDEXING

One important and useful feature of a database is its ability to transform randomly entered records into a more organized and useful form (Figure 9-9). For example, in a physician's office, patients' names are entered into a database in the order they come into the office. Rather than keeping the patient list in this random order, it makes more sense to alphabetize it. Database software uses two methods for alphabetizing or otherwise changing the order of records: sorting and indexing.

Sorting is a permanent reordering of the organization of a database, changing the actual arrangement and order of each record in the database. For example, a file sorted on the field LAST_NAME is permanently reorganized into alphabetized LAST_NAME order (Figure 9-10).

Sorting is useful when the organization of a database must remain constant. For example, a car dealer may enter the names and addresses of all customers visiting the dealership each day and then sort the data according to the specific criterion, by type of trade-in, by date, or by type of car desired.

• CHAPTER 9: Working with Databases •

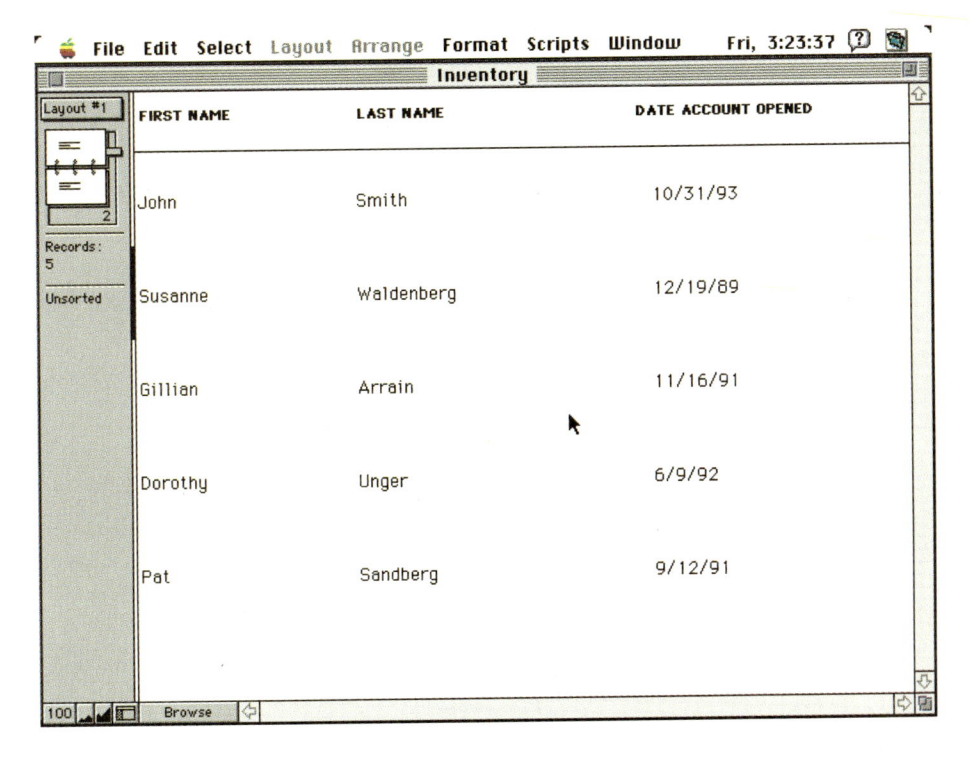

Figure 9-9
Information is usually entered into a database as it's received; thus, the records may not be organized in any convenient way.

The major disadvantage of a sort is time. Depending on the type of equipment and the number of records in the database, a sort can take from several minutes to hours.

Indexing organizes data temporarily. The results of indexing appear the same as sorting; however, the first record displayed may actually be (and remain) the 150th record in the database.

Because indexing is a temporary sort, it is possible to create multiple indexes for the same database file. For example, a file can be indexed alphabetically by last name, alphanumerically by zip code, and in date order

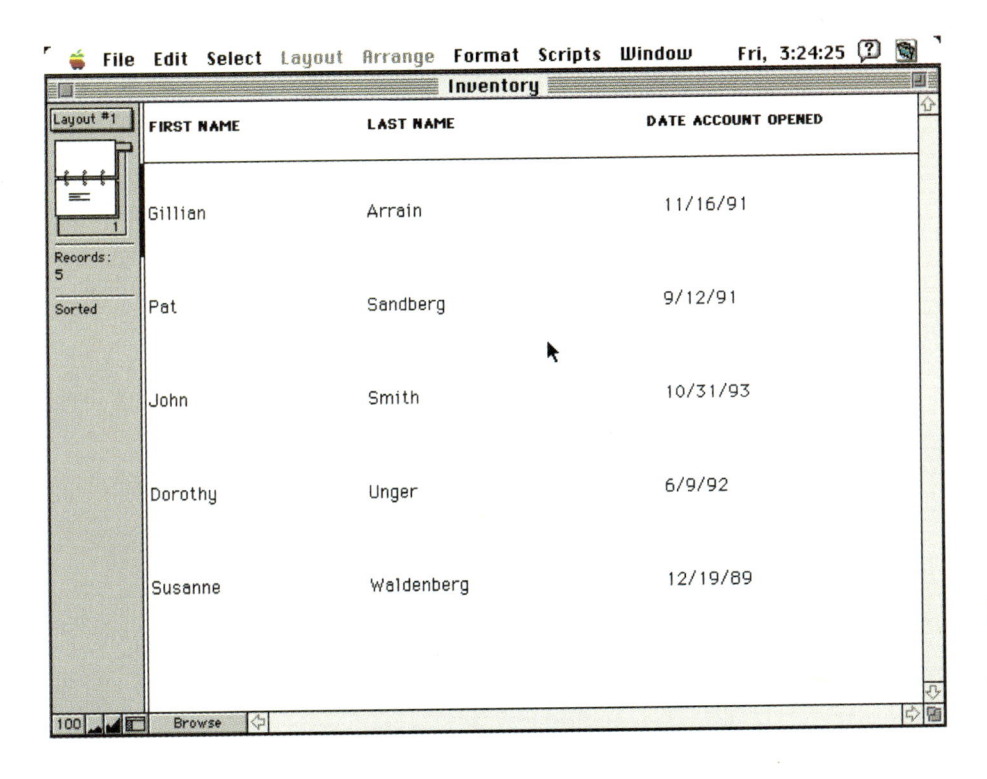

Figure 9-10
Sorting the database, as shown here, puts the records in the order you want; in this case, alphabetical by last name.

HISTORY

Ashton-Tate and dBASE II

Because a high-school dropout from the South got bitten by the computer bug, the computer industry got a brilliant, standard-setting program and several people ended up multimillionaires.

After dropping out of 12th grade because he was bored with school, George Tate spent the early part of his adult life "bumping around." When he got out of the Air Force, he went into the family furniture business in South Carolina, quit after a few months, and eventually moved to Los Angeles, where he supported himself by repairing stereo sets.

The now-legendary January 1975 issue of *Popular Electronics*, with its cover photo of the Altair computer, changed Tate's life. He ordered a kit and got the machine to run. "After that point, there was nothing in my life but computers," he said.

Since he had always enjoyed fixing TVs and stereos, it was a natural step to set up as a computer repairman. Only George Tate had a flair for marketing, so he billed himself as "The Computer Doctor"—complete with advertising photos of himself in a doctor's outfit.

Through a local computer club he met Hal Lashlee, and together—using Tate's garage as base—they started Software Plus, a discount mail-order firm for selling software to computer users. In 1980 one of their customers phoned, wanting to buy a copy of a program called Vulcan, and was so enthusiastic about it that the two men decided to investigate for themselves.

Vulcan had been developed by Wayne Ratliff, an engineer at Martin-Marietta's Jet Propulsion Laboratory, because he decided there must be a way to program a computer to pick the winners for the football pools. Within a few days he forgot about the football angle and began writing a program that would interpret a simplified set of a public domain database called JPLDIS. By 1979 he had developed a database program he called Vulcan, after the home planet of "Star Trek's" Mr. Spock.

One of Vulcan's chief selling points was that it allowed users to seek out and sort data by using an on-screen interface, rather than by typing in a list of rather cryptic commands. But Ratliff was not a marketer or a salesman, and his method of letting the world know about Vulcan consisted of taking out a few ads in computer magazines. In nine months he sold 61 units. He was embroiled in personal problems, still working full time at Martin-Marietta, so when he met with Hal Lashlee and George Tate in August 1980, Ratliff was happy to sell them marketing rights to his program. There was another program on the market called Vulcan, so Tate and Lashlee changed their program's name to dBASE (for *database*) and added "II," figuring people would have more confidence in a program that was already in its second generation. Tate also thought dBASE II should not be associated with a discount house such as Software Plus, so the firm Ashton-Tate was created. There never was an "Ashton" associated with the company—Tate just liked the sound of the name better than "Lashlee-Tate."

dBASE II shipped in February 1981. It became the most successful microcomputer database program of its time because of its astonishing versatility, combined with the fact it was the right program at the right time. Ratliff had hoped to make $100,000 from his deal with Tate. He made millions.

In August 1983, only a few months after introducing dBASE III, George Tate had a heart attack at his desk and died. He was 40 years old. ■

• CHAPTER 9: Working with Databases •

by purchase date, allowing customer listings to be produced in each specific order.

Multiple indexes also let you produce lists alphabetized in more than one field at a time. For example, a customer file indexed on CITY and LAST_NAME can produce an alphabetical list of customers within a city:

Chicago,	Bepper
Chicago,	Lowell
Chicago,	Meridith
New York,	Jones
New York,	Kale
New York,	May
New York,	Provall
San Francisco,	Allen
San Francisco,	Berger
San Francisco,	Valdez

Indexing is normally much faster than sorting and it provides greater flexibility. Indexing allows more than one kind or organization within one database file; permanent sorting tends to limit a file's organization.

DATA QUERIES

A request for data in a database is a **query**. Queries can be as simple as searching for a specific name in a field or as complex as searching for all customers who meet a precisely detailed set of specifications (Figure 9-11).

In a simple query, the first step is to identify the field to be used. For example, searching for a record of a specific customer is usually as simple as entering the customer's name or identification number.

The more precise the query entry, the more accurate the information located. Querying a large database using the last name Smith, for example, will return all Smiths in the database. Querying the same database for Smith as the LAST_NAME, Colorado as the STATE, and snowshoes in PURCHASE will produce all Smiths in Colorado who purchased snowshoes.

Queries work with database indexes to produce appropriately organized lists of data. Suppose you wish to find all customers who purchased a new

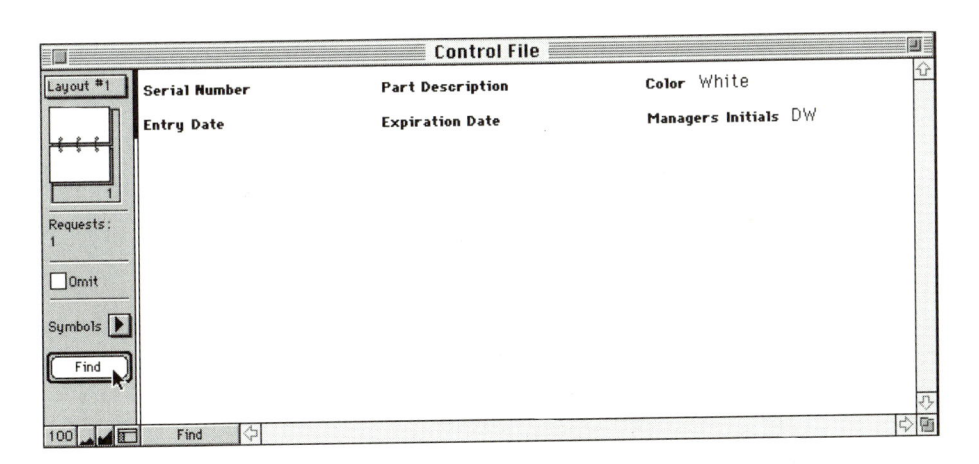

Keeping Track of the Voters

Elected officials can use databases to maintain better contact with their constituents. Since computers can store almost unlimited information, legislators can have lists of voters in their district segmented demographically or according to a voter's interests. For example, Senator Seymour knows that Henry Wallach hasn't voted for the past three elections, that Lilia Wallach opposed the logging of the Mendocino coast, and that Jerry Wallach contributed money to his last campaign. Accordingly, Jerry Wallach gets a letter every three months and Lilia gets a letter extolling the senator's support of the environment and informing her about current legislation he has introduced to save the spotted lizard. If Henry sent Senator Seymour a letter about crime in the streets, he might get back a letter describing the Senator's ideas on gun control.

Figure 9-11
Querying the database, as shown here, involves specifying what kind of information you're looking for and telling the database software to search the file for all records that meet your criteria. In this case, the program will find all records that contain "White" in the Color field and "DW" in the Manager's Initials field.

Art Database

A new art history database in Rome provides scholars comparing sculpture, painting, and architecture in the Ancient World and the Renaissance with a phenomenal amount of information in both text and visual form. Data can be viewed on two screens simultaneously, so that an ancient Greek work of art can be juxtaposed against a Roman copy from the 1450s. Any combination of images and text can be called up and compared. This is especially helpful to scholars of the periods, since it is unclear how much Renaissance artists knew of ancient art. The database—stored on a videodisc—was developed over ten years with the help of museums and libraries in three countries.

---

car in 1992. If the file is not indexed, the query will produce a list based on entry order rather than alphabetical or date order. If the file has been indexed by customer name, however, the query will produce a customer list in alphabetical order. If the file has been indexed by purchase date, the query will produce the list ordered by purchase date.

Structured Query Language (SQL)

Various databases approach the process of querying differently. Just as different word processors use different commands to accomplish the same task, different database programs use unique command sets for locating data. A standardized approach to data querying, the **structured query language (SQL)** crosses these barriers. Software that supports SQL can locate data within a variety of microcomputer and mainframe databases. Because SQL was designed for querying remote databases, not local ones, database software programs that implement SQL on microcomputers generally use it for accessing databases on mainframe computers and computer networks. Since these areas of microcomputing are growing fast, SQL has become more and more popular.

SQL is based on a series of standardized query expressions to specify the criteria for a data search. These expressions look very much like the commands in a programming language. It is beyond the scope of this book to teach you all the expressions in SQL and how they interrelate to produce queries; however, the following few expressions will give you some understanding of the basic SQL process.

Most SQL expressions have at least two **clauses.** For example, the SELECT clause determines the fields to use from the database and the FROM clause specifies which file will provide the fields.

```
SELECT TITLE, FIRST_NAME, LAST_NAME, STATE, AMOUNT
FROM CUSTLIST
```

This produces a list of all customers from the CUSTLIST file. It displays their titles, first names, last names, states, and purchase amounts.

Adding the WHERE clause puts a search restriction on an SQL expression.

```
SELECT TITLE, FIRST_NAME, LAST_NAME, STATE, AMOUNT
FROM CUSTLIST
WHERE STATE = 'MI'
```

This limits the query to customers in the state of Michigan. The name in single quotation marks in the expression identifies the data in fields that must match for the record to be included. The single quotation marks show that the data are alphanumeric (data without quotation marks are numeric).

Another useful clause is AND. AND follows the WHERE clause to show that two conditions must be met for a record to be included in the results of the query. For example,

```
SELECT TITLE, FIRST_NAME, LAST_NAME, STATE, AMOUNT
FROM CUSTLIST
WHERE STATE = 'MI'
AND AMOUNT > 15000.00
```

produces a list of all customers in Michigan who purchased a car valued at more than $15,000.

Several clauses are used to change data in the database. The clause INSERT places a new record into a database. DELETE removes a record, and UPDATE changes the contents of a record. For example,

```
INSERT
INTO CUSTFILE
VALUES ('DR.', 'Bill', 'Smith', 5634.23)
DELETE
FROM CUSTFILE
STATE = 'CO'
UPDATE CUSTLIST
SET COMMISH = .20
WHERE AMOUNT > 15000.00
```

will insert a new record for Dr. Bill Smith into the CUSTFILE, delete all records from the state of Colorado, and set the commission rate at 20 percent when the purchase amount exceeds $15,000.

GENERATING REPORTS

A **report generator** controls the display of information both on the screen and on paper. The simplest type of report is a list of the data in the database. More complex reports include titles, page numbers, subtotal and total calculations, column and row headings, and a variety of other information to make a database report both functional and attractive (Figure 9-12).

A database program's report generator contributes significantly to its overall usefulness. After all, it's not enough just to be able to store all this information; the information is useless unless you can get precisely the information you need and print it in a useful form. Together with queries, report generators are the primary method of extracting specific data from a database; their capabilities are crucial.

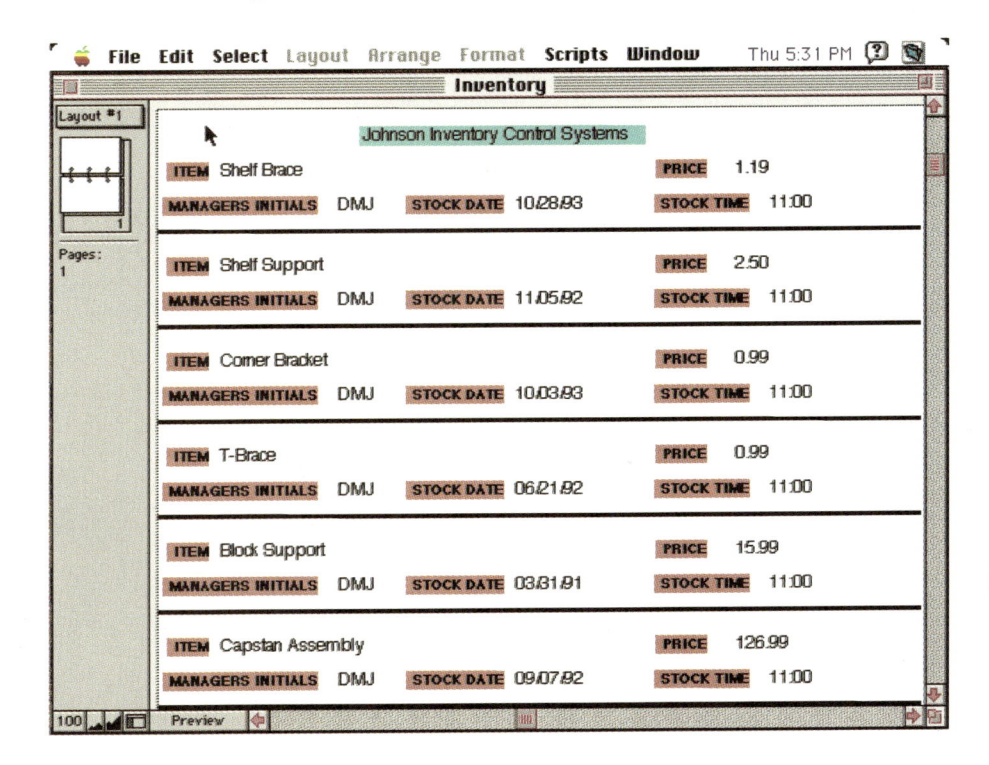

The Global Jukebox, a Singing Database

Want to find out how many people bought Madonna's latest hit, play Gregorian chants, or find the notation of Middle Eastern music? The world's greatest jukebox (more than 4,000 songs from 400 countries) allows the user to access statistical data, charts, graphs, dance videos—and most of the world's music. Intended as a research tool for museums and libraries, the Global Jukebox uses Cantometrics, a system of code words that define and analyze music. This computerized file cabinet for music and dance across time and cultures is part of New York City's Hunter College. Says Alan Lomax, director of Hunter's Association for Cultural Equity, "What we did was similar to the classification of plants and animals. We developed methods to describe and classify performances. And we can show the various cross-cultural evolutions of song and dance styles." Do lights flash while the Global Jukebox plays your request?

Figure 9-12
To print the information you've queried in a useful form, database programs provide report generators that let you specify how you want the records to be printed.

DATABASE ORGANIZATION

There are six major types of databases: relational, flat-file, HyperCard, hierarchical, network, and free-form.

Relational Databases

The database file in Figure 9-4 is a table showing a relation where the rows correspond to records and the columns correspond to fields. **Relational databases** organize information in this manner, which allows maximum flexibility of querying based on relationships between different fields.

By using this table structure, you can access and control more than one file at a time. Changes made to one record in one file automatically update linked records in another file.

Flat-file Databases (File Managers)

Many microcomputer users need only a simple method for storing limited amounts of data. To meet this need, **file managers**, sometimes called **flat-file databases**, are available.

Flat-file databases are **single-relation databases**. That is, these databases work with only one file at a time; there are no linkages with other files. One major advantage of flat-file databases is their ease of use: It is easy to set up a database, store records, and generate queries and reports. Another advantage is that flat-file databases are almost always much less expensive than any other type of database. As long as there is no need to cross-reference files, flat-file databases can be very efficient.

HyperCard

One fairly recent development in database management is a program called **HyperCard** (a limited version comes with the Macintosh). HyperCard combines many aspects of traditional database design with advanced graphics and the Macintosh environment.

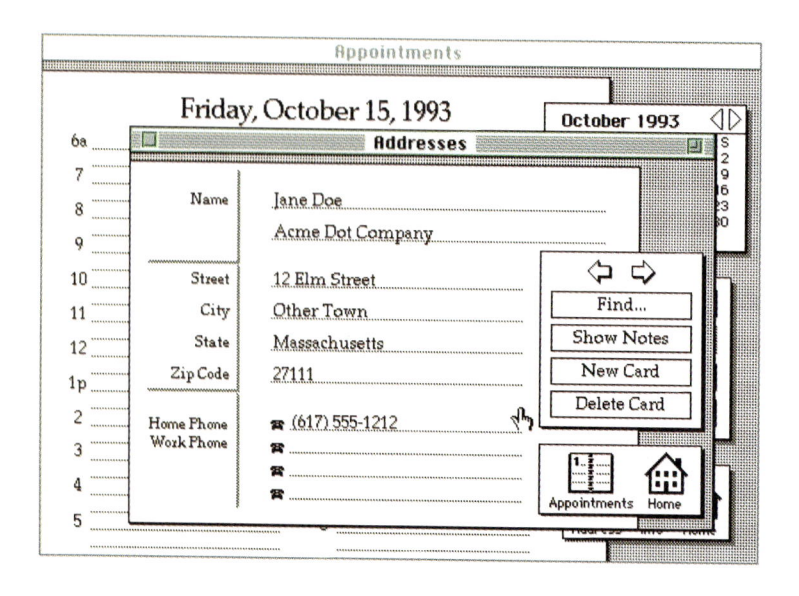

Figure 9-13
HyperCard's flexibility allows for a great variety of applications. You can design your own databases (called *stacks*) that can combine text, numbers, graphics, and sound. This stack is used for an address database.

HyperCard allows users to create individual screens filled with text from a word processor, other data, and graphics. Each screen displays a particular set of information with access to other screen displays (Figure 9-13). The term **card** describes an individual screen display, and a group of cards linked together form a HyperCard **stack.**

A card is equivalent, in database terms, to a record. Unlike traditional database records made up solely of fields, however, a card can be made up of fields, text from a word processor, or graphic images. For example, a user might design one card to welcome users to a database of the animal kingdom and another card with text about elephants, a picture of an elephant, and specific statistical elephant data. An individual card could be developed for each animal in the animal kingdom.

Linking cards in any order based on any criterion gives HyperCard its strength. A **button** links cards into a stack. A button can appear as a simple statement such as Continue, Next Card, Search, or even Change Kingdoms. It can also appear as a small picture or icon; moving the mouse pointer onto the icon and clicking causes a new card to appear. Buttons can cause cards to display sequentially or randomly.

One of HyperCard's features is its English-like language for setting up links between cards. Users do not have to be database or programming experts to use HyperCard, which—like its competitors, such as Linkway for the IBM—is very easy to learn and use.

Hierarchical Databases

Hierarchical databases are used mostly with mainframes. Data is organized with the broadest grouping at the highest level, followed by more specific subgroups (Figure 9-14). The structure is very similar to a family tree or DOS directory structure, where a parent, or root, directory houses several children,

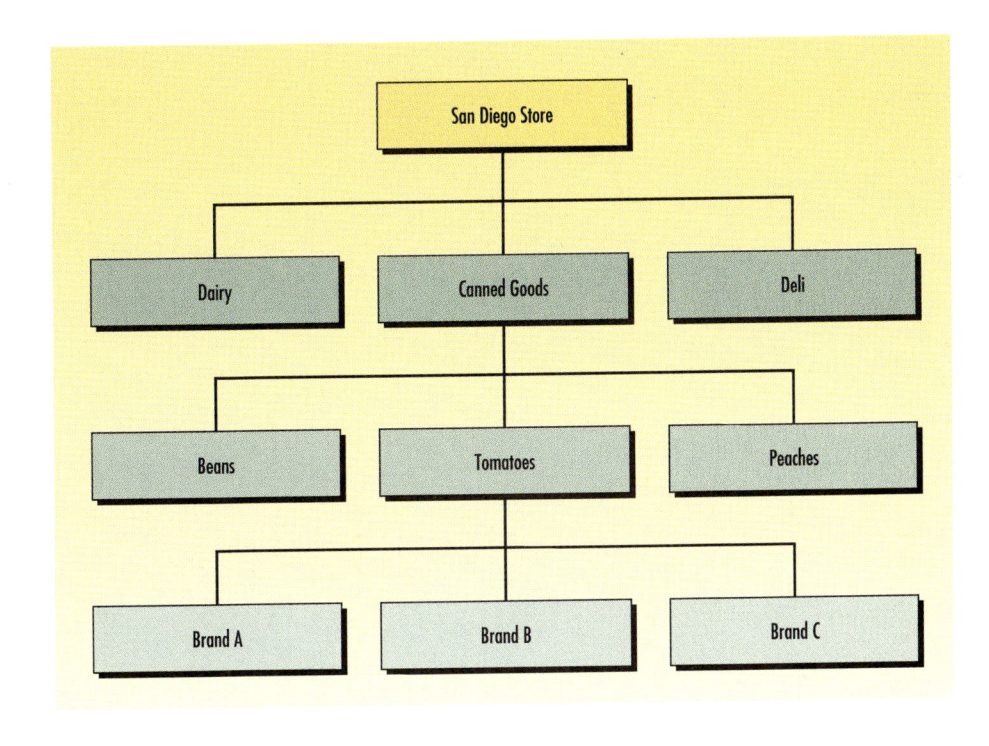

Figure 9-14
Hierarchical databases organize information in a tree-like structure, with each category of information containing subcategories. Here, brands A, B, and C are subcategories of Tomatoes, itself a subcategory of Canned Goods under the San Diego Store. This structure provides good organization of large volumes of information, but limits the ways in which you can access it.

or subdirectories. In turn, each subdirectory can house additional subdirectories. The top-down organization eliminates searching through all records; the program searches only the specified groups of data. The disadvantage is that, unlike relational databases, every relationship and link must be predefined. Adding any new field requires a complete redefinition of the database.

Network Databases

Network databases are similar to hierarchical databases with the additional feature of each subgroup having more than one root. That is, each child in a family tree can have more than one parent group. Network databases can branch from one group to several others or from one owner to several other members, making the search process easier.

Free-Form and Encyclopedic Databases

Except for HyperCard, all the databases discussed so far involve the storage of individual data in predefined fields. These are known as **record-oriented databases.** For many data applications the individual size of a record or a field within a record can cause problems; storing the Gettysburg Address in a table, for example, would be very difficult. **Free-form databases** are used for data that consists of large volumes of text.

Data entry in free-form databases is normally accomplished by moving word processing files into the database. Rather than specific fields, the search process uses **keywords**, words entered by user to determine the scope of the search. **Encyclopedic databases,** such as The Source or Dialog, are large

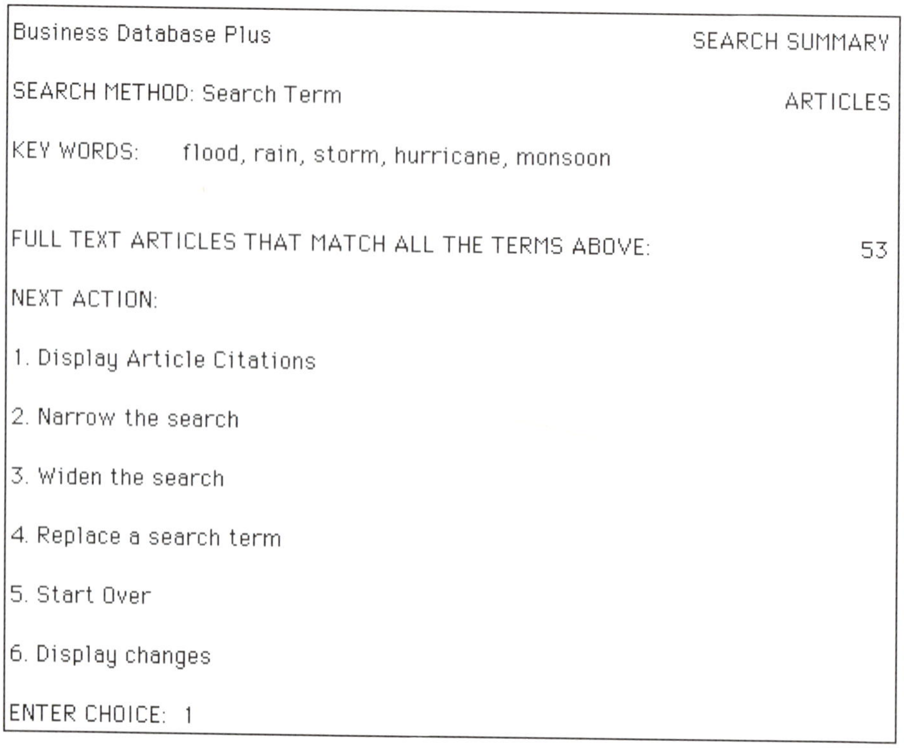

```
Business Database Plus                                SEARCH SUMMARY

SEARCH METHOD: Search Term                                   ARTICLES

KEY WORDS:     flood, rain, storm, hurricane, monsoon


FULL TEXT ARTICLES THAT MATCH ALL THE TERMS ABOVE:              53

NEXT ACTION:

1. Display Article Citations

2. Narrow the search

3. Widen the search

4. Replace a search term

5. Start Over

6. Display changes

ENTER CHOICE: 1
```

Figure 9-15
Keyword searches, such as this example from CompuServe, are the most common way to access large on-line databases.

databases, or data banks, containing information on a vast array of subjects. These databases are generally subscription services, allowing users access to the data (through communications links) for specific charges. Users begin their search with keywords. Any record that contains a specified keyword is included in the results of the search (Figure 9-15). For example, using the keyword **insects** causes the database to return a list of all records about insects. In a comprehensive biology database of research articles, this one word could produce a listing of several thousand records or articles.

The amount of time the host computer spends on this initial search varies according to the specificity of the keyword. For example, the keyword **baseball** will produce a much longer list of articles and citations than the keyword **Babe Ruth.**

Adding a third criterion such as **homeruns** to **baseball** and **Babe Ruth** will cut the number of citations even further. Each service provides guidelines to make searching the database more precise—and less costly.

Users with CD-ROM (compact disc read-only memory) drives can buy CD-ROMs with encyclopedic databases. The disks include tremendous amounts of instantly accessible information, including photographs, about an almost unlimited number of topics.

SUMMARY

Database software makes it possible for computers to store and retrieve large amounts of data. To do this, a database is organized into three levels: files, records, and fields. A file (the electronic equivalent of a filing cabinet) contains a group of records. A record (like a paper file folder) stores a group of data items, or fields, relating to a single specification such as a person, place, or thing.

Each field has a field name, size, and type. The field name is a unique identifier. Field size determines the maximum number of characters or numbers that can be stored in a field. Data type determines the kind of operation the computer can perform on the data; it can be alphanumeric, numeric, logical, or date. Alphanumeric data—addresses, Social Security numbers, and the like—can be alphabetized and sorted numerically but it cannot be subjected to any mathematical operations. Numeric data are numbers used in mathematical operations. Logical data identifies one of two alternatives—true or false, yes or no. The numbers stored in a date field represent a calendar date.

Planning is the single most important step in creating a successful database. A poor plan can make manipulating and controlling data difficult or impossible; a good plan leads to a database that is both easy to work with and efficient.

One of the most important steps in database planning is determining search factors and thus making the fields specific. It is also important to include every necessary field in the original plan. Although fields can generally be added later, it may require a significant amount of additional work. When dealing with large numbers of records, you can often group them into small files for easier manipulation. Using a common field name in each group allows access to data in each title.

Data is entered in the database through an on-screen entry form or a data file formatted to match the already-defined fields. Some programs offer list views, allowing the user to modify information in several records at once.

The order of the records can be permanently changed by sorting or temporarily changed by indexing. The latter allows the creation of multiple indexes within one file, providing greater flexibility.

A request for data in a database is a query. A simple query involves identifying a field and searching for all records that match the field name. Querying an indexed file produces an organized list of data.

Structured query language (SQL), a standardized language for querying, is based on a series of expressions that specify the criteria for a data search. Once data have been retrieved, a report generator can be used to control the display of information on the screen and on paper.

The six major types of databases are relational, flat-file, HyperCard, hierarchical, network, and free-form. Relational databases organize information in relational tables and let users manipulate or control more than one file at a time. Flat-file databases (file managers) work with single-file applications. HyperCard combines text and graphics to produce individual screens called *cards*. A hierarchical database organizes data into a family tree formation, with the broadest grouping at the parent (root) level; specific subgroups appear as their children (subdirectories). Network databases are similar to hierarchical databases; each subgroup has more than one parent. Free-form databases allow the entry of large amounts of text without specifying data type or size. Data are unstructured and are accessed through keywords. Encyclopedic databases are part of this group.

KEY TERMS

alphanumeric data	field type	numeric data
button	file	query
card	file manager	record
clause	flat-file database	record-oriented database
database	free-form database	relational database
database software	hierarchical database	report generator
date field	HyperCard	single-relation database
encyclopedic databases	indexing	sorting
field	keyword	stack
field name	logical data	structured query language (SQL)
field size	network database	

REVIEW QUESTIONS

1. What is a database field?
2. What is a database record?
3. List five ways a physician could use a database.
4. What is a file?

5. List four types of data stored in a database. Provide a brief explanation of each.
6. Describe an encyclopedic database.
7. Why does one use a keyword when accessing a database?
8. Describe how a file cabinet is like a computer database.
9. What is a report generator?
10. Describe the difference between indexing and sorting.
11. What is a relational database?

Working with Communications

10

OBJECTIVES

After completing this chapter, you will be able to
- Describe the role of computer communications.
- Describe the use of a modem.
- Explain the word *baud*.
- Explain why most microcomputers use asynchornous communications.
- Discuss byte length, stop bit, and parity.
- Name the major information services and their typical uses.
- Name and describe the two major types of networks.
- Identify the major components of a network.
- Describe distributed processing.

FOCUS

When a microcomputer stands alone, not connected to another computer, the only information it provides is on the hard disk or on manually inserted floppy disks. But if you connect that computer to other computers, you multiply its capabilities manyfold and gain access to a world of information.

The transfer of data from one computer to another is known as computer communications. This chapter describes the two most common microcomputer communications systems: telecommunications and networking.

Telecommunications, which uses telephone lines to connect computers to each other, takes on many forms for many uses. Chief among these are electronic mail, which sends messages from one computer to another; facsimile transmission, which sends electronic images of documents; access to various services, including on-line databases for supplying information; bulletin board services for posting public messages, sharing data files and software, and electronic conversation; and general on-line services, such as The Source, Dow Jones News Service, CompuServe, and Prodigy, among others, which provide a whole range of services, from financial information to on-line shopping.

Networking, which uses special wiring to connect computers locally and a mixture of private and public connections to connect computers over a wide area, is primarily used for sharing data, programs, and most importantly, processing power in a working environment. A local area network connects computers over short distances, say, within an office or between adjacent buildings; a wide area network connects computers and local area networks over many miles. Networks can be configured in a number of structures, called topologies: bus, in which all computers are on a single line of cable; star, in which computers are connected on branching lines from a central hub; and ring, in which computers are connected in a loop. Networks can also be administrated in one of two ways: client-server networks use a central computer to run the network and provide shared resources, and peer-to-peer networks give all computers on the network equal status and direct sharing of resources.

• CHAPTER 10: Working with Communications •

TELECOMMUNICATIONS

Telecommunications is the process of sending and receiving electronic data through telephone lines. This makes it possible for a computer to share and exchange data with another computer connected to a telephone line almost anywhere in the world. Users can communicate with each other directly, send and receive electronic mail and facsimilies (faxes), participate in electronic bulletin boards, and access large national databases.

Electronic mail

Electronic mail, or **E-mail**, is the sending and receiving of messages from one computer to another over telephone lines or across networks to other computers, computer bulletin board systems, and on-line services (Figure 10-1). Using E-mail software such as ccMail or InBox, you can write a short message with a text editor (similar to a word processor) and address it to a particular person or group of people. You can also attach items such as word processing files, graphics, or other computer files to your message and send them electronically, much like—but considerably faster than—mailing paper documents through the U.S. Postal Service.

Suppose a writer in New York City is working on a manuscript and wishes to have input from a colleague in San Francisco. It is 9:00 A.M. in New York, but it is only 6:00 A.M. on the West Coast—too early to send the chapter directly. In addition to their computers, both the writer and the colleague have E-mail software that can access a common **network** or on–line service (such as MCI Mail, an electronic mail network; Internet, a worldwide computer network; or on-line services such as CompuServe). The writer can create a message and attach the manuscript file, then send it electronically, in a matter of minutes, to the service they use. After dialing into the service and receiving and editing the manuscript, the colleague can send the file from San Francisco back to the service, from which it will be picked up by the writer in New York.

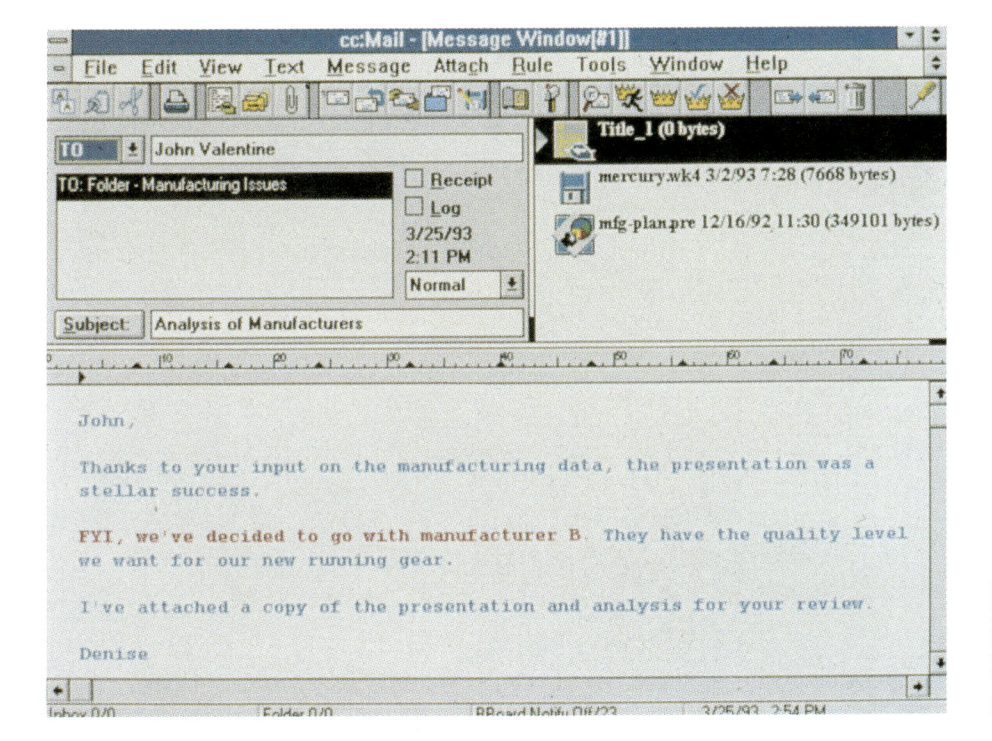

Ahead of the News

During the 1991 attempted military coup in the Soviet Union, information in faxes and E-mail often reached other countries ahead of the news media. Westerners who had been communicating via computer with Soviet citizens suddenly found themselves in an electronics crossfire of anxious messages. "The shooting has begun," read one E-mail message. "There have been many explosions outside the parliament building. The siege is underway." Since communications inside Russia were fragile, people in Europe and the U.S. could, in turn, relay what they had learned from TV, radio, and newspapers, offering encouragement and support for the freedom fighters. This vital electronic pipeline of information was greatly valued by those receiving it. "The new junta will try to impose censorship and cut the flow of information from our country," read one fax. "I suggest you take some measures in order to continue operating, even under highly adverse conditions."

Figure 10-1
E-mail packages such as cc:Mail Remote let you call in to mail services on remote networks and bulletin boards.

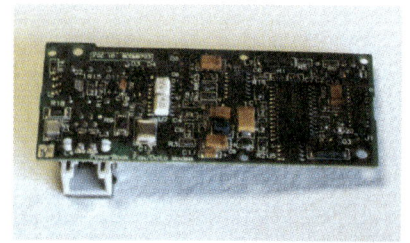

Figure 10-2
The fax card allows you to send and receive faxes on your computer just as you would on a fax machine.

Facsimile Transmission

Popularly known as a fax machine, a **facsimile** machine is essentially a copier that sends a receives copies over phone lines. An inexpensive alternative to a stand-alone fax machine is a fax card installed in a microcomputer. This arrangement generally allows you to use the card as either a fax or a modem (Figure 10-2).

With a computer fax, however, only computer files, rather than paper hard copies, can be transmitted. The faxed files differ from E-mail files in that, unlike a word processing file, faxes are received as graphic images and cannot be changed. Optical character reader utility programs convert the fax to a text file; they also print the faxes. Sending an already printed page requires a scanner and software to convert the scanned image to fax file format, enabling the fax card to transmit the scanned page.

Databases

Telecommunications provides access to news wire, financial, consumer product, and encyclopedic databases. Instead of calling a stockbroker for a stock quote, investors can get their own current information and can even schedule a stock trade (Figure 10-3). Users can reach others interested in trading products and services, shop by catalog, get information about topics from aerospace to specific laws, and make hotel and airline reservations.

Bulletin Boards

An electronic **bulletin board** serves the same purpose as any other bulletin board: it is a location for public messages (Figure 10-4). It provides a vehicle for users to share ideas ranging from computer use and software applications to stamp collecting and genealogy.

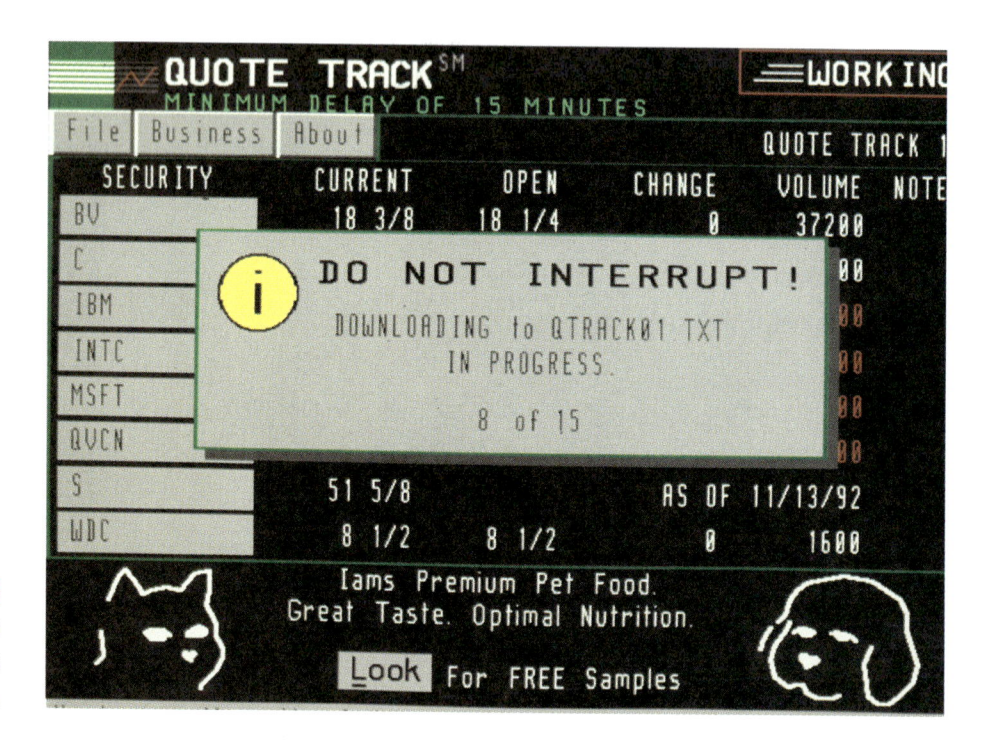

Figure 10-3
Quote Track from Prodigy lets users log in and receive a wide variety of financial news and information.

Figure 10-4

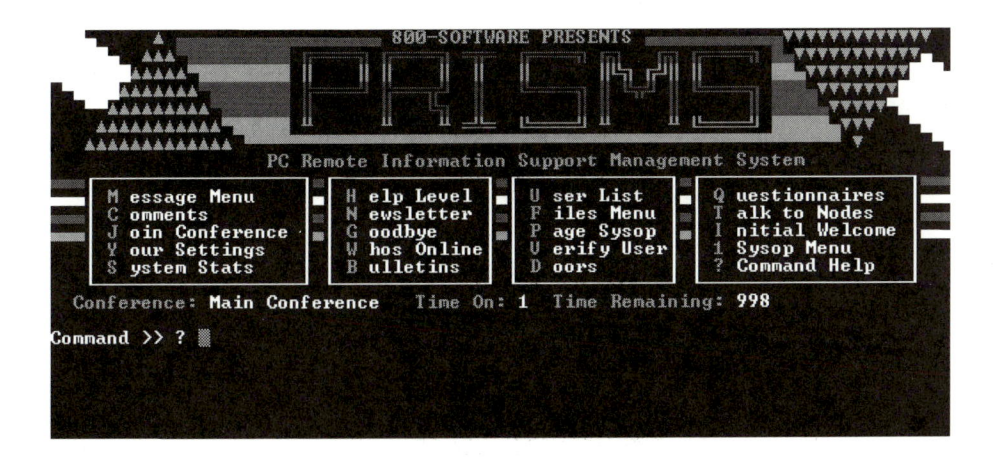

Electronic bulletin boards exist to serve a tremendous number of on-line needs; this one from 800-SOFTWARE provides technical support for its customers.

Subscribers access a bulletin board and scan the database for information. Job applicants, for example, can search for positions according to occupational groups, geographic locations, or salary requirements. For each job vacancy, an electronic mailbox indicates where applicants can send their resumes.

Computer user groups—groups of people who use the same type of computer equipment or software—are frequent users of bulletin boards. These groups use bulletin boards to announce meetings, ask each other questions, and offer solutions to computer problems. Some bulletin boards give users access to public domain software (which can be freely copied and used) and shareware (these also can be freely copied, but if they are used, compensation for the programmer is requested). Much of this is available at little or no cost.

Unfortunately, bulletin boards are also the primary method of transferring computer viruses. Viruses are computer programs, developed by unethical programmers, that destroy data stored on disk or otherwise interfere with the operation of your computer. They are discussed in the chapter on social issues. An infected bulletin board file copied to your computer can destroy all data on your disk. Before using a bulletin board, be sure to install software that can detect and destroy computer viruses.

Some bulletin boards, such as the WELL, offer users the opportunity to communicate with each other, either by leaving messages in public forums (generally organized according to topics) or by directly typing messages back and forth (what's called *chat mode* or *CB mode* on some systems). Using these capabilities, users can discuss anything from the news of the day to social issues, intimate affairs, and trivia. Computer bulletin boards have been the medium for social groups, political movements, clubs and organization, and even dating and marriage. Thus, **virtual**, or **on-line, communities** develop among people who have never actually met but know each other better than their own neighbors.

On-line Services

On-line service companies provide access to electronic mail systems, bulletin boards, and databases. Individuals who subscribe pay a flat fee or use fees. Popular on-line services include the following.

The Source. Subscribers to **The Source** can select database information for managing investments or analyzing financial markets (Figure 10-5, p. 182), such as

Cafe Link

Not all communities have geographic boundaries; some only have networks. Thanks to electronic mail, there are communities of people around the world bound together only by shared interests and their computers. People discuss Kierkegaard or sell kittens via E-mail. People have even met through E-mail and married.

Cafe goers in Paris, Budapest, and San Francisco now have their own network, Cafe Link. For $1 users buy 20 minutes of interfacing time. The brainchild of a computer and cafe lover, the network can be accessed from home, as well as from cafes. One of the users who accesses Cafe Link from his home is Don Caca, who is blind. He uses a computer equipped with a voice synthesizer and a Braille keyboard. Not all cafe lovers are enamored with the service. They say cafes are supposed to be havens from modern life. But users of Cafe Link say it's just another sort of haven.

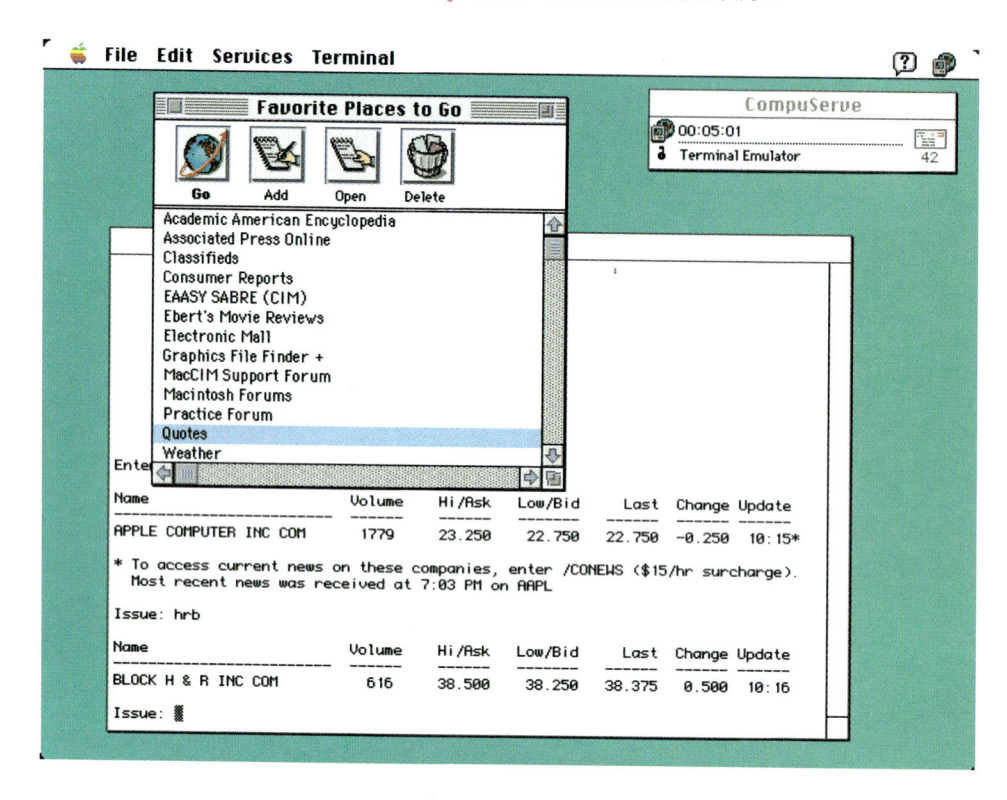

Figure 10-5
CompuServe provides, among other services, information from the New York Stock Exchange.

National Bedroom Communities

Once upon a time people lived in bedroom communities to escape from their jobs. Once on the 5:23 train home, work was no more. That was the idea anyway. But now, thanks to networked PCs, modems, and faxes, an opposite trend is developing: people who take their work home with them in a new way. At its most extreme are the urban professionals who commute several time zones to work a few days a week, and take care of business the other days by computer, such as Sherri Abend-Fels, a psychologist who lives four days in Los Angeles and three in Santa Fe. Some small towns are designing communities with state-of-the-art fiber-optic networks, regional microwave systems, and satellite links—all built into new homes. Opponents decry this creation of "yuppie ghettos," but supporters argue such places will attract more tax dollars for the community.

- Current stock market quotes from the New York Stock Exchange, American Stock Exchange, Standard & Poor's Index, and Dow Jones Index.
- Information on mutual funds and money market funds.
- Gold and silver prices.
- Commodity information from the Chicago Board of Trade, International Monetary Market, Chicago Mercantile Exchange, Kansas City Board of Trade, Minneapolis Grain Exchange, New York Mercantile Exchange, New York Futures Exchange, New Orleans Commodities Exchange, Coffee, Sugar and Cocoa Exchange, New York Cotton Exchange, and Commodity Exchange, Inc.
- Trends of major industrial groups such as aerospace, banking, computers, insurance, and real estate.

The Source also provides SourceMail, a service that allows users to access electronic mail or an electronic bulletin board.

Dow Jones News Service. The **Dow Jones News Service (DJNS)** provides financial information to business community subscribers. Initially, DJNS served brokerage firms with current stock market prices and stock market analysis. nitially, DJNS served As it expanded, DJNS added business information such as *Wall Street Journal* highlights, corporate earnings estimates, and weekly economic surveys.

CompuServe. **CompuServe** provides a broad spectrum of business and non-business information, including

- *The Official Airline Guide.* Subscribers can examine airline schedules, request information about specific flights, reserve seats, and even arrange for automatic credit-card billing.

• CHAPTER 10: Working with Communications •

- *Restaurant guides.* Users can select a restaurant according to price, name, type of food, features, and geographic location.
- *Hotel guides.* Users can select a hotel according to price and features; they can make their own reservations.
- *On-line shopping.* Users can access the catalogs of hundreds of merchants selling a broad spectrum of products and can purchase items directly.
- *Financial information.* CompuServe provides stock quotes and other financial reports similar to The Source or the Dow Jones News Services.
- *Computer-oriented services.* CompuServe is the leading forum for online technical support provided by producers of microcomputer hardware and software. CompuServe also offers large libraries of public domain software and shareware, and many of its on-line shopping vendors are computer suppliers.
- *On-line encyclopedias and databases.* Users can access a tremendous range of information and articles on subjects of general and technical interest.
- *Electronic mail and on-line conversion.*
- *Computer games.*

Prodigy. **Prodigy**, a telecommunications partnership between IBM and Sears, is one of the fastest-growing information services. It is more family oriented than other services; children as young as eight or nine can easily use the service because of its graphical interface (Figure 10-6). Unlike other services, Prodigy sells on-screen advertising to a variety of companies, many of which are also on-line as Prodigy merchants. Subscribers to Prodigy can

- Book their own seats on airlines, purchase tickets when there are discount opportunities, and make hotel reservations.
- Shop electronically from major stores and catalogs.

Telenurse

Thanks to computer communications, pregnant women can use their home telephones in new ways to get hospital help when they most need it. Pilot projects at Purdue University in Indiana and at Pennsylvania Hospital in Philadelphia have created a computerized phone system to monitor mothers at risk for early labor while they stay at home. The patients can answer questions by punching the numbers on their phone; the answers get sorted, recorded, and analyzed by a computer, which also alerts a nurse if necessary.

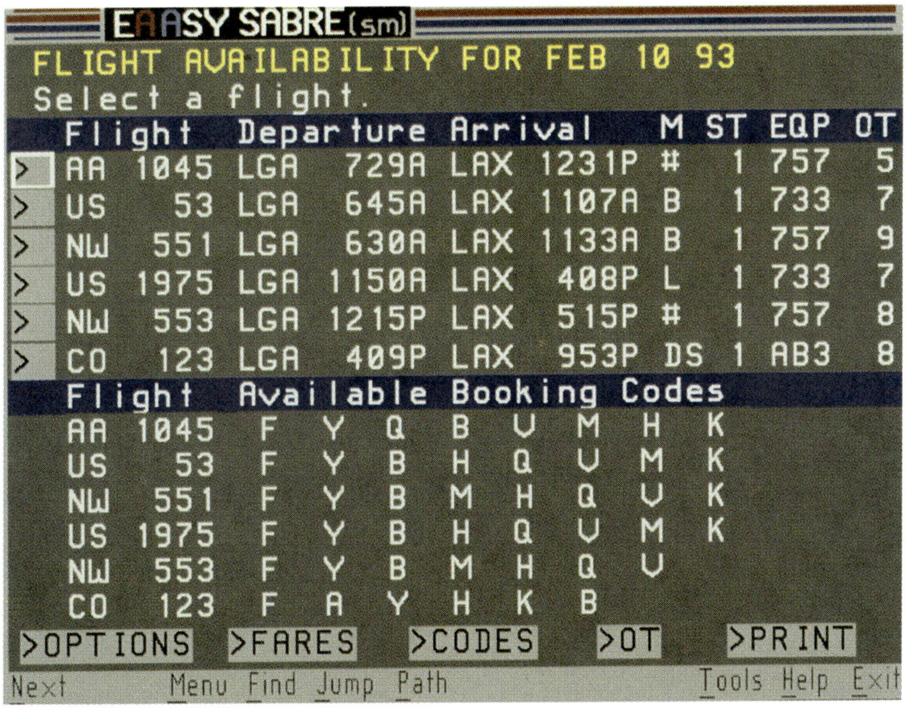

Figure 10-6
Prodigy's many consumer-oriented features include access to the EAASY SABRE airline booking service.

Computer Bidding

Now companies can advertise their garbage by computer. An Ohio firm, Team-W, provides an on-line service that lists companies' recycleable waste material and lets other companies bid for it. If Acme Yogurt has some leftover corrugated cardboard that Flowers First can use, the florist can use the computer to arrange to pick up the cardboard and give the yogurt company $25. Not only does the service save landfills from unnecessary objects, it's good for business. A similar service allows art lovers to bid on works via computers. Using an ID number to log on, they can browse through available works by title or by artist. Bids are made by punching in the code for the work, and sales are finalized by fax—all without ever leaving home.

Figure 10-7
An external modem is a self-contained unit and requires connection to the microcomputer through a serial port; the internal modem occupies an expansion slot on the microcomputer's motherboard.

- Track stocks through the DJNS.
- Access electronic games.
- Access an encyclopedia, the *Weekly Reader*, and *Consumer Reports* abstracts.
- Access news and weather information.
- Access *USA Today*.
- Participate in home banking services, including paying bills without writing checks, transferring funds, and checking their account balances.

TELECOMMUNICATIONS HARDWARE AND SOFTWARE

To communicate across telephone wires, a microcomputer needs both a modem and telecommunications software.

The **modem** is an absolutely essential piece of equipment for telecommunications (Figure 10-7). The modem translates binary (digital) informational to audible (analog) tones for transmissions over phone lines; it also receives these tones from the phone line and translates them back into binary information the computer can use (Figure 10-8).

Controlling the flow of information to and from the modem requires **telecommunications software.** A variety of telecommunications software packages are available for microcomputers, each with specific capabilities, such as linking to several different types of modems, providing automatic controls for accessing different computers with modems, and a host of technical features. As with all software, the more demanding the requirements, the greater the need for a package with sophisticated capabilities.

Synchronous and Asynchronous Communications

Synchronous communication is a method of transmitting data in serial fashion (one bit at a time) in which the bits are sent in digital form at a constant rate. To make this work, both ends of the transmission, the sender and receiver, must know the data transmission rate and what kind of data to expect (binary numbers, ASCII characters, etc.). Synchronous communication thus can operate at very high speeds (up to several megabits per second); however,

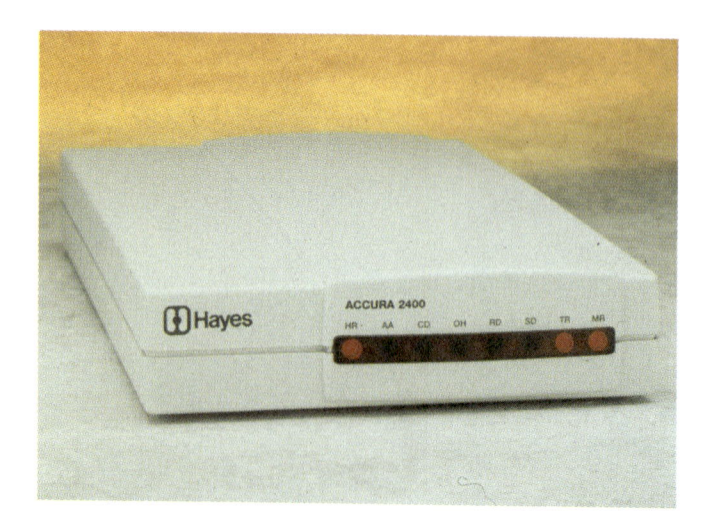

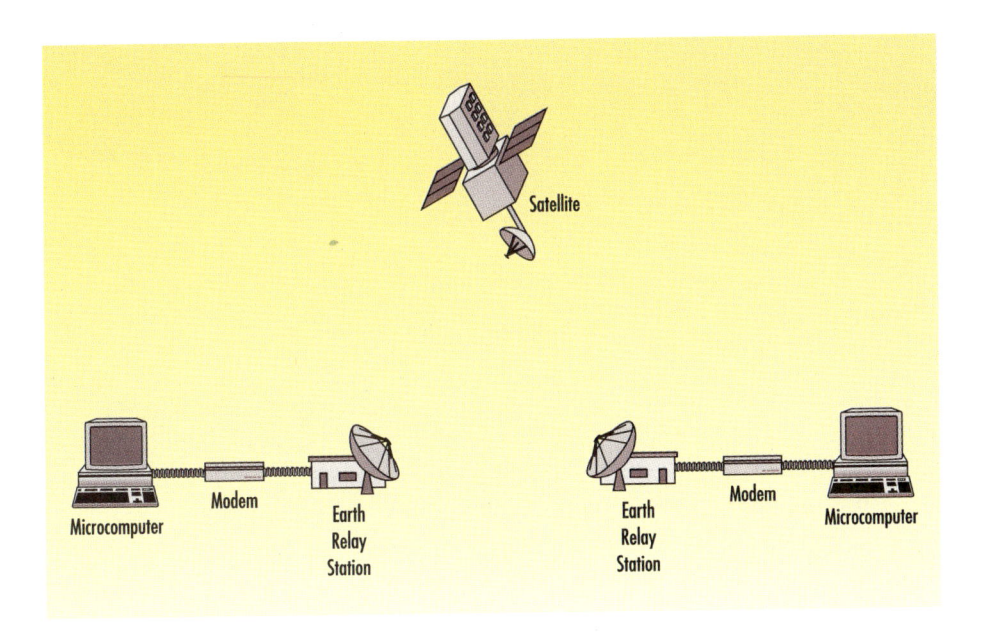

Figure 10-8
Telecommunications takes advantage of the phone company's extensive communications system. A typical modem connection may go out through the phone company's lines to an Earth relay station, which takes it up to a satellite that transmits the signal back to another relay station and then to the lines that connect to the other modem.

it requires special communications lines and equipment, which are generally too expensive for use with microcomputers. Synchronous communication is therefore used mainly for communicating in large computer networks and, within a computer, between its various components.

Asynchronous communication is the most common pattern for telecommunications with microcomputers. In asynchronous communication, the hardware assumes that the data coming over the line has no particular interval. Therefore, as the data comes over the line one bit at a time, the modem must have some way to know when a character starts and stops. A **start bit** indicates that the next set of bits forms a single byte, or character, and a **stop bit** indicates the end of a byte. For each byte of data that is sent, asynchronous communication confirms that the byte received was actually the byte sent. This ensures accuracy over telephone lines that have static, called **noise.**

Asynchronous communication can be implemented with inexpensive hardware and software, and in most cases can meet the needs of the individual user. That is why it's so widely used on microcomputers. However, the disadvantage of asynchronous communication is speed; its maximum transmission speed over standard telephone lines is 14,400 baud. This is very much slower than can be achieved with synchronous communication over dedicated (used only for this purpose) lines. Recent developments in asynchronous communication include data compression and error-checking standards that allow modems to pack more information into the bits they transfer, allowing for effective transmission speeds of 57,600 baud. These standards are designated V.32bis and V.42bis.

With asynchronous communications, users of the sending and the receiving computers must agree on three pieces of information:

- **Byte length**, the number of bits that make up a byte. Most modems and telecommunications software support bytes of 7 and 8 data bits.
- **Parity**, the method used by the computer to check that the byte sent was the byte received. Parity can be set to even, odd, or none.
- The number of **stop bits**, which indicate a byte has been sent. This can be set to one or two.

Getting Out of a Jam

Drivers may soon be able to use a computer in their cars to avoid those seemingly endless traffic jams. Some people already use the Global Positioning System, a computer mounted in cars, boats, and bicycles, to tell them exactly where they are. But a pilot project in Los Angeles, home of the country's first freeway, takes this idea the next logical step. The Department of Transportation has begun testing a program that picks up data from the California Highway Patrol, sensors and television cameras on the road, air surveillance, and information from radio stations. A screen mounted on the dashboard of the car allows the driver to access a map that highlights alternative routes that avoid reported trouble spots. Right now it is only being tested on a 14-mile stretch of road in Los Angeles and in Japan, but it seems like an idea whose time has come.

HISTORY

Hayes

It almost seems as if Dennis Hayes was predestined to make his name synonymous with modems.

Both his parents worked for Southern Bell in Spartanburg, South Carolina, when Hayes was growing up; his father as a lineman and his mother as a telephone operator. When Hayes got to Georgia Tech in 1968, he enrolled in the engineering department's co-op program, which allowed students to work full time for three months, followed by three months of school. Hayes's first three-month work assignment was with AT&T Long Lines, figuring out how to transmit radio signals over the Florida Everglades with its constantly fluctuating water level.

Hayes dropped out of Georgia Tech for financial reasons and began working in the telecommunications department of National Data, an Atlanta-based company that was involved with providing computerized data services for credit card companies, airlines, and banks.

During that time he and a friend, Dale Heatherington, bought an IMSAI computer. They were also founding members of the Atlanta Area Microcomputer Hobbyist Club. Hayes realized that sooner or later all his fellow computer hobbyists would want to be able to communicate with each other via their computers. Although modems were a well-known commodity in the commercial word, there was nothing similar for personal computers.

Hayes was still working full time for National Data when he and Heatherington came up with a schematic of a microcomputer modem and together, the two men built several. After showing fellow club members their product, about 10 people agreed to buy one.

Hayes would buy the necessary parts with what little money they had and assemble the modems, then take them to Heatherington, who would test them on the IMSAI computer. Hayes would take the modems back to his house, box them, and send them out, checking to see if any more orders had arrived at the post office since he had sent out the previous batch.

Finally the part-time business became too much of a burden to be just a sideline, and Hayes quit his full-time job in 1977, about the time the company moved out of his dining room and into a separate building. For a couple of years things were tight financially. Today Hayes recalls that his then-fiancee earned more money as a newspaper reporter than he did, and often had to give him gas money back to Atlanta when he visited her. But by 1983, Hayes Microcomputer had sales of $50 million—from the original Smartmodem, and three best-selling telecommunications software packages. Today Hayes and Heatherington, who became Hayes' senior engineer, are millionaires many times over.

Equally important to Hayes is that his company is a place where people like to work: a company that nutures talent, whether engineering or managerial. Hayes Microcomputer encourages each employee to create an educational path, whether night school or seminars or even just buying videos on special topics, all as part of the benefits package. In 1984 the company was voted one of the best places to work in Atlanta by the *Atlanta Business Chronicle*.

"Modern business needs people who can solve problems," Hayes has said. "Our best asset is our ability to think, and the best way to develop a disciplined thought process is through education." ■

The term 8N1, meaning an 8-bit byte, no parity, and one stop bit, is the most common telecommunications software setting for microcomputer users.

Selecting Transmission Speed

Modems can operate at several transmission speeds. The unit of measure for data transmission speed is the **baud** (named after the telegraphy communications pioneer, J. M. E. Baudot), which approximately equals the number of bits that are transmitted each second (bits per second—**bps**). With the 8 bits that form a character byte, plus the bits used to signal the start and stop of each character, it usually takes 10 bits to send a single character. Thus, modems operating at 2,400 baud can send data at 240 characters per second; 1,200 baud is about 120 characters per second. Most microcomputers use modems that operate at 1,200, 2,400, 4,800, or 9,600 baud.

The baud rates for both the sending and receiving computers must match. If one modem normally operates at a higher rate, the telecommunications software must be adjusted so that it transmits at the slower speed. Some telecommunications software packages can detect the transmission speed of the other modem and adjust the speed to match it.

Setting Duplex and Echo

Microcomputers can use one of two **duplex** settings: full-duplex or half-duplex. With a half-duplex setting, data are sent in only one direction at a time. With a full-duplex setting, the most common, data can be sent and received at the same time.

Echo settings determine whether or not the characters you type online are not only transmitted, but also show up on your own screen. They also determine whether the characters sent by the other end of the transmission link are sent back (echoed) to verify that they've been received.

Problems in these settings are indicated when you can't see what you type or get double characters when you type. If either of these happens, changing the duplex or echo setting on your computer will usually solve the problem.

Setting File Transfer Protocols

There are a variety of procedures, or **protocols**, for transferring files to and from other computers. Protocols specify how one computer will send a file and how the other computer will receive it. Protocols inform the computers on each end of the transmission that they're dealing with a file to be read and stored, for example, rather than simply text to show on the screen. File transfer protocols also let each end of the transmission verify that the file received exactly matches the file sent. The protocols organize the bits of the file into groups, called **blocks**, or **packets**, and give each block a key code that allows the receiving computer to check that the block received is what was sent. If the block doesn't check out, the receiving computer requests that it be resent until it is correct; this allows the file to be transmitted without errors.

As with other asynchronous settings, it is important that both the sending and the receiving computers have their telecommunications software set to the same file transfer protocol (Figure 10-9, p. 188). Some of the more popular file transfer protocols are **XMODEM, YMODEM,** and **ZMODEM**, each offering advantages and disadvantages. XMODEM, for example, one of the

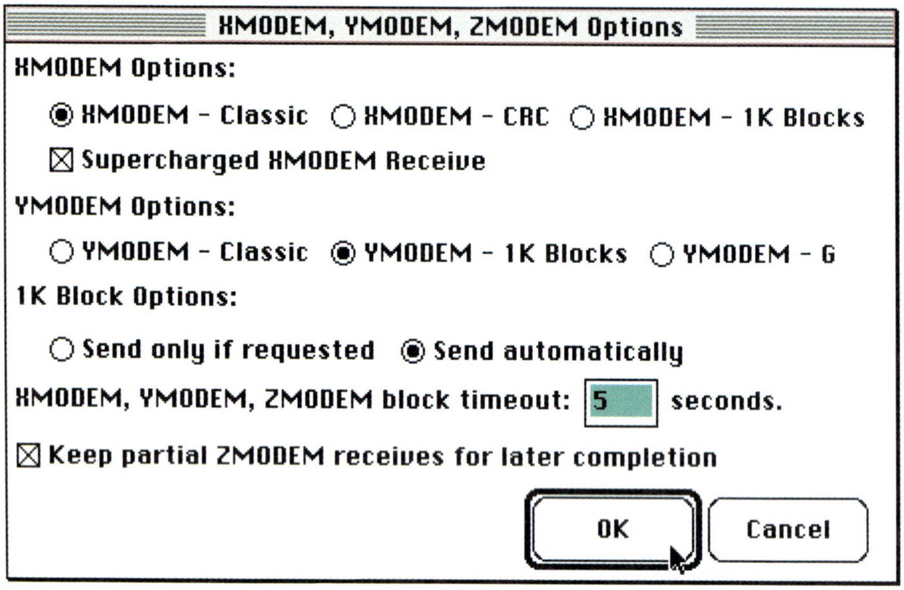

Figure 10-9
There are many different file transfer protocols. Most on-line services support a number of them; when transmitting files, make sure that both ends of the transfer are set to the same protocol.

first protocols designed for microcomputers, is reliable but very slow. YMODEM, based on XMODEM, is faster, but less stable and more susceptible to line noise. ZMODEM is designed to make XMODEM more efficient and flexible by using larger data blocks, allowing the sending computer to command the receiving computer; it also allows several files to be sent in one transmission. It sends the file names and sizes to the receiving computer, allowing the receiver to monitor transmission speed and estimate the time remaining for completion; this is very useful for transmitting large files. Another increasingly popular protocol is **Kermit**, which was developed on mainframe computers and is widely used on microcomputers to transfer information to and from mainframe databases. It is also becoming popular for micro-to-micro file transfers. Its sophisticated control language permits a variety of custom file transfer operations to be controlled by the user.

You can also capture incoming data using a **capture buffer,** a special allocation of memory controlled by the telecommunications software. Turning on a capture buffer lets the receiving computer store text or data there; this special memory can also be turned off at any point. For example, if you were receiving bibliographic citations from an encyclopedic database, the citations could be stored rather than sent directly to a printer. You could turn the capture buffer on when the desired information was being received and turn it off for information that you didn't want. After completing the telecommunications with the database, you could print the contents of the capture buffer or save it on a disk for future use and reference.

Setting Terminal Emulation

When a microcomputer accesses a large mainframe, it often needs to act like a specific type of terminal directly wired to the computer. Many telecommunication software packages support **terminal emulation** for a variety of different types of terminals. Thus your IBM 386 computer can "think" it is a DEC VT100 or VT102 terminal, a VIDTEX, and ANSI, or another terminal required by the mainframe you are accessing. This lets you run applications on remote mainframes and control the screen, rather than just watching text

> SECOND OPINION

Computer Communication In Learning

Telecommunications has changed the way students learn in Arizona's Maricopa Community Colleges. Whether through the local computer conference system called the Electronic Forum (EF) or through information sharing on the Internet, many students in the Phoenix metropolitan college system are learning through the networks.

Students in the Maricopa Community Colleges are taking control of their own learning and research by participating in class discussions on the Electronic Forum, corresponding via electronic mail, and accessing remote databases of primary source materials on the Internet for course papers. Networked terminals and personal computers are provided for student use in state-of-the-art high-tech centers, open access computer labs, libraries, and the student unions. Karen Schwaim, English faculty member at Glendale Community College and designer of the Electronic Forum, contends that increased participation in electronic communications media provides a social contact dimension for commuting students that would otherwise not be available to them.

Other colleges within the Maricopa system are providing "global classroom" activities for students by using the Internet. The first global classroom project at Mesa Community College focused on foreign language and intercultural communication. Students could choose from several language groups (including Spanish, German, and French), work from a hypercard stack that held a list of willing "pen pals" in countries where those languages are spoken, and use electronic mail to begin exchanges. English students are also participating in pen pal exchanges. Freshman English students communicate with students at Sangyo University in Kyoto, Japan.

Rio Salado Community College used the Internet to provide an opportunity for students in Moscow, Russia, to take a Freshman English Composition course without leaving home. The instructor sent eight Russian students preliminary instructions and textbook materials by mail, then used electronic mail to conduct the majority of her teaching and receive assignments from students.

Some of the newer applications of the Internet are "real-time" in nature. Glendale students recently participated in an introduction to Internet Relay Chat (IRC) in their English class. They joined with a group of Australians who were discussing the location of the 2000 Olympic Summer games. During the discussion, the games were actually awarded to the city of Sydney, Australia, which brought many on-line cheers from the Australians.

The MUSE, or Multi-User Simulated Environment, is another system that is changing students' control of their learning. Combining real-time conversation ability with the ability to create simulated spaces with words and programming instructions has provided groups of students and faculty a way to build their own learning environments. Led by faculty members from Phoenix College and Mesa Community College, students in computer science, education, and honors classes have learned to write instructions that describe objects and virtual "places" such as transportation devices, castles, libraries, and "classrooms." Participants can connect to MariMUSE, the name for Maricopa's MUSE, from anywhere on the Internet, so the MariMUSE citizens have been from several states in the United States as well as from other countries. Other college students and professors have contributed to the "building" of MariMUSE, thereby extending the Phoenix College and Mesa learning community to other places in the world. The latest MariMUSE project has been the extension of access to local urban elementary school children in third through fifth grade. The children learned to create learning spaces in MariMUSE, did research to be sure their creations were "true" to reality, and expanded their understanding of what computers can do.

These are but a few examples of the opportunities for network exploration provided to Maricopa's students. These students are being prepared for their future work lives, where electronic communication will be the norm for almost every position. ■

Janet Whitaker,
Mesa Community College

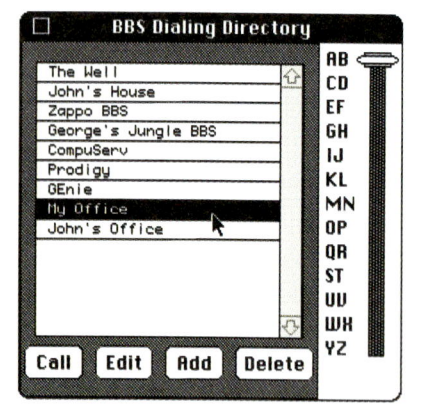

Figure 10-10
A dialing directory lets you enter all the pertinent settings for a particular on-line service, such as the Well, and save it so you can dial the service automatically merely by selecting its name from the directory.

Computer people *do* speak another language—it's called emoticons and it's very serious indeed : –). If you tilt your head to the side and examine that last punctuation sequence, you'll see it resembles the ubiquitous smiley face of the seventies. On an electronic bulletin board it has a more nineties meaning, such as "*NOT!*" or "just kidding." Also called smileys, emoticons first started showing up ten years ago, but with the popularity of E-mail, the range of emotions conveyed by emoticons has also grown. Writers on the subject say emotions convey nuances, individuality, or charisma that is otherwise lacking in computer conversation (: # = my lips are sealed). Movie critic Roger Ebert believes that "smileys might be a real help for today's students, raised on MTV and unskilled at spotting irony without a laugh track." (5 : –) = I'm Elvis). David Sanderson has been collecting smileys for four years and currently has 664 of them from around the world. His favorite? C=>: * ')). Guessed yet? It's "I'm a drunk demonic chef with a cold and a double chin."

scroll down the screen in one stream. A plain terminal, with no screen control, is usually called a TTY terminal and is controlled entirely with standard ASCII characters.

Dial Control and Packet-Switching Services

An important consideration when using telecommunications software is the method of calling another computer. For example, some software lets users create automatic dialing and access menus. Users record the phone number and all other appropriate settings for a particular computer (Figure 10-10). Then, all the user need do to contact another computer is select the desired item from the menu; the software does the rest.

Using a computer, a modem, and telecommunications software to access other computers has one major drawback: telephone toll charges. To decrease expenses, several communications services provide direct connections to distant computers through local telephone numbers.

One of the most common methods for providing such access is through a **packet-switching service**, which allows several computer users to share the same line. Charges are usually much lower than standard long-distance charges. Two of the most common packet-switching services, **Tymnet** and **Telenet,** charge as little as $2 per hour to access national information services. Standard long-distance toll charges might cost $10 to $15 per hour.

NETWORKING

Instead of telephone company lines, networks use specially designed cables that physically connect two or more computers. This makes it possible for one computer to house all the application software for all the computers in an office. Each connected, or **networked,** computer can share information from one central computer, access the same printers, and send electronic mail messages from one user to another.

The dedicated cables connecting a network carry information in a digital format, unlike the analog transmission over phone lines. This provides high-speed synchronous transmission of data.

Two types of computers make up the most common type of network, the **client-server network:** a host computer and a workstation (Figure 10-11). The **host** computer, or **file server,** is the central computer with all the network's files and programs. All computers on a network are connected to the host, which is usually the network's most powerful computer, requiring a great deal of disk storage capability. The host computer controls who can have entry to the network, which programs are available for operation, and file sharing. With its large hard disk, it also provides a common data storage space for users. In the past, a mainframe or minicomputer was used as a host computer. Today, high-speed microcomputers with large-capacity disk storage capability can serve as hosts.

Workstations are all the microcomputers linked to the host computer. Typically, the host computer requires workstation users to enter an identification code and password for security protection. This is known as logging on to the network. Once a workstation user logs on, the user can access programs and files stored in the host computer.

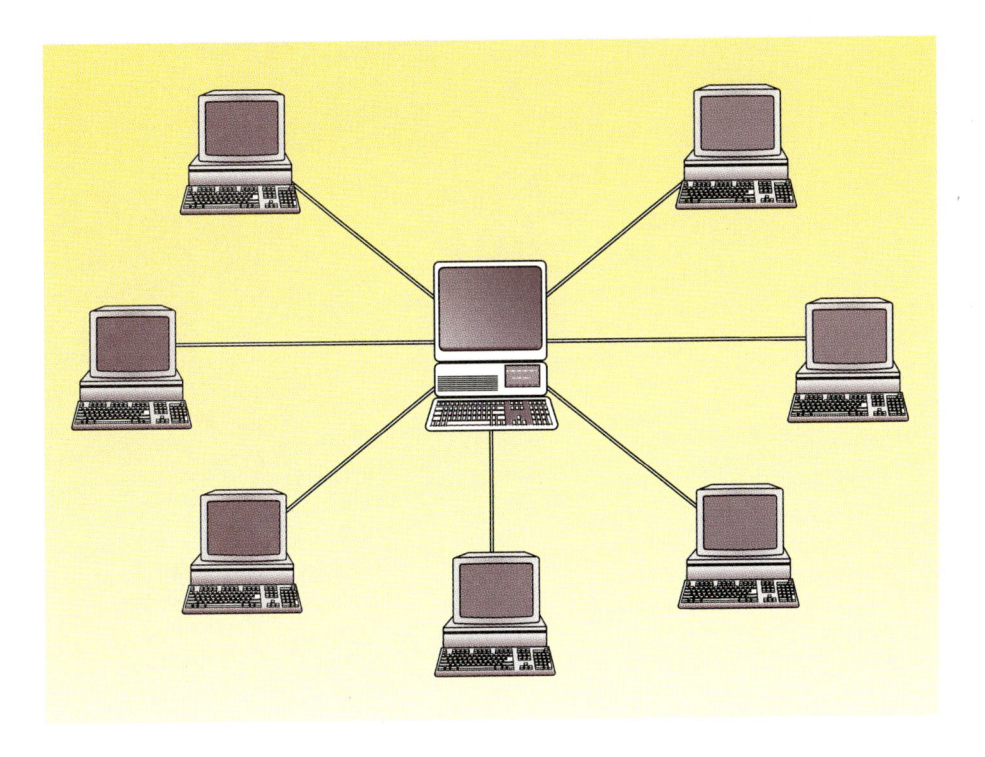

Figure 10-11
In a typical client-server network, the host computer functions as a file server, providing its hard disk space and other services to client workstations; workstations are typically connected only to the server, not to each other.

Because passwords are assigned to users rather than workstations, an authorized user can use any workstation on the network. Users can have differing levels of authorization; for example, some users can access any word processing files and others can access financial records. By limiting who has access to which programs and data, the network provides additional data security.

The primary disadvantage of this type of network occurs when the host computer becomes damaged or disabled. All access to information and programs on the network stops when the host stops. Another type of network, often used by businesses and organizations, is the **peer-to-peer network.** Here all stations on the network have equal status, and individual stations can choose whether to make their disk storage available to other users. As no station is host, the network doesn't stop when the host computer is off or damaged. Peer-to-peer networks, however, generally have less sophisticated services for the station. They also provide less security, as files are transmitted directly instead of through a host computer. Anyone whose disk is accessible is thus susceptible to having data lost or damaged.

LANs and WANs

Another way to describe networks is in terms of the area covered. A **local area network (LAN)** connects computers in the same building or within about a one-half-mile radius around the host computer. A **wide-area network (WAN)** can serve computers several—or hundreds—of miles apart (Figure 10-12, p. 192).

Local area networks are more common than wide area networks. Because WANS's often connect over long distances via dedicated communications

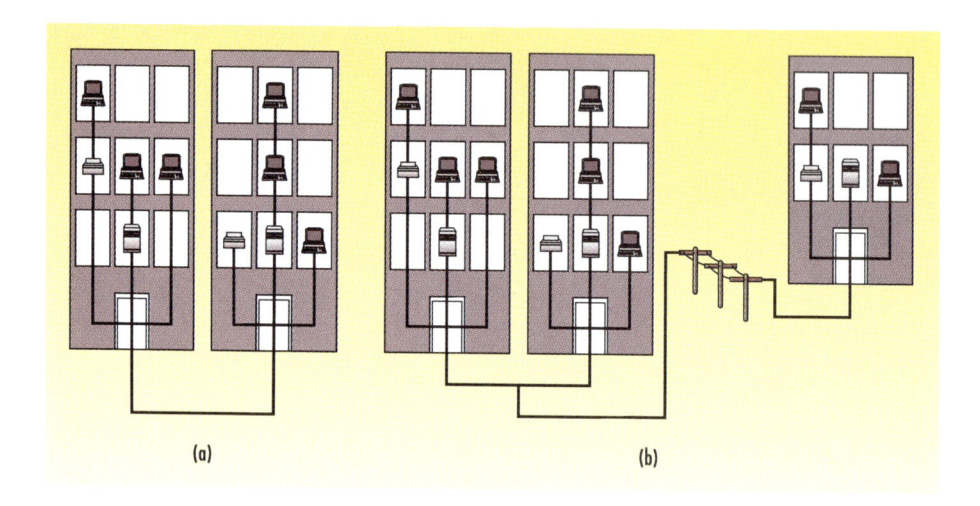

Figure 10-12
LANs and WANs: (a) A LAN connects computers within a building or between buildings near each other. (b) A WAN connects computers (including LANs) across long distances, even thousands of miles.

lines and satellites, they tend to be expensive. The LAN is less expensive, but it is an option only when an organization's networking needs can be met by connecting the computers in one location or adjacent locations.

Network Design

A network's **topology** is the way the various elements of the networks are wired together. The most common network topologies are bus, star, and ring.

Bus Network. In the **bus network**—the simplest network topology available for microcomputers (and common in peer-to-peer networks)—all computers are connected with a single line cable (Figure 10-13). For example, a 50-foot cable

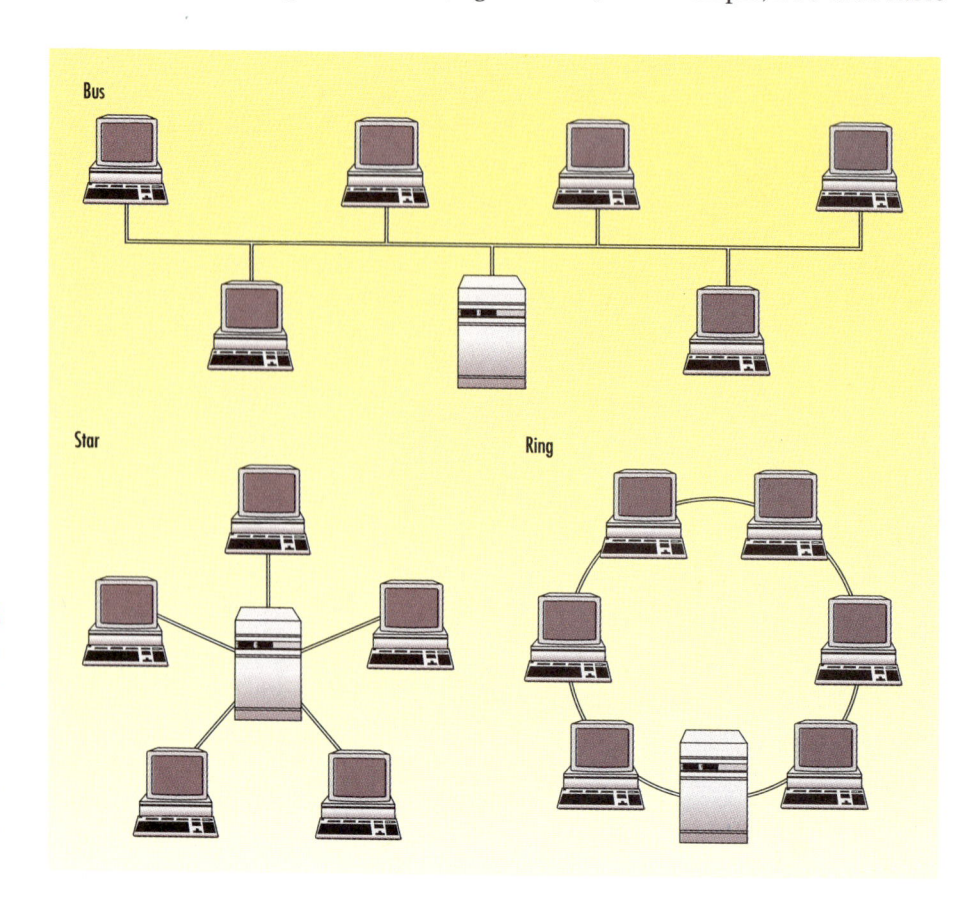

Figure 10-13
The three basic network topologies: bus, in which all computers on the network are connected to a single communications cable; star, in which client computers are individually connected to the central file server; and ring, in which the computers pass information around a central ring cable.

might connect a series of five computers, with the first computer at one end of the cable and the fifth computer at the other end. Data on a bus network travels from one computer directly to another.

Star Network. The **star network** is most commonly used to connect a central host computer to workstations in a client-server network. Each workstation is connected to the host computer by a separate table (Figure 10-13). Each workstation communicates directly with the host; workstations cannot communicate directly with each other.

Ring Network. In a **Ring Network,** all computers are connected on a central cable ring (Figure 10-13). This configuration is similar to the bus network, except there is no beginning point or ending point. The ring configuration is becoming more common for local-area networks, because adding computers is a simple process and the ring provides an efficient flow of data. Much as traffic flows on a highway around a major city, data enters the ring cable and travels around until it finds its desired computer, or exit. Both client-server networks and peer-to-peer networks use this topology.

Distributed Processing

In traditional network designs, all common processing is handled by one host or file server. **Distributed processing** is a decentralized approach in which processing requirements are shared among several smaller computer systems. Distributed processing uses more than one host; each computer has a different data processing role. The distributed processing network allows data sharing, but most computer operations remain independent of one another. Thus, while separate computers may perform accounting, research and development, inventory control, and marketing functions, they can still share other activities and resources through networking.

A distributed processing system has several strengths. Failure of one computer does not interfere with the operation of other computers. In addition, each department can work independently without worrying about the processing needs of other groups. This differs from centralized networks in which several departments in a business can compete for processing time on the host computer and activities must be prioritized. Distributed processing also incorporated the strengths of a stand-alone system. Each independent computer in the system can have software specifically tailored to fit its user's exact needs and requirements. Because the computers are independent, there is no need to use standardized software.

SUMMARY

Connecting computers allows computer communications. Two approaches are most common for microcomputer users—networking and telecommunications.

Telecommunications uses existing telephone lines and modems to send and recieve data, making it possible for computers to share and exchange data with other computers almost anywhere in the world.

Telecommunications allows sending and receiving electronic mail (E-mail) and facsimiles (faxes), participating in bulletin boards, and accessing databases. On-line services provide one or more of these services to their subscribers, including access to stock and bond data, encyclopedic information, news, sports, and even airline schedules. Some of the more popular information services include The Source, Dow Jones News Service, CompuServe, and Prodigy.

Data communication is either synchronous or asynchronous. Synchronous communication is faster, but it requires more expensive and specialized equipment and is therefore most commonly used in mainframe communications and networks. Asynchronous communication is slower but less expensive and easier to implement; it is the common choice for microcomputer telecommunications.

Telecommunications software controls the speed at which data are transferred (the baud rate, roughly equal to bits-per-second); whether the data flows in one direction (half-duplex) or both (full-duplex); whether you see what you type or only what the other computer sends you (echo); file transfer protocols (XMODEM, YMODEM, etc.) that help ensure error-free transmission; and emulation choiced that make your computer act like a specific terminal attached to a mainframe computer.

Networking—the other major type of computer communications—involves physically connecting two or more computers with specifically designed cables. Computers can then share information from one central computer, and access the same printers, and users can send messages to one another. Networking makes it possible for one computer to house all the application software for all computers in an office.

A client-server network includes the host, or file server, and the workstation. The host computer is the central computer that maintains and controls access to the files and programs used by all other computers—the workstations—on the network. On peer-to-peer networks, however, all stations have the same status and share information directly; such networks are simpler and less secure than client-server networks.

Two types of networks are commonly used with microcomputers. A local area network connects computers within a limited physical area. Computers in a wide area network can be several to hundreds of miles apart.

Local area networks commonly use three types of topology. A bus network connects all workstations to the host with a single cable; data travels from one computer directly to another. In a star network (the most common), each workstation is connected to the host by a separate cable. A ring network connects all computers in a large loop, with data flowing around the loop from one computer to another.

Distributed processing is a decentralized approach to networking in which processing requirements are shared among several smaller computer systems, each with a different processing role.

KEY TERMS

asynchronous
baud
block
bps
bulletin board
bus network

byte length
capture buffer
client-server network
CompuServe
computer communications
distributed processing

Dow Jones News Service (DJNS)
duplex
echo
electronic mail (E-mail)
facsimile

• CHAPTER 10: Working with Communications •

file server	peer-to-peer network	terminal emulation
host	Prodigy	The Source
Kermit	protocol	topology
local area network (LAN)	ring network	Tymnet
modem	star network	virtual (on-line) communities
network	start bit	wide-area network (WAN)
networking	stop bit	workstation
noise	synchronous	XMODEM
packet	telecommunications	YMODEM
packet-switching service	telecommunications software	ZMODEM
parity	Telenet	

REVIEW QUESTIONS

1. What is the difference between half-duplex and full-duplex?
2. What is the difference between asynchronous and synchronous communications?
3. What is the purpose of a local network?
4. What is the difference in characters per second (cps) speed between a 1,200 baud modem and a 2,400 baud modem?
5. What are the three common network configurations?
6. What is electronic mail, and what are the advantages of using it?
7. To use telecommunications, a computer must have two important elements. What are these elements, and how do they work?
8. What is the advantage of using a packet-switching service such as Tymnet or Telenet?
9. What are three popular information services?
10. List five activities common to information services.
11. What are the differences between client-server and peer-to-peer networks? What advantages do client-server networks have over peer-to-peer networks?
12. What are three popular network topologies?
13. What is distributed processing?
14. What does *baud* mean?

11

Programming

OBJECTIVES

After completing this chapter, you will be able to
- Define the terms *program* and *programming*.
- Describe the five steps in the programming process.
- Explain how a programmer goes about defining a problem.
- Define the term *algorithm*, and explain how a programmer constructs an algorithm.
- Explain structured or top-down programming.
- Describe the testing and debugging procedure.
- Explain syntax and logic error.
- Explain how programmers document programs internally and externally.
- Explain on-line documentation.
- Explain what a programming language is.
- List the categories of programming languages.
- Identify common procedural languages.
- Explain what problem-oriented languages are, and name some examples.
- Describe what a natural programming language might look like.

FOCUS

The most effective use of many popular software applications requires some knowledge of programming. In particular, spreadsheet, database, telecommunications, and some word processing programs encourage you to apply programming procedures when using them. Spreadsheet and word processing "power users" in business, finance, and scientific industries pride themselves on their extensive macro creations. Accountants and librarians create unique and customer-specific data input interfaces with elaborate automatic report-generating capabilities from their database applications. And some telecommunications enthusiasts have gone so far as to set up extensive electronic bulletin boards.

This chapter provides an overview of the program development process. It focuses on the definition of a program and programming, describing the programming process and the different types of programming languages. It is not meant to teach programming, but to provide an understanding of programming concepts that can be applied in many areas of microcomputer use.

• CHAPTER 11: Programming •

PROGRAMS AND PROGRAMMING

A **program** is a set of instructions written in a programming language and designed to make a microcomputer perform a series of specified tasks. These instructions tell computers exactly what to do and exactly when to do it. A **programming language** is a set of grammar rules, characters, symbols, and words—the vocabulary—in which those instructions are written.

Programming is the designing and writing of programs. It is a process that involves much more than writing down instructions in a given language. The process begins with identifying *how* a program can solve a particular problem. It ends when the written documentation has been completed.

THE PROGRAMMING PROCESS

The program development cycle involves five processes: problem definition, algorithm development, coding, program testing and debugging, and documentation (Figure 11-1).

Defining the Problem

The first step in developing a computer program is determining exactly what it is that you want the computer program to do. What tasks will it perform? What kind of data will it use, and where will it get its data from? What will the

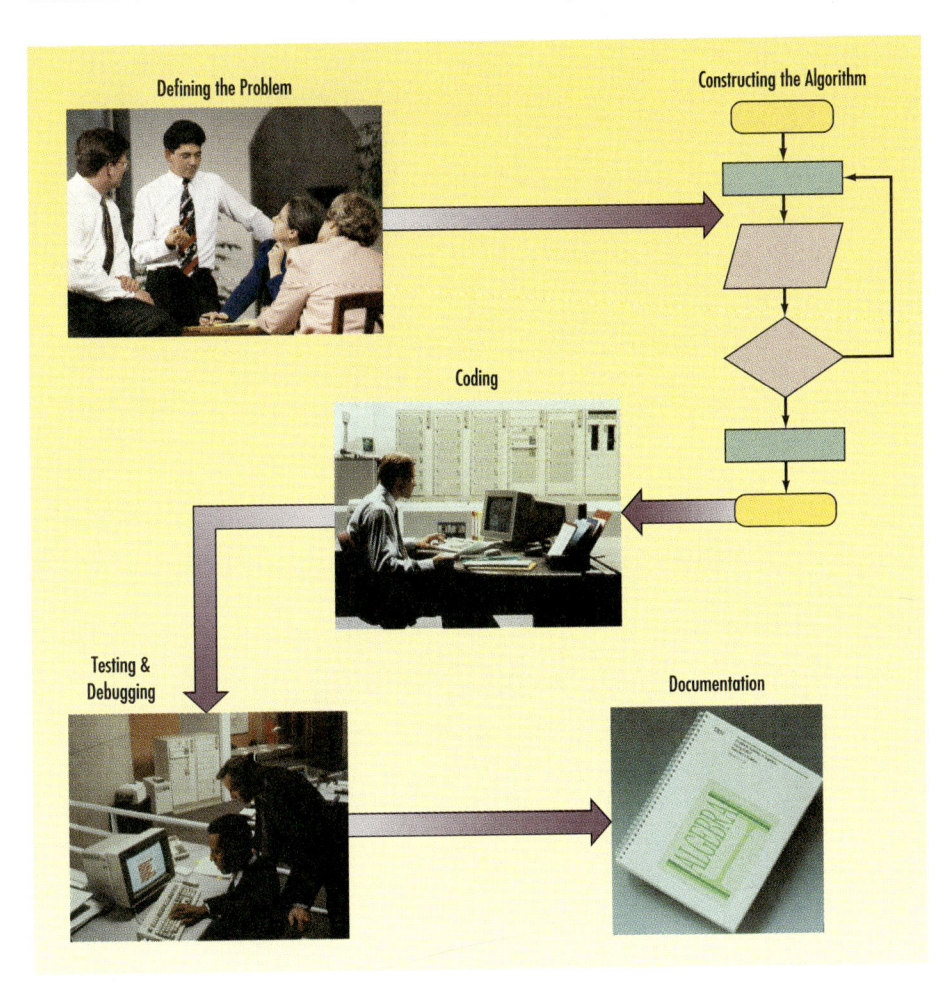

Living Computer Programs?

Tomorrow's state-of-the-art computer software won't be written; it will be grown. At least that's the current thinking of a number of computer scientists who are involved with open-ended programming. First developed to model weather patterns and global economics, open-ended programming was next turned toward the field of artificial life. Scientists treat the computer as an environment and the programs as organisms that must evolve over time or die. Programmers give the software certain traits and then design constraints within which the software will evolve. "All we do is define the puzzle," says one programmer. "We don't have to be smart enough to figure out the way the program solves the puzzle." At UCLA Rob Collins and David Jefferson used artificial life programming to build a computerized colony of ants who must go out, find food, and bring it back. Some ants never left the nest; others found food but did not bring it back. Only those colonies whose ants found food and brought it back thrived. Artificial life is not only changing computer programs, it is changing computer programmers. As one observer put it, "Programmers will be more like gardeners than engineers."

Figure 11-1

The five-step programming development cycle. First, programmers define the problem, often consulting users regarding desired specifications and output. Next, the programmer constructs the algorithm. The algorithm is then coded using the selected programming language. The code is tested and debugged until it runs correctly. Finally, the program is thoroughly documented, both for users and for future maintenance of the program.

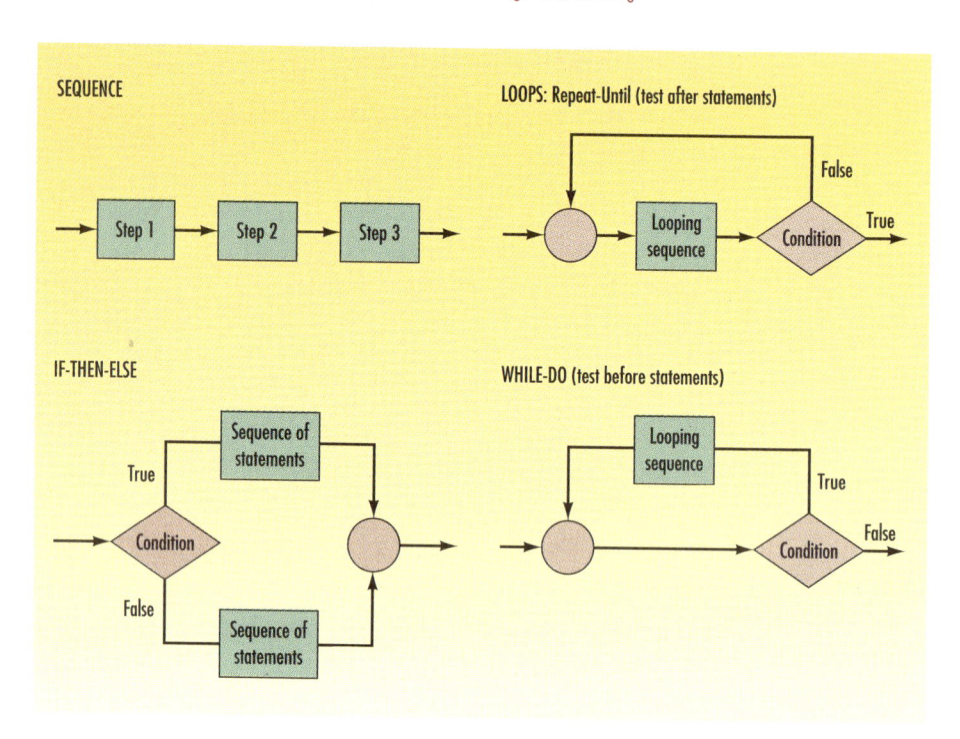

Figure 11-2
The programmer constructs the algorithm using three basic logic structures: sequence, selection, and looping, or repetition.

```
Checking Engine Oil

Open hood.
Pull dipstick.
Repeat:
    Wipe dipstick clean;
    Dip dipstick;
    Read oil level;
    If oil level is low, add
       appropriate amount;
Until oil level is correct.
Replace dipstick.
Close hood.
```

Figure 11-3
An algorithm can be developed for preforming any task. Here is a simple algorithm for checking engine oil and adding oil if needed.

output of the program be? How will the program interact with the computer user? Answering these questions, and thereby defining exactly what you want the computer to do, is what we call *defining the problem.*

To define the problem, programmers meet with the intended users to develop the program's objectives. The resulting **outline** includes information about how the output should look, what kind of data the program will use as input, and the processing requirements (how the data will be manipulated and what kind of hardware will be used to run the application). The more information programmers can learn at the beginning of the programming process, and the more specific that information is, the more likely the resulting application will meet user's needs.

To help in defining the problem, users are also asked to draw a picture of how they wish the final output to appear. The programmer can then begin to plan what input, data, and processing are necessary to get the desired results from the application.

Constructing the Algorithm

An **algorithm** is a prescribed set of well-defined instructions for solving a problem in a finite number of steps. The programmer, understanding how a microcomputer works, conceives how data must be entered, how it must be processed, and how the data must be presented to produce the required output. The algorithm spells out when the computer is to start and stop the program, where input is needed, where output is needed, when to perform arithmetic operations, and when to perform comparison operations. It also indicates what the microcomputer is to do if certain answers are derived from these operations.

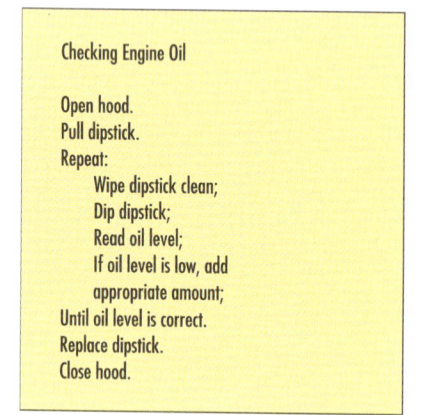

To control the sequence of steps the algorithm performs, the programmer uses **logic structures**, the rational constructs that control the steps from beginning to end (Figure 11-2). The logic structures used control the sequence of events, when a decision must be made, and what to do after the decision is made. The **sequence** structure is the simplest logic structure: One program statement follows another, instructing the microcomputer to perform tasks in a linear (sequential) manner. When a choice of actions is possible, a selection structure is written into the algorithm; this calls for the computer to make a decision and act accordingly. For instance, *IF* the data being received is within a given range of values, *THEN* use that data, *ELSE* (otherwise) do not use it. The algorithm may also require that a particular sequence of steps be repeated, either for a given number of repetitions or until a particular condition is met. This repetition requires a **looping** structure.

When working out the precise description of the algorithm, the programmer can write it in pseudocode and/or draw it in a flowchart. **Pseudocode** is a narrative description of the flow and logic of the intended program, written in plain language that expresses each step of the algorithm (Figure 11-3). A flowchart is a diagram, using symbols, lines, and arrows to show the movement of logic through the algorithm (Figure 11-4). Both methods of working out program logic are useful; which one is used is generally the programmer's choice. In a commercial programming environment the choice is often a matter of policy.

In constructing the algorithm, programmers use the techniques of top-down design and structured programming. **Top-down design** is the process of starting with the most general outline of how the algorithm will work, refining it by sketching in the details on smaller and smaller scales. Once a general outline is constructed, the programmer treats each of the steps as another algorithm to be developed and thus constructs an algorithm for executing all the steps in the general outline. By continuing to refine each step at lower and lower levels of the program, the programmer creates a plan for how the program should be organized. This is often drawn up on a **structure chart** (Figure 11-5).

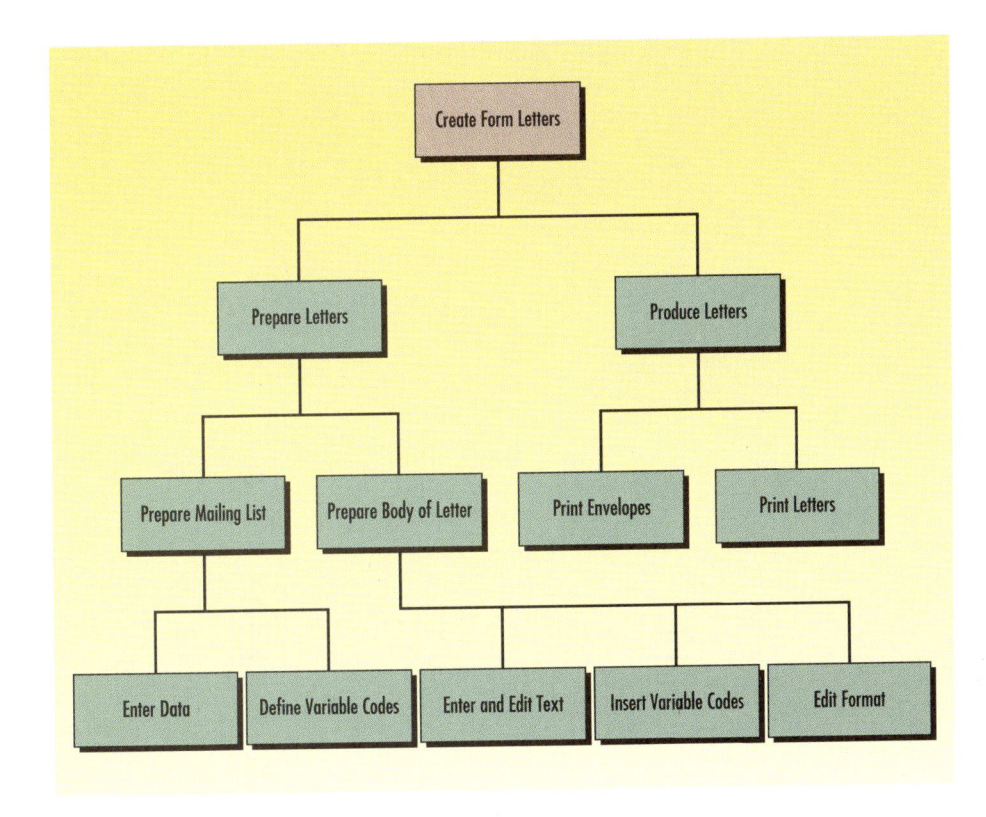

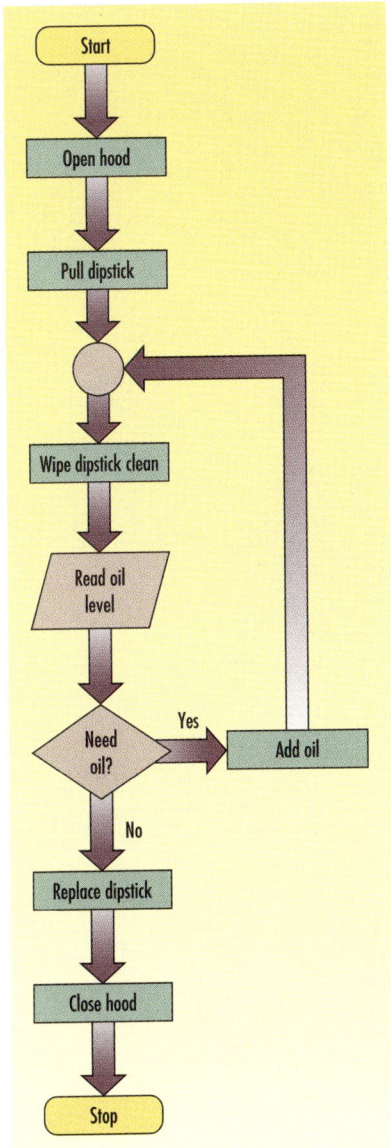

Figure 11-4
The flowchart uses graphic symbols and arrows to express the algorithm. Here the algorithm for checking engine oil is shown in flowchart form.

Figure 11-5
Structure charts are a different way of looking at the algorithm, showing not the sequence of steps to be performed but the way the steps are organized. Each successive level of the structure chart shows a greater level of detail in the algorithm, and the program is structured according to the form of the chart.

Structured programming uses the programming language to organize the code according to the top-down design. Most programming languages today let the programmer define each part of the program as a separate, self-contained block of code called a **procedure**. Procedures are written for each task the program must execute. These small procedures are grouped under larger procedures, and all the procedures are called in sequence by the the main body of the program, which is written to implement the top level of the program design. By providing a means of organizing code according to the logic and structure of the algorithm, structured programming makes programs easier to develop, debug, and document.

Coding

Coding is the process of translating the algorithm into the syntax (grammar) of a given programming language (Figure 11-6). In developing its programs, a software publishing company often specifies that its programmers must use a particular language, especially as most major applications are a group effort that involves many programmers. Independent software developers often choose a favorite language to work with for most of their projects. In some cases (such as a program developed for a specific client), which programming language to use is decided according to the needs of the user, who may refine or modify the program later. When possible, the decision should be made objectively; different programming languages have their strong and weak points that make them better for some programming tasks, worse for others. In any case, selecting a programming language is a crucial decision in the program development cycle. Programming languages appear later in this chapter.

Figure 11-6
Once the algorithm is constructed, it must be translated into a programming language: this is called coding. This algorithm performs the mathematical function of raising a number to a power; e.g., $2^2 = 4$.

Testing and Debugging

Program **testing** means running the program, executing all its functions, and testing its logic by entering sample data to check the output. **Debugging** is the process of finding and correcting program code mistakes. The term comes

```
Program in Pascal:

Program Exponential (input, output);

var      number, exponent: real;

function Power (var base, pow: real): real:
```

```
begin (Power)
    if base = 0.0 then
            Power: = 0.0
        else if base > 0.0 then
                    Power: = Exp(pow * Ln(base))
                else Power: = 1.0/Exp(pow * Ln(base))
end; (Power)

begin (main)
            writeln ("This program computes the result of raising a");
            writeln ("number to a power.  Please enter two numbers");
            writeln ("separated by a space, e.g. 3 6");
            readin (number, exponent);
            writeln ("The result is", Power(number, exponent)
end.
```

from an episode in the early days of modern computing when programmers for the Mark I computer in 1945 were trying to discover why their program didn't work. Examining the computer, they found a moth stuck between the contacts of an electrical relay. Nowadays any error in code is called a *bug*. Two general types of errors are syntax errors and logic errors.

A **syntax error** is a transgression (breaking) of the grammar rules of the programming language; like other languages, all programming languages have rules of grammar. A programming language's grammar is even stricter, however, and any deviation from the rules causes a program to not work.

A **logic error** is a transgression of the basic logic structure. It can involve missing a step in the algorithm, having an error in the algorithm's logic structure, using an erroneous formula, or any number of other subtle problems with the design or execution or the program steps. If the microcomputer cannot follow the logic, at some point the program will not operate properly. Logic errors can be so serious that entire programs must be redone.

The testing and debugging process follows a least-risk procedure (Figure 11-7). First the programmer reads the code in an attempt to edit (correct) any errors. Next the programmer tries to follow the program's procedures by hand, possibly using a calculator and sample data, to see whether the algorithm produces the product desired *without* the microcomputer. Next, because the program must be translated into machine code in order to use it, the programmer tries to have the code translated by the translating program. If it cannot be translated, it has syntax errors; even if it is translated, however, it doesn't mean the code is free of logic errors. Finally, the program is tested by running the program using sample data. If the program operates correctly and produces the desired output, logic errors are ruled out. If there are logic errors, here is where structured programming gives the programmer an advantage: Because the program is organized into short modules, it's easy to trace problems in logic to the specific procedure involved, rather than having to search the whole program for one erroneous statement.

Another round of testing involves actual software users. **Field testing** involves letting users operate the software with the purpose of locating problems, which can range from minor details to the broad approach of the software. Logic errors show up better under actual real-life use of the program—and the testers may find the program too difficult for its intended users to use.

Documenting the Program

Program documentation is a written record of the program's development; it is also a set of directions for using the program.

Internal documentation consists of instructions and comments within the program itself, for use by the programmer and other programmers when they are looking at the program code (Figure 11-8, p. 204). It includes comments that explain the program's logic, identify the significance of variable names, and highlight specific codes responsible for key features. If other programmers wish to make changes in the program, they need to know the meaning of acronyms and other abbreviations used by the original programmer. When testing the code or modifying it later, the original programmer may also need reminders of what various things mean and how the program works.

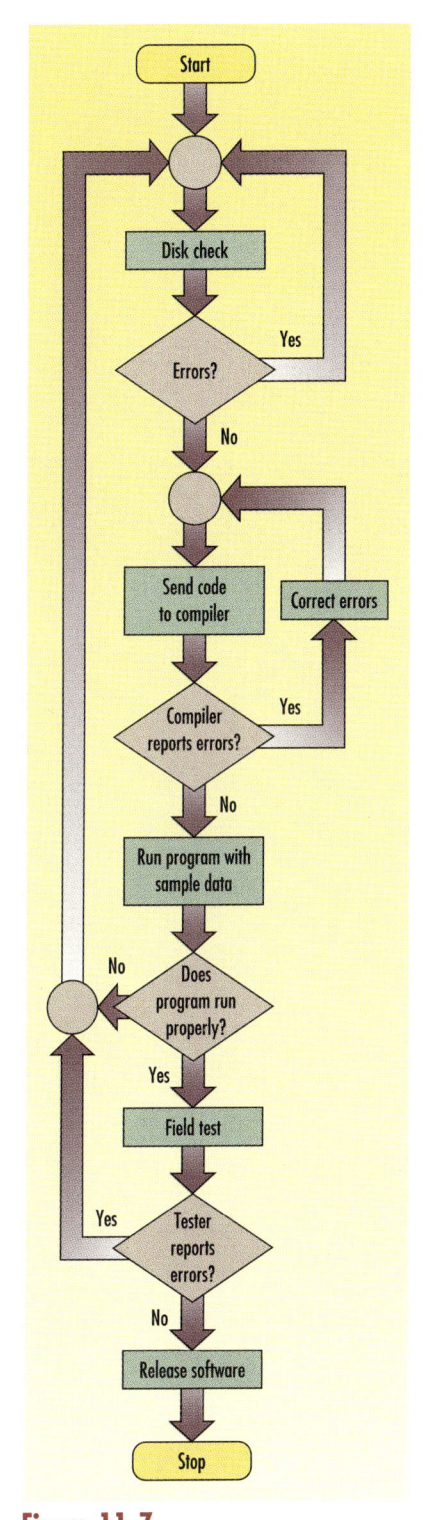

Figure 11-7
The testing/debugging process. Any error can force the programmer to start over; this is why testing and debugging often take more time than any other part of the process.

```
Program Skidspeed (input, output);
    {This program gives speed of a car before a crash by calculation based upon the length of the skidmarks and
    the strength of the brakes.}

const    Brakefactor = 0.70;           {brake strength: 1.0 = new}
         pi = 3.1416;

var      Skidlength: real;             {length of the skidmarks}
         slopedeg: real;               {steepness of a hill, in degrees}
         sloperad: real;               {steepness converted to radians}
         slope: real;                  {steepness converted to rise/run}
         speed: real;                  {speed of the car}

begin
         writeln ('Please enter the length of the skidmarks in feet.
                   You may use a decimal approximation: ');

         readln (Skidlength);

         writeln ('Please enter the road's slope in degrees:');

         readln (slopedeg);

         Sloperad := slopedeg · pi/180;
                   {converting slope to radian measure for use with trig functions}

         slope := sin (sloperad)/cos (sloperad);
                   {converting slope to ratio of rise over run}

         speed := sqrt(30 · Skidlength · (slope + brakefactor));
                   {the formula for finding the speed of the car}

         writeln ('The car was traveling approximately ',speed:3:2, 'miles per hour.')
end.
```

Figure 11-8
This Pascal program shows use of internal documentation. All text enclosed in braces is commentary, explaining what the program is for and what various parts of the program do.

External documentation is the printed set of instructions (the manual) describing how to operate the program. Early drafts of external documentation may occasionally be written while the program is being developed. Many programmers, however, wait to write precise instructions until after debugging the program with test data. Many good programs fail, not because of poor design or coding, but because the documentation is inadequate. Documentation explaining how to use the program is as important for most users as the program itself.

Many sophisticated applications add a third type of documentation that is directly accessible to users while operating the program. **On-line documentation** often provides—or amplifies—much of the information found with external documentation, in the form of help keys, topic indexes, and other features to guide users to successful operation of the software (Figure 11-9).

TYPES OF PROGRAMMING LANGUAGES

Programming languages are classified as first-, second-, third-, fourth-, or fifth-generation languages, according to when they were developed and how sophisticated they are. The first- and second-generation languages are very difficult to use and are considered low-level languages. The others are sometimes called high-level languages.

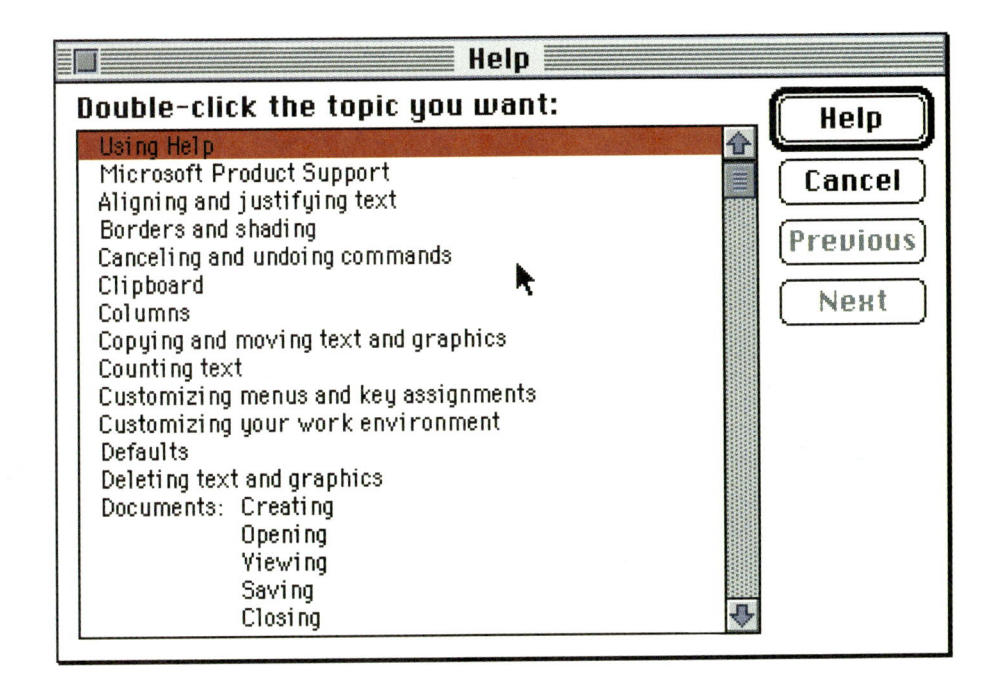

Figure 11-9
Online documentation, such as this screen from Microsoft Word's help index, gives users immediate access to instructions for using the program.

Machine Languages

Machine languages are the first generation of programming languages; these languages consist of instructions the computer is actually built to execute. Since at the hardware level computers understand only binary notation (1s and 0s), programming with a machine language requires writing out the binary values of the program instructions. A simple machine-language command might be "10101001 10101010 1011101011010100." Machine languages vary from one model of computer to another, as each model of processor is built differently. Machine languages are difficult to understand and use, so they are rarely used directly by programmers today. Since the computer understands only machine language, however, any program written in any other language must be translated into machine language in order to run.

Assembly Languages

Assembly languages are the second-generation programming languages and the first to use alphanumeric symbols to write code. The creation of assembly languages depended on the development, using machine language, of an assembler. An assembler is a program that translates the assembly code into machine language. It is necessary to have one assembler for each kind of assembly language and for each kind of computer used.

Assembly languages are the simplest improvement over machine language; their commands are simple mnemonic codes that stand for the binary instructions of machine code (Figure 11-10, p. 206). When programmers need to deal with the computer directly, they use assembly language; because it is so close to the hardware level, it is possible to write very efficient programs in assembly language. That same closeness to the hardware level, however is what makes assembly language difficult to use for large programming projects. Therefore, most assembly programming today is used for writing small modules that can be included in larger programs written in more convenient languages.

Tools for Programmers

The cost of developing an information system for a large company is staggering, but the cost of doing a bad job is even worse. Computer-Assisted Software Engineering (CASE) tools have been touted as the savior of corporate programmers since they incorporate all kinds of software tools into a single package. But there are still problems. For example, CASE tools are designed to foster structured programming, but in doing so they can force programmers into predefined structures that do not necessarily suit the needs of the system being developed. Another problem with CASE tools is that they are notoriously difficult to learn. Finally, programmers are generally used to working alone, and CASE tools encourage team effort, forcing users to change their style. But CASE tools are still in their infancy, which gives programmers hope that more sophisticated CASE tools will be even more useful.

Figure 11-10
The binary codes of machine language translate directly into assembly language statements. Note that the three lines of machine or assembly language code translate into one Pascal statement; obviously, this makes it easier to program in high-level languages.

```
Machine code                          Assembly language
10100001  00000000  00000000          MOV  AX,A
00000101  00000100  00000000          ADD  AX,4
10100011  00000000  00000000          MOV  A,AX
```

The commands instruct the computer to:
1. Fetch the contents of memory location A and move them to AX.
2. Add 4 to AX.
3. Move the result from AX back to A.

Pascal equivalent: A := A + 4

Procedural Languages

Procedural languages are the third-generation languages. They are also called **high-level languages** because they represent a higher level of abstraction from machine code than do assembly languages. Procedural languages employ more human-like words, and each has its own set of syntax rules. They are also more efficient, allowing the programmer to express with one statement what would take several commands in machine language. They are called *procedural languages* because they allow the programmer to create procedures that implement structured programming. Procedural languages are by far the most widely used programming languages.

The development of procedural languages was started by the invention of translation programs that could convert the syntax of the high-level language to machine code that the computer could execute. These translators are compilers and interpreters. A **compiler** converts an entire program written in a high-level language to machine language, storing it in what is called *executable file*, to be run later at the user's discretion. The original code is then called the *source code*, and the machine-language code is called the *object code*.

An **interpreter** reads each high-level program statement, then translates it to machine language and instructs the computer to execute the statement immediately. It creates no object code and no executable file; from the programmer's or user's standpoint, the computer executes the original code. This method of execution gives the programmer more immediate control of the machine and lends itself to an interactive method of programming and refining code and testing it immediately. The interpreter program does not permanently change the code, allowing users or programmers to make additions and other modifications to the program more easily. However, interpreting the code takes more processing than running a compiled program, so interpreted programs generally run slower than compiled programs.

Some of the most frequently used procedural languages include the following:

BASIC. The beginner's all-purpose symbolic instructional code (**BASIC**) is a high-level programming language developed in 1964 at Dartmouth College. An interpreted (rather than compiled) language, it is the first language designed to make programming easy for the novice programmer. It is a general-purpose language used for microcomputer programming and developing business data processing and education applications. BASIC's simple syntax is

---

A Flowering Computer

Computers are aiding a new branch of mathematics, biomathematics, which seeks to use numbers to describe nothing less than the growth of plant life itself. Sets of mathematical formulas describe not only the plant's outer shape, but also duplicate the way the plant grows. The result is a series of biologically correct computer pictures that trace the life of the plant from a tiny seed to maturity. One advantage of these computer programs is that processes that cannot be observed in nature can be visualized through computer modeling. Another advantage is that as the programs become more sophisticated, scientists can watch a 500-year growth cycle within a few minutes on a computer screen.

```
10      REM Program to compute integer sum.
20      MAXINT% = 32767
30      TOTAL# = 0#
40      PRINT "This program calculates the sum of all integers"
50      PRINT "from 1 to whatever integer you specify."
60      PRINT "Enter any positive integer up to "MAXINT%":";
70      INPUT NUMBER
80      IF (NUMBER > 0) AND (NUMBER <= MAXINT) THEN GOTO 90 ELSE GOTO 150
90      FOR COUNT% = 1 TO NUMBER
100     TOTAL# = TOTAL# + COUNT%
110     NEXT COUNT%
120     PRINT "The sum of all integers from 1 to "NUMBER
130     PRINT "is "TOTAL#
140     GOTO 160
150     PRINT "This number is out of bounds!"
160         END
```

Figure 11-11

A simple program in BASIC. BASIC was intended to make programming easy for beginners, but its lack of sophisticated control structures makes it more difficult to program large applications.

easy to learn, but its lack of sophisticated structural features makes it less useful for commercial programming applications (Figure 11-11). In the microcomputer era, BASIC has been popularized as the programming language packaged with the computer, but it has also suffered from the fact that many different versions of it exist, making it difficult for programs to be used on different computers. New versions of BASIC, such as VisualBASIC for Windows, promise a new generation of novice programmers an easy tool for developing applications.

Pascal. Pascal (named after the French mathematician Blaise Pascal) is a programming language developed in the late 1960s specifically as a teaching tool. It has subsequently developed into a very popular language for use with a variety of programming applications, because of the clarity of its syntax and its strong features for structured programming development (Figure 11-12). Standard Pascal is used on mainframes and minicomputers; the microcomputer programming field is dominated by Turbo Pascal for both DOS and

```
Program NumberCount (input, output);

var count,
        number: interger;
        total: real;

begin
        total := 0.0;
        writeln ('This program calculates the sum of all integers');
        writeln ('from 1 to whatever integer you specify.');
        write ('Enter any positive integer up to ',maxint, ':');
        readln (number);
        if (number > 0) and (number <= maxint) then
            begin
                for count = 1 to number do
                    total := total + count;
                writeln ('The sum of all integers from 1 to ',number);
                writeln ('is ', total)
            end
        else writeln ('This number is out of bounds!')
end.
```

Figure 11-12

This sample Pascal program implements the same algorithm as the BASIC program in Figure 11-11. Pascal was designed for clarity of syntax and structure; do you find this easier to read?

Hard Times for Russian Programmers

Since the collapse of the Soviet Union, the plight of the Russian computer user has been unpleasant at best. Personal computers are far from a household item, and the falling ruble has made it almost impossible to buy foreign-made hardware. The big-name software titles are especially tough to find because companies selling them are wary of the widespread software piracy in Russia. The country did not pass its first law protecting software copyrights until June 1992. Under communism, the best programming jobs were with the government or the universities (which were, of course, controlled by the government). Now that public money is drying up, those jobs are suffering. Nonetheless, talent seems to abound among Russian programmers, who are, of necessity, quickly learning the Western skill of marketing their talents.

Windows and ThinkPascal for the Macintosh. The latest versions of these Pascal packages include object-oriented programming features (see discussion later).

C. One of the fastest-growing high-level programming languages is **C**, developed in the early 1970s. Its developers were especially conscious of the flow of data to and from storage devices. Because C can control this flow especially well, it is a popular language for developing database software, operating systems, and general applications, providing both strong structured programming features and tools for close control of the hardware (Figure 11-13). C has spawned new versions, C+ and C++, for use in object-oriented programming, and it has become the most popular language for developing Windows and Macintosh software.

COBOL. The common business-oriented language (**COBOL**) is a language used for business applications such as accounting, inventory control, payroll, and banking systems. Initially developed in 1959 by a panel of government and business experts, COBOL was designed around the needs of common business reporting. Programs are based on four major divisions: identification, environment, data, and procedure (Figure 11-14). The identification division states the name of the program, who wrote it, and other distinguishing data. The environment division states the computer or computers to be used. The data division lists the data used in the program. The procedure division is the actual algorithm. While COBOL has never achieved great popularity in microcomputer use, it is still one of the most important programming languages for mainframe computers in business.

FORTRAN. The formula translator (**FORTRAN**) language was the first high-level programming language, developed in 1954 for applications in mathematics, engineering, and science (Figure 11-15). As its name implies, FORTRAN works very well with sophisticated mathematical formulas. FORTRAN has gone through several stages of standardized revision since its creation, keeping it up-to-date with advances in programming techniques and hardware development. FORTRAN is still the most popular language for scientific and

Figure 11-13
The same algorithm coded in C. C's power for including programming modules and packing dense meaning into statements makes for efficient code; its object-oriented extensions make it currently the most popular microcomputer programming language for professionals.

```c
/* numbercount.c */
#include <stdio.h>
#define MAXINT 32767

main ()
{
    int count, number;
    long int total;

    total = 0;
    printf("This program calculates the sum of all integers\n");
    printf("from 1 to whatever integer you specify.\n");
    printf("Enter any positive integer up to %d:",MAXINT);
    scanf("%d",&number);
    if (number > 0 && number <= MAXINT)
        for (count = 1; count <= number; count++)
            total = total + count;
        printf("The sum of all integers from 1 to %d\n",number);
        printf("is %d\n",total);
    else printf("This number is out of bounds!\n");
}
```

```
IDENTIFICATION DIVISION.
PROGRAM-ID. NUMBERCOUNT.

ENVIRONMENT DIVISION.
CONFIGURATION SECTION.
SOURCE-COMPUTER. IBM-PC.

DATA DIVISION.
WORKING-STORAGE SECTION.
01      WORK-FIELDS.
        10      NUMBER  PIC 99999.
        10      COUNT   PIC 99999 VALUE 1.
        10      TOTAL   PIC 999999999 VALUE C.
        10      MAXINT  PIC 99999 VALUE 32767.

PROCEDURE DIVISION.

        DISPLAY "This program calculates the sum of all integers"
        DISPLAY "from 1 to whatever integer you specify."
        DISPLAY "Enter any positive integer up to ", MAXINT
        ACCEPT NUMBER
        IF NUMBER > C AND NUMBER <= MAXINT
            PERFORM UNTIL COUNT > NUMBER
                ADD COUNT TO TOTAL
                ADD 1 TO COUNT
            END-PERFORM
            DISPLAY "The sum of all integers from 1 to ",
NUMBER
            DISPLAY "is " TOTAL
        ELSE
            DISPLAY "This number is out of bounds!"
        END-IF
```

Figure 11-14
A COBOL version of the same algorithm. Note the four fundamental divisions of the program. COBOL was designed for business use and handling large amounts of structured data.

engineering applications in business, institutional, and government settings and is used frequently by microcomputer programmers in these fields.

Ada. **Ada** (named after Ada Lovelace, the first programmer) was developed from the foundation of Pascal, and is primarily used in the defense industry for developing weapons systems and in industrial environments for controlling

```
*   Program to total integers to a given limit.

        INTEGER COUNT, MAXINT, NUMBER
        REAL TOTAL

        MAXINT = 32767
        TOTAL = 0.0
        PRINT *, 'This program calculates the sum of all integers'
        PRINT *, 'from 1 to whatever integer you specify.'
        PRINT *, 'Enter any positive integer up to ', MAXINT, ': '
        READ *, NUMBER
        IF (NUMBER .GT. 0) .AND. (NUMBER .LE. MAXINT) THEN
            DO 100, COUNT = 1, MAXINT
100             TOTAL = TOTAL + COUNT
            PRINT *, 'The sum of all integers from 1 to ',NUMBER
                PRINT *, 'is ',TOTAL
        ELSE.
```

Figure 11-15
A FORTRAN implementation. FORTRAN's syntax is modeled on algebraic notation, since it was designed for scientific and engineering use.

A Brainless Robot

For years scientists have used computers to try and create artificial intelligence by mimicking the human brain electronically. But at MIT researchers are trying a vastly different approach, called "bottom-up" AI, and the result is Genghis, a six-legged, foot-long robot without a brain. What Genghis does have is a network of small, simple control programs, each dedicated to a single function; say, lifting one limb. Though the programs operate independently, they communicate with each other rather like bees in a hive. Genghis is programmed to learn through avoiding negative feedback, a vastly simplified version of an infant learning to walk by not falling down. Information is provided by sensors in the robot's belly that provide feedback to the small programs that lift and lower its legs and change its direction. Scientists hope that someday collections of such robots could be used to do such things as clean up oil spills or explore other planets.

---

real-time systems and automation. Ada is very highly structured, which forces programmers to use a standard procedural approach for program design. This programming language is still primarily used in the defense industry, with its larger computer systems. Because of its highly structured approach, however, it is gaining popularity in other areas.

RPG. The Report Program Generator (**RPG**) is a business-oriented programming language designed to automate many input and output features. Users are encouraged to use it to retrieve data and generate reports. Many of the processes used to input and output data are integrated into small sets of commands. Using these small sets of commands allows programmers to avoid writing protracted instructions for each programming task. RPG is popular among programmers who need to design sophisticated reports from well-defined input. RPG's automation of input and output functions and use of standardized procedures served as a precursor to later techniques of object-oriented programming and authoring systems.

LISP. The List processing (**LISP**) language was the first interpreted language; although a structured language, LISP is nonprocedural in the sense that the programmer doesn't implement a sequence of algorithmic steps, but instead develops a group of functions that work together to solve the programming problem. LISP syntax consists primarily of lists, where the first item in the list is the name of a function, and the other items in the list are data items on which the function operates. LISP is also unique in that the programmer can not only define new functions, but also rewrite the language's built-in functions. Together with the fact that the program is interpreted, this allows programs to modify both themselves and the language—a crucial component of intelligence. Since its inception, LISP has been used primarily for artificial intelligence research and the development of expert systems (where a computer is programmed to function as an expert resource in a given subject area or occupation); it has also been used for some commercial applications, such as databases. LISP has not become very popular on microcomputers yet, but that may change as the hardware becomes increasingly sophisticated and thus better able to handle the processing demands of the language.

Problem-Oriented Languages

Fourth-generation languages, the **problem-oriented languages**, are a mixed bag of strategies to make programming easier and place them within the grasp of nonprogrammers. They were created to solve specific user and programming problems rather than to achieve the broad general usability of procedural languages. This group of languages includes object-oriented languages, application generators, authoring systems, HyperTalk, and query languages.

Object-Oriented Programming. **Object-oriented programming (OOP)** takes a different approach to creating applications. Traditional programming treats data and instructions as separate items with the instructions controlling the data; the instructions are active controls on passive data. In object-oriented programming, an object is created by joining data and instructions in a process known as *encapsulation*. Once an object is made and debugged, it will work. Objects can then be linked together with messages (*calls* to the object to implement its instructions on its data) to form full-fledged applications.

Common OOP languages include C++, Smalltalk, Loops, and Objective-C. OOP is contributing greatly to the development of the newest GUIs, including programs using the Macintosh, OS/2, and Windows operating systems as well as the operating systems themselves.

Application Generators. **Application generators,** also called *programming environments*, can be used to create programs without writing any code. An application generator provides an example of the interface for the intended environment. A Macintosh application generator first shows a standard Macintosh window with menu bar and slide bars; a Windows application generator shows a Windows interface. A DOS or UNIX character-based application generator may have a menu bar, but it could be much more limited. With Windows and Macintosh, for example, you can name menu items, pull down the menus, click on an add-command message, and be given a dialog box to name a new command and designate what the command will do. When you finish, the application generator writes the code necessary to add that feature to the application. You can also design the window and dialog boxes as you go along. Then, at any time in the process, the code can be tested for syntax and logic errors, and these can be brought to your attention. You can even type the code directly, in a text editor provided by the tool. This editor, using the search and replace feature, is a great help when you are making broad, sweeping changes.

Authoring Languages. **Authoring languages**, also called *authoring systems*, are popular application generators for creating educational and instructional software. They are designed to create question-and-answer screens and develop instructional material according to principles of instructional design. For example, an authoring system may be used to create an instructional module on forecasting economic trends. This type of module may display a screen that asks a question and provides four different answer options. As the user selects an option, a message such as **correct**, followed by a brief reinforcing statement, may be displayed.

HyperTalk. The **HyperTalk** programming language, a control language for the HyperCard system (see the chapter on databases) combines the GUI with object-oriented programming (Figure 11-16, p. 213). Behind HyperTalk is the concept of **hypertext**, which uses the microcomputer's ability to present information in a nonlinear way. Books and other written material can generally give information only in a linear, straight-line method. Computers can present text, images, sounds, and actions in any order and can be controlled by the user from moment to moment. In hypertext development software, users and programmers are given objects represented by index cards on screen. These cards may have lists of people or animals or other data; they may also have graphics; and they have one or more buttons with pictures or text that tell what pushing each button will do. You link these cards together to make new applications.

HyperCard is a programming application that implements hypertext on the Macintosh. Several Windows and OS/2 programming environments, such as Smalltalk, Toolbook, and IBM's Linkway, make use of the hypertext concept as well.

HISTORY

HyperCard

One of the most talked-about hypermedia database systems is HyperCard, which Apple introduced on August 11, 1987. The software development environment and interface builder for the Macintosh was created by a team headed by Bill Atkinson, the person largely responsible for MacPaint and widely believed to be the brains behind both the Lisa and Macintosh computers.

Atkinson was at the time one of the three or four people closest to Steve Jobs, the maverick founder of Apple. Atkinson had gained Jobs's trust in an unusual way, according to Apple lore. He stood up in a meeting where Jobs was spewing what Atkinson considered ridiculous statements, shouted an obsenity at Jobs, and walked out. The next day Jobs invited the disgruntled employee to dinner.

Atkinson, who once had a very promising career in neurochemistry, is considered something of a god when it comes to writing code, and HyperCard is a project close to his heart. It combines features of both structured and freeform databases in an attempt to give users a more natural, intuitive access to the program and data.

HyperCard uses the image of a stack of cards. Each card—which fills the screen—can contain text, graphics, or input fields. One kind of field is known as a *scroll field*. This serves as a window through which any amount of freeform text can be viewed. Since stacks can be linked together (as can cards within a stack), the program allows users to browse much more freely than is the case with other databases without being so rigidly bound to the usual way a computer operates.

Cards can also contain buttons that allow users to select an option, start a process, or jump from one card to another. HyperCard comes with its own programming language, called HyperTalk, which allows application programs to be incorporated into a HyperCard database.

Atkinson himself has described HyperCard as being "both an authoring tool and sort of a cassette player for information" which also allows the user to create programs as they are necessary.

"I started thinking that many more people would have a use for a computer if it did some different things than it does right now," Atkinson says. "I started thinking about gradually unfolding a path that starts with clicking and browsing—something that anybody could do and that would be useful for a lot of things. The HyperCard program itself is an authoring tool, but the things it creates are applications in their own right."

Some early users of HyperCard were film-editing students at Standford. After shooting all the scenes for a movie with a video camera, the scenes were transferred to a video disk. Using a HyperCard stack as a storyboard, one miniature picture for each sequence that had been shot, students could edit the film. Manipulating the stack of cards allowed students to splice the film any way they wished, making scenes shorter or longer, moving scenes to different sequences, all via computer.

In the end, each student had a HyperCard diskette of his or her film—without ever going into the darkroom and doing any splicing of actual acetate film.

Typically, Bill Atkinson has a rather philosophical view of his brainchild: "I'm really more interested in the worldwide sharing of information. My reward will come when I get stacks from the people who have the information, but don't have the tools to get it out now." ■

Figure 11-16
HyperCard can work as both a database and an application generator. HyperTalk, the scripting language used for developing applications based on HyperCard, is an example of a fourth-generation programming tool.

Query Languages. **Query languages** are used specifically within the realm of databases. These languages are designed to instruct the computer to retrieve and manipulate database information and can be used to develop specific applications based on databases, such as database publishing and project management. The most important query language is structured query language (SQL; see the chapter on databases), but most major database packages for the microcomputer have their own sophisticated query languages.

Macros. Although not, strictly speaking, a language, macros use the ability of existing applications such as Lotus 1-2-3, Excel, WordPerfect, and dBASE to automate tasks. Many programs now come with *scripting languages* for users to write macros. Others have macro recorders. Extensive macros can be used to query database information and to generate many of the products that in the past required programmers to write new programs; they can even be compiled with macro compilers.

Natural Languages

The fifth and final generation of programming languages does not involve the generation of any code. These **natural languages** use the normal grammar of the spoken language to create programs. Some natural programming languages include Intellect, Broker, and Explorer. Although they don't yet meet their inventors' ideal, they are showing promise, and continued advances in this area may someday radically change the way we use computers and how we create programs.

SUMMARY

A program is a set of instructions written in a programming language and designed to make a computer perform a series of specified tasks that solve a particular problem or achieve a specific goal. Programming is the act of designing and writing programs in a development cycle that has five processes: problem definition, algorithm development, coding, program testing and debugging, and documentation.

In defining the problem, programmers meet with users to identify the output desired and other expectations for a program; they also determine the input and machinery to be used. The programmer constructs the algorithm—the prescribed set of well-defined rules or processes for the solution of the problem—that describes the program's process from start to finish, including the logic structures used. The algorithm can be written in pseudocode or drawn as a flowchart. Programmers use a structured programming approach, building the program in modules in a top-down manner; structure charts show the relationships among the program modules.

The algorithm is coded—translated—into statements in a programming language whose choice is sometimes crucial to the success of the program. Once written out, the program is tested to find bugs, or errors in the syntax or logic. Program testing and debugging involves desk checking, compilation, running the program with sample data, and field testing.

A program's internal documentation covers the trail of development, including comments within the code to remind the original programmer of (or tell other programmers) the meaning of each line of code and the flow of the program's logic. External documentation is prepared for user manuals; on-line documentation supports users while they use the program.

Programming languages are classified as first-, second-, third-, fourth-, or fifth-generation languages. The first generation of languages, machine language, is written in the binary 0 and 1 values the microcomputer can process. The second-generation assembly languages use alphanumeric mnemonic codes to replace machine commands and need an assembler to translate their code to machine language.

The third-generation procedural languages dominate the programming field and require compilers or interpreters to translate their code to machine language. Compilers translate the whole program at once, storing object code in an executable file. Interpreters translate the source code line by line; the computer can run each line as it's translated. Common third-generation languages in use today include BASIC, Pascal, C, COBOL, FORTRAN, Ada, RPG, and LISP.

The fourth-generation problem-oriented languages bring programming more within the reach of nonprogrammers, starting with object-oriented programming, then the use of application generators and authoring systems, on to the use of HyperTalk, and finally to query and scripting languages.

The fifth-generation natural languages do not produce code but follow human language grammar rules. They are not yet well developed.

KEY TERMS

Ada	BASIC	debugging
algorithm	C	external documentation
application generators	COBOL	field testing
assembly languages	coding	FORTRAN
authoring language	compiler	high-level language

HyperTalk
hypertext
internal documentation
interpreter
LISP
logic error
logic structures
looping
machine language
natural language
object
object-oriented programming (OOP)
on-line documentation
outline
Pascal
problem-oriented language
procedural language
procedure
program
programming
programming language
pseudocode
query languages
RPG
selection
sequence
structure chart
structured programming
syntax error
testing
top-down design

REVIEW QUESTIONS

1. What is a program? What is programming? What processes are involved with programming?
2. How does a programmer define the problem? What information does a programmer need to begin the programming process?
3. What is a program's algorithm? In constructing an algorithm, what logic structures does a programmer use? How would these logic structures appear in pseudocode and on a flowchart?
4. What is structured programming? What is a top-down approach?
5. What is coding? How does a programmer choose one programming language over another for any given program?
6. What is program testing? What is debugging? What kind of errors are found in program code? Describe the errors.
7. What kind of documentation is necessary for programs? How is each used?
8. What are the low-level languages? What does an assembler do?
9. What are the procedural languages? How do they differ from first- and second-generation languages?
10. What do compilers and interpreters do?
11. Make a list and describe five common procedural languages.
12. What are the fourth- and fifth-generation languages? Describe object-oriented programming and two other fourth-generation programming strategies.

12

Microcomputers and Social Issues

OBJECTIVES

After completing this chapter, you will be able to
- Describe the various types of computer crime.
- Discuss how the use of computers relates to problems of privacy.
- Identify some organizations that acquire and store personal information.
- Discuss the reasons for and against sharing such information.
- Identify the dangers inherent in electronic trespass.

FOCUS

As you've read this book, you've seen the many uses to which computer technology has been and can be applied. We've looked at hardware and software and operating systems; explored the nonmysteries of word processing, graphics, desktop publishing, communications, and databases; and discussed the less arcane aspects of programming.

Like most other technological advances, the computer is a tool, one that can be used for good or ill. You can save time with computers, write better—or at least write better spelled and better typed—papers. You can balance budgets, from the personal to the professional; input and store and process and output all kinds of information; and send it around the world as fast as telephone lines and satellites can carry it. You can also use computers frivolously, by typing up notes that would be better handwritten while co-workers mutter in the background. We can use our computers to spy. To lie and cheat. To steal. To do harm.

These last uses are the uses that concern us in this chapter. As the power of even the smallest laptop microcomputer increases, so does the danger of misuse increase. We have an obligation to use computers responsibly—in ways that are not harmful to the society in which we live and work.

• CHAPTER 12: Microcomputers and Social Issues •

COMPUTER CRIME AND SECURITY

The headlines tell us about **computer crimes** *after* they have been discovered. Hackers are arrested for using telephone and credit card numbers other than their own to acquire goods and money; someone with a distinctly different sense of humor infects software with a virus that causes fish to swim across the spreadsheet. Another someone changes all the scholarship information in the financial aid office, and yet another uses the company computer—on company time—to do a little freelance writing or software development for an outside client. These are not jokes. They are crimes.

Electronic Trespass

Although peeking at someone's private records may not seem a heinous crime, **electronic trespass** is a crime. Peekers who gain access to a co-worker's personnel file or to a neighbor's checking account records are trespassing, just as they would be if they were physically in the file or the bank. They have entered another's computer system or file without permission—hence, illegally. Among its other provisions, the Computer Fraud and Abuse Act of 1986 makes it a felony to willfully access a computer without, or in excess of, authorization.

The problem of trespassing is compounded when data is altered or destroyed (Figure 12-1). Although there may sometimes be no intent to alter data and the changes are only the result of striking the wrong key, this is a very rare occurrence. In most cases, the trespasser has something to gain from the

Computer Crime

As technology has outpaced the law, it is sometimes almost impossible to prosecute computer crimes, which often fall into rather gray legal areas. Some fraud is straightforward; for instance, forging checks with magnetic ink character recognition (MICR) numbers at the bottom, or the false inputting of data. Such crimes can easily be prosecuted as forgery, theft, or extortion. However, consider the case of a studio employee who sold story ideas and gossip to the tabloids. The information came from the studio's database, but there were no company guidelines on how the database should be used, so no rule had been broken. Criminal cases against hackers are often lost because, although it is easy to prove intentional access, it is almost impossible to prove intentional damage. Hackers contend their motivations are intellectual rather than criminal and that they are an annoyance rather than a serious threat to business. Britain has recently passed the Computer Misuse Bill and the Data Protection Act in an effort to cope with computer crime. But it remains to be seen how successfully these laws will deter computer criminals.

Figure 12-1
In the movie *War Games*, Matthew Broderick played a computer hacker who mistakenly breaks into the Department of Defense, nearly starting WWIII.

alterations. The gain may be real, as in changing bank records to reflect a higher balance (discussed later), stealing company secrets, erasing long-distance charges, or changing that grade from an "F" to an "A." The gain may be strictly personal and vengeful: changing hospital records or credit ratings, destroying social security records, or inserting false and defamatory information in a personnel file. These crimes are serious, and they are costly.

Electronic funds transfers (EFT) take money from one account and move it to another. Banks do this when authorized to do so by legitimate customers. But bank employees have also been known to do it without authorization, directing the funds into their own accounts or those of an accomplice. The transfer of a million dollars will be quickly noted, but the transfer of one-tenth of a cent from every customer's monthly interest will not—and those fractional cents can quickly add up to many dollars.

Business and industry also have much to lose through electronic trespass. Information about new products, stock transfers, plans to acquire another company—or to head off such an acquisition—and other proprietary information can be worth millions of dollars to the company or its competitors.

Data encryption—using a code—when transmitting information is one way to help stop would-be electronic thieves. The data encryption standard, a code that was considered unbreakable a dozen years ago, has been broken. It is still in use, however, because the high cost of intercepting the coded data pushes would-be intruders into using less costly and more detectable methods. More recent advances offer codes based on the product of two large prime numbers and on the use of quantum theory. The latter uses some aspects of the uncertainty principle to encode messages; both new methods are currently considered unbreakable.

Internal Security

Protecting data from electronic invaders is one thing—but how do you protect your data from people inside the organization? One obvious control is to limit access. Personnel who use computers must be carefully screened—just as they would be for any sensitive position within the company. Just as auditors inspect a company's financial records, so too can they inspect a computer log to determine who has had access to what, and when. Have there been too many data corrections? Are the same people who wrote the programs running them? An old data security rule was never to let the programmer operate the computer—and beware of any computer operator who refused to take vacation or sick days.

Passwords are an old means that still work for limiting access (Figure 12-2, p. 224). If you share a computer or are in the habit of leaving it on while you go to lunch, you can foil trespass by making entry into the program or file contingent on a password. True, passwords can be guessed or worked out by determined spies, but changing them frequently makes such exercises more difficult. Other cautions include not posting your password on the computer or jotting it on the edge of your desk calendar and not using such easily guessed combinations as your birthdate or your mother's maiden name.

Waste—from used printer ribbons to printout—should be routinely shredded or otherwise disposed of safely. If it isn't done routinely, the day you forget to do it will be the day proprietary secrets land in the wrong basket.

HISTORY

Computers Under Siege

In the wee hours of the morning of November 3, 1988, computers all across the country—from NASA's Ames Laboratory to Harvard's Observatory to Berkeley, California—began acting strangely. Security experts who had programmed their computers to notify them when something went wrong began getting phone calls. But when they tried to log into their computers, the machines were too busy doing something else to act on the log-in commands.

On the West Coast it was slightly before midnight, and a few programmers were still at their computers when the trouble started. "Something's eating the system," they warned friends by phone, "it's starting a lot of programs and running all kinds of processes. Whatever it is, it's slowing the system down to almost a standstill. We've probably got a virus."

Computer viruses work the same way as biological viruses. Like a flu bug in a human being, a virus spreads on contact, and continues replicating itself in the new host.

To a host computer, the virus often looks harmless, like just another series of legitimate commands. But rather than running a series of program, the computer virus may merely duplicate itself, taking up valuable space in the computer—or it might be more malicious, lying in wait until the appropriate time to spring to life and follow its instructions, which may be something like "Erase all word processing files" or "Make six copies of yourself, and wipe out all files containing numerals." Often the virus's commands are buried within ordinary programs, then executed when the program is run. Viruses can spread from program to program within a computer, or between computers when they talk to each other.

For instance, if a virus has infected a bulletin board or a network, when users copy an infected program—say, a game—from the bulletin board or network onto their personal computer, the virus comes along too. Copy the game onto a floppy disk for a friend, and the virus is copied too.

Within a couple of hours that November morning, concerned computer experts realized that as soon as they deleted one infected program from their computer another would instantly take its place and begin growing—right before their eyes. The 80,000 computer DARPANET network was infected. So was the Army's Ballistics Research Lab. All were being brought to a virtual standstill by the mysterious bug.

Frantically programmers tried to isolate the virus and to break down its code to find out how it was entering computers. They did not know if the virus only replicated itself, or if there was a time bomb still hidden somewhere in the code that would do even more damage when it went off. Like turn off all NSA computers, effectively shutting down our national defense system?

One thing programmers learned quickly was that the commands in the virus did not look like machine codes. Another was the fact that it was exploiting a security hole in UNIX systems, sneaking in through the Sendmail command. They also discovered that the infection was more of a worm than a virus. It did not modify other programs, as a virus does, but merely replicated itself, creating havoc by eating valuable space and slowing down the infected networks.

Eventually the worm was traced to Cornell University and to Robert T. Morris Jr., son of the chief scientist at NSA's computer security center. He admitted writing the program specifically to break into computers, but it was not supposed to happen overnight. Had his program worked correctly, it would have slowly infected computers over months, even years—a much more insidious occurrence.

In January 1990, Morris went on trial in Syracuse and was convicted of a felony, the first conviction for writing a computer virus. He was sentenced to three years probation, 400 hours of community service, and fined $10,000. ∎

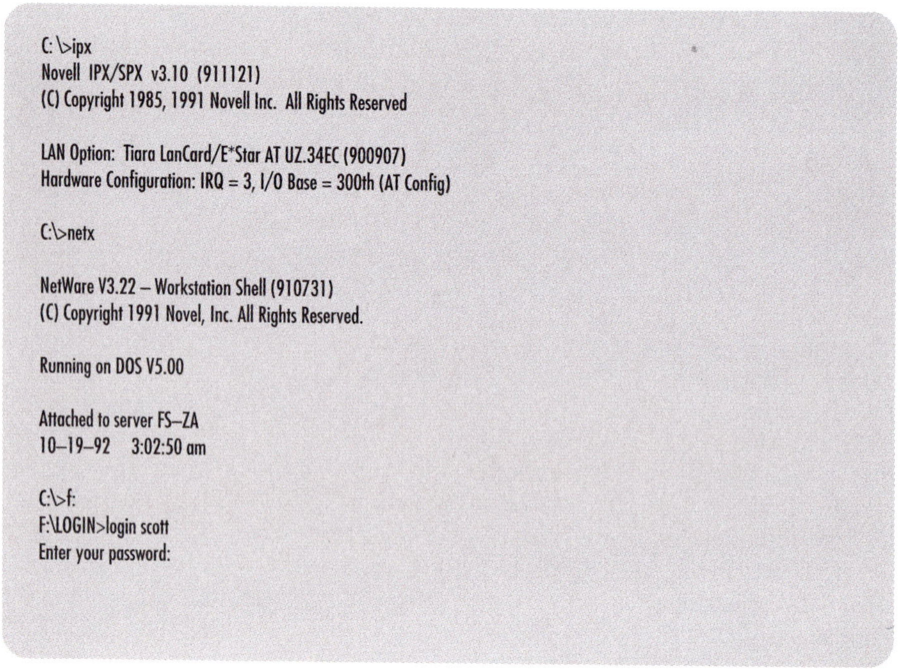

Figure 12-2
Passwords, such as for logging on to a network, are the most common way to discourage unauthorized use of computers. However, passwords should be carefully chosen and changed frequently to ensure security.

```
C:\>ipx
Novell IPX/SPX v3.10 (911121)
(C) Copyright 1985, 1991 Novell Inc. All Rights Reserved

LAN Option: Tiara LanCard/E*Star AT UZ.34EC (900907)
Hardware Configuration: IRQ = 3, I/O Base = 300th (AT Config)

C:\>netx

NetWare V3.22 – Workstation Shell (910731)
(C) Copyright 1991 Novel, Inc. All Rights Reserved.

Running on DOS V5.00

Attached to server FS–ZA
10–19–92   3:02:50 am

C:\>f:
F:\LOGIN>login scott
Enter your password:
```

Laptop Theft

As computers become more popular, so does computer crime. And now that laptop computers have shrunk in size, swiping a computer has become even easier. Laptops have been stolen from people like the chairman of Compaq Computer Corporation, Ben Rosen, and even from General Norman Schwarzkopf! The real danger for many corporations is not so much the loss of the equipment, as annoying as that is, but the loss of valuable—perhaps irreplaceable—information. Thieves can earn $10,000 per laptop, provided it belongs to the correct corporate or government official. Companies do, of course, have ways of protecting themselves from such crime. Methods range from the computer equivalent of locking a bicycle up with a chain, to elaborate procedures to ensure a stolen laptop cannot be connected to the corporate database.

Any microcomputer—not just a laptop—can be picked up and moved out of the door and into a waiting car or truck. Too often, a uniform or a smudged signature on an official-looking form is enough to gain a thief entrance. To prevent such thefts, microcomputers can be locked to desks; laptops can be placed in secure closets. And proprietary data can be kept on floppy disks that can also be locked away, rather than allowed to remain on the hard disk.

Many microcomputers have locks that will keep unauthorized personnel from even turning them on. Identification badges with photographs or magnetic stripes, combination or card locks, sign-in and log-on sheets, and physical means of identification such as fingerprints, voice recognition, or retinal scanning—all these can limit unauthorized access to the computer.

Although many of these deterrents seem more suited to a computer center than to one small computer sitting on your desk, neglecting computer security at any level is a costly error.

Safety

Although today's microcomputer is sturdy, it is not indestructible. Dropping ashes or liquids into it is frowned upon; so is using magnets to hold messages to it, clipping disks together with magnetized paper clips, or placing the disk you just spilled coffee on in front of an electric heater. Surge protectors—usually multiple-outlet extension cords with built-in circuit breakers—are wise investments. They prevent electrical spikes from harming either the computer or your data; some also protect your telephone-modem line. Uninterruptible power sources provide backup power that will keep the computer running at least long enough to save your data; some let you keep working even longer.

Fire is another danger. Large computer centers are generally protected by smoke detectors and fire extinguishers; they often use commercial off-site storage for their backup records—especially copies of sensitive data and customized software. Smoke detectors and fire extinguishers are a good idea in general; placing them conveniently close to your own computer may make it possible for you to extinguish a small fire quickly with no danger to yourself. Off-site storage of your backup records—even if it's in the barn or a friend's closet—can also save you grief and hours of trying to reconstruct lost files.

Viruses

Computer **viruses,** like physical viruses, are invidious, insidious, and often deadly. They're programs on a computer disk that generally remain undetected until their damage is done; they move from an infected disk (usually a floppy, although some hard disks were infected during the Michelangelo epidemic) to the system disk or another disk in the system, and they replicate themselves, turning data into unusable nonsense when they become active. The damage is typically permanent, and anyone who has lost important files to a virus understands how serious the problem is. Other viruses have been created that aren't quite so deadly to your data, but do such things as slowing your computer to a crawl, putting prank messages on the screen, and the like. Some viruses wait until a particular date or other condition before becoming active; others act immediately to inflict harm on your computer.

Viruses are often spread through shared disks; some bulletin boards were apparently infected with Michelangelo and Stoned (or other viruses) and unknowingly passed them on to subscribers who downloaded files—or even simply logged on to the system. Some viruses, known as **Trojan horses,** are designed to act like a legitimate piece of software when first used; once on your system, though, they usually destroy all your data.

The effect of a **worm** is much like that of a virus: you lose disk space and computer capability. The difference—which doesn't much matter if you've lost the use of the computer—is that a worm does not attach itself to other programs while it spreads. It does, however, write itself to each computer it encounters in a network, establishing itself on the hard disk, and using up memory until the affected computer becomes disabled.

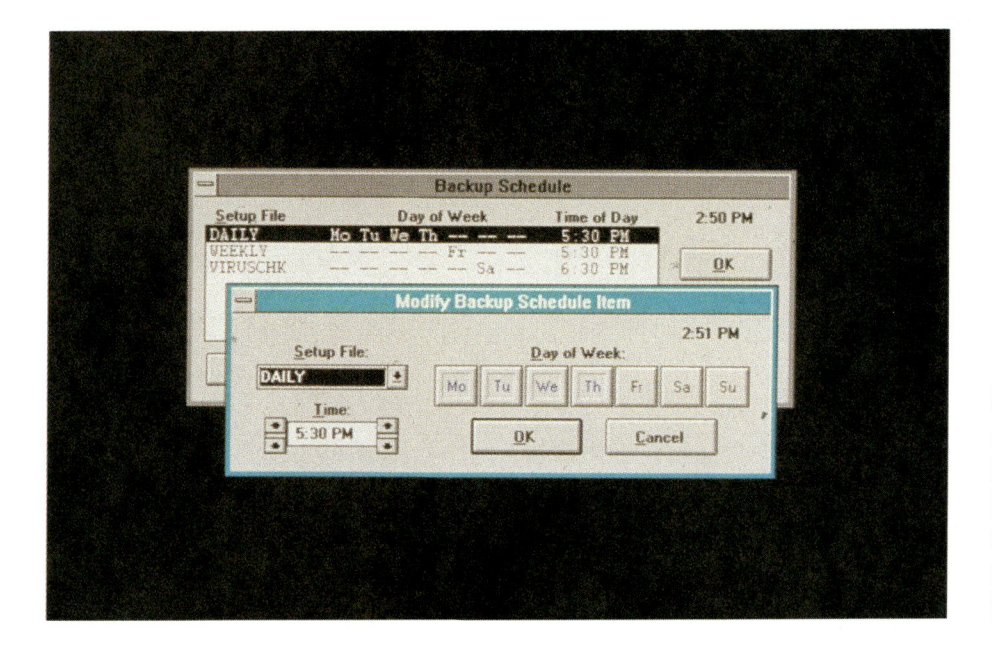

A Computer Amendment?

Harvard law professor Laurence H. Tribe has called for a 27th amendment to the U.S. Constitution to protect privacy and other individual rights being threatened by the spread of computer technology. Because the law has not kept pace with technology, Tribe says it needs to be made clear that the Constitution as a whole "protects people, not places." Speaking before high-tech cops, indicted computer hackers, civil libertarians, and corporate security experts at a California conference on Computers, Freedom, and Privacy, Tribe pointed out that it took the government over 40 years to recognize that conversations on telephones were as protected by the Constitution as any other form of speech. Cyberspace, the nonphysical area where communication and business takes place via computers, is equally in need of protection, Tribe said. Though normally wary of Constitutional amendments, the professor feels the computer revolution has created "substantial gray areas" that need to be carefully explored.

Figure 12-3

Many utility programs, such as Central Point Backup for Windows, include data-protection features such as delayed-scheduling backup and virus-checking programs to detect and remove known viruses on your computer's hard disk or floppy disks.

> ### Computers, a Hazard to the Environment?
>
> Computers were supposed to create "the paperless office," but things don't seem to have worked out that way. The spread of the PC, plus high-speed copiers, laser printers, and FAX machines, have all dramatically *increased* the consumption of paper in the office. Many companies are recycling their paper, and some paper products are made using recycled materials, but paper is only one of the problems. In an effort to recycle hardware components, some companies are now accepting empty toner cartridges and selling refurbished ones. Batteries are another problem. Though they only constitute two-tenths of one percent of the total volume in landfills, their toxic heavy metals make them account for 20 percent of the hazardous waste from households and offices. Some companies are collecting worn-out batteries and others are developing batteries that do not use heavy metals.

Recovering data that has been lost can be expensive and time-consuming; it can also be impossible. A number of software vendors have developed programs that detect viruses on a new or suspect disk and can then clean the the disk (Figure 12-3). The cost ranges from virtually free (public domain) to $100 or more (from some established vendors). The major limitation, aside from cost, is that the programs may be virus-specific; that is, they can detect and destroy only already-known viruses. New viruses, worms, and time bombs will undoubtedly be written and new detection software will follow; although the cost of acquiring the latest virus-killer may be high, the cost of not using it may be even higher.

Piracy and Counterfeiting

Not too many people would buy a book, photocopy it, and then return the book to the store. Yet many otherwise honest citizens buy a software program, copy it, and return the original to the computer store. Or they buy a program that is so useful they wish to share it with all their friends and classmates, passing out multiple free copies.

Sometimes illegal copies are sold as original work; this is **electronic counterfeiting**—a more sophisticated crime than sharing your new spreadsheet—and often involves a major criminal effort. It is a surprisingly big business. The package is hard to distinguish from the original, the disks may perform well, and the manual may be a direct copy of the book in the original box. The initial outlay by the dealer and consumer is lower, of course, but the users who couldn't resist the bargain of the century may find themselves with no backup—or recourse—when the program fails.

Given that software prices are often high, we must still remember that those prices include development costs, testing at several levels, and, usually, technical support. Like other authors and publishers, those who develop and publish software have a right to be compensated for their work; whether we call copying software without paying for it **piracy** or theft, it is still a crime. And it is, in part, responsible for the high prices charged.

There are, of course, legitimate copies that can be made of software: shareware and public domain software. Shareware, which can be purchased inexpensively both in stores and through mail-order catalogs, ranges from games to databases. Some of these programs cost no more than the small purchase price, but the software usually includes a request for an additional small payment to the software writer. Public domain software is generally spread from friend to friend—no one quite remembers who originally wrote the neat little program that blanks the screen or lets you type with one hand, but there's rarely a charge (maybe the cost of a disk), and it's all quite aboveboard and legal. A word of caution: check the disk immediately to make sure it carries no viruses or worms.

It is also legal in certain situations to copy commercial software: to make backup disks, for example, or to make licensed copies for many users in an organization. In the latter case, the company gets a multiuser license or site license; the particular arrangement varies with the vendor, who receives a given percentage of the cost of a single package for each additional user.

Stealing Time

At first glance, it doesn't seem like much of a crime: a little solitaire or a quick battle to save the home planet before you start work. If it's your own computer on your own desk—and if you are not charging anyone else for the time you spend—it's not a crime. But if you use your employer's computer on your employer's time to play games or do a little outside consulting work, it is a crime. It's theft, and it's wrong—even if you're only doing a flyer for the church rummage sale. Although this is more of a problem in organizations with mainframe computers, where access is limited and time is rationed, the company computers—of any size—should be used only for the company's business. At the very least, ask permission.

PERSONAL INFORMATION: STORAGE, USE, AND ABUSE

If you have bought a battery at a widely known chain store and given the clerk your name and address, you are listed in a computer database. If you've applied for insurance or subscribed to a magazine or filled out a warranty card, you are listed in a computer database. It is almost impossible for anyone to avoid having **personal information** stored in a computer. Businesses collect personal data about current and potential customers to increase sales and reduce credit losses. Government agencies collect and store a vast amount of information, from tax records to driving records to criminal records. Most of the time the information and its uses are benign and sharing it can be beneficial. Sometimes, however, sharing or releasing such information can be harmful.

A number of laws have been enacted to guarantee privacy. Some federal acts forbid the exchange of personal data (**data sharing**) between government agencies. Others restrict access to such information to authorized users only; loopholes and exclusions, however, often make these laws virtually ineffective. Some states have also passed laws dealing with computer crime and privacy.

Credit Bureaus

Credit bureaus collect data about people from banks and other financial institutions, department stores, small businesses, and credit card companies; they also supply data to them. The data includes indebtedness and loan-repayment history, marital status, whether the person's residence is rented or owned and how long he or she has lived there, next of kin, military service, employment history, and other personal information. The Fair Credit Reporting Act of 1970 allows you access to your record and grants you the right to challenge it, to explain marks against you, and to have incorrect information changed.

Although the individual's authorization is supposedly required before any personal information is released, such permission may be part of a charge card application or presumed by the bureau itself. Problems arise when the record contains false or incorrect information or when there is illegal access—electronic trespass—or when the information is simply no one else's business.

Border Crossings

In Europe, plans to create a continent-wide database that would contain information on terrorists, criminals, illegal immigrants, and asylum seekers have triggered objections from civil rights groups and others. Opponents contend the system may criminalize legitimate refugees. By tracking people who seek asylum, governments are keeping records on innocent people that might be used against them unfairly. Opponents also say the database may violate human rights and run counter to principles of national public accountability. Three different systems have been proposed. One is based in Strasbourg, France, with satellites in six other countries. Police and immigration officials would have access to information such as fact of sighting, place, time, route and destination of journey, passengers, vehicle used, luggage, and context of the sighting. Another system would concentrate on criminal records and details of visas. The third proposed database would code people who have sought asylum many times so that, after a certain amount of time, they would be denied access to a country.

Have We Lost Our Physical Intelligence?

One of the reasons we are often so unhealthy physically, according to some scientists, is that our bodies were not designed for the way we live today. The body we walk around with is the same one our ancestors had 30,000 years ago. Societies were hunter-gatherers for 100,000 generations, agriculturists for only 500 generations, industrialized for 10, and computerized for only one. This has resulted in a sophisticated brain being housed in a body that is designed to be on the move all day, facing physical and mental challenges, while subsisting on a diet low in fat, sugar, and salt. In our pursuit of an easier way of life, we have taken a machine designed to run, walk, and be physically active all day and made it sedentary, straining instead the small muscles of the eyes and fingers, injuring the spine through continued sitting, the wrists through continued flexing. Some doctors feel that an hour at the gym (often, ironically, using computerized equipment) simply cannot restore our physical selves, since often there is little mental or emotional satisfaction in doing routine squats and sit-ups. Our bodies were built for challenging labor and free play. They were not built to be ignored.

Banks

The repayment record of your student loan not only is reported to one or more credit bureaus but becomes part of the bank's own database. This allows access to your credit history when you apply for a credit card, a mortgage, or another loan. Your credit record at Bank A thus becomes part of your record at Bank B—and accessible to an additional group of people. There are some limitations, however. The Right to Financial Privacy Act of 1978 limits the government's access to your bank records; the Comprehensive Crime Control Act (1984) goes even further in keeping other unauthorized users from accessing those protected records. It also forbids the unauthorized use, disclosure, manipulation, and so on of information stored in the government's computers.

Internal Revenue Service

It seems that everyone tells the IRS everything; the interest on your savings account; the amount you earned last year; how much you received in alimony, child support, workers' compensation, or unemployment compensation; how much you spent on other taxes, doctors and prescriptions, alimony and child support; how many children you have at home. Almost everything that affects the amount of tax you ultimately have to pay goes into the IRS's computer system. Theoretically, this information cannot be shared with another government agency; in actuality, however, access to it may still be granted.

Federal Bureau of Investigation

The files of the FBI, with information that ranges from missing children to interstate criminal activity to the last known address of a potentially dangerous individual, are open to law enforcement agencies throughout the country. Although much of the data, such as that gathered from police, court, and prison records, is accurate, some—that provided by informants, for example—may not be. Access to and dissemination of inaccurate or false data can lead to serious errors, sometimes causing innocent people to be arrested or fired from their jobs.

Other Agencies

The Social Security Administration has records of where people have worked, how long they've worked, and how much they've earned. The Selective Service folks know who has registered for the draft—and who has not. The Computer Matching and Privacy Protection Act of 1988 is supposed to keep the government from trying to match records between agencies, but IRS records (which are supposed to be confidential) have been compared with draft registration records. The information you supply when you apply for unemployment compensation is checked against records from your former employer(s). Workers' compensation databases include not only your employment data but confidential medical data as well.

Health Care and Insurance

Hospitals and clinics keep computerized records about their patients' medical conditions, medications, family members, insurance coverage, and ability to pay. Pharmacies frequently use computerized databases to list the patient's medications and allergies. These medical databases can speed hospital admissions, provide crucial data in an emergency, prevent serious drug reactions and interactions, and help physicians to make diagnoses and prescribe medications.

The insurer who pays the bill will most likely report the patient's condition to a medical-insurance clearinghouse, making information available to other insurers.

Businesses

"The last car you bought was a red Tercel in 1984," says the car salesman. And although this is the first time you've set foot in the showroom in all those years, he's right—and he also knows how often and for what problems you took the car in to the service department. Computerized databases provide businesses with information about customers' purchases—what they buy, when they buy, how much they spend. A listing from the database of people who buy large, expensive cars every two years can be sold to a mailing list company, whose database, in turn, can provide other businesses with information about personal finances and preferences in clothing, cars, or food.

Politics

Register to vote, volunteer at the polls, or send someone a political contribution: there's your name in a database and more than likely on a mailing list. Political organizations keep—and share—databases on voters, volunteers, and contributors; they may also maintain records on elected officials' voting patterns and base their support (or nonsupport) on those records. Poorly maintained databases can result in voters who have changed registration, receiving friendly solicitations from both major political parties; even death may not remove a potential contributor's name.

GUARDING OUR PRIVACY

Given this proliferation of databases in credit bureaus, banks, department stores, government agencies, political organizations, hospitals, insurance companies, and businesses, we must wonder whether there is any such thing as **privacy.**

Each of these organizations has the right, given by us when we deal with it, to develop a profile or history. The bank must know our credit record, the hospital must be aware of all our medical problems, the landlord must know whether we habitually move at midnight. The problem—other than electronic trespass, which is patently a crime—lies in the dissemination of confidential information to others who have no clear right to it (Figure 12-4, p. 228).

Privacy

An increasing amount of controversy has developed around the ability of computers to watch and record us. Caller-ID and E-mail eavesdropping are two of the latest examples. Caller-ID enables a telephone to display and record the caller's telephone number and address. This can be particularly helpful in tracing 911 calls or catching obscene phone callers. But many people are concerned that marketing companies will use this information to hound people. The service can be blocked, but some states disregard the need to offer blocking while others require it. Pennsylvania recently ruled that Caller-ID was unconstitutional since it violated privacy rights and wiretapping laws. Phone companies contend the information is the equivalent of a telephone book and so violates no laws.

The violation of E-mail privacy has been cited by some employees in suits against their former employers. Employees say E-mail was presented to them as an alternative to the U.S. mail system, telephones, or fax. However, all E-mail messages can be printed out, and employees say when they complained of this, they were fired.

Health Hazard

With new technology has come new work-related physical injuries. Even such an innocuous activity as typing at a computer keyboard can be hazardous to your health. Carpal tunnel syndrome and wrist tendinitis are afflictions new to the computer era. Carpal tunnel syndrome is an inflammation of the tendons leading from the fingers and hand to the wrist; this can deaden sensation, incapacitate movement, and cause extreme pain. Though surgery, physical therapy, cortisone injections, and wrist braces can provide some relief, there is no cure other than not to type. Such diseases did not affect people who used manual typewriters because using a manual typewriter requires a different set of movements, which gave relief to the wrist tendons. Manual typewriters also did not encourage the same kind of prolonged use that a computer does. The best method of prevention is to take frequent rest breaks and to adjust the keyboard so your wrists remain straight while typing.

Does the car dealer *need* to know that his customer has asthma or that her sister failed the Bar examination three times? As far-fetched as that may sound, that is precisely the type of information that can be gathered through shared data and used to develop a profile that tells more about a person than any one organization or individual needs to know.

There is obviously a need for information. Credit bureaus, for example, exist to provide financial information that will enable their customers to extend credit wisely. But should they supply it to anyone who asks? Which information should they supply? And how much information do they really need? Is there a need for the credit bureau—or the department store—to know about your mother or your sister-in-law or the fact that 20 years ago you refused to cross a picket line?

Is it necessary for government agencies to keep files on all the country's citizens? Do they have an inherent right to know what we read, where—or if—we worship, and how we vote? There have been some legislative efforts to safeguard our privacy. In addition to the laws just mentioned, the Federal Privacy Act (1974) mandates that people must be allowed to know what information is on file about them—not only with government agencies but with their subcontractors—that they can know the uses of the information, and that they must be allowed to correct errors. None of these laws, however, protects us from the gathering of the data in the first place. And while the Freedom of Information Act (1970) gives you the right to access your federal files, actually getting the information can be a difficult, time-consuming, and—if legal action is needed—costly process.

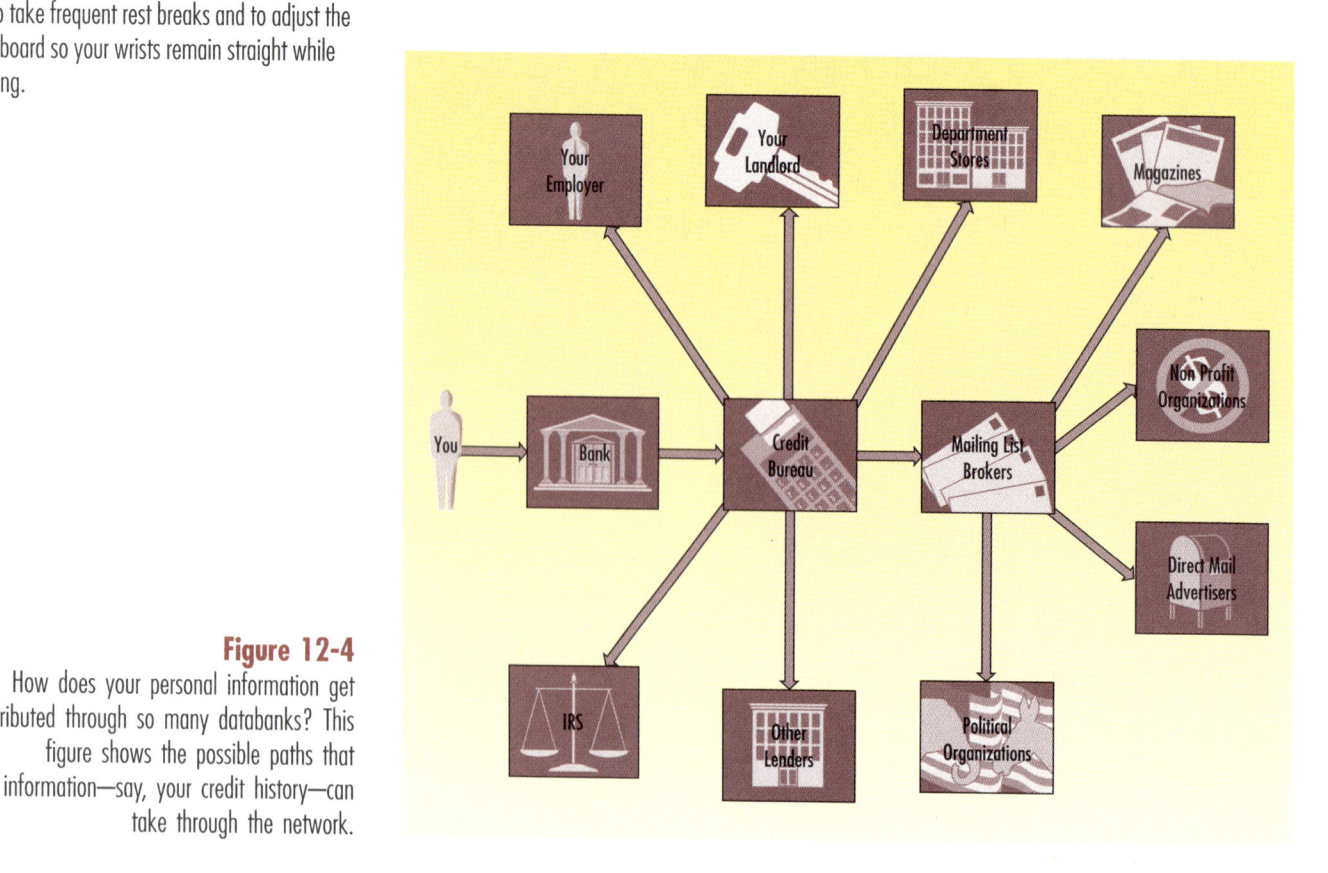

Figure 12-4
How does your personal information get distributed through so many databanks? This figure shows the possible paths that information—say, your credit history—can take through the network.

When files were simply paper files, sharing information was a slower and more complex process. Finding the assessed value of a neighbor's house, for example, might have required taking a trip to the county hall of records and persuading the guardian of the records—which are public records—that you indeed had a need to see them. Now you can access that information quickly—and often with no questions—through your own computer and modem.

The potential for abuse, for invasion of privacy, has increased tremendously with the increase of computerized databases. Ultimately, the right to privacy may have to be addressed in the courts as well as the legislatures.

PEOPLE AND COMPUTERS

The introduction of computers to the workplace was greeted some years ago with cries of fear: The computer was going to replace the typist, secretary, machinist, accountant, executive, and so on. If it didn't take your job away, it was instead going to kill you with radiation and damage your wrist, back, eyes, internal organs, and any other vulnerable portion of your anatomy.

Job Insecurity

The early rush to automate the office did result in the loss of some jobs. The buzzword in the early 1980s was *productivity*, and it seemed that one could achieve it by counting a typist's keystrokes. Some secretarial and typing positions were eliminated with the idea that fewer people, working on wonderfully fast machines, could do the same—or a greater—amount of work. The idea proved erroneous as the workload increased, and in many instances additional—and different—jobs were created (Figure 12-5, p. 230). The stress of trying to learn a new skill or to achieve the required number of keystrokes per minute proved too much for some employees, however, and some eventually left—or lost—their jobs.

Part of the problem, then and now, is the lack of training. Software vendors provide manuals, many of which are comprehensible; they may also provide on-site training classes for organizations that purchase multiple copies (Figure 12-6, p. 230). Too often, however, the office worker finds a new computer or a new software program on his or her desk and is expected to master it by the close of business that day. Graphical interfaces and menus of commands tend to make using new programs easier, but training is still important—and reading the manual is essential.

Computer Errors and Waste

One obvious result of a lack of appropriate training is operator error. The misplaced decimal point, the incorrect entry of a name or address or Social Security number, or the entry of critical data into the wrong file can lead to errors that range from the ludicrous to the tragic. Entering data carefully, following the program's instructions or documentation, and checking the results for errors that the software may have missed (or caused) are all essential.

The best training in using the computer cannot make up for errors in judgment or a lack of common sense, however. If the billing department's

Radiation

The jury is still out on whether the radiation produced by computers is harmful to your health. A 1988 study found that a large percentage of women who used computers more than 20 hours a week had miscarriages or abnormal births; but the study has not been replicated, nor did it establish a causal link between computer use and reproductive abnormalities. It is true that the safety standards for computers are lower in the U.S. than they are in Europe. For U.S. companies to produce terminals that comply with Sweden's MPR II standard would raise prices by 2.5 percent. One of the problems is the difficulty of measuring radiation emissions. Another is that it is simply not known how much radiation is actually harmful. Also, emissions are higher from the back of terminals, and they vary depending on the image on the screen and conditions around the computer. One thing that is known is that radiation emissions dissipate rapidly the further you are from the screen, so sitting two feet from the screen will keep you out of any real—or imagined—danger.

Figure 12-5
Early fears that computers in the office would replace people have been allayed by experience, as the new technology has demanded new job skills related to computing, creating new jobs.

software automatically generates a bill whenever there is a balance, it would be wise to put a bottom limit on the amount. Sending a bill—with interest charges—or threatening a customer with a collection agency when the remaining balance is under a dollar, for example, can lose the company a customer very quickly. It will also cost more than that dollar to send and defend the bill. If the program cannot be modified, sound judgment is required, and the person using the program should be given the appropriate instructions.

Computer waste can also be blamed on improper training. There is not point in having a microcomputer on everyone's desk if half of them are never used because the people behind those desks are afraid to use them or never learned how to use them. On the other hand, it is not necessary to use a computer for every facet of one's life. Some arithmetic calculations can still be done mentally, manually, or on a hand-held calculator. Some notes and memos can and should be handwritten.

Computers for white-collar workers were going to provide the world with paperless offices, said many experts in the 1980s. What they have provided instead has been countless reams of paper, often with information that could have been easily provided either verbally or through the computer network within the office.

Health and Ergonomics: Fact or Fancy?

The wrist brace seems to be a sign of the times. Once worn mainly by athletes and jackhammer operators, we now see it worn by supermarket cashiers, office workers, and other who perform repetitive wrist motions. (Figure 12-7). The culprit in most instances seems to be a keyboard that is too high and that requires constant flexion of the wrist. The resulting trauma, whether carpal tunnel syndrome or another disorder, sometimes becomes severe enough to require surgery. Lowering the keyboard is a simple but often ignored preventitive measure; some new keyboards have been

Figure 12-6
Training is a crucial element of successful computer use, and makes a big difference in productivity and profitability in corporate environments. The home user or student can also benefit greatly from computer training.

designed to allow typing with a more natural position for the hands, arms, and shoulders.

Other health-related questions have to do with the placement of the monitor, the chair, and the desk. Will the operator have to squint or stoop? Is his or her back supported properly? Is there radiation from the front of the monitor on our desk or from the back of the monitor behind us? What will the effect be in the short term? The long term? Will working in this environment cause unbearable stress? Sterility? Migraine headaches? What about the noise of half-a-dozen impact printers all going at once? Are there harmful fumes escaping from the laser printer or the copy machine? Is the air circulation adequate? How well is the office designed? What are the safety features? Should employers be required to supply furniture designed **ergonomically** (that is, with the comfort and safety of people in mind)?

These are real questions. They deserve real answers.

Figure 12-7
Carpal tunnel syndrome has become a serious work-related health issue, and the wrist brace is becoming commonplace. New customizable keyboards and ergonomic designs can help, but true relief requires rest.

SUMMARY

The pervasive use of microcomputers in modern society has engendered a number of social issues that affect our security, privacy, and well-being.

The computer can be a wonderfully practical tool, but it can also be misused. Computer crime is growing rapidly: electronic trespass, hacking, and espionage all make use of illegal access to private computers and data. Some electronic trespassers are relatively benign, but others destroy data or appropriate data for unauthorized use. Viruses and worms, two types of programs written specifically to invade and disrupt computer systems, are becoming an increasingly serious problem; and perhaps the most common misuse of computers is the illegal copying of software. Computer equipment itself has become a valuable target for theft. Finally, computers in professional settings are sometimes used inappropriately by those in the organization, effectively stealing productive time from the organization.

With the risk of electronic trespass, viruses, and illegal copying and theft of computer equipment and time has come increased need for computer security. Protecting access to machines and data takes the form of passwords to prevent access to the system, locks on hardware, secured storage of data disks and tapes, limiting personnel access to equipment, and proper handling of waste.

Computer safety is also an issue, chiefly with regard to protecting against catastrophic loss of data. Regular backups of data files rotated off-site are the most common means of ensuring that important data isn't lost when the computer is damaged due to fire, water, or other calamity.

Another area where computers are creating new social issues is privacy. With computers being used to store personal information and marketing data, and with networks in place to exchange that data, there is the potential for personal, private information to be distributed without the person's knowledge to those who have no clear need for it, but would use it for their own purposes. Credit bureaus, banks, government agencies, hospitals, insurance companies, retail businesses, direct-mail advertisers, political parties, and nonprofit organizations all have access to personal information on million of people. Although privacy laws have been enacted to protect the public, enforcement is problematic at best. Being highly selective about the information you provide to companies, credit bureaus, and others can help restrict the access these entities and others have to your personal information.

Computer's impact on productivity and employment is another source of controversy and social change, as the computer replaces some jobs and creates other, different ones, thus changing the nature of work and the skills required of both blue- and white-collar labor. Organizations have also found it difficult to translate computer use to real gains in productivity, as computers create new needs for personnel training and cause organizations to rethink the way business is done.

Finally, an issue especially focused on microcomputers is that of health effects of prolonged microcomputer use. As more and more people spend their entire working day staring at a computer monitor and typing on a keyboard, occupational injuries such as carpal tunnel syndrome, back problems, and eyestrain are on the rise. Radiation from computer monitors is suspected, although not proven, to have harmful effects on health, possibly including increased risk of cancer and birth defects or miscarriages.

KEY TERMS

computer crime	ergonomics	privacy
data sharing	passwords	Trojan horse
electronic counterfeiting	personal information	virus
electronic trespass	piracy	worm

REVIEW QUESTIONS

1. List as many kinds of computer crime as you can. Why are they criminal activities?
2. Define electronic trespass.
3. What is data encryption?
4. What is a computer virus? How is one transmitted?
5. What is software piracy?
6. When should personal data be shared between businesses?
7. Define ergonomics.
8. What is electronic counterfeiting?
9. What is a Trojan horse?
10. What rights to privacy are we guaranteed as citizens of the United States?

Index

@ sign, 147

A
A: drive, 43, 44
Abend-Fels, Sherri, 182
Absolute reference, 149
Ada, 209–210
Adobe, 11, 103
Aldus, 122
Algorithm, 200–202
Allen, Paul, 24
Alphanumeric data, 161–162
Alt key, 83
Altair, 5, 24
Apple, 5, 27, 42, 59, 62, 68, 72
Apple II, 5, 27
Application generators, 211
Application packages, 61, 63–66
Application programs, 42, 43, 45
Application software, 7–8
Arithmetic/logic unit (ALU), 21, 23
Arrow keys, 81
Art, 28, 100, 168, 184
ASCII, 21, 22
Ashton-Tate, 166
Assembly languages, 205, 206
AST, 73
Asynchronous communication, 184–185, 187
Atkinson, Bill, 212
Authoring languages, 211
Authoring systems, 211
AutoCAD, 102, 113
AUTOEXEC.BAT, 44, 45
Automatic teller machine, 3

B
B: disk drive, 43
Backslash (/), 46
Backspace key, 81, 85
Backup files, 91, 224
Balance of the Planet, 71
Banc One Corporation, 161
Banks, 226
  databases of, 159–160
Barnaby, Rob, 82
BASIC, 206–207
Batch file, 44
Batman, 123
Batteries, 224
Baud, 187
Bicycle, computerized, 9
Binary system, 21
Biomathematics, 206
BIOS, 28, 43, 44
Bit(s), 21, 69, 100
Bit-mapped fonts, 125, 126
Bit-mapped images, 99, 100, 101, 103, 104, 109, 111, 112, 113
Blindness, 26, 43
Blocks, 85–86, 187
BMP (bit-map) file format, 101
Boldface, 88, 125
Book production, using application software, 8
  development, 9–10
  planning, 8, 9
  production, 10–11, 13
  research, 9, 10
Books, talking, 8
Boot, 43
Boot up, 28

Borland, 66
Bps (bits per second), 187
Braille printer, 36
Brainerd, Paul, 122
Bricklin, Dan, 153
Broderbund Software, 14
Bug, 203
Bulletin boards, 180–181
Burk, Greg, 161
Burson, Nancy, 106
Bus, 26, 27, 69
Bushnell, Nolan, 62
Busicom, 12
Business databases, 159, 227
Bus line, 26
Bus network, 192–193
Button, 171
Byte, 21
Byte length, 185

C
C, 208
C: drive, 43, 44
CAD (computer-aided design), 103
Cafe Link, 181
Caller-ID, 227
C&C Music Factory, 66
Canon, 36
Cantometrics, 169
Capture buffer, 188
Cards, 25, 26, 171
Carmen Sandiego, 14
Carpal tunnel syndrome, 22, 228, 230, 231

CD (Change Directory), 49
CD-ROM, 7, 29, 30, 31, 32, 66, 80
Cell, 145
Cell address, 145
Centered, 87, 128
Central processing unit (CPU), 12, 21, 23, 26, 69
CGA (color graphics adapter), 35, 72
Chart(s), 151
Charting and representation graphics, 63
Charting software, 106
Chat mode (CB mode), 181
Chernobyl, 6
Chess, 15
Chips, 25–26
CityGuide, 16
Clauses, 168
Clicking, 112
Clients, tracking, 162
Client-server network, 190, 191
Clip art, 104
Clones, 73
CLP (ClipBoard) file format, 101
COBOL, 208, 209
Coding, 202
Collins, Rob, 199
Colon (:), 46
Color, 103–104
Color monitors, 35
  characteristics of, 36
Columns, 85, 123, 145, 146
  inserting and deleting, 149–150
COMMAND.COM, 43, 44, 45
Command-driven software, 120
Command interpreter, 44
Command line, 44
Command processor, 44
Commercials, 99
Commercial software, 224
Communications software, 8, 10, 66
Compaq, 72, 73
Compiler, 206
Comprehensive Crime Control Act (1984), 226
CompuServe, 10, 182–183
Computer(s), 80
  characteristics of, 3
  at home, 14–15
  at the office, 15
  in the schools, 13–14
  where to buy, 72–74
Computer-aided design (CAD), 33, 34, 113–114
Computer animation, 99, 103
Computer-assisted software engineering (CASE), 205

Computer crime, 219
Computer errors, 229–230
Computer family, 59
Computer Fraud and Abuse Act (1986), 219
Computer Matching and Privacy Protection Act (1988), 226
Computer Terminal Corporation, 12
Computing cycle, 6
CONFIG.SYS, 44, 45
Control (Ctrl), 83
Control unit, 21, 22, 23
Conventional memory, 28
COPY, 49
Copying, 149
Counterfeiting, 224
CP/M, 47
Credit bureaus, 225
Crime. *See* Computer crime
Crop, 129
Crosstalk for Windows, 9
CRTs (cathode ray tubes), 34
Cursor, 81, 145
Cyberspace, 223

D
D: drive, 43
Daisy-wheel printers, 36, 88, 92
Data, 6
  entering, 146–148
  manipulating, 148–151
Database(s), 14, 66, 180
  bank, 159–160
  communications with, 160
  design of, 160–162
  encyclopedic, 172–173
  flat-file, 170
  free-form, 172–173
  general business, 159
  government, 159
  hierarchical, 171–172
  home, 160
  law enforcement, 159, 160
  network, 172
  organization of, 170–173
  planning, 162–164
  record-oriented, 172
  relational, 170
  single-relation, 170
Database software, 8, 159
Data encryption, 220
Data entry, 164
Data files, 45
Data-generated graphics, 104, 105, 106, 108–109
Data queries, 167–168
Data sharing, 225
Date field, 162

dBase II, 166
dBase IV, 66
Debugging, 202–203
Default drive, 44
Default settings, 155
DEL (Delete), 49
Deleting
  files, 51
  rows and columns, 149–150
  text, 85
Dell, 72, 73
Delome Mapping Company, 11
Desktop computers, 5
Desktop monitors, 35
Desktop publishing (DTP), 11, 64–65, 110, 114, 131–132
Desktop publishing (DTP) software, 8, 61, 63
  description of, 119–120
  designing with, 133–135
  as tool of expression, 120–121
  types of, 120
  users of, 133
Deviant text, 126
Device-driver programs, 45
Device-generated graphics, 104, 109–111
DFX extension, 101
Dial control, 190
Dialog box, 124
Digital, 73
Digital camera, 111
Digital Research, 47
Dimon, Roz, 100
DIP (dual-inline package), 25
Direct-access storage device (DASD), 29
Directories, 45
Directory command, 48
Disabled, 26
Disk(s)
  floppy, 7, 29, 91
  hard, 7, 44, 45, 91
Disk cache, 71
Disk drives, 29–32, 37
  floppy, 29, 30, 31, 43, 71
  hard, 29, 30, 31, 43, 71
Diskettes, 30
Distributed processing, 193
DOS
  birth of, 47
  entering commands, 46, 48–49
  file structure of, 45–46
  GUI or, 60–61
  loading, 43–44
Dot matrix printers, 36, 37, 88, 92, 93
Double-sided pages, 123
Dow Jones News Service (DJNS), 182

INDEX

Draft quality, 92
DRAIN.COM, 54
Draw programs, 63, 64, 111–113
Drop cap, 126
Duplex, 187
Duvall, Shelley, 66
Dvorak keyboard, 22

E

E: drive, 43
Ebert, Roger, 190
Echo, 187
Editing, 85–87, 148
EGA (enhanced graphics adapter), 35, 72
86-QDOS, 47
Electronic Cadaver, 68
Electronic counterfeiting, 224
Electronic databases. *See* Databases
Electronic Forum (EF), 189
Electronic trespass, 219–220
EL (electroluminescent) screen, 36
E-mail (electronic mail), 15, 179, 181, 227
Emoticons, 190
Encapsulation, 210
Encyclopedias, 29
Encyclopedic databases, 172–173
End key, 83
Enter key, 81, 83
Entering text, 81, 83
EPS (encapsulated PostScript), 101
Equal (=) sign, 147
Ergonomics, 230–231
Excel, 44
Executable file, 206
Expanded memory, 28
Expansion boards, 26, 29, 32
Expansion slots, 26
Extended memory, 28
Extended VGA, 35, 72
External documentation, 204

F

Facing pages, 123
Facsimile, 180
Faggin, Federico, 12
Fair Credit Reporting Act (1970), 225
FAO Schwartz, 59
Federal Bureau of Investigation, 226
Federal Privacy Act (1974), 228
Field(s), 161–162
Field name, 161
Field size, 162
Field testing, 203
Field type, 161

File(s), 46, 161
  deleting, 51
File conversion, 110
File Manager, 50, 170
Filename, 45, 46
File server, 190, 191
File transfer protocols, 187–188
Finder, 42, 50, 51, 60
Firmware, 28
Flat-file databases, 66, 170
Floppy disk(s), 7, 29, 91
Floppy disk drive, 29, 30, 31, 43, 71
Flowcharts, 108, 201
Flush left, 87, 128
Flush right, 87, 128
Fodor's travel books, 16
Fonts, 88, 125–126
Footers, 85, 123
Footnotes, 89
FORMAT, 48
Formatting, 87–88
Form letters, 90–91
Formulas, 147–148
  ranges in, 148
FORTRAN, 208–209
FoxPro, 11, 66
Frankston, Bob, 153
Freedom of Information Act (1970), 228
Free-form databases, 172
Full-duplex, 187
Functions, 83, 147–148
  ranges in, 148
Fylstra, Dan, 153

G

Gas-plasma screen, 35, 36
Gates, Bill, 24, 47
Gateway 2000, 73
General business databases, 159
General-purpose computers, 3, 4
Genghis, 210
Geographers, 109
Geologists, 109
Glendale Community College, 189
Global Education Network, 59
Global Effect, 71
Global Jukebox, 169
Global Positioning System, 185
Government databases, 159
Graph(s), 151, 152
Graphical user interface (GUI), 26, 42, 49, 67
  DOS or, 60–61
Graphics
  description of, 99
  importing, 89–90
Graphics card, 71–72

Graphics controls, 128–131
Graphics monitors, 35
Graphics software, 8, 14, 15, 61, 63–64, 109
Graphics tablets, 34
Graphing, 106
Grid, 145
Grolier's Encyclopedia, 8
Group organization software, 108

H

Half duplex, 187
Hardcopy, 36, 91
Hard disk(s), 7, 44, 45, 91
Hard disk drive, 29, 30, 31, 43, 71
Hard return, 83
Hardware, 6–7, 67
  disk drives, 29–32
  ports, 32
  system unit, 23, 25–29
Harring, Phil, 164
Hayes, Dennis, 186
Hayes Microcomputer, 186
Headers, 85, 103, 123
Health care, 227, 230–231
Heatherington, Dale, 186
Hierarchical databases, 171–172
High-level languages, 204, 206
Hijaak, 11
Hockey, David, 100
Hoff, Ted, 12
Home key, 83
Home databases, 160
Host, 190, 191
HyperCard, 14, 170–171, 211, 212, 213
Hypermedia, 14
HyperTalk, 211, 212, 213
Hypertext, 211
Hyphenation, 128
  automatic, 83, 84
Hyphenation zone, 128

I

IBM, 5, 36, 43, 47, 52, 68–69, 70, 72
IBM-compatible computers, 59, 68–69
IBM PC, 47, 49, 59, 73
IC DRAM (integrated circuit dynamic random access memory), 27
Icons, 49, 50, 51, 112
Image-editing software, 63, 64
Image file formats, 101, 103
Image origination, 104–105
Image processing software, 110
Image types, 99–101

Indent, 84, 128
Indexes, 89
Indexing, 164–165, 167
Ink jet printers, 37
Input, 6, 21, 32–34, 37–38
Inserting
 rows and columns, 149–150
 text, 85
Insert mode, 83, 85
Insurance, 227
Integrated circuits (ICs), 25
Integrated packages, 61, 66–67
Intel, 12, 24, 43, 70
Interact, 102
Interactive video storage disks, 29, 30, 31, 32, 66
Internal documentation, 203, 204
Internal memory, 27
Internal Revenue Service, 226
Internal security, 220, 222
Internet, 189
Internet Relay Chat (IRC), 189
Interparagraph spacing, 127
Interpreter, 206
IO.SYS, 43, 44, 45
Italics, 88, 125

J
Japanese language, 7
Jefferson, David, 199
Job kiosk, 88
Job insecurity, 229
Jobs, Steve, 62
Johnson & Johnson, 161
JPLDIS, 166
Junk mail, 164
Justification, 83, 84, 128

K
Kermit, 188
Kerning, 127
Keyboard, 6, 22, 32–33, 81, 83
Keywords, 172, 173
Kildall, Gary, 47
King, Catherine, 161
Kodak, 29
Kramlich, David, 106
Kriss Kross, 66
Kuwait, 6

L
Labels, 146–147
Landscape, 93, 123
Language, 7
Laptop computers, 5, 27, 35, 36, 222

Laserdiscs, 31, 80
Laser printers, 36, 37, 88, 93
Lashlee, Hal, 166
Law enforcement databases, 159, 160
Leading, 127, 128
Letter-quality printers, 36, 92
Letter-spacing control, 127
Light pen, 33–34
LCD (liquid crystal display), 35, 36
Line(s), drawing, 89
Line art, 129–130
LISP, 210
Livermore Labs, 6
L.L. Bean, 29
Local area networks (LANs), 191–192
Logical data, 162
Logic error, 203
Logic structures, 200–201, 203
Log on, 190
Looping, 201
Lotus, 65
LotusWorks, 67
Lowercase characters, 46
Low-level languages, 204
Lucas, George, 66

M
MAC file format, 101
Machine languages, 205
Macintosh, 5, 27, 42, 43, 50–51, 59, 61, 68, 92
Macintosh Classic, 68
Macintosh LC, 68
Macintosh Performa, 68
Macintosh Quadra, 68
Macros, 88, 151–152, 213
Magnetic disk storage, 29, 31
Magnetic tape, 7, 37
Mainframes, 4, 5
Main memory, 27
Manipulating text, 85–87
Mapping programs, 111
Margin(s), 83, 84, 123
 ragged, 128
Margin guide, 123
Maricopa Community Colleges, 189
MariMUSE, 189
Mazor, Stan, 12
McEwen, Dorothy, 47
MD (Make Directory), 49
Memory, 21, 23, 27
Mesa Community College, 189
Microcomputers, 4, 5–6, 24
 description of, 3–5
MicroPro, 82
Microprocessors, 3, 4, 6, 26
 types of, 26

Microsoft Corporation, 24, 43, 47, 52, 89
Microsoft Project, 11
Microsoft Word, 8, 10, 44, 205
Millard, Bill, 82
Minicomputers, 4–5
MIRROR, 53
Missing children, 106
Mitchell, Artie, 103
MITS, 5, 24
Modem, 6, 9, 10, 38, 184, 186, 187
Mona Lisa, 28
Monitor(s), 34–35, 72
Monitor screen, 7
Monkees Memories and Media Madness, 124
Monochrome monitors, 35
Monospaced font, 127
Motherboard, 26
Mount Pinatubo, 6
Mouse, 6, 33, 51, 81, 85, 112
Moving text, 149
MS-DOS, 42, 43, 47. *See also* DOS
MSDOS.SYS, 43, 44, 45
Muchen, Dennis, 26
Muckraker, 133
Multifinder, 51
Multimedia, 80, 107, 114–115
Multitasking, 50, 51
MUSE, 189
Music, 37, 54

N
Natural calculation, 150
Natural disasters, 6
Natural languages, 213
Navarro, University of, 132
NCR, 73
Network, 38, 179
Network databases, 172
Network design, 192–193
Networking, 190–191
Noise, 185
Noninterlaced monitor, 72
Northgate, 73
Notebook computers, 35
Numbers, 89
Numeric data, 162

O
Object code, 206
Object-oriented graphic files, 101
Object-oriented images, 99, 100, 103, 104, 108, 111, 112
Object-oriented programming (OOP), 208, 210–211

Official Airlines Guides, 16
Oil wells, 6
Olympic Committee, 132
On-line documentation, 204, 205
Online services, 10, 181–184
Open architecture, 26
Open-ended programming, 199
OpenLook, 51
Operating systems, 7, 42, 43, 45
Optical character recognition (OCR), 34
Optical storage devices, 7, 29, 30–32, 37
OS/2, 42, 50, 52, 59, 60, 61
Outline, 200
Outline fonts, 125, 126
Output, 7, 23, 34–38, 131–132

P
Packets, 187
Packet-switching service, 190
Page(s)
    double-sided, 123
    facing, 123
    number of, 123
    single-sided, 123
Page layout, 119, 121, 123–125
PageMaker, 64, 122, 124, 128
Page numbers, 85, 123
Page orientation, 123
Page setup, 124
Page size, 121
Paint programs, 63, 64, 111–113
Paper, 224
Paradox, 9, 66
Paragraphs, 127–128
Parallel ports, 32
Parity, 185
Pascal, 207–208
Pass, 13
Passwords, 191, 220, 222
Paterson, Tim, 47
Path, 46
PC. *See* IBM PC
PC-DOS, 43, 44
PCMCIA (Personal Computer Memory Card International Association), 44
PCX/PCC (Paintbrush), 101
Peer-to-peer network, 191
Pentium, 70
Peripheral devices
    for both input and output, 37–38
    input devices, 32–34
    output devices, 34–37
Personal computers, 4
Personal Digital Assistant, 48
Personal information, 225

Peterson's Career Options, 88
Piracy, 224
Pixels, 34, 35, 100
Plotters, 37
Plug-in boards, 26
Plus (+) sign, 147
Point, 125
Point and click, 81
Political asylum, 225
Politics, 227
Popular Electronics, 24
Port(s), 32
Portable computers, 35
Portable monitors, 35–36
Portrait, 93, 123
PostScript, 101, 103, 126
Powerbook, 68
Preschoolers, 59
Presentation applications, 114
Primary memory, 27
Printed circuit boards, 25–26
Printers, 36–37, 88, 92
Printing, 91–93, 154–155
Privacy, 227–229
Problem-oriented languages, 210–213
Procedural languages, 206
Procedure, 202
Processing, 6, 21–23
Procomm Plus, 190
Prodigy, 38, 183–184
Program, 7, 199
Program files, 45
Program Manager, 49
Programming, 199
    coding, 202
    constructing the algorithm, 200–202
    defining the problem, 199–200
    documenting the program, 203–204
    testing and debugging, 202–203
Programming environments, 211
Programming languages, 199, 204–213
Project management software, 108
Proportionally spaced fonts, 127
Protocols, 187
Pseudocode, 201
Publications, types of, 132–133
Public domain software, 224

Q
QuarkXPress, 13, 120, 124, 128, 129
Query, 167
Query languages, 213
QWERTY, 22

R
Radiation, 6
Ragged margins, 128
Raised cap, 126
RAM (random access memory), 21, 27–28, 69, 71
RAM cache, 69
Range, 145, 148
Ratliff, Wayne, 166
Read-only memory (ROM), 28–29
Recalculation, 150
Record(s), 161
Record-oriented databases, 172
Recycling, 224
References, 89
Relational databases, 66, 170
Relative reference, 149
Rename command, 48
Replacing, 86–87
Report generator, 169
Resolution, 72, 104
Résumés, 161
Reverse type, 126
Riddle, Mike, 102
Right to Financial Privacy Act (1978), 226
Rightwriter, 10
Ring network, 192, 193
Rio Salado Community College, 189
Roberts, Ed, 24
Roberts, Steve, 9
Robotic arm, 37, 38
Root directory, 45, 46
Rotated text, 126
Rows, 145
    inserting and deleting, 149–150
RPG (Report Program Generator), 210
Rubinstein, Seymour, 82
Ruling lines, 123
Russian programmers, 208

S
Safety, 222–223
Sams, Jack, 47
Sanderson, David, 190
Sans serif, 125
Save, 91, 154
Scaling, 129
Scanners, 6, 34, 85, 104, 105, 109, 110
Scanning, 54
Scanning software, 109–110
Schwaim, Karen, 189
Schwartz, Lillian, 28
Screen(s), 34
Screen captures, 111
Screen pattern, 130

Scripting languages, 213
Scroll field, 212
Search and Replace, 86
Searching, 86–87
Seattle Computer Products, 47
Sectors, 29
Security, 219
   internal, 220, 222
Selection, 200, 201
Semiconductors, 25
Sequence, 201
Serial ports, 32
Serif, 125
Setting up, 83–85
Shakespeare, 8
Shareware, 224
Shells, 49
Silicon-gate technology, 12
SimEarth, 71
Single-relation databases, 170
Single-sided pages, 123
Sizing, 129
Slots, 25–26
Smart printer, 36
Smileys, 190
Social Security Administration, 226
Soft return, 83
Software, 6, 7–8
   application, 8–13
   choosing, 59–60
Solomon, Les, 24
Sorting, 150–151, 164–165, 167
Sound effects, 54
Source code, 206
Spacing, 83–84, 127
Special characters, 88
Special effects, 126
Special-purpose computers, 3
Spelling checker, 87
Spreadsheets, 8, 9, 14, 15, 65, 89–90, 106
   functions of, 141–144
   home, 144
   talking, 146
Stacks, 170, 171
Star network, 192, 193
Start bit, 185
Stop bit, 185
Storage, 7, 21, 23, 71
Street Atlas, 11
Street maps, 11
Structure chart, 201
Structured programming, 202
Structured query language (SQL), 66, 168–169, 213
Styles, 128
Subdirectories, 45, 46
Supercomputers, 4, 5
Super VGA, 35, 72

Synchronous communication, 184–185, 187
Syntax error, 203
System, 42, 43, 50, 61
System board, 26, 69, 71
System bus, 26
System clock, 26–27
System 7, 50, 61
System unit, 23, 25

T
Table of contents, 89
Tabs, 84–85, 128
Tags, 128
Tate, George, 166
Tax forms, 87
Team-W, 184
Telecommunications, 179
Telecommunications software, 184
Telenet, 190
Templates, 124, 152, 154
Terminal emulation, 188, 190
Testing, 202–203
Text
   editing, 85–87
   entering, 81, 83
   manipulating, 85–87
Text blocks, 85–86
Text wrap, 130
Thesaurus, 80
The Source, 181–182
TIFF (tagged image file format), 101
Token, 88
Top-down design, 201
Topology, 192
Touch pads, 34
Touch-sensitive displays, 34
Track(s), 29
Trackballs, 34
Tracking, 127
Transmission speeds, 187
Travel guides, 16
TREE command, 46
Tribe, Laurence, 223
Trojan horses, 223
TrueType, 126
TTY terminal, 190
Tymnet, 190
Typeface, 125
Typeover mode, 83, 85
Typesetting, 119
Type size, 125
Type style, 125
Typing modes, 83
Typographical controls, 125–128

U
Undelete, 53
Underline, 88, 125
UNFORMAT command, 48
UNIX, 42, 50, 51
Uppercase characters, 46
User-created batch files, 45
User-generated graphics, 104, 111–115
Utility graphics software, 115
Utility programs, 45, 52–53

V
Values, 147
VDTs (video display terminals), 34
Vector images, 99
Vectorized, 111
Ventura Publisher, 27, 64, 124
VGA (video graphics array), 35, 72
Video, 71–72, 104
Video editing software, 33
Video grabbing, 111
Virtual (on-line) communities, 181
Virtual reality, 52
Viruses, 181, 221, 223–224
VisiCalc, 153
Voice-recognition software, 34, 43
Voice synthesizer, 26
Voters, 167
Vulcan, 166

W
Wait state, 69
Walden, 152
Walker, John, 102
Waste, 229–230
Weather information, 109
Webster's Ninth New Collegiate Dictionary, 8
What if?, 141
White space, 121
Wide area networks (WANs), 191–192
Winchester disks, 30
Windows, 42, 49–50, 59, 60, 61
Word for Windows, 89
WordPerfect, 9
Word processing, 8, 15, 61
Word processors, 79–80
   choosing, 80–81
   using, 81, 83–93
WordStar, 82
Word wrap, 83

Workplace Shell, 52, 60
Worksheet, 145–146
Workstations, 190–191
Worm, 223
Wozniak, Steve, 62
Wrist tendinitis, 228
"Writing to Read," 83
WYSIWYG, 120, 121, 123

X
Xbase, 66
XMODEM, 187–188
XWindows, 51

Y
Yeltsin, Boris, 130
YMODEM, 187–188

Z
Zagot travel guides, 16
Zeos, 73
ZMODEM, 187–188